OLD FASHIONED CHARM

WITH MODERN COMFORT

The Artdeco is a unique hotel in Rome. In fact, in the entire world there are only three other hotels with a similar charm and originality. Every detail has been carefully carried out according to the style of the first decades of the century, which culminated in the famous exhibition of decorative arts held in Paris in 1925.

The care taken in selecting the interiors and the attention to detail (lamps, lights, fabrics, paintings, etc.) make it all seem intended to bring the hotel's guests nearly a century back in time.

The first priority is to give the guests a sense of being in a friendly, cosy atmosphere. Guests are given every attention, from the daily paper brought to your room in the morning, to the evening chocolate left on your pillow to end the day in sweetness. There is also a very full breakfast selection: bacon and eggs, yoghurt, various jams and marmalades, savoury or sweet breads, croissants, fresh fruit and fruit juices.

The hotel is just a few steps away from the history city gate called Porta Pia, in the centre of Rome. Each of the 49 rooms has a radio, satellite television, telephone, mini-bar air conditioning, a hairdryer and a safe. Some of the rooms also have a hydro-massage bathtub or a sauna shower.

The Artdeco also has an excellent restaurant which offers a traditional menu with products, flavours and aromas from Italian cuisine, especially Roman cuisine.

It is well connected with public transportation, with a metro station just 200 metres away and the city's main bus lines just nearby.

TERMINI TRAIN STATION - 5 MINUTES
FIUMICINO AIRPORT - 45 MINUTES

LAST MINUTE RATES
Call for information

Your room, Our hospitality
In Rome's historical center

Hotel ★★★
IL PICCOLO
DI PIAZZA DI SPAGNA

(near Piazza di Spagna)
Single rooms from 90,OOO to 140,000 li:
Double rooms from 150,000 to 290,000 li

Via Due Macelli, 47 - 00100 Rome - Tel. +39 6 69200560 / 69200847

★★ Hotel
SANTA PRASSEDE

(between Termini railway station and the church
of Santa Maria Maggiore)
Single rooms from 50,000 to 120,000 lire
Double rooms from 80,000 to 160,000 lire

Via di Santa Prassede, 25 - 00184 Rome - Tel. +39 6 4828804/4814850 Fax +39 6 4746859

Hotel ★★
NARDIZZI AMERICANA

(between Termini railway station and the Trevi fountain)
Single rooms from 50,000 to 120,000 lire
Double rooms from 90,000 to 160,000 lire

Via Firenze, 38 - 00187 Rome - Tel. +39 6 4880668 / 4880035

♦ THE HERITAGE GUIDE ♦

ROME

The Eternal City and the Vatican, their churches,

museums, monuments and archeological sites

Touring Club of Italy

Touring Club of Italy

President and Chairman: *Giancarlo Lunati*

Chief executive officer: *Armando Peres*

Managing Director: *Marco Ausenda*

Editorial Director: *Michele D'Innella*

Coordination: *Anna Ferrari-Bravo*

General Consultant: *Gianni Bagioli*

Jacket Layout: *Federica Neeff*

Map Design: *Cartographic Division - Touring Club of Italy*

Authors: *Gianni Eugenio Viola* (Rome in History and in Art; from chapter 1 to chapter 4); *Laura Giallombardo* (Rome: Instructions for Use and Information for Travellers); *Alessandra Andresen* (museums).

Translation and adaptation: *Antony Shugaar*

Copy Editor: *Derek Allen*

Drawings: *Antonello* and *Chiara Vincenti*

Layout: *Studio Tragni*

Production: *Stefano Bagnoli*

Picture credits: *Archivi Alinari*: 17, 47, 153, 156, 178; *Archivi Alinari / Archivio SEAT*: 124, 178; *Archivio Bertarelli / Foto Saporetti*: 13, 45, 75; *Archivio T.C.I. / G. Berengo Gardin*: 112, 144, 167; *Archivio T.C.I. / F. Radino*: 49; *M. Fraschetti*: 28, 31, 35, 36, 39, 42, 61, 73, 81, 83, 90, 92, 93, 99, 102, 106, 147; *Image Bank / G.A. Rossi* 8, 53, 149; *G. Neri*: *R. Bettini* 176, *K. Guedbrandsen* 135, *M. Yamashita* 137; *PhotoMovie* 117; *L. Ronchi*: *A.E.L. Images* 111, 151, *V. Martegani* 89; *L. Ronchi / T. Stone*: *L. Grandadam* 105, *B. Schio* 115; *Scala, Firenze*: 3, 11, 12, 14, 20, 41, 51, 55, 62, 65, 68, 79, 85, 86, 94, 123, 128, 132, 140, 143, 155, 165; *L. Sechi*: 18, 24, 27, 59, 70, 120, 131, 174; *Ag. Sintesi-F. Fiorani / L. Ronchi*: 76; *Stradella*: *D. Ceresa* 23, *Mozzati* 162.

Cover: Fontana di Trevi, by *B. Schio (L. Ronchi)*.

We have taken great pains to ensure that the information provided in this guide is accurate. Some schedules, numbers, and addresses may have changed; we cannot accept responsibility for those changes, nor for any loss, injury, or inconvenience sustained by any traveller as a result of information or advice contained in the guide.

Typesetting and colour separations: *APV Vaccani - Milano*

Printed by: *G. Canale & C. - Borgaro Torinese (Torino)*

© 1999 Touring Editore - Milano
Code L2C
ISBN 88-365-1523-1
Printed in April 2000

Foreword

Rome has been called the Eternal City. It is the capital of Italy, but it has been the capital of ancient empires and universal churches.

It is a timeless meeting ground of cultures and peoples. It was the epicenter of the international jet set, and it remains a watering place for those who appreciate fine living.

Rome boasts palaces, churches, and monuments that mirror its centuries and millennia of continuous history. Rome is one vast museum, with a collection of artworks unparalleled on earth. Virtually every great artist of the past either worked or left traces in Rome.

After a brief but thorough introduction to the history of Rome and a chapter devoted to suggestions on seeing the city, this guidebook, part of "The Heritage Guide" series, offers a variety of tours, with an array of 21 routes. One route is devoted entirely to the Vatican, the papal city, with the famous cathedral of St. Peter's and the remarkable Vatican Museums. The guidebook is completed by a section abounding with helpful hints and useful addresses, which suggests, quarter by quarter, the finest hotels and restaurants, stores for excellent shopping, cafes and pastry shops, and the most important art galleries and cultural institutions.

A rich array of maps and illustrations accompanies the text; it is further completed with photographs and drawings, floor plans of buildings and monuments, and an extensive 35-page city atlas.

Etruscan sarcophagus "degli Sposi", in the Museo Etrusco di Villa Giulia (Rome)

Contents

Maps and Plans

How to Use this Guidebook

■ We have attempted to use the original Italian names of all places, monuments, buildings, and other references where possible. This is for a number of reasons: the traveller is thus made more comfortable with the names as he or she is likely to encounter them in Italy, on signs and printed matter. Note also that maps in this book for the most part carry the Italian version of all names. Thus, we refer to Battistero and Casa di Livia rather than to Baptistery and House of Livia. On first mention, we have tried to indicate both the Italian and the English equivalent; we have renewed this dual citation when it is the first mention in a specific section of text. In Italian names, one of the most common abbreviations found is "S." for "saint" (and "Ss." for "saints"). Note that "S." may actually be an abbreviation for four different forms of the word "saint" – "San", "Sant'", "Santo", and "Santa". Many other terms, while generally explained, should be familiar: "chiesa" is a church, "cappella" is a chapel, "via" is a street, "ponte" is a bridge, "museo" is a museum, "biblioteca" is a library, "torre" is a tower, "campanile" is a bell tower, "giardino" is a garden, "parco" is a park, "pinacoteca" is an art gallery, "teatro" is a theatre, "piazza" is a square, "ospedale" is a hospital, "porta" is either a door either a city gate.

Introductory Chapters. This guidebook opens with a chapter on the history of the city and its artistic development. Another chapter, "Rome: Instructions for Use", contains all the information you will need to organize your tour – from advices on how to find the entertainment places to tips on how to use public transportation, from shopping suggestions to descriptions of the cuisine, from hints on the best times of year to visit to the most noteworthy cultural and folk events.

The Places to Visit. This section comprises 4 chapters, 3 of which are devoted to the historical city; the 4th is dedicated to the new quarters built beyond the walled perimeter, after the unification of Italy. Each chapter contains several walking tour.

In all descriptions of monuments or landmarks differences in typography (names shown in **bold** or in *italics*) larger or smaller type size, and one asterisk (*) indicate the importance of each monument, museum, or other site. Written descriptions are accompanied by drawings and photos that help the reader to visualize works of art or architecture which he or she should not miss.

Information for travellers. A compendium of useful addresses, hotels and restaurants which suggests a selection of the finest hospitality facilities. Specific criteria are described on page 180. We provide information which is up-to-date as of the writing of this book. The reader should be aware that some subsequent changes may have occurred in hours or schedules.

Maps and plans. Monuments, hotels, restaurants, and other public facilities are marked on the Rome city atlas maps that appears at the end of this guidebook. Throughout this volume numeral in parentheses (5) indicate the map in question, while a letter and a number in parentheses (E2) refer to the sector of the map. The notation *off map* indicates that the specific monument or location is not shown on the map.

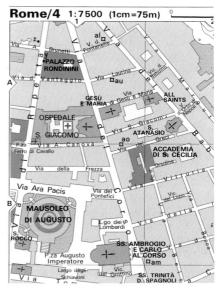

Notice regarding telephone numbers. As of the 18th December 1998, each location's telephone code must also be dialled for local calls and are listed next to the symbol ☎ in the section Information for Travellers, page 180. For those calling from abroad, the local code (06 for Rome) must be dialled after international code for Italy, followed by the subscriber's number.

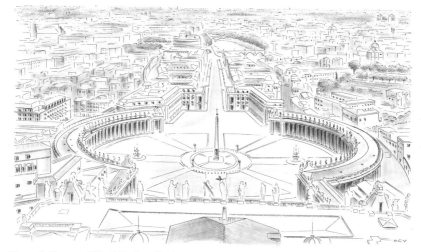

Piazza S. Pietro and Via della Conciliazione

Rome in History and in Art

If a city could be described in words, if its color, its light, its atmosphere could be translated onto the page, then the centuries of effort on the part of thousands of artists, travellers, idlers, and antiquarians of every sort, striving to capture the image of Rome, might appear less of a vain attempt; but leaving the image aside, not even the complete history of this city – aside from a ragtag assemblage of legends – can be properly conveyed and composed. Archeology, from Lanciani to Muñoz, has demonstrated this for many years now: the history of Rome – as written by Livy, and there is no need to take into consideration later and less accurate authors – is a fount of contradiction. Camillus, the "second founder" of the city, following the devastation wrought by the Gauls, does little to diminish the monarchic legend; already in this instance, as in other phases and points of tran-

Aerial view with Castel Sant'Angelo and the Tiber

sition in the city's history, we seem to glimpse the idea of a nature and a life of the "Urbs" that is entirely separate from those of its people: and perhaps we should place in this context the special nature of the relationship that bound the "cives romani" to the ideals of Rome, a select body of subjects summoned to celebrate the civil religion of Romanity.

Ancient Rome

The city to become the largest metropolis in the Mediterranean and to dominate the entire ancient world sprang up from a series of small settlements along the river Tiber, documented as far back as the Bronze Age which from mid 9th c. B.C. gradually came to constitute an urban structure.

Rome appears to have been ruled, in its first historical incarnation, by an elected monarchy, guided by a senate composed of 100 senior members ("patres") and by a popular assembly which elected that senate. This structure seems to date back at least as far as the time of the mythical "foundation" of Rome in 753 B.C. (according to the traditional chronology, which is of course entirely unreliable, Romulus ruled until 715 B.C.; Numa Pompilius until 673; Tullius Hostilius until 641; Ancus Marcius, builder of the first bridge – the "Pons Sublicius" – until 616). The struggle against the Etruscans to the north and the Greeks to the south was alternately successful and disastrous; it is thought that during the reigns of the last monarchs – especially, under the last three: Tarquinius Priscus, king until 578; Servius Tullius, king until 543; and finally Tarquinius Superbus, until 510 – there may have been a period of Etruscan domination over Rome, which ended with the popular revolt, led – according to legend – by Lucius Junius Brutus, and caused by the rape of Lucretia by the son of the king (Sextus Tarquinius).

From the monarchy to the republic

The decline of the monarchy is marked, according to tradition, by great public works (the embankment of the Cloaca Maxima, the temple of Capitoline Jove, the Circus Maximus, the Servian walls), by successful military campaigns, and by the entrance – under Servius Tullius – of Rome into the Latin League. Junius Brutus and Tarquinius Collatinus are said to have served in 509 B.C. in the earliest republican magistracy – the consulate – which took over the power of the kings; it was an annual office, tempered by a stronger system of competing powers, and divided with another equal; the office especially had a strong military connotation. Greek culture, even more than Etruscan culture, increased its importance in Rome: we see it, for instance, in the construction and adornment of the temple of Ceres on the Aventine, the hill that was assigned to the "plebs" in antiquity, and which from Augustus on, instead, was to become the preferred residence of the high patricians, and from the age of the Flavians on, the site of the residence of the emperor himself.

Early in the period of republican rule, Rome already held uncontested leadership within the Latin League, and over the next two centuries defeated and largely assimilated all the peoples which attempted to withstand its rule; before long, Rome's expansionistic policies brought it face to face with the contrasting ambitions of one of its most formidable adversaries: Carthage, with which a first treaty was sealed probably as early as the turn of the 6th c. B.C., and a second in 348 B.C., shortly after the subjugation of southern Etruria and of the Latin cities, then engaged in a widespread revolt.

Rome was shaken, ever since the dawn of the republican age, by the harsh conflicts between the tribes of the "plebs," or plebeians – a sort of entrepreneurial "bourgeoisie" – and the patricians. The end of this period of turbulence witnessed the evolution of the sacred and inviolable nature of the tribunes, who served as a mighty counterweight to the free-wheeling power of the patrician state magistracies. When the most serious threat to the state occurred that is, to the Punic invasion (in 211 B.C., Hannibal came within one mile of the walls of Rome), i.e., the sack of Rome by the Gauls of Brenno in 390 B.C., this process of assimilation and pacification had already been completed: the patrician class still maintained its power through the regulation of credit for commercial activities, a field it controlled entirely, as well as control of the army. Not until the passage of the "Lex Hortensia" (287 B.C.) was there finally total parity (at least on paper) between the plebeians and the patricians.

The conquest of the Mediterranean

By the turn of the 3rd c., Rome had definitively subjugated the Etruscan and most of the Greek colonial cities in southern Italy, while the conquest of the Greek colonies in Sicily took until 216 B.C. (except for Syracuse, which fell only in 211 B.C.; Sardinia was taken in 238 B.C.); by the end of the Punic Wars and the Macedonian Wars (282-132 B.C.) the city was the greatest power of the Mediterranean. In the meanwhile, a great road system had developed to link the city with the provinces, and a network of aqueducts was begun in the 4th c. B.C., to supply the water needs of the ever-growing capital; progress in engineering led to further benefits and quality in Roman buildings, with the use pozzolana (a water-based mortar) for the foundation, the development of the key-stone arch, and improvements in mining and quarrying, leading to use of the finest materials.

The end of the campaign against Carthage – razed to the ground in 146 B.C. after a 3-years siege – along with the definitive subjugation of Spain and vast territories in Africa, the acquisition of Macedonia, Greece, the kingdom of Pergamum, and northern Italy, gave Rome standing as the absolute power in the civilized world as well as opening it to the influence of exceedingly diverse cultures, often rich with vital ferment. Greek thought in particular, loomed above Roman thought, and was of considerable influence in literature and the arts, in philosophy and in science. The true marvel is not so much the adoption of Greek culture and thought by the Romans, but by the Roman ability to synthesise the two, finally evolving a "unicum" that served to engender new political forms indispensable to the administration and progress of territories that had become mind-bogglingly vast, and were often multiethnic, multicultural, and multilinguistic.

The influence of Greek Culture

The concept of a Roman art and architecture is difficult to pin down at its origins, and even up to a fairly late stage in the history of the city and the Roman state; at least until the 1st c. B.C., it seems that the chief dynamic was the influence of Hellenistic art and architecture, while it was not until the period of Empire that this relationship was to be reversed, and

Roman official architecture, which had assimilated a number of Italic features, spread out across the Mediterranean world. Generally speaking, Roman art and architecture, during the first centuries of their history, elaborated a number of principles of expression that were taken from the Greek world, first during the classical period and later during the Hellenistic age, without being rigidly bound by them. Indeed, a bit at a time, over the course of historical development, the Romans freely introduced the arch and the vault, mixed and blended orders and styles, abandoning toward those orders and styles the religious respect shown by the Greeks toward proportions and limits. The Romans, in contrast, gave increasing importance to the practical aspects of building, trending toward a fairly schematic monumental style, comprising fairly elementary features, though rich in its volumetric composition, and at times stunning in its magniloquence. This monumentality, toward the end of the 1st c. B.C., was underscored and heightened by the new monarchic character of centralized power, which was desirous of endowing all its public manifestations a grandiose appearance. For that matter, Roman culture soon imposed a number of "standards," not only in the urban layout of colonial cities, which – in accordance with the military nature of their organization – tended to mirror the topography of the "castrum," but also in the architecture of public complexes (amphitheaters, baths, etc.).

Patricians and "plebs"

In Rome itself, this new cultural condition came to affect the social situation that had developed at the end of the age of the Gracchi. The nephew of Scipio Africanus, Tiberius Sempronius Gracchus, named tribune of the "plebs," had proposed a law in 133 B.C., that called for the redistribution of the lands that had been confiscated; this law went against the interests of the patricians with major landholdings. The serious opposition encountered was overcome by Tiberius by the deposition of his fellow tribune and the law's principal opponent (Marcus Octavius); this was considered by the senate to be a truly revolutionary act. In the tumult that ensued, Tiberius was assassinated, an event which inaugurated the grim period of the civil wars. His brother Caius met a similar fate during a riot; Caius had attempted a direct reform in order to outflank the economic preponderance of the senatorial class – hoping thus to reestablish the political equilibrium that had pivoted on the tribunate of the "plebs." To attain this end Caius had attempted to gain the support of the equestrian order. This class was a new and dynamic factor in Rome, made up as it was by "capitalists," not members of the noble class, that had acquired wealth over time through a number of means (including the concession of loans) and the subcontracting of tax collection.

The conflict between the optimates and the "plebs" within Rome, covered a much broader ground outside of Rome, in the serious question of citizenship; by recognizing citizenship, it became possible to confer privileges to which many classes in the subjugated nations greatly aspired.

The conflict between Marius and Sulla

This conflict exploded during the consulate of Sulla (88 B.C.), and which took place in Rome, involved the democratic party under the leadership of Marius and Sulla as the champion of a restoration of senatorial powers. The dictatorship of Sulla, established following the death of Marius, and in the wake of a year of hard military and political campaigning inside the city and out, was marked by a long series of bloody vendettas (thousands of opponents were slaughtered, and an even greater number were banished from Rome; entire regions, in particular, Samnium and Etruria, were devastated for having dared to oppose resistance); the army became a major political force as well, and the subsequent actions of the dictator (a title he officially requested and received at the end of 82 B.C.) reinforced the close linkage between military command and the political leadership of the nation.

Having restored to the senators their judicial function, having limited the legislative power of the assemblies of the "plebs," and having suppressed in fact the right to veto of the tribunes, Sulla felt that he could safely expunge the fledgling democratic reforms of the Gracchi and the new conquests of the "plebs" and the magistracy of the tribunes. The "reform" was destined for failure: on the one hand, the democratic yearnings were well and deeply rooted, and on the other the senatorial class was already showing advanced signs of degeneration, while the equestrian order was a constant source of instability due to its tendency to act solely in consideration of its own mercantile interests. A few years after his exit from the political scene (in 80 B.C., having resigned the dictatorship, he became a consul, and then retired to private life), Sulla was sharply shown to have erred by the terrible servile revolt that exploded in 73 B.C. It was only after two years of hard fighting that Marcus Licinius Crassus succeeded in defeating Spartacus, leader of the revolt, while the surviving rebels were brought to battle and destroyed by Gneaeus Pompeius Magnus, or Pompey, in 71 B.C. Crassus and Pompey became consuls for the year 70 B.C., and together passed a series of reforms that overturned those passed under Sulla; in particular they reorganized the judicial system.

The fight between Caesar and Pompey

The last decades of the Republic were troubled by new civil conflicts that represented, with increasing intensity, the need for a linkage between the military "imperium" and political power in some sort of institutional form. While Pompey enjoyed success in the war against pirates who were dominating Rome's sea-borne trade, and triumphed again in the campaign against Mithridates VI of Pontus, assigned him in 66 B.C., Crassus and Gaius Julius Caesar had together taken control of the capital; placing themselves at the head of the popular party, with the assistance of a remarkable orator and politician, Marcus Tullius Cicero, they thwarted the efforts of the patrician Catiline to take power by manipulating malcontents in the provinces.

With the return of Pompey, fresh from his triumphs in the East, it became necessary to find a "modus vivendi" among the three powerful men who by this point controlled the state (First Triumvirate: 60 B.C.): Caesar, who the year previous had been "propraetor," or governor, in the province of Spain, was named consul for the year 59 B.C., with the agreement that he would then be given the government of the Gallic provinces for five years, while Pompey and Crassus remained in Rome at the head of the state. But Caesar was already back by 56 B.C., having conquered all of Gaul and having accumulated immense wealth. The pact of the triumvirate was therefore renewed: Caesar was thus to be given the rule over the Gallic provinces for another five years, while Pompey and Crassus were to be consuls for 55 B.C., and immediately thereafter they were to take over the government, respectively, of Spain and Syria. Crassus attacked the Parthians in Syria, where he was defeated and slain. Pompey remained in Rome, where the political situation was white hot, due to the implacable hostility among the various factions; the Roman Senate entrusted him with the maintenance of public order, which he did with the support of the "optimates" and in the unusual position of serving as sole consul. The envy of the two surviving "triumviri" soon exploded. Caesar's command in the Gallic provinces ended in 49 B.C. and Caesar requested for himself the consulship for 48 B.C., declaring, against the demands of the consuls, that he did not intend to relinquish his command before being assigned this new office. The Senate entrusted Pompey with the defense of the Republic. Surprised by a quick march on Caesar's part, who was in Ravenna and within a few days had reached Arezzo, Pompey marched to Brindisi and there took ship. His adversary, rather than pursue him, reinforced his power in Rome, and only the following year succeeded in drawing Pompey, his enemy, into a pitched battle in the plains of Pharsalia; Pompey, having escaped from this disastrous defeat, sought refuge in Egypt, but he was killed at

Statue of Augustus (Musei Vaticani)

the orders of Ptolemy XII. Establishing an alliance with Cleopatra, sister of Ptolemy XII, Caesar defeated Ptolemy, and placed the young woman on the throne (47 B.C.); after defeating the rest of Ptolemy's forces, he returned to Rome, where his absolute power soon took on a monarchic dimension. Among the reforms that he quickly introduced was the concession of citizenship to vast portions of the subject peoples, but a considerable extent of his efforts were directed to the embellishment of the capital city: although many of the public works that he planned were never implemented, their number and complexity (consider the projects for the deviation of the course of the river Tiber and the plans to enlarge Rome's walled perimeter) are sufficient to indicate the mark that Caesar hoped to leave upon Rome; this intent was hindered by a group of conspirators, led by Marcus Junius Brutus, who assassinated Caesar on 15 March 44 B.C.

The rise of Octavian

The "popular" character of Caesar's actions and the remarkable personal prestige nonetheless contributed to salvage much of the body of his reforms, while the intervention of Mark Antony, consul, and the exceedingly young Caesar Octavian, son of a niece of Caesar, and adopted by Caesar himself, served to crush the revolt and to force the con-

spirators to flee. With the defeat of the assassins of Caesar near Philippi (42 B.C.), and after Mark Antony lost much popular favor, in contrast with the growing popularity of Octavian, the Second Triumvirate was established, in which Mark Antony and Octavian were associated with Lepidus. Octavian worked, gradually, to acquire absolute power and the monarchy. As the conflict sharpened between him and Mark Antony (in 36 B.C. Lepidus was forced to resign as "triumvir" and withdraw to private life), the military situation took Mark Antony to the East, where he became involved with Cleopatra. The great freedom with which he disposed of the Asiatic provinces and the growing scandal caused by his concessions toward the queen of Egypt led to open war. The battle came on the western coast of Greece, near Actium, in 31 B.C.: in the naval battle, Mark Antony and Cleopatra were defeated, and the land army was also forced to surrender to Octavian, who pursued the pair as far as Egypt, conquering the region in the sum-

Bust of Commodus (Musei Capitolini)

mer of 30 B.C. (Mark Antony and Cleopatra both committed suicide) and transforming it into his own personal domain.

The three-fold triumph with which the return of Octavian to Rome was greeted in 29 B.C. marked the establishment of a monarchy and the end of the republican way of government.

The imperial age

The ideological, and in certain respects sociological core of the shift from republic to empire can be singled out – as early as the lifetime of Julius Caesar – in the emergence of a power base in the proletarian army, in the sharp reduction of the distance between Rome and the provinces, and the increasingly hazy boundaries between military power and civil government. The problems that afflicted a state born of so diverse a blend of component parts could only be solved by the rise of a single powerful man, backed by the army and placed at the head of all civil and military magistracies; only such a man would have the power to regulate the various forces summoned to constitute the immense state. Octavian, like Pompey before him, decided to bind his own power to the old republican tradition, having the senate confer upon him exceptional powers; all the same, he based his power also upon the army and on the direct relationship with many areas of the provinces. The shift from republic to empire was gradual, then, though clearly defined: the senatorial class and the equestrian class were in no sense humiliated; indeed, they were summoned to occupy the highest offices of the imperial administration; the old Roman virtues, especially the religious virtues, were invoked as the principles underlying public action.

There were truly an extraordinary number of reforms and a great deal of urban construction under Octavian Augustus, in the Rome over which he ruled. And a clear sign of the general consensus that only a monarchical constitution could assure stability for the Roman state can be seen in the relatively secure manner in which dynastic succession was accepted. Augustus gave the city an appearance that fundamentally remained unchanged until the late empire: the Campo Marzio was definitively occupied, the theater of Marcellus was completed; a mausoleum was built, in which the imperial family was to be lain to rest; the theater of Balbus was erected; a sundial was built (the "Horologium Augusti"), so large that it had an Egyptian obelisk as its dial; the Ara Pacis Augustae was consecrated; all the projects that Julius Caesar had planned to carry out in the Foro Romano, or Roman Forum, were completed; a temple was built to Caesar; the network of the aqueducts was improved greatly; the Palatine was partly built. Augustus's successors continued his work, reinforcing the new structures of the immense Roman dominion, and, in the capital, improving and embellishing the creations of the first emperor of Rome: Tiberius built the temple to the Divus Augustus in the Velabro, and confirmed the selection of the Palatine as the imperial residence; Claudius added two new structures to the network of aqueducts (among them was the famous Aqua Claudia) and built a perimeter wall around the Aventine; Nero planned and partly completed the immense Domus Aurea, which was later almost entirely dismantled by the Flavians.

The Pantheon in a drawing of 1831

The city – for the most part built of wood, with a population density that was spiralling ever upward over the last century of the republic – was often subject to great fires, occasionally immense ones; in A.D. 64, under Nero, the flames devastated ten of the fourteen regions into which Rome had been divided by Augustus. Vespasian and Titus, and to a greater degree Domitian, pursued the spirit of transformation that had already been shown by Augustus, replacing wooden structures with stone and masonry buildings, with a renewed thoroughness and determination. New fires – the Campidoglio in A.D. 69 and in the Campo Marzio in A.D. 80, the same year in which Titus was ending his war against the Hebrews, and in which the Flavian amphitheater was being inaugurated – eased the transformation and reconstruction; a signal of this progress can be seen in the arch of Titus, the forum known as the Forum of Nerva, the new imperial palace upon the Palatine hill (Domus Flavia), and the first restorations, which became an increasingly common feature of the building activity of the later Flavians, the Antonines, and the Severi.

The empire during the second century

A new crisis arose with the conspiracy that attempted, with the murder of Domitian in A.D. 96, to restore the aristocratic rule of the empire. One exponent of this faction was Nerva (96-98), an elderly senator who nonetheless had the wit to assure himself the support of the army and the provinces by naming as his own successor a provincial general of great renown, Marcus Ulpius Trajanus, or Trajan (98-117). And it was beginning with Trajan that – for the next century – while the empire attained its greatest expanse and Rome filled up with abundant and splendid new monuments – the power shifted overwhelmingly to the provincial aristocracy. Under the Antonines (138-193), perhaps, the city enjoyed its greatest splendor: the Pantheon, the temple of Trajan and the temple of Antoninus and Faustina, the column honoring Marcus Aurelius in the Campo Marzio, the major restorations. All the same, the economic crisis, which was already beginning to strangle the empire at the time of the transition from the rule of the Flavians to that of the Antonines, worsened around the end of the 2nd c. Following Trajan, who had encouraged investment in Italy, Hadrian (117-138) reversed the priorities, beginning that slow shift eastward of the cultural center of the empire that was later sanctioned definitively by Constantine in the 4th

c. Although there were attempts to stem the rising tide of philhellenism as early as under Antoninus Pius (138-161), we may safely say that the movement begun by Hadrian was to prove irreversible; Marcus Aurelius, in association with Lucius Verus, was to begin the development of a division of powers that was to lead to the break-up of the empire.

Even prior to the division of the empire, the eastern regions were acquiring growing importance and power, and became especially critical in the moments of contested succession to the imperial throne; one particularly astonishing case was the elevation to the throne, in A.D. 218, of the young Helagabalus, nephew of Septimius Severus through his wife (who was Syriac) and priest of the Sun god at Emesa. As early as the rule of Septim-

Portrait of Innocent X (Galleria Doria Pamphilj)

ius Severus, the Eastern elements, and especially the Syriac elements, had become more numerous in Rome; with Helagabalus, while religious practices were being introduced that clashed with both the Roman tradition and the increasingly widespread Christianity, those Eastern cults tended to become predominant. Alexander Severus (222-235) tried in vain to provide a political equilibrium to balance the restlessness of the army, as economic difficulties multiplied, and as new cultural elements made their way into the Roman world.

The crisis in the ancient world

The crisis of the ancient world came about from the failure of this attempt by the last Severi, marked by numerous military mutinies and peasant uprisings increasingly bound up with the state of economic disarray, the precarious state of the public finance, the growing burden of taxes, and the disorders in the coinage introduced by the decline in quality of the alloys used in coins (with the inevitable result, later noted by Gresham, of the hoarding of the purer, more valuable coins) – this decline in quality was undertaken in the hopes of increasing the money supply, but only triggered further inflation. Despite the effort to extend Roman citizenship to larger groups, in the hope of satisfying some of the demands from the provinces (Edict of Caracalla; 212) and the minting of a new coin (the Antoninianus), insufficient all the same to halt the devaluation and general lack of confidence, in time it was almost natural that heavy repression would be the next step taken.

Eastern preponderance was significantly evident in Christianity, which even in Rome was to maintain Greek as its language until the 3rd c., which did nothing to impede contradictory efforts to restore the old ways: Philip the Arabian – who, by a twist of destiny, presided over the thousandth anniversary of the foundation of Rome – was said to have been a Christian; Decius, who was to kill Philip in battle near Verona, obliged all Roman citizens to make sacrifices in honor of the ancient gods. The economic disaster (during the reign of Gallienus – 260-268 – the Antoninianus, or chief unit of currency, had only 5 percent silver in the alloy) was accompanied and worsened by an outbreak of plague, which raged for decades around the mid-3rd c. And it was none other than Gallienus, a practitioner of an Eleusian mystery cult, who recognized Christianity as a legitimate form of worship, restoring to Christian bishops the property of which their churches had been deprived. Efforts to provide reforms, or at least stability, tended to last no longer than the average reign of an emperor, who often succumbed to palace revolts, or unsuccessful military campaigns, or even the plague, during the 50 years that led up to the rule of Constantine.

Oriental cults and Christianity

Aurelian (270-275) was the last to attempt with any success the reunification of the empire under the rule of Rome: he built a new walled perimeter around the city, he encouraged once again the pagan cult of the Sun God, but in disputes with eastern regions he always sustained the primacy of the Church of Rome. Efforts to reassert the supremacy of Rome, however, were undercut symbolically, to an ever increasing degree, by the orientalization of customs and ways. It is worthy of note that Diocletian, proclaimed emperor by his soldiers in A.D. 284, insisted on being crowned with a diadem (an eastern symbol of absolute rule), while the power of the senate declined constantly, as the sovereign claimed divine investiture (again, as early as Diocletian). After establishing government by tetrarchy (the two Augusti each designated an adoptive son and successor, the two Caesars), Diocletian was also the first emperor to abandon Rome entirely as the capital and seat of the empire; he also succeeded in gradually stripping of military and political power the Praetorian Guard (the Guard was dissolved entirely under the rule of Constantine); above all, he succeeded in lightening the burden of tributes upon the provinces, transforming them into payments in kind. Diocletian was an adept of the cult of Mithras, a further indication of the orientalization of imperial customs; Christianity, especially at the behest of one of the Caesars (Galerius), underwent between 302 and 304 restrictions, if not actual persecution.

After about five years of turmoil, culminating in the victory over Maxentius at the Milvian Bridge (Ponte Milvio) on 28 October, A.D. 312, Constantine, the son of Costanzo Cloro, and serving as Augustus together with Galerius, took power. In his rule, he showed a new and tolerant attitude toward the Christian church, in which he probably saw a possible new foundation for the unity of the Roman state. The empire was still, for the most part, pagan, and certainly Constantine never considered abdicating the ideal of an emperor who was the absolute and supreme regulator of all things; although Constantine himself was persuaded by Christianity only in the very last years of his life, he gave the Christian church a position of some privilege early on; at the same time he reformed the central institutions of the state: the imperial court became increasingly eastern in style, and the fact that he personally opened the proceedings of the Council of Nicaea (325) did nothing to prevent him from employing pagan rites just five years later when he inaugurated the "New Rome," Constantinople (330). The new imperial residence, whose position reflected the now definitive shift of the empire's center of gravity, nonetheless could not replace the old Rome in importance nor in privilege: though a new senate was created, the senators of Constantinople did not enjoy the same rank as the senators of Rome. As early as A.D. 381, at any rate, the episcopal see of the eastern capital was to play a special role in the rule of Christianity, and in 484 the first schism took place.

Rome under the Popes

The medieval city, especially between the 13th c. and the 14th c. (in the year 1300 the first Jubilee was celebrated), was a major cultural center due to the activity of the religious schools; in fact, it may have rivalled Florence and Venice in its intellectual and artistic flourishing. The various religious orders settled in the city (the Cistercians at the Tre Fontane, near the site of the martyrdom of St. Paul, as early as the mid-12th c.), bringing new influence and vigor to the architecture of that period (one need only think of the various Franciscan buildings, including, we may note, the Aracoeli, as early as the mid-13th c.; this church constituted the prototype of all churches built by and for the mendicant orders). The new style of construction was not limited to houses of worship, but could be seen in the civil architecture as well, with the gradual introduction in Rome of a number of typologies that had long been common in the Italy of the Communes, to the north (consider the work on the Palazzo Comunale Capitolino, the stairway of the Aracoeli, etc.). This activity attracted artists of great renown, from Arnolfo di Cambio to Giotto, and laid the groundwork for the development of a Roman school of art that, at least at this early stage, had in Pietro Cavallini a major figure. From this point forward, there was no interruption in construction in Rome, with the possible exception of the so-called Babylonian captivity, when the papacy was moved to Avignon – and even during that period, things revived during the "seigneury" of Cola di Rienzo (1347-54).

Transformations for the Jubilee celebrations

The Jubilee year of 1400, which occurred despite the lasting Western Schism, was marked by major construction projects aimed at making the city capable of accommodating the great flow of pilgrims expected, especially those from the north: as early as May 1395, Pope Boniface IX was busying about the reconstruction of the roads needed to get from one church to another within the city and in the surrounding territory, paying for the repairs with the money taken in from offerings and charity. The circuit of churches which were to be visited in order to obtain holy indulgences grew to include S. Lorenzo Fuori le Mura, S. Maria in Trastevere, and S. Maria Rotonda; the last-named church was in the heart of the commercial district – especially cloth merchants, bankers, and craftsmen – and certainly the decision to unleash a vast crowd of pilgrims upon that area must have represented a conscious business decision in terms of economic development (shortly thereafter, at S. Eustachio, in fact, the Dogana di Terra was established, corresponding to the Dogana di Ripa, respectively, and literally, the customs yards of land and riverbank). With the Colonna pope, Martin V, at the end of the schism, work was shifted to focus on bridges and the roads that were to lead toward St. Peter's, as well as on restoration of St. John Lateran (beginning in 1425), on S. Maria Maggiore, and on S. Paolo Fuori le Mura (St. Paul's Without-the-Walls), which was subject to the depredations of brigands because of its distance from the city and the declining population of the monastery.

Toward the middle of the 15th c., there were two events of particular importance in the life of the city, aside from the Jubilee year of 1450: the coronation in St. Peter's of the Holy Roman Emperor Frederick III (1452) and the fall of Constantinople (1453) to the Ottoman Turks; both events seemed to restore Rome to its old "imperial" status. Pope Nicholas V therefore appeared as the restorer of Christian universalism, and his vast construction projects were a sign of that view – the reconstruction and restoration of churches (especially the patriarchal basilicas) and city walls, construction of the Palazzi Vaticani, fortification of Borgo, and so on.

The Roman Renaissance

It was between the end of the papacy of Nicholas V and the end of the century that Rome began to lose its medieval character, with the disappearance of the baronial fortresses marked by towers; in this same period, new aristocratic residences began to be built, generally with some aspiration to elegance, and in some cases sheer splendor, in the general state of mind linked to the new condition of supremacy in the civil and political standing of this great apostolic see. Rome, in brief, became – or tried to become – the capital of a state, with clear territorial boundaries, that was to subsist for a good three and a half centuries, within those same boundaries. The restorations of the bridges (Ponte Milvio, Ponte Nomentano, Ponte S. Angelo, and Ponte Cestio), the great plan for the rebuilding of the "borghi," the cobblestone paving of a number of squares and streets (the Via Flaminia between S. Maria del Popolo and the Ponte Milvio), and the embellishment and restoration of the city gates are all further signs of this mindset.

The transformations of the city are nicely summarized in the various uses to which Castel S. Angelo has been put: from an imperial mausoleum to a house of worship dedicated to the Archangel Michael, palace, and fortress set at the edge of the city's fortifications (this building, in fact, presents itself as a sort of entranceway to Borgo and, as it surveys the Tiber and the most heavily traveled bridge across the Tiber, it also controls the links between the two sections of the city of Rome). These years were characterized, as St. Peter's became the prime focus toward which the flow of pilgrims was increasingly directed, by increasingly monumental projects affecting the medieval urban structure, leading to the opening of new roads and boulevards, and the expansion and improvement of roads and boulevards that already existed; at the same time a new culture, antiquarian and learned, sprang up, encouraging the exaltation – and in some cases, the re-use of artifacts and finds dating from antiquity; nor should we forget the routes of devotion that the city was partly shaped to accommodate.

Beyond Ponte S. Angelo, in the heart of medieval Rome, reclamation work continued in the first half of the 16th c. (Parione and S. Eustachio), while the route of Via del Pellegrino was being improved, and the construction of the Palazzo della Cancelleria was being completed. Cardinal Carafa, who had the "talking statue" of Pasquino installed at the corner of his palazzo, offered the Roman people a brand-new mouthpiece, very close to the Piazza Navona, where toward the end of the previous century the most important Roman market had been moved, from its older site on the Campidoglio and in surrounding areas. In the 16th c., the new headquarters of the university was built and began operations (the "Studium Urbis") and, as a result, there was a rapid expansion of land being reclaimed and reconstruction of the buildings in the area between S. Eustachio and Piazza Navona. Antonio da Sangallo the Younger, and Peruzzi both put their mark on this great complex of buildings, linked by a series of renovations of aristocratic palazzi (and we need only mention the Insula dei Massimo as an example); Pollaiolo, Antoniazzo Romano, and Andrea Bregno seem an obvious prologue to the remarkable work done in Rome by Michelangelo, who was commissioned to carve the *Pietà* in 1497.

The Sack of Rome

The Roman Renaissance was stricken by the sacking and plunder of 1527, but around the Jubilee year of 1525 and the Jubilee year of 1550 the city experienced two high points. The city around the year of the Sack of Rome (1527) had a sharply composite population. Ac-

The Delphic Sibyl by Michelangelo in the Sistine Chapel

cording to the data produced by the first modern census of the city, under Pope Clement VII, it appears that there were slightly fewer Romans than there were subjects of the Duchy of Milan, while there were nearly as many Tuscans and nearly as many subjects of the Duke of Savoy; the census also revealed the presence of a great number of Spanish, Portuguese, Frenchmen and Germans, as well as Albanians and Slavs, Greek exiles, and many other, smaller colonies, making up a total population of about 55,000, a number that was decimated by the war and violence of the invaders. Despite the terrible destruction of archival documents, we do know that when the population began to flow back into the city, its makeup was substantially different: we can form some idea of these changes from popular language, if we consider that the language used in the "Cronica," a chronicle written by an anonymous Roman in the 14th c., was a dialect not unlike the Neapolitan idiom, while the new dialect used commonly in Rome at the end of the 16th c. was assuredly a dialect from central Italy. Despite the fact that Pope Leo X de' Medici opened the new thoroughfare of Via della Scrofa-Via Ripetta, greatly concentrating the power and wealth of the zone of S. Eustachio (probably one of the few areas in which there were tall buildings of some architectural note), much of the city was still, in the middle of the 16th c., made up of low hovels, each housing a single family, here and there overshadowed by an aristocratic residence or the ruins of a building dating from antiquity. The city was tolerant: the year previous to the Sack of Rome, nearly 2,000 Jews lived unhindered between Regola and S. Angelo. Around the middle of the century, the flow of foreign visitors coming to Rome began to increase in volume, in parallel, and undistinguishable in terms of precise numbers, but already marked by literary documentation; these travellers came to Rome out of cultural curiosity; we can take a fairly well grounded guess, that Rome in this period had four taverns for every one thousand residents.

S. Giovanni dei Fiorentini, the Palazzo dei Conservatori, S. Silvestro al Quirinale, S. Marcello al Corso, S. Maria della Pace – all mark the new artistic cityscape of Rome, while the commission established by Clement VII (1523), after the debate between Antonio da Sangallo the Younger and Peruzzi, resumed work on the new St. Peter's; in the meanwhile, work continued on the Via del Babuino, civil architecture was enriched with the Palazzo della Zecca, and Peruzzi, Raphael, Giulio Romano, and Perin del Vaga all frescoed and painted some of the most illustrious works produced by Roman art in the entire century.

The rediscovery of antiquity

It was Pope Paul III Farnese (1534-39) who first gave a new cultural meaning to the rediscovery of antiquity in the new city; his attitude and his plans find wonderful expression in Michelangelo's renovation of the Campidoglio, where the statue of the Roman emperor serves as a seal to the synthesis of the ancient with the modern created in this new space now overlooking the city. And the urban itinerary created for the procession of Charles V, designed with massive demolitions, improvements, and reclamations, is rich in examples

The Basilica of S. Paolo Fuori le Mura

of the ancient restored to new lustrous meaning in the furnishings of the city (the arches of Constantine, Titus, and Septimius Severus, and more in general the entire area of the Forum). Shortly before the battle of Lèpanto (1571), when the Turkish threat looming over Christendom was at its most menacing, the bastions of Castel S. Angelo were built, reinforcing the Leonine walls, even though the residential section of Rome then expanded with the new settlement of Borgo Pio; after Lèpanto, with the lessening of the Turkish threat, there was a general renewal of work on monuments and urban improvements (Via Gregoriana, Via Merulana, and so on).

The transformer, though hardly a revolutionary transformer, was certainly Sixtus V; especially in symbolic terms, a level that was clearly understood by the European intellectuals between the Renaissance and the Baroque period; this second and greater Sistine age was marked by the demolition of the ruins of the Settizonio – a demolition that was entrusted not to navvies or diggers, but to a "prince" among architects: Domenico Fontana – and by the creation in the city's fabric of the penitential circuit of the basilicas – which included, beyond S. Pietro, S. Paolo Fuori le Mura, S. Sebastiano, S. Giovanni in Laterano, S. Croce in Gerusalemme, S. Lorenzo Fuori le Mura, and S. Maria Maggiore – and by a new relationship with urban space, conceived as a monumental form even in the freer aspects (squares and perspectives) – by the importance given to the concerted workings of the arts in the cultural development of the city (the rule of Sixtus V also saw Palestrina as chapel-master of the Basilica Vaticana and the development of publishing and the visual arts in Rome).

All of this allows us to indicate late-16th c. Rome as the site of the development of a true cultural policy that, for most of the succeeding century, was to influence the decisions of the popes.

When Sixtus V Peretti died after just five years as pope (1585-90), the work he had done proved to be so solid and thorough that even his greatest successors (Paul V Borghese – 1605-1621; Urban VIII Barberini – 1623-44; Innocent X Pamphilj – 1644-55; Clement X Altieri – 1670-76; and Innocent XIII, the last Roman pope for more than two centuries) were able to do little more than confirm and reinforce the new relationship between the Holy See and the city of Rome that was established once and for all by Sixtus's policies; a relationship that was to govern all possible art commissions over time.

The Baroque age

The turn of the new century (17th c.) was symbolically marked by the work done by the Carracci on the frescoes of Palazzo Farnese, a circumstance that therefore seemed symbolically to distinguish the new style that was to have in Rome one of its greatest fields of endeavor.

The great Roman 17th c. was the age of Gian Lorenzo Bernini. Perhaps no architect in history has left so deep an imprint on a city as Bernini did upon Rome in the 17th c., and it is significant that this happened in the period of the most thoroughgoing secularization of the arts – a period in which, all the same, in the year 1600, Giordano Bruno was burned at the stake for heresy, and later in the century Galileo was condemned and forced to abjure. If Michelangelo was the "divine Michelangelo," as Giulio Carlo Argan once observed, then Bernini was "il cavalier Bernini," proud of his knighthood; if the Campidoglio was the finest theater of expression of Michelangelo's conception of the city, then Piazza S. Pietro was the same for Bernini's. Pietro da Cortona is another major figure in this 17th-c. school, theatrical and triumphal, while the great adversary of Bernini, Francesco Borromini, sought out contracted spaces and unreal perspectives, which prevail over the fairly recherche' relationships between buildings and contexts. False perspectives slipping away into imaginary depths (as in Palazzo Spada and S. Agnese in Agone), great allegorical fountains that are reminiscent of the fanciful "machines" found in the theaters, which are enjoying ever growing success, up to the "ephemerals" thrown together for sumptuous festivals in which the square was no longer a place, but a theater. The great canvases in the Museo di Roma that depict the feasts held for queen Kristina of Sweden are an elegant illustration of these conditions, while the engravings of Falda offer a charming idea of the city in the last few years of Bernini's activity.

The illustrating of Rome in the 1700s

Between the end of the 17th c. and the turn of the 18th c., although the overall number of architectural and urbanistic projects may have declined, their nature tended to have a greater impact on a now-clearly defined urban layout. The Spanish Steps, or Scalinata di piazza di Spagna, completed in 1726, the port of Ripetta, the Piazza di S. Ignazio, the Fontana di Trevi, and above all, the giant edifice of S. Michele, at the turn of the 18th c. already completed and partly redecorated, these are the various steps in the further development of the city. The great illustrator of Roman life in the 18th c. was Giovanni Paolo Pannini, whose canvases display the splendor and lively existence of the high aristocracy and the papal court; but the most remarkable artist working in Rome in this century was probably G.B. Piranesi, whose engravings – and few pieces of built architecture – never fail to astonish and unsettle the viewer, now as they did then. The century was captured by a remarkable family of artists and view painters: the Vanvitelli (Gaspar van Wittel, followed by his son Luigi, and finally Luigi's son, Carlo). If Gaspar did some of the loveliest view paintings of the turn of the 18th c., Luigi was responsible for a number of noteworthy architectural projects (restoration of the cupola of S. Pietro, 1742), as well as remarkable drawings representative of Roman Baroque, which were to be translated into theatrical solutions for churches and palazzi. Gaspar, who arrived in Rome in 1674 and decided to stay, marrying a Roman woman and Italianizing his surname, has left us some of the most enchanting drawings of that period, drawings which cast light on the antiquarian style that was spreading (suffice it to mention the drawings done on the occasion of the discovery, in Piazza di Montecitorio, in September 1705, of the Antonine Column). This dynasty of artists of Dutch origin, who were the most prolific artists in the Rome of that period, along with the Florentine Ferdinando Fuga and the Roman Alessandro Specchi – outdone perhaps only by the Ticino-born artist Carlo Fontana – were responsible for some of the most influential works of the Roman 18th c.: a remarkable offspring – almost a throwback – of the style of Bernini. Borrimini's work left its mark too however: suffice it to think of the work done by the Jesuit artist Andrea Pozzo, the inventor of the false cupola in the church of S. Ignazio.

A "romantic" illustration by G. P. Pannini: "Ruins with the Statue of Marcus Aurelius"

Rome in the 19th c.

Rome under the French (actual rule under Napoleon lasted for only five years, from 1809 to 1814) witnessed the first contrasts between the demands of a secular state and the temporal power of the Church. The confiscation of major ecclesiastical landholdings and the transfer of non-religious French and Italian officials of the administration made it possible to make considerable strides on the path to an embryonic industrialization and rationalization of agriculture. Archeological excavations and new urban planning projects were also carried forward: the renovation of Piazza del Popolo and the partial rebuilding of churches and palazzi with a clear Neoclassical imprint, are the lasting sign of this short but intense period; the attention devoted to public hygiene after centuries of neglect was an indication that was to have lasting consequences.

The restoration of Pope Pius VII was not enough to cancel the new trend of things, which to some extent was to continue over the course of the 50 years that separated the return of the pontiff to Rome (1815) and the annexation of the territory of the papal state by the new kingdom of Italy.

The fairly brief reign of Pope Leo XII marked the definitive decline of the political significance of temporal power, even though that pope made every effort to render the temporal power popular once again with a reform of the legal codes – and especially of penal law and administration of justice (the bull known as "Reformatio Tribunalium," also known as "the bull of Cheap Justice"; 5 October 1824) – and later with lavish donations to the Biblioteca Vaticana, or Vatican library and with the foundation of the core of the Museo Etrusco, or Etruscan museum; nor should we neglect to mention his reform of the university system (the bull known as "Quod Divina Sapientia"; 28 August 1824); note that Leo XII gave the order to remove the works of Galileo Galilei from the Index of Forbidden Books.

All the same, the air of suspicion that the outbreak of liberal revolts introduced in the government, a number of measures designed to restore dignity to houses of worship – and which may have been given intentional bad publicity – and the controls imposed on pilgrims, who had gathered from all over the world for the Jubilee Year of 1825, excavated an unbridgeable gap between the government and the curia on the one hand and the populace of the city and the state on the other. When, upon the death of Leo XII (the "papa limone," or lemon pope, who was always a sickly yellow cast from his diseases, was commemorated by Pasquino as follows: "Tre dispetti ci festi, o Padre Santo, / accettare il papato, viver tanto, / morir di carnevale per esser pianto" – "You played three nasty tricks on us, o Holy Father: you accepted the papacy, you lived so long, and you died during Carnival, forcing us to mourn you instead of celebrating"), Pope Pius VIII (Castiglioni) was elected, it was clear that this degeneration of the papal state, made up of institutional hardening of the arteries and economic parasitism, was destined to become more pronounced: Pope Pius VIII seemed to sum up all the defects of the previous papacy, without even making the same efforts at reform.

Social and intellectual life in the 19th century

Despite this general state of affairs, the flow of Italian and non-Italian visitors intensified throughout the century, although travelling to Rome was truly anything but easy, even following the opening of the great Alpine passes carved out during the campaigns of

Napoleon. Though it was difficult to get there for even the wealthiest of travellers, life in Rome in the 19th c. remained a glittering whirl; there were famous balls and receptions, held by Don Alessandro Torlonia, where the most prosperous passing foreigners, many of them customers and clients, were invited to meet high prelates, and at which it was common to see both cardinal Mai and cardinal Mezzofanti. Social life in Rome followed the turning of the seasons, since the idea was already common back then that remaining within the walls of Rome during the summer was not particularly salubrious; mountains of treatises were written, as late as the mid-19th c., to explain the origins and dangers of the "miasmatic infections" that afflicted the city, a result in part – as was generally recognized – of the awful health conditions that encouraged the spread of the terrible cholera outbreak of 1837. Rome – especially in comparison with large cities such as Naples – remained a relatively small city, though it did have a high birth rate; in 1826 the population was just 139,847, rising by 1835 to 152,457, but dropping again, following the cholera epidemic (1838), to 148,903. What is more, the city managed its medioce resources – many of which were used for costly restoration projects – in an almost parasitical manner. Among the most noteworthy projects were those done under the supervision of a dynasty of Roman architects, the Camporese family, for nearly a century, and virtually right up to the "Breccia di Porta Pia," with the capture of Rome by the new Italian state: Giuseppe Camporese (1763-1820) excavated the Foro di Traiano (Trajan's forum), supervised work on the buttress of the Colosseum (under Pope Pius VII), reinforced the three columns of the temple of Vespasian, and excavated the platea of the Flavian amphitheater; his son Pietro (1807-1863) continued his work by erecting the building known as the "Palazzo del Ferro di Cavallo" – named for its horseshoe shape – in Via di Ripetta, rebuilding the Teatro Argentina, a theater, rebuilding the side of the hospital, or Ospedale di S. Giacomo, and by designing, and often building, numerous buildings, some of them among the most interesting in the century. There were other architects in 19th-c. Rome doing noteworthy work, such as Pasquale Belli, who rebuilt the church of S. Paolo Fuori le Mura (St. Paul's Without-the-Walls) after it was badly damaged by the fire of 1823, and Luigi Canina, who renovated the Villa Borghese, or Giuseppe Valadier, certainly the architect who left the largest imprint upon the city, both in terms of civil and religious architecture; and we cannot fail to mention archeologists such as Nibby and antiquarians such as the Muñoz family.

The papacy of Pope Cappellari, the jovial Gregory XVI, was not marked by the disorder or great events that were seen at the beginning and the end of the century (indeed it fits almost precisely between the uprisings of 1830 and those of 1848), and may well have been the only tranquil period in the century; all the same, he promulgated the encyclical "Mirari vos" (1832), a firm condemnation of liberal ideas. Control of the press was, and remained, quite strict: only a few unimportant publications were printed in Rome, the most significant of them being the "Diario di Roma," which came out on Thursdays and Saturdays, along with the weekly publication, "Notizie del Giorno"; all the same, the cultural life of the city was not entirely dull, if there were such figures as, in the first half of the century, Carlo Fea, the abbot Francesco Cancellieri, Antonio Nibby, and diplomats such as Niebuhr or the baron de Hubner, and learned cardinals of the Curia. When Pope Gregory died, in June of 1846, the long-repressed energies were about to explode: the statue that stood on his bier, just shortly before the funeral ceremony in St. Peter's, toppled to the ground with a roar, and seemed to foretell the urgent change that was to take place within the next two years. After French troops re-occupied Rome, to put an end to the Roman Republic inspired by Mazzini and defended by Garibaldi, the city lived on under a sort of protectorate. In fact, France prevented united Italy's definitive annexation of Rome, which finally took place in September 1870 shortly after the fall of Napoleon III.

The character of modern Rome

The topographic peculiarities intertwined with the monumental vestiges, of which this city is a true quarry, have also heavily conditioned modern expansion, especially the expansion following the unification of Italy. Rome presents, at least by and large, the coexistence of two major cores: one of exceedingly dense construction along the left bank of the Tiber and the Mura Aureliane, or Aurelian walls, and the other made up of villas and gardens belonging to patrician families and of green belts that formed integral parts of the urban layout, and which only gradually were acquired by the city, in part or entirely. The villas, even during the earliest years of unified Italy, were a sort of counter-altar to the monumentality of both ancient and modern monuments, and saved the city from demolitions and ravages greater than those done under King Umberto or the Fascist regime.

It is certainly true that for centuries, the appearance of the city, both in terms of what is seen by a sightseeing visitor and in terms of its urban layout, has been dominated by the contrast between the "tono aulico" and "tono popolare," or what we might call "high" and "low" tones, in the terms that Benevolo established, fixing a contrast between the "minute, compact, and irregular structure of the medieval habitat" and the "grandiose structure of the shattered imperial city," a contrast that engendered a "permanent dramatic effect"; but it is equally true that, despite the many and repeated urban renovations, some of great scope and scale – such as the great straight thoroughfares or the "tridenti," the demolitions and redistribution schemes – the plan of Rome still shows that the various projects have not been coordinated to give the vast urban agglomeration a unified character. On the other hand, the contrast between a city that is the capital of a nation, with its requirements for centralization and bureaucracy, and the exaltation of historic and monumental values of the ancient tradition (often likewise functional to political instrumentalization) led to further imbalances, still evident, which would have been even greater had the urban regulatory plans of 1873, 1883 and, above all, 1931 ever been fully implemented.

Rome as the capital of a unified State

The difficulties of identifying a "Roman" style and character became evident when the city was made the capital of newly united Italy, increasing the pressure to produce a reflection of a national Italian art and culture; if we leave aside episodes such as the exhibition of the Secessione, which offered a new space to a Roman aspect of art (Palazzo delle Esposizioni; 1913), or the Rome Biennials of 1921 and 1923, most public projects were dedicated to a "national" art (and already the first Quadrennial, assembled under Oppo in 1931, was "national"); indeed, as early as 1877 Ettore Ferrari had suggested that the city be made the center of national exhibitions, and it was finally agreed that Rome was the focal point of all promotion of art in Italy, with the recognized contribution of the various regional schools. All the same, the great centralization that followed, with the particular support of the Italian right, under Quintino Sella, though it did manage to attract the financing needed for the great projects of urban renewal, was insufficient to create a genuine cultural awakening; it should be said that the project to make Rome the great intellectual center of Italy, with a great university, or "università principalissima," and a renewed thrust toward a universalist mission, certainly did little or nothing to encourage the local and idiosyncratic character of Rome. A new city rising alongside the old one, with the urbanization of the eastern areas, was the goal of the urban projects of the Italian right; the left wing, on the other hand, demanded new quarters along the Tiber and in the Prati di Castello. The succession of parties led to a succession and overlapping of designs: Sella did nothing more than to continue and expand upon the project of Monsignor de Merode (urbanization of the higher areas of the city and the Esquiline hill); the left continued work, but added, during the rule of Depretis, the break-up and development of the great city villas (Villa Ludovisi, Villa Massimo, Villa Spittower) and completed the process in the quarters of Testaccio and Prati, with the encouragement of Pianciani, who was mayor from 1872 on.

The urban and demographic history of the city of Rome is marked by periods of expansion and frenzied building, and by periods of neglect and decay, with drops in population that were in some cases dramatic. If the Eternal City had a population of more than a million – as it appears – during the reign of Hadrian, at the turn of the 2nd c. A.D., the population could be counted in the tens of thousands when the eastern emperor Costans II visited in A.D. 663. In the 6th c., amidst the devastation of the Gothic war, it remained entirely devoid of population for a number of years. At the end of the great Western Schism of Avignon (1418) the population may have been as little as 20,000. In 1527 the imperial armies of Charles V sacked a town of just over 50,000.

A growing city

It was to take about a century and a half before this number doubled. Ten years after the arrival of the house of Savoy (Savoia), Rome was the third-largest city in Italy: it had just over a quarter million inhabitants, half the population of Naples, and a third less than Milan. The year before the March on Rome, the last "rioni" were established, and the city had a population of 660,000; ten years later, in 1931, the population had risen by a third and continued to grow, despite economic difficulties. Just six years after the end of WWII, in the census of 1951, Rome had a population of over 1.6 million, an increase of half-a-million in the course of a decade. In the two decades that followed, the population continued to grow, reaching 3 million in the mid-1980s, and then began a slow drop, in the context of which the abandonment of the historic center appears particularly serious; in 15 years, the center lost nearly two-thirds of its residents.

The history of "demolitions" in Rome is an odd and lengthy one, and dates back to Augustus. In the Renaissance, the destruction ordered by Pope Sixtus V is notorious (though before him, Bramante had earned the dubious honor of the title, "maestro ruinante"), and the Colosseum itself was slated for demolition; Pope Urban VIII seriously considered demolishing the tomb of Cecilia Metella, and even commissioned Bernini to do it, though the architect luckily had other things to do. The various regulatory plans of Rome, the new capital, and the demolition prescribed by many of those plans, are clear indicators of the odd relationship that Italian urban planning has always had with this city: conflicted between the

The temple of Aesculapius and the small lake in the park of Villa Borghese

exaltation of the city's great symbols and the rationalization of the various settlements and road networks.

Nearly three-quarters of the population of the province now (1993) lives in the city of Rome; as opposed to the province of Milan, where less than a third of the population lives in the city, and Turin, were the figure is roughly 40 percent, and the forecast is for things to remain roughly the same by the end of the century, when for that matter the number of retired persons will have grown considerably (with 17 percent of the population over age 65). In the decade from 1981-91 those working in industrial occupations declined by more than 14 percent in the province of Rome, where already industry is fading away, save for limited areas. As is already the case in many urban settings, the richer and newer quarters are those where the average age of the inhabitants is rising sharply (in one decade, the number of elderly people living in EUR has risen by more than a third), while in the quarters with the highest density of inhabitants, there has been a decline in the younger population (at the Portuense, in the same decade, the number of young people under the age of 20 declined by 25 percent).

At the turn of the new millennium, Rome appears as a city that has succeeded in preserving its artistic heritage, but which is undertaking a great modernization, that for now is proving to be an overwhelming challenge.

Rome: Instructions for Use

Over 200 years ago, on 1 November 1786, Goethe wrote in his diary: "Yes, I have finally arrived in this, the capital of the world! ... Certainly, outside of Rome, you cannot have an idea of what you can learn here. It is necessary, so to speak, to be reborn; and once you have, you look back at the ideas you once held, and they seem like the short pants you wore as a child."

To rediscover the emotions described by Goethe may seem impossible if we consider the tumultuous demographic and urbanistic progress that, in little more than a century, has transformed the sleepy capital of the realm of the popes into a modern metropolis of roughly 3 million, scattered across a greater metropolitan area of 208 sq. km., a maelstrom of traffic and pollution, a rapidly and carelessly growing urban structure.

And yet there remains the old center of Rome, still enclosed by the walled perimeter erect-

The public rose garden on the Aventine hill in front of the ruins of the Palatine

ed nearly 2,000 years ago, and it is there that a visitor must go to find the remarkable allure – visual and mental – that has attracted people to this city over the centuries. A city center that may be the largest in the world, where many different cities coexist, stacked one atop the other. A gigantic open-air museum, as well as a real and living city, that is a two-fold capital – of Italy and of the Roman Catholic Church. A center that is still alive, inhabited by roughly 150,000 persons, a center – perhaps for the lack of any serious urban planing – has not been reduced to a mere stage and backdrop for gawking tourists. There has been no breakdown of the city into various sectors, as there has been instead for many other European capitals; rather, at a distance of just a few yards, there may be buildings that are focal points of religious or political power, the temples of business and finance, international shopping streets, museums, art galleries, neighborhood markets, and even flea markets. And all this is distributed in a way that may seem troublesome or anything but functional for those who have to live in this city, but full of charm and fun for the passing tourist.

And so it may be useful to forget your car, to walk or even to take to bicycling. As you wander through the center of Rome – an odd puzzle made up of a dozen different, interlocking cities – why should you not give yourself up to the spontaneity of the moment, and create your own, unusual tours? Why not go from one antiques shop to another? Why not seek out all the creations of Borromini, or go visit all the works of Caravaggio, scattered throughout the churches and museums of Rome? Or why not visit the smaller art galleries, or wander through the many marketplaces of Rome, or seek out little restaurants, obscure theaters, unusual shops or craftsmen's workshops, in Trastevere, Campo de' Fiori, Monti, or Testaccio, the quarters populated by the young, by the intellectuals, and by artists? Go on a tour of the myriad staircases and stairways, the fountains and drinking fountains, the portals and the heraldic crests of old aristocratic palazzi, which appear suddenly at every street corner?

And in order to find some peace and quiet, you may seek out the little network of pedestrian malls, havens that are too often violated by vehicles, but which allow you to sit at a little table in the open air at one of Rome's more famous bars, watching the flow of strollers in this age-old capital, where the brand new comes to mingle with the homely and ancient flavor of the old "rioni."

When you should go. The Roman climate is one that favors tourism: there is nice weather during the winter, generally clear and sunny, "ottobrate" – literally, "Octobering" – that tends to be warm and bright, and in the springtime there is intense color and perfume of budding plants, in the summer there are "ponentino," or western evening breezes to clear away the muggy air of summer. Rome, in every season, offers something special. You may choose to visit the city in the springtime because there are generally a few days of pure summer even in the early season, and because there are the spectacular liturgical celebrations of Easter, or for the shows and exhibitions: there is a vast azalea show in Piazza di Spagna and an orchid show in the Orto Botanico in April, a huge antiques show and market in Via dei Coronari and the famous exhibition of 100 painters in the Via Margutta in May. Between May and June you can also tour the splendid collections of the Roseto Comunale (city rose garden) on the Aventine. Sports fans will not want to miss the international horse show between April and May in Piazza di Siena, and in May the international tennis championships are held at the Foro Italico.

Those who would rather go in the summer should know that July is the hottest and most frenzied month in Rome. In August, on the other hand, the city is finally empty, traffic comes to a virtual standstill, and the city emerges in all its splendor. There are difficulties, of course, with so many restaurants and other businesses closed, but then there are the numerous events of the "estate romana," or Roman summer, including the popular high-fashion runway presentations on the Spanish Steps of Trinità dei Monti and the Tevere Expò, an annual exposition of craftsmanship along the banks of the Tiber, between the bridges of Ponte S. Angelo and Ponte Cavour.

In fall, the weather is mostly sunny, though there are occasional cloudbursts. The spectacular sunsets over the Tiber tinge the old palazzi with pink and orange hues. But Rome is also lovely at Christmas: the cold "tramontana" wind that sweeps the sky clear and blue does not keep you from strolling; this is when the main streets of the center fill with refined decorations, when the stalls are out in the Piazza Navona, and when the main exhibitions and films open. And, when the frenzy of Christmas is over, the sales begin: January and February are ideal shopping months for those interested in making fine purchases.

How to get there. Rome is connected with the major cities of Italy by a very good **highway system**, the main branches of which are: *the Autostrada del Sole* Milan-Naples, which links up with the *GRA* (Grande Raccordo Anulare, Rome's beltway) near the capital, the *A16* Rome-Civitavecchia, and the *A24* Rome-L'Aquila. You can also get to Rome on one of the old consular roads ("strade consolari"), which converge on the city like spokes, from every corner of Italy. For those who decide to drive to Rome, we recommend selecting a hotel with its own parking area, or with a nearby parking structure, quite rare. The largest parking areas with attendants are: the underground parking areas of *Villa Borghese* (Via del Galoppatoio 33) and *Villa Ludovisi* (Via Ludovisi 60, tel. 4740632), the parking areas of *Piazza Mancini* (not far from the Stadio Olimpico), the *Villaggio Olimpico* (in Via Flaminia), and on the *Piazzale della Stazione Tiburtina*.

For those who prefer to reach the capital by **train** the *Stazione Termini* (Piazzale dei Cinquecento, tel. 4775) is the major station, and from here trains leave for all the major destinations in Italy and the rest of Europe. The stations arranged around the city are minor stations for local traffic and, often, for interregional trains.

There are different ways of getting into the city for those who choose to **fly**; best to land at the *Aeroporto Leonardo da Vinci* (tel. 65951) in Fiumicino, for national and international flights, or at the *Aeroporto di Ciampino* (Via Appia Nuova, tel. 794941), which is smaller and not as busy. Transportation to and from Fiumicino, which is roughly ca. 50 minutes from the center of Rome, leaves from the Air Terminal of the FFSS (Italian National Railway

Company): there are trains from the Stazione Ostiense every 20 minutes that arrive directly at the Aerostazione; you can also take a coach from Via Giolitti, alongside the Stazione di Termini. For Ciampino (ca. 30 minutes from the center of Rome) you can take the Metropolitana Linea A (subway) to the Cinecittà stop, where you can catch a COTRAL motor coach to the airport.

We should mention the *Aeroporto dell'Urbe*, for private planes and touring planes (Via Salaria 825, tel. 8120524).

Information. Listed here are a series of addresses of public and city offices and institutions that can provide information or permits to visit a number of monumental complexes that are usually closed to the public.

Ente Provinciale per il Turismo di Roma, or tourist board of Rome: Via Parigi 11, tel. 4881851.

Posta Centrale, central post office: Piazza di S. Silvestro 19, tel. 6771.

Posti Telefonici Pubblici, phone offices: Piazza di S. Silvestro 20, tel. 6795909; Piazza dei Cinquecento (inside the Stazione Termini), tel. 4775.

Transportation. Is it easy to get around Rome? That question is difficult to answer, considering the layout of this city, that developed on the slopes and peaks and valleys of seven surrounding hills, with different characteristics and stratifications of centuries of history in a succession of concepts of urban planning that have diverged greatly over time. The *ATAC* (which stands for Azienda Tramvie Autobus Comune di Roma, literally trolley and bus company of the city of Rome, tel. 4824451) is not exactly famous for its efficiency, even though serving a city that is "extra-populous" with too many cars and too-narrow streets, hard to get through for larger vehicles, does present daunting obstacles. The main bus terminal points are scattered through the central sections of town: Piazza dei Cinquecento, Piazza Venezia, Largo Augusto Imperatore, Piazzale Flaminio, Piazza Risorgimento, Piazzale Clodio, and Piazza Mancini (near the Stadio Olimpico). Tickets are valid for 90 minutes, riding anywhere on the transportation network; you can purchase 24-hour tickets, which are also good for the Metropolitana, Rome's subway system.

The Roman *Metropolitana* is run by an agency called *COTRAL* (Cooperativa Trasporti Lazio, or cooperative for transportation in Latium, tel. 5915551) and has only two lines: the "A" running from the Vatican (Ottaviano station) to Tuscolana (Anagnina station) and the "B" from Rebibbia to the EUR (EUR Fermi station). From the "B," Magliana station, trains set out about every 30 minutes – in the morning, less frequent throughout the day – for Lido di Ostia, which can be reached from the Termini station approximately every 30 minutes. COTRAL also offers a thorough network of motorcoaches running to areas around Rome and in the neighboring provinces.

Tickets for the motorcoaches and for the Metropolitana can be purchased at tobacconist's shops, at newsstands near the stations and bus stops, or in ATAC kiosks, found near the main terminuses.

One pleasant and unusual way of touring the city is to hire one of the historic "botticelle," traditional Roman carriages that can be found at "carriage stands" (the main ones are in Piazza S. Pietro, at the Colosseum, in Piazza Venezia, Piazza della Rotonda, Piazza di Spagna, at the Fontana di Trevi, at Villa Borghese, and in Piazza Navona) at official rates; you should take advantage of them while you can; it is a piece of Roman folkways that in time will very likely vanish.

Accommodations. In the capital of Italy, there is a wide array of hotels. Thre are of course many luxury hotels, most of them situated in historic areas of the city: buildings designed and furnished by the finest architects of the late-19th c.; ancient aristocratic homes; 16th-c. inns, cunningly renovated; all of them offer a central location, fine panoramic views (often enjoyed from magnificent roof-gardens), and excellent service. Equally exclusive hotels can be found on the outskirts of Rome, offering other services to outweigh their location. Excellent alternatives for those who wish to keep to a smaller budget can be found in the many mid-level hotels, the countless "pensioni," the "residences" and the hotel/homes run by religious organizations; these latter are generally in the area around St. Peter's (the Ente Provinciale per il Turismo will provide listings). No matter the season, you should make reservations.

The two international youth hostels are insufficient to satisfy the growing demand of travelling young people (especially in the summer and at Easter); but not far from the city there are functional and well organized camping areas, located in ample greenbelts along the coast and the main thoroughfares.

In the last few years, some hotels and campgrounds have been converted into facilities for housing the flood of immigrants from outside of Europe.

Shopping. The "Eternal City" is also the biggest shopping city in Italy, and is a major international marketplace. Above all, it is the surprising variety of what you can find, much more than the actual Roman quality of the products, that will strike the visitor most forcefully. In Rome, the complete array of exclusive Italian and European haute-couture can be seen alongside a wide array of products at every level of price. Outrageous fashion and classical sobriety merge and mix in the display windows, suited to every taste and every pocketbook.

Piazza del Popolo, Piazza Venezia, and Piazza di Spagna form the three corners of the shopping triangle in which you will find the highest quality and most expensive stores. The best known jewelers and the more refined boutiques of Italian and European high fashion are located along the Via dei Condotti, Via Frattina, Via Borgognona, and Via della Croce: Bulgari (fine jewelry), Fendi (leather goods), Gucci, Battistoni, Valentino, and Laura Biagiotti (pret-a-porter). Not far off, in the Via Veneto, the atelier of shoe-designer Raphael Salato is a drawing card for visitors from around the world.

The most exclusive shops selling artworks and antiques and fabrics for interior decoration are chiefly found in the Via del Babuino and Via Margutta, but also – if you step outside the "triangle" – in the Via dei Coronari and Via Giulia.

Stores selling objects linked to religious iconography and souvenir shops are scattered throughout the center of Rome, but there are two specialized areas in which you can actually find objects of considerable quality – Via della Conciliazione and the area around the Pantheon. The latter of these two areas also has a solid crafts tradition and an array of shops of all sorts, selling quality goods.

For visitors interested in Italian fashion and design, but reluctant to spend heavily, the Via Nazionale offers an unbroken series of shops with products of average quality. Other thoroughfares with a sharply commercial character – more popular with Romans than with tourists – include Via Cola di Rienzo, Viale Libia, and Viale Eritrea, which are veritable bazaars, with merchandise of every type and description.

Lastly, a note on open-air markets: the largest and most colorful in the city is in Piazza Vittorio Emanuele II, famous for its competitive prices as well; in the old section of Rome, note the market in Campo de' Fiori; used items of all sorts can be found in Via Sannio. The most traditional and crowded flea market in Rome, however, is certainly the one in Porta Portese – here you should be prepared to stroll and rummage every Sunday morning.

Rome by night. Unlike London, Berlin, and New York, which have quarters devoted to entertainment and nightlife, here you must learn to find your way through a vast and fragmentary network of clubs and meeting places, scattered through various zones of the city. We recommend reading the "pagine degli spettacoli," or entertainment pages of any

Window shopping

of the daily newspapers (some have special supplements) or else obtaining those publications that list events day-by-day; those who wish to attend the theater should enquire about tickets well ahead of time.

There are roughly 100 movie houses, including about 15 art houses, which offer the possibility of seeing the latest films, sampling retrospectives of the work of certain directors, or finding films that you cannot normally see, and even seeing movies in their original languages; even Rome has begun to adopt multiplex cinemas, increasing the selection of titles.

Flea Market at Porta Portese

There are about 60 theaters and concert halls, ranging from a classic repertory to cutting edge avant-garde productions, from musicals to cabarets; there is an interesting array of productions at the Teatro dell'Opera, which has in recent years offered enchanting summertime concerts and productions at the Baths of Caracalla.

Pubs, night clubs, and discotheques are set up and shut down in Rome with remarkable speed. To list the latest ones is practically impossible in this context: around the Via Veneto you will find the more exclusive and sophisticated spots, in the historical center there are discotheques and private clubs that are popular with upper class Romans, known here as "Roma bene," while the more daring and entertaining discotheques and clubs – in the quarters of Flaminio, Parioli, and Pinciano – offer wild music and exotic settings.

We should devote a separate chapter to the cocktail bars of Rome, a term, used in Italian, that fails to do justice to one of the most attractive aspects of Roman nightlife. You can find them just about everywhere (in Trastevere and Testaccio, in the Rione Monti, around Piazza Navona and Piazza del Pantheon, behind the Via Cavour) and, generally open from 10 pm to 3 am, they are meeting spots where people can drink or snack while listening to music or watching videos, where you can watch rock, jazz, blues, or funk concerts, or many other exotic forms of music, with the performance of well-known or less-well-known groups, though always of some note.

Lastly, we should point out the recent development of "centri sociali occupati," or, literally, occupied social centers, small self-run squatters' outposts, generally on the outskirts of town, popular with young people, where the newest Roman musical groups perform.

Festivals and celebrations. The Roman calendar is studded with noteworthy events, must-sees for those who wish to have some sense of the flavor of old traditions. There are many religious and non-religious feasts and festivals, though quite a few have been lost; those that survive have lost the solemnity and universal participation that once distinguished them.

The night of 6 January, for the feast of the Epiphany, creches in the churches are visited by the Three Magi, and in the Sala del Bramante adjoining the church of S. Maria del Popolo there is an interesting exhibition of 100 creches from every place on earth.

For the feast of S. Antonio Abate (St. Anthony), on the 17th of the same month, benedictions are given for animals in the church courtyard of S. Eusebio, while the two lambs that are sheared for the wool for holy banners ("sacri palii") to be given to the pope are blessed on the 21st in the basilica of S. Agnese Fuori le Mura (St. Agnes Without-the-Walls). During the feast of the "Candelora" (Candlemas; 2 February), candles are blessed and distributed in commemoration of the rite of purification of the Virgin Mary.

Amidst processions and public illuminations, on 19 March Rome celebrates S. Giuseppe, the popular feast of St. Joseph, which has perhaps lost in recent years the solemnity and color of bygone years; during this feast, the Quartiere Trionfale (St. Joseph being that quarter's patron saint), in an explosion of the sacred and the profane, holds a procession that winds through the streets, lined with stalls of food vendors – "porchettari," "frittellari," and cotton-candy stands.

And then there is Easter, a major holiday in Rome, especially with the rites of Holy Week, the Via Crucis from the Colosseum to the Palatine hill, and the traditional benediction by the pope in Piazza S. Pietro. There are all sorts of cultural events and ceremonies, bands and fanfares, fireworks and banners, to commemorate the foundation of Rome, on 21 April. On 23 and 24 June, in S. Giovanni, there is another old and authentically Roman festival, with games, singing competitions, illuminations, and, in the taverns of the Quartiere S. Giovanni, great feasts of roast pork ("porchetta") and snails. Also noteworthy are the feasts of the patron saints, St. Peter and St. Paul, on 29 June, with the vestition of the statue of St. Peter in the Basilica Vaticana.

Decidedly more heartfelt and working-class is the Festa de' Noantri which takes place in Trastevere. The traditional procession transports the Madonna del Carmine, a richly adorned statue of the Virgin Mary, from the church of S. Agata to the church of S. Crisogono. On 5 August, on the other hand, during the spectacular ceremony of the Madonna della Neve, in the basilica of S. Maria Maggiore a shower of white rose petals descends upon the faithful at the moment of "Gloria" in commemoration of the snowfall on the Esquiline hill on 15 August, in A.D. 352.

Dining out. You can have everything from "nouvelle cuisine" to the old Roman cooking. After years of paté, mousse, "escargot," and "quiche lorraine" Rome is finally rediscovering its culinary roots. Not only "osterie" and "trattorie," which have always been temples of rustic cuisine of Italy's capital, but even the most refined restaurants offer the old dishes of Roman tradition: rigatoni with "pajata" (innards of beef or veal), an old favorite of local cuisine, the famous "bucatini all'amatriciana," the "spaghetti alla carbonara," or the "spaghetti a cacio e pepe" (pancetta, egg, pecorino cheese, red pepper, and fresh black pepper); and then there are chickpea and lentil soups, "gnocchi alla semolella" and "fettuccine paja e fieno," literally, hay and straw. Baked lamb – or lamb "a scottadito" or lamb "brodettato," tripe, "porchetta" (a savory roast pig), "coda alla vaccinara," or oxtail, and "pollo con i peperoni" (chicken with peppers) are all familiar flavors and smells. Particularly savory are "carciofi alla giudia," a wonderful artichoke dish, a heritage of Italian Jewish cooking, and a mixed fry ("fritto misto") of meat and vegetables (sweetmeats, brains, filets of cod, artichokes, and zucchini). Side dishes: "cicoria e puntarelle," chickory and other typical vegetables of the Campagna Romana, or Roman countryside, seasoned with oil and anchovies or with a sauce of egg yolks, oil, salt, and lemon.

The wines are the fine standards of the Castelli: Frascati, Marino, and Colli Albani.

Among the pastries and sweets, try the "maritozzi," little puffs with pignoli, raisin, and candied fruit (the Romans often fill them with whipped cream); it was once a custom for young lovers to give these to their sweethearts during Lent.

And for those who wish to relive an ancient Roman tradition, one of the largest and finest bakers in Rome, in Via Merulana, every year, the first Thursday of June, offers free bread to the citizens of Rome, in honor of Ceres, the goddess of fertility (as was the custom in ancient Rome).

When dining in Rome, the array of Roman restaurants is both wide and diversified: there is alternative cuisine and new flavors, from regional food to exotic food; there are hundreds of "rosticcerie," "tavole calde," and pizzerias, where for a reasonable amount of money you can eat a pizza, "bruschetta," and "crostini al prosciutto" or "crostini alle alici."

Italy: Useful Addresses

Citizens of Australia, Canada, New Zealand, and the United States can enter Italy with a valid passport, and stay for a period of not more than 90 days; citizens of Great Britain and Ireland, as members of the European Union, can travel either with valid passport or with valid identification card.

Foreign Embassies in Italy

Australia:
Via Alessandria 215, Rome, tel. (06) 852721

Canada:
Via G.B. de Rossi 27, Rome, tel. (06) 445981

New Zealand:
Via Zara 28, Rome, tel. (06) 4404035-4402928

United States of America:
Via Vittorio Veneto 119/A, Palazzo Margherita, Rome, tel. (06) 46741

Great Britain:
Via XX Settembre 80, Rome, tel. (06) 4825441

Ireland:
Largo Nazareno 3, Rome, tel. (06) 6782541

Foreign Consulates in Italy

Australia:
Via Borgogna 2, Milan, tel. (02) 76013330 - 76013852

Canada:
Via Vittor Pisani 19, Milan, tel. (02) 6758001

New Zealand:
Via F. Sforza 48, Milan, tel. (02) 58314443

United States of America:
– Lungarno A.Vespucci 38, Florence, tel. (055) 2398276
– Via Principe Amedeo 2/10, Milan, tel. (02) 290351
– Piazza Repubblica 2, Naples, tel. (081) 5838111
– Via Re Federico 18/bis, Palermo, (consular agency), tel. (091) 6110020

Great Britain:
– Via S. Paolo 7, Milano, tel. (02) 723001
– Dorsoduro 1051, Venezia, tel. (041) 5227207

Italian Embassies and Consulates Around the World

Australia:
12 Grey Street - Deakin, Canberra, tel.(06) 273-3333
Consulates at: Adelaide, Brisbane, Melbourne, Perth, Sydney.

Canada:
275 Slater Street, 21st floor, Ottawa (Ontario), tel.(613) 2322401

Consulates at: Montreal, Toronto, Vancouver.

New Zealand:
34 Grant Road, Wellington, tel.(4) 4735339 - 4736667

United States of America:
1601 Fuller Street, N.W., Washington D.C., tel.(202) 328-5500
Consulates at: Boston, Chicago, Philadelphia, Houston, Los Angeles, Miami, New York, New Orleans, San Francisco.

Great Britain:
14, Three Kings Yard, London W.1, tel.(0171) 3122200
Consulates at: Edinburgh, Manchester.

Ireland:
63/65, Northumberland Road, Dublin 4, tel.(01) 6601744

ENIT

In order to have general information and documentation concerning the best known places in Italy, you can contact the offices of the Ente Nazionale Italiano per il Turismo (ENIT), run by the Italian government; they are open Mon.-Fri., from 9 to 5.

Canada:
Office National Italien du Tourisme/Italian Government, Travel Office, Montreal, Quebec H3B 3M9, 1 Place Ville Marie, Suite 1914, tel. (514) 866-7667/866-7669, fax 392-1429

United States of America:
– Italian Government Tourist Board c/o Italian Trade Commission, New York, N.Y. 10022, 499 Park Avenue, tel. (212) 843-6884/843-6885, fax 843-6886.
– Italian Government Travel Office, Chicago 1, Illinois 60611-401, North Michigan Avenue, Suite 3030, tel. (312) 644-0996, fax 644-3019
– Italian Government Travel Office, Los Angeles, CA 90025, 12400, Wilshire Blvd. Suite 550, tel. (310) 820-0098/820-1898, fax 820-6357

Great Britain:
Italian State Tourist Board, London W1R 6AY, 1 Princes Street, tel. (0171) 408-1254 fax 493-6695

1 Entering Rome

If surprise and wonderment were once the almost immediate result of entering through the city walls of Rome, the different nature of travel nowadays and the immense development and growth of the city no longer allow a modern-day visitor to experience a similar first contact with the remarkable cultural presence that Rome has always been and continues to be. And yet, the perception of just how remarkable a place this is cannot long elude the visitor, even the hastiest tourist, whether visiting the most classic of tourist attractions or simply wandering at hazard through the city, if that tourist or visitor will merely consider the incredible layers of buildings, cultures, and traditions that the city still reveals almost at every step, even in areas that have been developed only relatively recently. A city unlike any other on earth, Rome displays, even on the more usual routes into the historical center – which to all intents and purposes is still the center of the modern city – the evidence of a succession of ancient, medieval, and modern settlements in an unbroken series, in a substantially unified network of buildings dating back over almost three thousand years; the best way to examine them might be "stratigraphic" in approach.

The "decumanus maximus" in Ostia Antica

In whatever manner you choose to tour it, Rome offers – since it is the only city on earth that for nearly 30 centuries has developed and grown on the same site, notably larger only over the last century, and even so with most of the same landmarks and locations – a unified image, a clear indication of a certain continuity, and almost of some mysterious purpose: the ancient ports, long since buried or silted over, may accommodate much larger and faster craft than the old Roman cargo ships, as is the case with Fiumicino, once a river port and now an airport; huge baths, which were once the site of vineyards and hunting preserves during the Middle Ages and in the Renaissance, now overlook a bare railroad marshalling yard. This transformation has in no way altered the relationship that this city maintains with its own history, toward which, one might say, it tends periodically to return, to find new reasons for expansion.

The three routes recommended for this chapter are intended to show this character to its best advantage. From whatever part of the world travellers may arrive, they will probably find in Rome traces of their own native culture: "universal" in this way as well, Rome was the capital of a political empire that later became the center of a universal faith, that over the centuries, has succeeded in gathering, amalgamating, and in some sense, retransmitting, at least within that faith, cultural contributions from all over the planet, the heritage of every conqueror and ruler – and every sightseer and tourist. And everyone who has passed through Rome has nurtured the hope that the sign of their passage should be preserved in the immense experiential melting pot that is Rome, to be glimpsed by future generations. And that is just one more reason – and not the least – for the allure and interest of any trip to Rome.

1.1 From the Stazione di Termini to Piazza Venezia

In the final decades of the 19th c., the new capital of the kingdom of Italy arranged a new approach for visitors and for important guests, who no longer arrived along the old consular roads, but rather descended from trains at the new terminus, or Stazione di Termini. The groundwork for this great terminus was laid, under Pius IX, first of all with the decision (1860) to unify at Termini the existing railroad lines, and later with the overall urban project drawn up by Monsignor Francesco Saverio de Merode, who devised and laid out the first stretch of an avenue linking up with the historical center and the various side streets along the way. The route followed by this "Via Nazionale" – including the stretch of road later named after Vittorio Emanuele II, or Victor Emmanuel II of Savoy, the king, and originally called the "Via Nazionale" – was conceived and implemented with a view to creating an impressive and representative approach to the city. This route celebrated the new monarchy with public buildings, with the Altar of the Fatherland, and with two non-Catholic churches, allowed inside the walls, but it also represented the new "national" middle class, or bourgeoisie, with the palazzi, stores, cafes, and theaters, without neglecting – in the second section – the old papal nobility that displayed its elegant homes here.

The axis of Via Nazionale-Corso Vittorio Emanuele II, lined with buildings designed by the best professionals of the era, established an urban and architectural model for Rome under king Umberto, both in the areas being newly developed and in the work done in the heart of the historical center.

From Piazza dei Cinquecento, which spreads out before the Termini railroad station, along with the impressive ruins of the baths of Diocletian and the new site of the Museo Nazionale Romano, the walking tour runs to Piazza della Repubblica, nowadays, as in bygone times, commonly called the Piazza dell'Esedra and embellished by the church of S. Maria degli Angeli, by Michelangelo; from here, the Via Nazionale runs off to the SW, a long straight avenue that runs past the Palazzo delle Esposizioni, by Piacentini, and the medieval tower, or Torre delle Milizie, and changes direction, angle, and name (Via IV Novembre and Via Battisti), before leading into Piazza Venezia.

Piazza dei Cinquecento (5 D2-3; 14 B1). The layout of this vast tree-lined square,

named after the 500 victims of Dògali (the *monument* honoring those 500, by Francesco Azzurri, 1887, was moved in 1925 to the gardens in the nearby Viale Einaudi), was a consequence of the changes in the structure of the new station (1948) and has been modified repeatedly in subsequent years to accommodate auto and pedestrian traffic. This square is in fact the main terminus of public transportation in Rome, where many bus lines converge, and the intersection point of the two lines of Rome's Metropolitana, or subway.

Stazione Centrale di Termini (5 D-E3; 14 B1). The architecture is noteworthy for the horizontal extension of the remarkably long front elevation (232 m.), faced with travertine and emphasized by the continuous band of windows (two on each floor, except for the top floor), and for the canopy roof made of reinforced concrete (the so-called "dinosaur"); the ticket atrium is open on three sides, with full-height sheet glass, while the well-lit gallery at the head of the tracks behind that atrium allows passengers to reach the trains, and links Via Marsala with Via Giolitti.

Mura Serviane*, or Servian walls (5 D3; 14 B1). Tradition dates these tufa-stone walls back to the reign of the king Servius Tullius; to the left of the station, you can see a well-preserved section; reinforced by an embankment ("agger"), the walls ran during the Republic for a length of about 11 km., with a height of nearly 10 m. and an average thickness of 4 m.

This system of fortifications, largely destroyed during the invasion of the Gauls, was restored during the Second Punic War, and again under the reign of Augustus – who rebuilt the gates – by which time the walls had lost their military value; they were later incorporated into buildings dating from imperial times.

Museo Nazionale Romano*. This museum, which possesses one of the most important archeological collections on earth, was inaugurated in 1889, in the complex of the baths of Diocletian, with a collection of artifacts unearthed after 1870, to which were added the antiquities of the Museo Kircheriano and those of the Ludovisi Collection, acquired in 1901, and the various materials found in later excavations. The main core of the collection is now on display in the *Palazzo dell'Ex Collegio "Massimiliano Massimo"* (5 D2), a building that was erected in 1883-87, a copy of the aristocratic palazzi of early Roman Baroque; this building, in the context of the project of a larger Museo Nazionale Romano and at the end of a complex restoration (1983-92), will become the most important section of the museum; it stands next to the "historic building" in the baths of Diocletian (see below) and to Palazzo Altemps (see page 109), destined respectively to hold the Epigraphic Department and the historical sculpture collections, among which the Ludovisi.

The thematic sections document the salient aspects of the art practiced in Rome between the time of Sulla and the end of the empire. On the ground floor, note an inter-esting series of artworks that illustrate the iconographic styles found in the transitional phase between the late Republican age and the age of Augustus; alongside the numerous busts, the inscriptions, and the coins from the Republican era, note the *statue of August Pontifex Maximus** and the *Niobid* from the "Horti Sallustiani", a Greek original, dating about 5th c. B.C.

A number of different halls on the second floor illustrate the development of tastes and iconographic styles in the Roman world, from the 1st to 4th c. A.D., and the various sculptural decorations of the imperial villas, aristocratic residences, and gardens; of particular interest is the *young girl of Anzio* and the statue of Apollo (Roman copy from a Greek original from the 4th

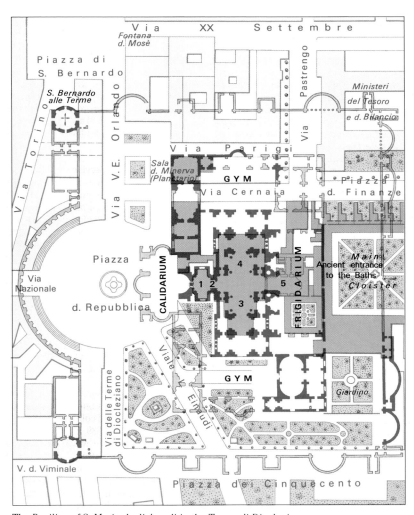

The Basilica of S. Maria degli Angeli in the Terme di Diocleziano

c. B.C.) from the villas of Nero at Anzio et Subiaco, the *Aphrodite Crouching*, an *Amazon* and a *Dionysus* (Roman statue based upon a Greek original from the 4th c. B.C.) from Hadrian's Villa; the **Lancellotti discus thrower**, the **discus thrower of Castel Porziano** and the *Apollo Chigi**. Aside from the theatrical masks and the Dionysian reliefs, the bronze decorations of the so-called *Ships of Nemi** stand out, floating platforms on the lake infront of Caligola's villa. Then there is large section devoted to official portraits, including: the *bust of Julia Domna*, with its distinctive hairstyle, the *statue of a boy on a horse*, in marble and alabaster, and the colossal *head of Alexander Severus* (3rd c.); also, of special note, the *sarcophagus of Portonaccio* with scenes of battle between Romans and barbarians, the *sarcophagus of Acìlia* from the second half of the 3rd c., the *sarcophagus of Claudianus* with scenes from the Old and the New Testaments, and the colossal *krater** decorated with one of the earliest images known of the Virgin Mary with Christ Child.

On the second floor are decorative series, painted and in mosaic, dating from the 1st c. B.C. to the late empire: alongside the splendid **frescoes** (late-1st c. B.C.) **from the Villa "ad Gallinas Albas"** of Livia, depicting a luxuriant garden and orchard, you can also admire the **stuccoes** and the **frescoes of the Villa della Farnesina**, characterized by delicate miniature architectural landscapes, set between slender candelabra and plant festoons, and the frescoes taken, along with a group of *mosaics*, from the Villa di Castel di Guido.

The subterranean level contains a section devoted to goldsmithery and a major numismatic collection, including such exceedingly rare items as the *medallion of Theodoric*, silve *plaques* with views of the city, the Papal State, and the four *ducats* of Pope Paul II depicting St. Peter's boat.

Terme di Diocleziano*, or baths of Diocletian (5 C-D2). Begun in 298 and completed between 305 and 306, these were the largest baths in Rome (covering a surface area of 376 x 361 sq. m.); the structure could accommodate ca. 3,000 persons, and it copied – in the central wing, surrounded by gardens with nymphaea, exedrae, and groups of rooms on the interior – the layout of the baths of Trajan. Of the complex, an exceptional example of the reutilization of structures, there survive – aside from the rooms transformed into the Basilica di S. Maria degli Angeli (see below) and those adapted for the Museo Nazionale Romano

– two rotundas from the outer perimeter and the main exedra, which served as a cavea from which to watch people exercising, reiterated in the lines of the buildings erected by Gaetano Koch in Piazza della Repubblica.

The historic site of the Museo Nazionale Romano is currently under expansion and re-organization, linked to the new site, in the former Collegio "Massimo"; in the general context of reinstallation of the museum, the complex of the baths of Diocletian and the charter house will be largely reserved for a *Dipartimento Epigrafico*, or epigraphic department, which will contain the major epigraphic collection (ca. 10,000 inscriptions). The four sections, arranged chronologically, will illustrate the significance of epigraphic production and the techniques linked thereto: the birth of epigraphy and its development, until the late Roman republic; epigraphy as a mirror of political, social, and religious change during the empire; Rome and other cities in epigraphic terms. The museum will also feature an interesting collection of sarcophagi (dating from the 1st to the 4th c.), busts and reliefs.

Piazza della Repubblica (5 D1-2). Once called the Piazza dell'Esedra, or Exedra, inasmuch as it followed the large curving structure with tiers, belonging to the nearby thermal complex, this square was renovated at the end of the 19th c. as a major "entrance" from the station into the city. At the center stands the *Fontana delle Naiadi* (or Fontana dell'Esedra), the most monumental fountain of all those created following the unification of Italy: on the basin (1888) note the four bronze *groups with nymphs riding sea monsters* (1901).

S. Maria degli Angeli* (5 C-D2). The first stirrings of the idea of transforming the baths of Diocletian into a church date back to Giuliano da Sangallo and Baldassarre Peruzzi (ca. 1515), but it was not until 1561 that the priest Antonio Del Duca obtained from Pope Pius IV the consecration of the place of worship, dedicating it to the angels and to the Christian martyrs who, according to legend, worked on the construction of the baths. Michelangelo was entrusted with this project, while at the same time the Carthusians, to whom Pope Pius IV had assigned the complex, built the convent (the main cloister, known as the "Chiostro di Michelangelo," dates from 1565).

The later transformation of the complex began in 1700, with the creation of the Cappella di S. Brunone, named after the founder of the Carthusian order, while the redecoration done by Luigi Vanvitelli for the Holy Year of 1750 resulted in the present-day appearance of the interior.

You should observe in particular: in the aedicules of the interior vestibule (plan, 1), on the right, are the *funerary monuments of Carlo Maratta*, executed to his own design, and with a bust by Francesco Maratta (ca. 1704), *and of the cardinal Francesco Alciati* (d. 1580) by G.B. Della Porta, and, on the left, the *funerary monument to Salvator Rosa* (d. 1673), with sculptures by Bernardino Fioriti; in the passageway (2), note the *statue of St. Bruno the Great of Cologne*, founder of the Carthusian order, by Jean-Antoine Houdon (1766-68); in the right arm (3) of the cross-aisle, note the *funerary monuments* of the three leading figures behind Italy's role in WWI: *of Vittorio Emanuele Orlando* (d. 1953) by Pietro Canonica, *of the admiral Thaon di Revel*, again by Canonica (1950) and *of the marshall Armando Diaz* (d. 1928) designed by Antonio Muñoz; in the left arm (4), note the *Fall of Simon Magus* by Pompeo Batoni (1755); in the presbytery (5), on the right wall note the *Martyrdom of St. Sebastian*, an oil painting on stucco by Domenichino, while on the left wall, note the *Baptism of Jesus* by Carlo Maratta (1697).

A short detour to the left of the entrance to the church allows one to reach the hall – beyond Via Cernaia – known as the **Sala della Minerva** (5 C1), in a corner of the complex of the baths. In 1928 the hall was converted into a planetarium.

It houses sculptures from the Museo Nazionale Romano, originally from the baths, including a *satyr's head* and a *Cnidean*

Aphrodite – copies from originals by Praxiteles – and the *Aphrodite of Cirene**, derived in style during the age of Hadrian from the prototype of the Venere Anadiomene by Praxiteles, and the two bronze *statues* of the so-called **Greek Prince*** (2nd c. B.C.) and of the **Seated Boxer** (1st c. B.C.).

Via Nazionale (4 D-E-F4-5-6; 5 D1). This was the first road of modern Rome; it follows the route of the classical "Vicus Longus," from the baths of Diocletian to the Forum of Augustus; the segment that runs as far as the intersection with Via delle Quattro Fontane, along with three cross-streets, was built under the auspices of Monsignor de Merode between 1864 and 1866, while the city government saw to the urbanization and completion of the road all the way to Piazza Venezia, after 1871.

Torre delle Milizie* (6 E6). This tower is a significant piece of civil architecture of medieval Rome; it was erected by the Conti family at the turn of the 13th c., and later purchased by Pope Boniface VIII, who fortified it as protection from the Colonna family.

The earthquake of 1348 caused the collapse of the fourth floor and the shift in the soil beneath its foundations, which is why the tower still leans sharply. In the 16th c., it once again belonged to the Conti family; from 1619 it was owned by the nuns of S. Caterina (St. Catherine), who incorporated it into their convent; following the restoration and consolidation by Antonio Muñoz in 1914, the tower was incorporated from 1927 on into the Mercati di Traiano, or Trajan's Market.

1.2 From Fiumicino and Lido di Ostia to Piazza Venezia

This route features the ancient – and paradoxically exceedingly modern – approach to Rome as experienced by long-distance travelers; the maritime docks of the ancient imperial capital and the modern intercontinental airport are in fact located quite near each other. Every day, hundreds of aircraft and tens of thousands of modern travelers pass each day over the archeological digs of ancient Ostia.

Throughout the tour you will experience this intertwining of themes, from the most ancient to the most modern: the route of the Via Ostiense, which runs parallel to the great modern thoroughfares toward the sea, intersecting the motorway ring roads, alternates memories of the classical era

A sculpture in the Theater of Ostia Antica

with the futuristic settings of EUR and the more modest settings of the quarters and outlying villages that have been built in the last few decades; beyond Porta S. Paolo and the pyramid of Caius Cestius, which were the settings of some of the most dramatic episodes in the war of liberation during WWII, the broad thoroughfares built in the first third of the 20th c. run past some of the most impressive relics of Roman antiquity. Setting out by car from the "Leonardo da Vinci" airport (though from the Circus Maximus, this can also be a walking route), you will pass Lido di Ostia and the excavations Ostia Antica.

Following the Via Ostiense back to Rome after a stop at the Basilica di S. Paolo Fuori le Mura, or St. Paul's Without-the-Walls, you

port in the Mediterranean area – and it was built on the site of the ancient *Port of Claudius*; the structures of the ancient port, unearthed during the construction of the airport, were later buried again.

The airport has been in operation since 1961, and it has undergone continuous expansion and improvements, with some examples of remarkable architecture (*Alitalia aircraft hangars* di Riccardo Morandi, 1960-63 and 1970). Since 1990, those exiting the airport will find a railroad terminal, for the line that connects the airport to the train station of Roma Termini, where Lines A and B of the Roman underground, or Metropolitana cross.

In the area immediately surrounding the air terminal, moreover, you will find the

The sandy shore of the Lido di Ostia, a much loved seaside resort

will pass through the Aurelian walls of Rome; within that enclosure you will take the Viale della Piramide Cestia – which is named for the pyramid of Caius Cestius, a famous monument, now part of the walled perimeter – and the Viale Aventino until you reach the Circo Massimo, or Circus Maximus, a first "taste" of the long series of monument lying near the Velabro (church of S. Maria in Cosmedin, Arco di Giano, or Arch of Janus) and along the Fascist-built Via del Mare (Casa dei Crescenzi, theater of Marcellus) which – with the names of Via Petroselli and Via del Teatro di Marcello – leads to Piazza Venezia.

Aeroporto Intercontinentale "Leonardo da Vinci". The airport of Fiumicino is one of the largest intercontinental airports in Europe – and, when work is finished, the largest air-

Museo delle Navi, a museum containing the remains of five of the seven ships found at the mouth of the Port of Claudius.

Necropoli di "Portus" *. This necropolis, or vast cemetery (1st to 3rd c.; open: 9-4 or 5; in the summer 9-6) abounds in chamber tombs, often featuring cornices that frame funerary inscriptions; the interiors are decorated with stuccoes, paintings, or mosaics.

In some cases, there is an enclosure with two beds in masonry, for the funerary banquets; the terracotta reliefs on the fronts – now replaced by cast copies – indicated that those buried in these chamber tombs were craftsmen, doctors, and merchants. The less well-to-do were buried in chest-shaped tombs or in aedicules; the poor were simply buried under shed-roof overhangs, "a cappuccina," or even in an amphora.

The necropolis takes its name from the little town of "Portus," which developed in the 2nd c. around the *Lago di Traiano**, or Trajan's Lake, a harbor basin built by that emperor to deal with the silting up of the Porto di Claudio (port of Claudius; of the structures built by Trajan, we know the layout of the storehouses and the perimeter line of walls built by Constantine); the town itself, which served chiefly to store goods for the nearby trading port of Ostia, declined at the end of the 8th c.

Lido di Ostia. The "lungomare", or waterfront promenade, is marked by the *Piazza dei Ravennati*, originally the terminus of the Via Ostiense (the modern plaza was designed in 1939-40 during the construction of the landing facilities). One notable landmark of the Lido di Ponente is **Tor S. Michele**, a fortress designed by Michelangelo and built by Nanni di Baccio Bigio prior to 1568 (it can be reached from Piazza dei Ravennati by following the NW stretch of Lungomare Toscanelli, Via Giuliano da Sangallo, Corso Duca di Genova, and Via dell'Idroscalo and Via degli Atlantici).

If you take the SE section of the Lungomare Toscanelli toward the Lido di Levante you will see, along the *Lungomare Duilio* (1931), the three "historic" *bath houses* of Lido di Ostia: the *Plinius*; the *Tibidabo* (1936), rationalist in plan; and the *Kursaal* (beyond the Piazzale Mediterraneo, which marks the beginning of the Castel Fusano), designed with umbrella roofing, by Attilio La Padula and Pier Luigi Nervi, in 1950.

As you continue along the "lungomare" toward Anzio you can just glimpse – beyond the Piazzale Cristoforo Colombo at the terminus of the Via Cristoforo Colombo – the *presidential estate of Castel Porziano* (not open to the public), extending over 4,800 hectares, with an exceedingly old castle.

If, from the Piazzale Cristoforo Colombo, you return toward Rome, you will instead cross the *Parco di Castel Fusano*, 1,100 hectares of pine forest and Mediterranean maquis, open to the public since 1933. This is a traditional destination for Sunday outings and picnics, a custom which is seriously damaging the ecosystem here.

Archeological digs of Ostia Antica*. This colony – documented by archeological finds dating back to the end of the 5th or the beginning of the 6th c. B.C. – was founded as a rectangular, fortified citadel ("castrum") as a naval base for the Roman fleet; over

time it became increasingly important in the supply of provisions for Rome. Inscriptions tell of colonial independence from the 1st c. B.C. on, and as early as the beginning of the empire, Ostia possessed a theater, a forum, and an aqueduct; its true development began with the construction of the ports of Claudius and, later, of Trajan (under Hadrian it may have reached a population of 50,000); Ostia remained a major port until the second half of the 3rd c., when "Portus" overtook it, and the silting of the Tiber pushed the shoreline further away (it now lies about 2 km. away).

The disastrous flood of 1557 marked the abandonment – and virtual oblivion – of the town, where the latest rebuilding was done during the reign of Theodoric. Excavations began at the turn of the 19th c., during the reign of Pope Pius VII and, continuing through the middle of the century, became systematic and determined only after the unification of Italy; work intensified in preparation for the planned Esposizione Universale of 1942 (Universal Exposition); following WWII, more emphasis was placed on restoration than on new excavations, though some digs continue.

The tour (ore 9-4 or 5, in the summer, 9-6; see map) largely follows the "decumanus maximus," along which are arrayed the most important buildings in Ostia (the frescoed homes are not, for the most part, open to the public); for this reason we shall first describe those arrayed along the right side of the street, while the landmarks along the opposite side of the street will be described during the return to the entrance of the archeological area.

Immediately to the left of the entrance, the last stretch of the Via Ostiense, after you pass the *Porta Romana* (a gate flanked by two square towers; the *statue* dating from the age of Domitian *of Minerva-Victory* which once adorned it is now in the large plaza), continues as the *decumanus maximus*; on the right side, half-concealed by a masonry portico, are the *Terme di Nettuno**, or baths of Neptune, one of the largest public baths in the city, built during the reign of Hadrian. Behind it is the *barracks of the "Vigiles"* (along the Via dei Vigili that leads here there is a mosaic – from the age of Claudius – with *symbols of the winds and provinces that supplied Rome*), from the age of Hadrian; these barracks housed a detachment of about 400 men; the far side of the porticoed courtyard was occupied by the *"Caesareum"*, a place of worship for the emperor cult.

Also on the right of the "decumanus" is the

Teatro, a theater first built by Agrippa but rebuilt in brick in 196 (its present-day appearance, in any case, is the result of a modern restoration). From the corridors on either side of the "orchestra" you will reach the **Piazzale delle Corporazioni**, which was used by spectators during intermissions between performances; the name – plaza of the guilds – derives from the professional guilds ("collegia"), which installed the mosaics set in the portico.

From the plaza, a passageway runs, to the left of the Domus di Apuleio, or home of Apuleius, to the *Mitreo dei Sette Cieli*, a mitraeum and one of the better preserved santuaries of the 17 in Ostia devoted to the Mithra cult, which spread at the end of the 2nd c. and in the 3rd c. from Persia; facing it, on a podium, stood four small *temples*, dedicated at the turn of the 1st c. B.C. to female deities (Venus, Ceres, Fortuna, and Speranza; the last three being goddesses of the harvest, luck, and hope) connected with trade and shipping.

The Via dei Molini, which splits off from the "decumanus maximus," runs to the right around the area of the *Grandi "Horrea"*, the largest commercial structure in Ostia; built in brick, it dates from the age of Commodus. The Via della Casa di Diana, which splits off to the left, takes its name from the *Casa di Diana* (dating from the age of Antoninus Pius), or house of Diana, named for a terracotta statue in the courtyard of the fountain; the last building on the left side contains the "**thermopolium**," a 3rd-c. tavern with wine counters and a fresco depicting food and drink. The nearby *Caseggiato dei Dipinti*, an enormous residential block, is split up into three independent "insulae": the so-called *home of Jove and Ganymede* contain frescoes from the age of the Antonines and, in the garden, a handsome *mosaic of the Months* (4th c.).

The *Museo Ostiense**, or museum of Ostia, which is located in the *Casone del Sale* (a 15th-c. salt storehouse; the elegant facade dates from 1868), contains an interesting collection of the applied arts, with objects intended for domestic life and manufacturing and crafts. There are also the most important archeological finds from the last 40 years of excavation. In the vestibule is a body of documentation concerning the successive phases of excavation. The halls contain marble and terracotta reliefs, depicting episodes of everyday life (2nd c.), sculptures inspired by the Eastern cults, Roman copies of Greek and Hellenistic originals, and a collection of imperial portraits and sarcophagi (2nd c.); one of the most interesting is the sarcophagus of a child, with *dancing putti*; behind displays windows are bronze and terracotta statuettes, oil lamps, vases, instruments for writing and weaving, dice for gaming, and a small assortment of glass and ivory objects and jewelry. Lively and colorful paintings and mosaics, from various eras, are assembled in the last hall, along with a large marble *mosaic* in "opus sectile" (4th c.), discovered not far from Porta Marina.

At the intersection of the "decumanus maximus" and the "cardo maximus" lies the *Forum*, lined with porticoes; the structure that you see dates from the age of Hadrian, in the same years that witnessed the urban reform that involved the renovation of the quarters betweeen the Forum and the Tiber. Overlooking it are: the "**Capitolium**," Ostia's largest and most important temple, also built under Hadrian; the *Caseggiato dei Triclini*, originally perhaps a hotel, and under Septimius Severus, the head office of the guilder of builders. Nearby are the *Terme del Foro*, or baths of the Forum, the most important baths in Ostia, built during the rule of Antoninus Pius, and restored until the 5th c.; the *Tempio di Roma e Augusto*, or temple of Roma and Augustus, built during the reign of Tiberius; the *Basilica Giudiziaria*, a hall of judgement, erected under Domitian or Trajan; before it stand the remains of a portico.

In the next stretch of the "decumanus maximus," you will see on the left the *Tempio Rotondo*, a round temple of the emperor cult, with a 10-column pronaos and a cella with seven niches for statues; opposite is the *Caseggiato del Larario*, which enclosed a marketplace, with shop/homes.

Near the crossroads of the "castrum," the Via della Foce leads to the *sacred area** from republican times, used ever since the 3rd c. B.C.; it comprises the *Tempio di Ercole* (temple of Hercules; late-2nd c. B.C.) and, to the right of that, the *Domus di Amore e Psiche* (named for the statue of Amor and Psyche now in the museum), a fine example of a decorated home of the wealthy (4th c.). From the *Caseggiato di Serapide*, or apartment house of Serapis, named for the sacellum containing an image of that god, set on the opposite side of the Via della Foce, you have a good view of the *Quartiere delle Casette Tipo*, a residential quarter dating from the period of expansion that followed the construction of the port of Trajan; behind it extend the *Terme della Trinacria*, baths built during the reign of Hadrian. The adjoining *Terme dei Sette Sapienti*, are baths that formed part of the complex built between A.D. 126 and 140; they abound in paintings (in an "osteria" near the "frigidarium" are satirical paintings of the Seven Wise Men of ancient Greece); these baths are connected with the *Caseggiato degli Aurighi* (a residential block, with depictions of victorious charioteers in the corridor), a residential block with a handsome courtyard with two registers of arches.

The "caseggiato" gave its name to the nearby "cardo," from which you can enter – by passing through the Insula delle Volte Dipinte – the *insula delle Muse**, an elegant house from the middle empire. It features a hall, overlooking the handsome porticoed courtyard, with a series of frescoes of *Apollo and the Nine Muses*, an exceptional example of Roman painting from the age of Hadrian. The adjoining Insula delle Pareti Gialle leads into the complex of the *Case a Giardino*, or Garden Houses, a rectangular quarter with gardens, embellished by fountains, built in A.D. 128.

Pass through the *Porta Marina*, a gate opened in the walls dating from the Republic, to the left of which is the *"caupona" of Alexander Helix* (the erotic mosaics date from the 3rd c.); here the "decumanus maximus" once reached the beach; just before the elevation that once marked the arrival of the road to the coast, branching off to the left is the Via di Cartilio Publicola, which offers a view of the excavations of the baths, or *Terme della Marciana*, also known as the Terme di Porta Marina, inaugurated under Trajan and Hadrian, and still in operation until the 6th c.; from them you can see, to the east, the remains of the **Sinagoga**, or Synagoge, a remarkable relic of the ancient eastern Mediterranean; we have documentation of phases of construction in the 1st and the 4th c.

The "decumanus maximus," which you will follow toward the Forum, runs past, in sequence, the *Schola del Traiano* (or Schola of Trajan, where a niche contains a cast of a statue of the emperor); this was probably the site of the guild of ship builders, and on the left, the so-called *Basilica Cristiana*, or Christian Basilica, a late-4th-c. building with two fore-aisles and two flanked aisles (on an architrave, note the names of the four rivers of the earthly Paradise).

The corner of the "decumanus" and the Via del Pomerio near the intersection of the "castrum" is marked by *"Macellum"*, a meat market dating back at least the 1st c. B.C., and restored until the 5th c, A.D.; the portico on the "via" contains two *tabernae of fish-vendors**, decorated with mosaics with sea scenes.

The *Santuario di Cibele**, or Sanctuary of Cybele (you can reach it by taking, in succession, the Via del Pomerio and the "cardo maximus" to the SE), also known as the Campo della Magna Mater, dates from the age of Hadrian or the Antonines; it comprises the Tempio di Cibele, or Temple of Cybele, the *Tempio di Bellona* (warrior goddess associated with Cybele), the *Schola degli Hastiferi* (these were spearbearers who maintained the cult of the goddess) and the *sanctuary of Attis* (son and lover of Cybele, whose cyclical resurrection was linked to the vernal rebirth of the earth).

Along the stretch of the "decumanus maximus" that runs from the Forum to the entrance to the excavations, a detour along the *Via degli Augustali* (named for the priesthood established by Augusto for the emperor cult) allows one to visit – in an area that was under exploration in 1993 – the largest **"fullonica"** (cleaners) excavated in Ostia, dating from the age of the Antonines:

The Theater of Ostia Antica

at the center are four wash basins, on the sides a portico with 35 terracotta recipients used to press and solidify old cloth, to convert it into new fabrics. Along the "decumanus," past the Teatro, or theater, note the *"horrea" of Hortensius*, perhaps the oldest grain siles in Ostia (Julian-Claudian era), with an elongated courtyard surrounded by columns.

Ostia Antica*. The settlement of ancient Ostia developed around and upon the ruins of Gregoriopolis, a fortified citadel built at the orders of Pope Gregory IV during the first half of the 9th c. as a commercial port and customs yard; it was sacked in 1408, whereafter the citadel was further reinforced by Pope Martin V, by the cardinal Guglielmo d'Estouteville, and lastly by the cardinal Giuliano Della Rovere. After the great flood of 1557, the town declined and dwindled in population. Nowadays, it is possible to tour the *Rocca*, or fortress, which preserves its 15th-c. appearance; note the handsome church of S. Aurea, the Palazzo Episcopale, or bishop's palace, and the castle of Pope Julius II (Castello di Giulio II).

The church of **S. Aurea**, attributed to Baccio Pontelli, would appear to have once contained the relics of St. Aurea, a Christian martyr of the 3rd c., and of St. Monica, the mother of St. Augustine, who died in Ostia in 387. The facade features a handsome rose window; inside, in the single nave, there are 17th-c. altar pieces, an *aedicule* for holy oils (13th c.) and, to the left of the main altar, a *paschal candelabrum* comprising a relic of the earlier basilica (5th c.). The *Palazzo Episcopale* (1472), set behind the church of S. Aurea, is particularly noteworthy for the series of *frescoes** (1508-1513) by Baldassarre Peruzzi, discovered in 1977-79 beneath a layer of whitewashed plaster: the battle scenes are inspired by Trajan's column.

The restoration of the **Castello di Giulio II**, which was completed in 1991, restored the building's original massive appearance; it was built at the wishes of Pope Sixtus IV and actually ordered by the cardinal Della Rovere (1483-86) to plans by Baccio Pontelli (possibly with assistance from Giuliano da Sangallo). It has a triangular plan with a trapezoidal courtyard; there are two circular towers and a five-sided keep for last-ditch defense. The castle has features (use of scarped curtain walls; casemates connected by galleries), innovative at the time, that became common in the 16th c. The interior staircase was decorated by Peruzzi, together with Cesare da Sesto and Michele del Becca.

Via Ostiense (maps 10, 15). The route of a road that ran along the left bank of the Tiber, linking Rome to the sea, is certainly far earlier than the road for which we have documentation, dating back to the 3rd c. B.C. Sometime after the 6th c. A.D., this road declined in importance, as result of the concomitant decline of the port of Ostia. This route now runs – with the name of Statale 8bis – parallel to the faster *Via del Mare*, which was inaugurated in 1927-28 (one of the earliest Italian "autostrade," or highways). Just before S. Paolo Fuori le Mura, Via Ostiense coasts, on its left, an ex-industrial area; the ex Montemartini installation now exhibits a selection of items from the Museo Nuovo and the Braccio Nuovo (Capitolini Museums).

S. Paolo Fuori le Mura (15 C2). The church of St. Paul's without-the-walls is the largest basilica in Rome, second only to St. Peter's (S. Pietro). It stands on the site where legend has it that St. Paul was buried. It was consecrated by Pope Sylvester I in A.D. 324; it was rebuilt by Valentiniano II, Teodosio, and Arcadio.

It was reconsecrated by Pope Siricius in 390, and then it was finally completed – attaining its current size – by Onorio in 395. A village developed around the abbey in the 8th c. and took the name Giovannopoli, since it was fortified by Pope John – or Giovanni – VIII. The church was largely destroyed by fire (15-16 July 1823). All that survived were the transept, the arco santo and a part of the facade. Rebuilt to the original plan, it was reconsecrated by Pope Pius IX in 1854; Luigi Poletti designed and built the new facade (the surviving fragments of the old wall were demolished), as well as the left side, with portico and campanile (the original bell tower collapsed in the earthquake of 1348).

The church was partly rebuilt by Pasquale Belli (1825-33); the main portico was rebuilt by Virginio Vespignani (1890-92).

Before the facade there extends a quadriporticus with a narthex comprising 10 monolithic columns, each 10 m. tall; the high section of the facade features a mosaic (*Christ Giving Benediction, between St. Peter and St. Paul, Agnus Dei* and *prophets*) designed by Filippo Agricola and Nicola Consoni (1854-74).

Inside, there is a nave and four aisles (the nave is 24.6 m. across): overall, this church is 65 m. wide, more than 131 m. long, and just shy of 30 m. tall.

The *triumphal arch* is embellished with a mosaic that was moved here from the original arch, dating from the time of St. Leo the Great.

On the main altar, note the exquisite **ciborium** (1285) by Arnolfo di Cambio, possibly with the assistance of Pietro Cavallini; to the right of the ciborium, note the *candelabrum for Paschal candles**, signed by Nicolò di Angelo and Pietro Vassalletto (12th c.).

The large mosaic in the apse dates from the time of Honorius III (that pope is depicted at the feet of *Christ Giving a Benediction, between St. Peter and St. Andrew*, on the right; and *St. Paul and St. Luke* on the right). In the 1st chapel to the left of the apse (Cappella del Santissimo), by Carlo Maderno, you can see the *Crucifix** attributed to Cavallini, who is buried here, as well as a mosaic *Virgin Mary** from the 12th c. In the left niche, note the *statue of St. Bridget* by Stefano Maderno; the 1st chapel to the right of the apse (Cappella di S. Lorenzo), by Carlo Maderno, has an altar bearing a marble *triptych* of the school of Andrea Bregno (1494).

At the heads of both arms of the transept, note the *altars* faced with malachite and lapis lazuli, a gift from Czar Nicholas I.

The *art gallery*, which you enter from the right arm of the transept, still preserves notable art works from the 16th-c. Umbrian school, by Bramantino, and Cigoli, and a *Virgin Mary with Christ Child and Saints*, in the style of Antoniazzo Romano.

In the adjacent monastery is a *museum* with portraits of popes (5th/9th c.) and a collection of Christian inscriptions and burial plaques from the ancient basilica.

structed by Innocenzo Sabbatini in 1926-29, and to the *Albergo Rosso*, a hotel on the Piazza Biffi (from the Via Ostiense take a right onto the Circonvallazione Biffi), designed by Sabbatini (1927-29).

Porta S. Paolo* (10 D4-5). This gate now stands alone, due to the demands of modern traffic – and in part because of the damage done during combat in September 1943, as a plaque records – marking the beginning of the Via Ostiense. This was originally the Porta Ostiense, while its present name comes from the nearby basilica of S. Paolo Fuori le Mura; the two openings on the interior side, unified on the exterior face under Pope Honorius, indicated that in classical times the ancient Via Laurentina also started from this gate (see page 176).

The Pyramid of Caio Cestio, painting by G. P. Pannini (Galleria Nazionale d'Arte Antica)

Quartiere della Garbatella (15 A-B3-4-5). This quarter was built around 1920, in the area of the planned center of Via Ostiense (in reality, the project never quite materialized); it was intended for working-class residents, with plenty of green area and relatively few buildings; the project underwent numerous adaptations, with work done after WWII, modifying its original nature.

Special attention should be given to the two *polyfunctional buildings* on Piazza Bartolomeo Romano (from the Via Ostiense take a right onto the Via Rocco), con-

The structure, which includes two massive semi-circular towers, contains the *Museo della Via Ostiense*; this museum contains models and casts of Ostia, the ports of Claudius and Trajan, and other landmarks along the old Via Ostiense.

Piramide di Caio Cestio* (10 D4). This pyramid is now separated by a narrow gap from the Porta S. Paolo, but it was once part of the Aurelian walls (see page 171); it stands about 36 m. tall and has a base of nearly 30 m. per side. It was built as funerary monument to Caius Cestius Epulo (who died in 12 B.C.) in the space of just 330 days, as is noted in the inscription set on the facade overlooking the Piazzale Ostiense; we do not know where the original access to the frescoed funerary chamber was located (the visible door is a modern addition), which is not open to the public.

Piazza Albania (10 B-C5). Once named for the Porta Raudusculana, a gate in the Servian walls (see page 32; of those walls, a fragment survives at the corner of Via di S. Anselmo, about 42 m. in length), this square is adorned by a *monument to Scanderbeg*, by Romano Romanelli (1940).

Running NE from the square is the *Viale Aventino* (10 A-B6; 11 A-B1), a major thoroughfare which cuts through the quarter of the Aventine (on the right is the "piccolo Aventino," a hill crowned by the church of S. Saba: see page 132) along an ancient Roman road.

Piazza di Porta Capena (11 A1-2; 8 F4-5). This is one of the most intricate interchanges for vehicular traffic, and its name is taken from the gate in the Servian walls (see page 32) that marked the beginning of the ancient Via Appia, or Appian Way (see page 171).

Overlooking it is the *Palazzo della FAO* (11 B1-2), now occupied by the Food and Agricultural Organization, designed by Vittorio Cafiero and Mario Ridolfi in 1938 for the Ministero dell'Africa Italiana (ministry of Italian-ruled Africa), but completed in 1952; before the building stands the *stele of Axum* (11 A2; 8 F5), a monolithic structure 24 m. tall – dating from the 4th c. – from Ethiopia and erected here in 1937; on the opposite side of the square is the *Vignola* (8 F5), a small porticoed 16th-c. building.

Circo Massimo (8 D-E-F3-4), or Circus Maximus. The depression lying between the Aventine and Palatine hills (the archeological area that faces the Palazzi Imperiali here is described beginning on page 99) was used in athletic competitions and racing from the earliest times. A "circus," or race track, was supposedly first erected here under Tarquinius Priscus; the masonry structure was renovated by Julius Caesar (46 B.C.), enlarged and embellished by Augustus, who installed an Imperial box and erected the obelisk of Rameses II (now in Piazza del Popolo); it was rebuilt under Trajan (A.D. 100-104), enlarged under Caracalla, and restored again by Constantine, who ordered the installation of the obelisk

of Tuthmosis III (now in Piazza di S. Giovanni in Laterano). The Circus Maximus remained in use until A.D. 549. All that now survives is the outline (it is said that as many as 300,000 could watch a race here; the vast area that it once occupied has been converted into a garden).

Piazza della Bocca della Verità (8 D2). This square now stands where the old livestock market was once located (Foro Boario); it is embellished by an 18th-c. *fountain* that borrows the theme of Bernini's fountain in Piazza Barberini, as well as by two small temples (for a tour, contact the Soprintendenza Archeologica di Roma).

The rectangular one is the **temple of Fortuna Virile** (8 D2), now identified as the temple of Portunus, one of the best preserved buildings from that period (2nd/1st c. B.C.); in 872 it was transformed into the

The "Mouth of Truth"

church of *S. Maria Egiziaca* (the painting of the St. Mary of Egypt on the altar is by Federico Zuccari).

The round one is the **temple of Vesta** (8 D2), which however was probably dedicated to Ercole Vincitore; this is oldest marble building in existence in Rome (late-2nd c. B.C.); in the 12th c. it was transformed into the church of *S. Stefano*, also known – from the mid-16th c. on – as the church S. Maria del Sole, because of a miraculous ray of sunlight that flashed from an image found in the river.

S. Maria in Cosmedin* (8 D2). Cosmedin comes from the Greek word "Kosmidion," meaning lovely, and describes the spectacular decorations of what was originally called "S. Maria in Schola Graeca," built on the ruins of a 3rd-c. chapel; those ruins were incorporated in the 6th c. into a building that was subsequently enlarged under Pope Adrian I in 782, and was thereafter restored more than once, in particular by Pope Gelasius II after the sack of Robert Guiscard (1082).

The facade – restored to the appearance it had under Pope Calixtus II with the removal of 18th-c. additions – is flanked by a handsome Romanesque *campanile* (12th c.); before the facade extends a portico with arches set on pillars. Beneath it, on the left, is the renowned *Bocca della Verità**, or mouth of truth, a large marble disk with a mascaron representing a river god (in classical times, it was used as a manhole cover); for centuries it hung on the outer wall of the church; it was moved to its present location in 1632; aside from the legend that if a liar inserts his hand into the mouth of the mask, he will lose his hand, the Bocca della Verità has also been linked to the legends of Vergil the Magician, who supposedly created it to test the virtue of married women.

The interior has a nave and two aisles, divided by pillars and by 18 Roman columns, with ancient and medieval capitals. Note: the handsome Gothic *baldachin* that bears the name of Deodato di Cosma the Younger (1294), the *floor* dating from the 8th c., the frescoes in the apse wall from the 11th c., and the fragment of mosaic in the sacristy – from the ancient St. Peter's – that dates from the turn of the 8th c.

The *Via del Velabro* (it was near the Velabro that Faustulus supposedly found Romulus and Remus), which runs from the east side of the square, is occupied in the center by the **Arco di Giano** (8 D3), or arch of Janus, a four-faced monument with four piers supporting cross-vaults built in the 4th c.; in ancient times, it was completed with an attic, which was demolished by mistake when a tower built atop it by the Frangipane family was demolished.

Behind the arch is the church of *S. Giorgio in Velabro* (8 C-D3), founded in the 5th-6th c. but rebuilt by Pope Gregory IV in the first half of the 9th c. In the 11th/12th c., the five-story Romanesque *bell tower* was built (the portico was restored at the turn of the 13th c.). The interior, with a nave and two aisles, features a series of frescoes (*Christ, the Virgin Mary, and St. George, St. Peter, and St. Sebastian*) in the vault of the apse, attributed to Pietro Cavallini though it shows signs of repainting in the 16th c.

To the left of the church, note the **Arco degli Argentari** (8 D3), or arch of the silver changers, built by the money-changers' guild in A.D. 204 to honor the imperial family (note the depictions of

The Church of S. Maria in Cosmedin

Septimius Severus, Julia Domna, and their sons Caracalla and Geta, whose figure was cancelled after he was murdered by his brother): the monument consists of two pillars, faced in marble and travertine, supporting a marble architrave, abundantly decorated, largely with a plant motif.

At n. 3 in Via del Velabro you can tour (contact the X Ripartizione del Comune, Rome city council) the *Cloaca Maxima*, which conveyed water from the surrounding heights into the Roman Forum down to the Tiber; it was supposedly built by Tarquinius Priscus, but the modern vault dates back no earlier than the 2nd c. B.C.

Overlooking the Via di S. Giovanni Decollato is the church of *S. Giovanni Decollato* (8 C2; to tour the church, contact the church governor), built between the late-15th c. and the mid-16th c., and reconsecrated by Pope Benedict XIII in 1727. Inside, the single nave contains a major series of frescoes by Tuscan artists (Jacopo Zucchi, Pomarancio, school of Giorgio Vasari) as does the Oratory, where, on the left wall, you will note a *Beheading of John the Baptist* and a *Dance of Salomè* by Pirro Ligorio.

Casa dei Crescenzi* (8 C-D2). This rare medieval building now contains the Centro Studi per la Storia dell'Architettura, a center for architectural studies, was erected in 1040-65 by Nicolò di Crescenzio using ancient fragments. It was damaged when the Holy Roman Emperor Henry VII attacked Italy and restored in 1940.

On the same side of Via Petroselli, note the not so lovely *Palazzo dell'Anagrafe* (8 C2), a massive public records building made of brick, with travertin cornices, built in 1936-37.

S. Nicola in Carcere (8 C2). Rebuilt in 1128 atop an older building (dating from the

9th, or possibly, the 7th c.), this church was restored in 1808 by Giuseppe Valadier during the reign of Pope Pius X; it was then isolated from the surrounding houses during the renovation done by the Fascist regime. It stands on the ancient site of the Foro Olitorio (this was the vegetable market) and is the result of the medieval transformation of the temples (see below) that once stood here: the facade, the work of Giacomo Della Porta (1599), re-used two columns from the temple of Juno Sospita, while the interior, with a basilican plan, features a number of re-used columns (in the right aisle, note the *Virgin Mary with Christ Child*, fragment of a fresco by Antoniazzo Romano; the Cappella Aldobrandini, a chapel to the right of the apse, is decorated with paintings by Giovanni Baglione).

The temples of the Foro Olitorio, which date from the time of the Republic, can also be seen in the underground chambers of S. Nicola in Carcere (open: Thursday, 10:30 am-12 noon). In particular, the church contains the Ionic hexastyle *temple of Juno Sospita*, built in 197 B.C., while what may have been a *temple of Janus* – hexastyle but Doric – can be seen in the six columns embedded in the left flank of the Christian church; the *temple of Speranza*, built after the First Punic War and set to the right of the facade of the church, is visible in the podium with two Ionic columns made of peperino (eight more are embedded in the wall).

Opposite S. Nicola in Carcere and visible from the *Vico Jugario* (the name may come from yokes used for oxen) is the **area sacra di S. Omobono** (8 C2; to tour it, contact the X Ripartizione del Comune, Rome city government), unearthed during the demolition done in the 1930s, and excavated in 1959-64. The digs uncovered an archaic settlement (material was found dating from the 9th and 8th c. B.C.), possibly similar to that found on the Palatine; here, in the 6th c. B.C. stood the *temple of the Magna Mater* and the *temple of Fortuna*, connected to the development of the river port on the Isola Tiberina and restored as late as the age of Domitian. Like a backdrop at the end of the Vico Jugario, note the handsome facade of the church of *S. Maria della Consolazione* (8 C3), built in 1470 and rebuilt by Martino Longhi the Elder (1583-1600). The interior, with nave and two aisles, contains a number of noteworthy artworks: frescoes by Taddeo Zuccari, canvases and frescoes by Giovanni Baglione in the 1st and 3rd chapels of the right nave; a 13th-c. *icon* in the chapel to the right of the presbytery; a medieval fresco touched up by Antoniazzo Romano, a *Nativity* and *Our Lady of the Assumption* by Pomarancio in the presbytery; fragments of frescoes by Antoniazzo Romano in the sacristy.

Teatro di Marcello* (8 B-C1-2), or Theater of Marcellus. Begun by Julius Caesar and dedicated by Augustus (13 or 11 B.C.) to the memory of his nephew and son-in-law Marcellus, this was one of the largest theaters in ancient Rome: it could contain about 15,000 spectators, the cavea measured nearly 130 m. across, and the travertine facade was punctuated by 41 arches for each of the three registers.

Abandoned in the 5th c., this edifice was early on used as a quarry for building material, later as a fortress – first by the Pierleoni family and later by the Savelli family (hence the name of the nearby Piazza di Monte Savello).

For the latter family, Baldassarre Peruzzi built in 1523-27 the imposing aristocratic home, which later passed into the Orsini family (and it is still called *Palazzo Orsini*), that stands directly upon the arcades of the "cavea."

Via del Teatro di Marcello (8 B-C2). This road was built along the SW slopes of the Campidoglio between 1926 and 1941 to connect the "forum" of Rome (Piazza Venezia) with the new roads leading to the Lido di Roma (the modern Lido di Ostia), with the demolition of a dense quarter of medieval buildings.

At n. 40 is the *monastery of Tor de' Specchi* (8 B2; open only on 9 March), founded by St. Francesca Romana in 1433. Inside: at the foot of the Scala Santa or holy stair, a fresco (*Virgin Mary and Christ Child, St. Benedict and St. Francesca Romana*) by Antoniazzo Romano; in the church of the *Santissima Annunziata* (1596), *Our Lady of the Holy Annunciation*, a copy by Alessandro Allori of the Florentine original.

Piazza d'Aracoeli (8 B2). Now largely spoiled by the demolition done in 1928 – it is hard to imagine that a flourishing marketplace once thrived here – this square still preserves three buildings of great majesty and beauty: the *Palazzo Massimo di Rignano* (8 B2; N. 1), rebuilt by Carlo Fontana in the late-17th c.; the *Palazzo Pecci Blunt*, formerly Palazzo Ruspoli (8 A2; n. 3), built by Giacomo Della Porta (late-16th c.) along with the *fountain*, surmounted by the hills that were heraldic crests of Pope Sixtus V (1589), in the green area near the building; the *Palazzo Muti Bussi* (8 A2), completed by Giovanni Antonio de Rossi in 1642-62.

Adjoining the square is Piazza Venezia (see page 54).

1.3 From Piazza del Popolo Along the Corso to Piazza Venezia

A series of historical, architectural, and urban landmarks make this route fundamentally important in any tour of Rome. In part, this is because for centuries Piazza del Popolo and the thoroughfare of Via del Corso (running from Piazza del Popolo to Piazza Venezia) have constituted the most common access route into Rome for visitors, Italian and non-Italian, but also because, over the centuries, a dense network of religious and civil buildings has sprung up; and also because along this thoroughfare over the centuries several of the most important urban projects to shape Rome, even contemporary Rome, have affected this road. We need only mention the history, the buildings, and the construction projects that gave Piazza del Popolo its appearance as a great and theatrical entryway into Rome – a number of motifs, and not by chance, were buried for the renovation of Piazza dell'Esedra, the new and modern entranceway to the city. We might also cite the way in which traditional Roman events have been moved to the Corso (first and foremost the famous Roman Carnevale, culminating in races; Pope Paul II moved it here from Testaccio). Lastly, the way that the Corso was lined with squares and buildings central to the new economic and political power (numerous banks, the office of the prime minister, and – nearby – the Camera dei Deputati, or parliament) of the newly unified Italy.

The Roman aristocracy soon demonstrated that they had clearly grasped the importance of this thoroughfare by building their spectacular homes here, or moving them here (to mention only the most important families: the Aldobrandini, Chigi, Ruspoli, Sciarra, and Doria Pamphilj families), remarkable pieces of Renaissance and 17th-/18th-c. architecture; the Corso was also the site of the most remarkable examples of Roman eclecticism at the end of the 19th c. and turn of the 20th c. Between Piazza del Popolo and Piazza Colonna, from the unification of Italy until late in the 1920s, intellectual life in Rome flourished here, gradually replaced by business and trade, still thriving here.

This walking tour starts in Piazza del Popolo, where the church of the same name is one of the most remarkable concentrates of art in all Rome; it then proceeds along Via del Corso, punctuated by the churches (Ss. Ambrogio e Carlo al Corso, S. Marcello al Corso, and S. Maria in Via Lata) and palazzi (Palazzo Ruspoli, Palazzo Chigi, Palazzo Sciarra, and Palazzo Pamphilj); short detours allow you to penetrate the dense quarters on either side of the Corso (note the Palazzo della Borsa on the Piazza di Pietra and the Piazza di S. Ignazio, with the church of S. Ignazio, and the "Burrò") and to halt for awhile in Piazza Colonna, which, with the adjoining Piazza di Montecitorio, is one of the political nerve centers of Italy.

Piazza del Popolo in a drawing of 1831

Piazza del Popolo* (1 D1; 13 D6). One of the most spectacular and theatrical squares in all of Rome – it was indeed the setting for fairs, games, and popular performances of all sorts, including the "Corsa dei Bàrberi," a racehorse, during the Roman Carnevale – this was the grand culmination of a reorganization of this section of the city, undertaken at the end of the 15th c. with the reconstruction of the church of S. Maria del Popolo, and completed with the Neoclassical work done by Giuseppe Valadier (turn of the 19th c.). Closed off to the north by the gate known as the Porta del Popolo, and dominated to the east by the Passeggiata del Pincio (for both, see below), the center of the square is adorned by the **Obelisco Flaminio**, or Flaminian Obelisk (1 D1; 13 D6), the second-oldest and second-tallest obelisk in Rome (25 m.; with the base, 36.5 m.) after the Lateran obelisk; this granite monolith was erected at Heliopolis by Rameses II and by his son Merneptah around 1200 B.C. It was then brought to Rome at the orders of Augustus, who had it set up in the Circus Maximus; it was finally set up in this square at the behest of Pope Sixtus V, under the supervision of Domenico Fontana in 1589.

Set in the square's hemicycles are two *fountains* made of travertine, with basins shaped like giant seashells, surmounted by sculptural groups designed by Valadier and completed in 1818-21; Valadier also designed the buildings (1818-24) overlooking the Tridente (see page 48), which house two celebrated cafes – the *Caffè Rosati* (at the corner of Via di Ripetta) and the *Caffè Canova* (at the corner of Via del Babuino).

From Piazza del Popolo you can climb up to the Pincio along the handsome *Passeggiata del Pincio* (1 D1-2; 13 D6), built by Giuseppe Valadier in 1834, with handsome views, niches, and statues in the Neoclassical style.
At the end of the uphill climb, you will find yourself at the foot of the *Casina Valadier* (1 D2; 13 D6), a Neoclassical reconstruction of a building upon a cistern dating from Roman times, and now an elegant cafe-restaurant, exceedingly popular during the fine weather.
From the vast panoramic terrace on the left, high over Piazza del Popolo, one enjoys a stupendous view* of the city of Rome, dominated by Michelangelo's cupola of S. Pietro (St. Peter's).

Porta del Popolo (1 C-D1; 13 D6). This gate stands on the site of the ancient Porta Flaminia, opened in the Mura Aureliane, or Aurelian walls (see page 171), which marked the beginning of the consular road known as the Via Flaminia (see page 158); for centuries this was the main entrance to the city

for those arriving from the north.
The elevation facing the Piazza del Popolo was designed and built by Gian Lorenzo Bernini, at the behest of Pope Alexander VII, on the occasion of the triumphal entrance into Rome of Kristina of Sweden, on 23 December 1655 (the inscription "Felici faustoque ingressui" refers to that occasion); the festoon with sprays of oak-leaves and sheaves of wheat recalls the heraldic devices of the pope and the queen.
The rear facade, overlooking the Piazzale Flaminio, was designed by Nanni di Baccio Bigio, who built it for Pope Pius IV (1561-62), deriving the design from the Arch of Titus, with a Doric trabeation, a commemorative inscription, and the papal crest; the crowning crenelation is reminiscent of the crenelation designed by Michelangelo for the Porta Pia.

S. Maria del Popolo* (1 C-D1; 13 D6). This church is the most significant piece of ecclesiastical architecture of the last quarter of the 15th c. It takes its name – St. Mary of the People – from the people of Rome, who supported the cost for the construction of a small chapel built by Pope Paschal II, in the area later occupied by the church. In 1472 it passed into the hands of the Augustinian order of the Lombard Congregation, and it was rebuilt (1475-77), in accordance with the standards of Lombard church architecture, perhaps by Andrea Bregno. It was subjected to new renovations as early as the 16th c. (Bramante rebuilt the apsidal choir; the Cappella Chigi was built to plans by Raphael); these modifications were continued in the Baroque style during the following century, when the transept chapels were renovated, the main altar was replaced, and a new decorative array was created on the facade and interior – under the supervision of Gian Lorenzo Bernini – and the Cappella Cybo was built by Carlo Fontana.
The interior abounds in splendid works of art. The Cappella Della Rovere (1st chapel in the right aisle) contains the *tombs of the cardinals Cristoforo* and *Domenico Della Rovere* by Bregno (the *Virgin Mary* is by Mino da Fiesole).
In the sacristy, a *Virgin Mary* of the 14th-c. Siennese school is set in the marble *altar** created by Bregno in 1473.
The *main altar* was built in 1627 at the behest of cardinal Antonio Sauli, who ordered the lavish gilt stucco decoration of the large arch: note the Byzantine-style panel (*Madonna del Popolo*, or Our Lady of the People), dating from the turn of the 13th c.

On the walls of the *choir**, transformed by Bramante in two separate phases (ca. 1500 and 1505-1509), are the **monument to Cardinal Ascanio Sforza** (1505; left) and the **monument to Cardinal Girolamo Basso Della Rovere** (1507; right), two masterpieces by Andrea Sansovino: shaped like triumphal arches, they no longer display the dead as merely supine, but as sleeping, with the torso raised, and, in the niches and above the trabeations, allegorical figures. The windows above the monuments are decorated with exquisite *stained glass** (*Childhood of Christ* and *stories of the Virgin Mary*), unique in Rome in this period, by Guillame de Marcillat (1509). In the vault, note the handsome *frescoes** (*Coronation of the Virgin Mary, Evangelists, Sibyls*, and *Doctors of the Church*; 1508-1510) by Pinturicchio. In the 1st chapel in the left transept, on either side of the *Assumption* by Annibale Carracci (1601), note two masterpieces by Caravaggio (1601-1602): **Conversion of St. Paul** (right) and **Crucifixion of St. Peter** (left). The *Cappella Chigi** (2nd chapel in the left aisle), has a central plan, and is characterized by the contrast between the stark exterior and the rich interior; it was built to plans by Raphael at the wishes of Agostino Chigi, as a family mausoleum; construction was begun in 1513-14 under the supervision of Lorenzetto, and was completed by the future pope Alexander VII with the supervision of Bernini in 1652-56. Raphael, who was influenced by the work of Bramante, designed the mosaics in the cupola (*God the Creator of the Firmament Surrounded by the Symbols of the Sun and the Seven Planets*), executed in 1516.

S. Maria di Montesanto and S. Maria dei Miracoli (1 D1). The "gemelle", or twin churches, stand at the terminus of the central thoroughfare of the Tridente, framing the Via del Corso (for both the Tridente and the Via del Corso, see below), emphasizing the consecration to the Virgin Mary of the Piazza del Popolo; their facades are only apparently identical.

The construction of the first of the two churches – S. Maria di Montesanto – began in 1662, and was completed in 1679 under the supervision of Gian Lorenzo Bernini; the *campanile* was completed in 1761. The construction of the second of the two churches – S. Maria dei Miracoli – began in 1675 under the direction of Carlo Rainaldi and was continued after 1677 by Carlo Fontana, who completed it in 1681; the elegant 18th-c. *campanile* is by Girolamo Theodoli.

Via del Corso* (maps 1, 4). This straight thoroughfare extends 1,500 m. – now in

The "Crucifixion of St. Peter" by Caravaggio

part closed off to private car traffic – with, as backdrops, the obelisk of Piazza del Popolo and the monument to Vittorio Emmanuele II (Victor Emmanuel II; see page 57); it is the most representative street in the historic center of Rome.

It corresponds to the length of the Via Flaminia within the Mura Aureliane or Aurelian walls (see page 171) and runs across the Roman Campo Marzio, a vast area of public buildings and spaces, such as the mausoleum of Augustus, the Ara Pacis Augustae, the Pantheon, and the column of Marcus Aurelius; this thoroughfare – along which a number of the earliest churches were built in early-Christian times (S. Lorenzo in Lucina, S. Marcello al Corso) – continued to be of considerable importance, even after the fall of the Roman Empire, as the northern entrance into the city: the construction of the Palazzo di Venezia in the late-15th c. prompted Pope Paul II to restructure the first stretch of this road (the transfer here – from their original site at Testaccio – of the Roman Carnevale and the accompanying horse races gave this road the name of Corso, or race), while the popes of the 16th c. encouraged the transformation of ordinary residential buildings into great palazzi (Palazzo Sciarra, Palazzo Chigi, Palazzo Ruspoli) and the construction of churches (Santi Ambrogio e Carlo al Corso, Gesù e Maria).

In the 18th c. the Via del Corso, thanks to its numerous coffeehouses, or "caffè" (the Aragno was particularly renowned), became a major center in Italy's intellectual, political, and artistic life, while in the mid-19th c. the finer fashion shops, bookshops, and the offices of newspapers and magazines sprung up along the Via del Corso, making the beginning of the street's modern identity (fashion boutiques, which have almost entirely supplanted the historic coffeehouses, are the latest phase).

The Via del Corso constitutes the main axis of the *Tridente*, designed and implemented at the turn of the 16th c. on the southern side of Piazza del Popolo – which formed the point of the trident – and running toward the center; this structure was taken as a model of urban design in all of Europe during the Baroque period. This structure comprises – besides the Via del Corso – the *Via di Ripetta* (1 D-E-F1), built under Pope Leo X (1517-19) with the original name of Via Leonina, running along the right of the church of S. Maria dei Miracoli and skirting the oxbow curve of the Tiber (the modern name of Via di Ripetta, given it in the 18th c., is taken from the term "ripa," or river bank) and the *Via del Babuino* (1 D-E-F1-2), to the left of the church of S. Maria di Montesanto, which was opened under the reign of Pope Clement VII (hence the original name of Via Clementina) in 1525 and completed in 1543 under Pope Paul III (hence the other name of Via Paolina Trifaria).

A short detour along Via del Babuino, which links Piazza del Popolo with Piazza di Spagna (see page 110) and which was, much like the Via del Corso, a promenade for the nobility of Rome and for foreign visitors; here you can admire the art shops that for the past two centuries have made this street famous as the antiques row of Rome; you may note, just beyond the church of S. Atanasio, the *Fontana del Babuino* (a foun-

tain, topped by one of the "talking statues of Rome": see page 107).

Extending from the right side of the street is the Via Vittoria, where, in the monastery of the former church of Santi Giuseppe e Orsola, the *Accademia Nazionale di S. Cecilia* (1 E-F1), one of the oldest and most illustrious musical conservatories on earth is located.

Extending parallel with the Via del Babuino is the elegant *Via Margutta* (1 D-E1-2), whose name is commonly said to derive from Margutte, the shield-bearer of Morgante; ever since the 17th c. this has been a meeting place for Italian and non-Italian artists, who often had – and sometimes still have – their studios here; there is still an annual art fair here.

Ss. Ambrogio e Carlo al Corso (1 F1). The church itself, one of the most important monuments of Roman Baroque, was built to plans by Onorio Longhi, while Martino Longhi the Younger actually supervised its construction (ca. 1640); in 1668-69 Pietro da Cortona completed the tribune, built the stupendous cupola set on a tambour, and designed the stucco decoration on the interior.

Palazzo Ruspoli (3 C5-6). It dates from the second half of the 16th c., was built by Bartolomeo Ammannati and marks the right side of the Via del Corso with a stern and symmetrical elevation punctuated by windows; the majestic interior *stairway** was designed by Martino Longhi the Younger, around 1640; each of the 120 steps was carved from a single piece of ancient marble; the gallery on the main floor was frescoed by the Mannerist artist Jacopo Zucchi.

S. Lorenzo in Lucina (3 C6). On the site and foundations of the home of the Roman matron Lucina, a Christian "titulus" of the same name was built in the 4th c.; in the 5th c. it was transformed into a place of public worship, and was later rebuilt under Pope Paschal II (the portico and the *campanile*, with two levels of single-light mullioned windows and three levels of twin-light mullioned windows both date back to the turn of the 12th c.); the radical transformation of the interior (the side aisles were converted into aristocratic chapels) took place in the mid-17th c., and was done by Cosimo Fanzago.

The portico that stands against the simple facade – and which was renovated in 1927 – is decorated with mostly medieval marble fragments and inscriptions; the chilly interior bears the marks of the purism of the work done by Busiri Vici: he was also responsible for the frescoes.

If you turn left off the Via del Corso into the Via delle Convertite you will reach the Piazza di S. Silvestro, and the church of *S. Silvestro in Capite* (3 C6), built at the behest of Pope Stephen II in the mid-8th c. (the Romanesque *campanile*, which looms over the picturesque little interior courtyard, dates from the construction done in 1198-1216) and rebuilt between 1595 and 1601 by Francesco da Volterra and Carlo Maderno; the appellation "in Capite" derives from the fact that this church contains what is believed to be the head of St. John the Baptist. The altarpiece by Orazio Gentileschi in the 2nd chapel on the right and the frescoes by Pomarancio in the cupola are the most interesting works on the interior.

Palazzo Chigi (3 D6). Seat of the Presidenza del Consiglio, head of Italy's executive branch of government, this building, which links, politically speaking, with the Camera dei Deputati, or chamber of deputies, in the nearby Palazzo di Montecitorio (see page 50) was begun in 1580-86 by Matteo da Città di Castello and, after being purchased by the Chigi family in 1659, the courtyard and monumental stairway was added; it was finally completed by G.B. Contini; in the 18th c. the portal overlooking Piazza Colonna was added, and a number of the interiors were decorated with great lavishness. The history of this palazzo, in terms of function and renovation, parallels that of many other palazzi in the historical center, after Rome became capital. Of these various and numerous phases of construction, nothing can be seen from the exterior structure of the building, which is marked by the distinctive rigorous architecture of the late-16th c.
Facing it, also on the Via del Corso, is the *Palazzo della Rinascente* (3 D6), which was built in 1885-87, copying Parisian department stores of the same period; this building had the first escalators in Rome.

To the left of the department store, the *Caffè Alemagna* (3 D6) has, since 1955, taken the place of the celebrated Caffè Aragno, a meeting place for artists who used to gather in the so-called "terza sala," or third room.
On the right, serving as a backdrop to the chaotic Largo Chigi, is the church of *S. Maria in Via* (4 D2), which may date back as far as the mid-10th c., but which was rebuilt in the late-15th c. and again, in the current version, by Francesco da Volterra in 1594, to plans by Giacomo Della Porta (the same architect designed the facade, which was only completed by Carlo Rainaldi in 1670). Inside, with only a single nave and four chapels on each side, the 1st chapel on the right contains the greatly venerated image of the *Madonna del Pozzo* or Our Lady of the Well, a painted fragment of tile dating from the 13th or 14th c., linked to the legend from which the

church takes its name (the tile bearing the sacred image was supposedly seen floating in the water that poured forth from a deep well, located to the right of the present site of the altar; the water supposedly stopped flooding the rooms of the church when someone picked up the tile; the water is now thought to be miraculous, and is bottled and given to the ill); in the Cappella Aldobrandini (3[a]) three paintings by the Cavalier d'Arpino (1596).

Piazza Colonna* (3 D6). Adorned by the coclide column (see below) which stands at the center, and from which it takes its name, this square was one of the nerve centers of Papal Rome; in the 19th-c. it merged administrative functions (the main office of the Papal Post Office was located in the 19th-c. *Palazzo Wedekind* – 3 D6 – now the Palazzo de "Il Tempo," a newspaper, with a number of re-used columns in the portico, originally found at Veio) with social ones (there were numerous cafes in this square; concerts were also held here).

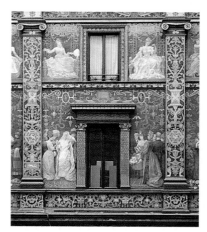

The Galleria Sciarra

The expansion of the Via del Corso called for in the urban plan of 1873 led to the destruction of the Palazzo Boncompagni Piombino; on the site of this building, in 1915-22, the *Galleria Colonna* was built (3 D6), copying the 19th-c. structure of the gallerias of Milan and Naples.

Colonna di Marco Aurelio*, or Column of Marcus Aurelius (3 D6). Erected in A.D. 180-193 in marble from Luni (the shaft stands 29.6 m. tall; the diameter is 3.7 m.), this column narrates in a continuous frieze the wars waged by the emperor against the Marcomanni, the Quadi, and the Sarmatians, between A.D. 172 and 175; the statue of the emperor, lost during the Middle Ages, stood on the top of the column, and could be reached by a stairway that climbed up inside the shaft of the column. The bronze *statue of St. Paul* that replaced it was commissioned – during the course of the restoration ordered by Pope Sixtus V and supervised by Domenico Fontana – and executed by Leonardo Sormani and Tommaso Della Porta; in the same period, Giacomo Longhi Silla and Matteo da Città di Castello refashioned many of the figures that had been lost in the central and upper part of the frieze; the most recent work dates from 1981-87.

Palazzo di Montecitorio* (3 D5-6). Overlooking the Piazza di Montecitorio, this building has housed the Italian Camera dei Deputati, or chamber of deputies, since 1871, and was built by Gian Lorenzo Bernini (he designed the convex elevation, with Baroque ornamental motifs) at the behest of Innocent X in 1653; construction was halted at the death of the pope, and the building was converted in the late-17th c. by Carlo Fontana into a courts building (Tribunali); renovation was done by Ernesto Basile from 1903-1927, resulting in the present rear facade overlooking the Piazza del Parlamento and the *Aula Parlamentare* (or hall of parliament, which is open to visitors only when the chamber of deputies is in session), adorned by an allegorical *frieze* on canvas, by Giulio Aristide Sartorio (1908-1912) and decorated with carved oak in the floral style. The various rooms of the building feature noteworthy works by Ottone Rosai, Carlo Carrà, Giorgio De Chirico, Lorenzo Viani, Giovanni Boldini, Massimo Campigli, and, to name one canvas in particular, the *Marriage at Cana* from the school of Paolo Veronese.

Before the palazzo looms, 29 m. tall, the *obelisk of Psamtik II* (3 D6; turn of the 6th c. B.C.), which Augustus brought from Heliopolis as part of his sundial; it was raised here again in 1792 by Giovanni Antinori, who restored it to its time-keeping function (traces on the pavement of the square can still be seen).

Palazzo Sciarra (3 E6). Recognizable especially by the handsome 17th-c. *portal* enclosed in the stern and austere facade, this building once overlooked a square, the Piazza Sciarra, which was eliminated at the end of the 19th c. in order to make way for the widening of the Via del Corso. On that occasion, the building – whose construction dragged on from the middle of the 16th c. to 1745 (completion of the library designed

by Luigi Vanvitelli) – was the subject of major renovation, overseen by Maffeo Sciarra, who also extended the work to the adjoining block: at the same time, the **Galleria Sciarra** (4 E2) was opened, a pedestrian passageway linking the Via Minghetti and the Piazza dell'Oratorio, planned with an iron-and-glass vaulting structure, decorated in the eclectic style.

On the opposite side of the Via del Corso (n. 320) is the *Palazzo della Cassa di Risparmio di Roma* (3 E6); when this headquarters of a major bank was built, in 1867-74, it marked the beginning of the change in the nature of this street.

If you take the Via di Pietra, which branches off to the right from the Via del Corso shortly before the Palazzo Sciarra, you will reach – after passing by one of the oldest hotels in Rome – the Piazza di Pietra, embellished by the **Palazzo della Borsa** (3 E6) which is perhaps the most remarkable example of re-use and redesign of a building that Rome offers. The building was originally the *temple of Hadrian*, dedicated by Antoninus Pius (the 11 surviving columns belong to the right side), but in 1695 it was transformed by Carlo and Francesco Fontana into the Dogana di Terra, a customs house, and in 1879 by Virginio Vespignani into the Camera di Commercio e Borsa Valori, a stock exchange and chamber of commerce.

Along the left side of the Palazzo della Borsa you will reach the *Piazza di S. Ignazio* (3 E6), squeezed somewhat by the facade of the church of S. Ignazio (see below) and rendered particularly distinctive on the opposite side of the square by the three small Rococo palazzi known as the *"Burrò*"*, which close off the square in accordance with the design by Filippo Raguzzini in 1727-28.

The church of **S. Ignazio** (3 E6) was dedicated by Pope Gregory XV to St. Ignatius of Loyola, who was the founder of the Company of Jesus, or order of the Jesuits. St. Ignatius had been canonized in 1622. Work on the construction of the church began under the supervision of Carlo Maderno, in 1626, and as late as 1685 it still had no cupola; to make up for the missing cupola, Andrea Pozzo planned and executed the remarkable perspective painting (*Glory of St. Ignatius**) that imitates the lighting and profundity of a cupola. The facade is a copy of the facade of the church of the Gesù, as is the interior, with a single nave, with three communicating chapels on each side, containing works by Alessandro Algardi (*Religion* and *Magnificence*, shown on the counter-facade bearing the commemorative inscription of the consecration of the church), Pierre Legros (*Glory of St. Luigi Gonzaga*, a marble relief on the altar of the right transept), Camillo Rusconi (*Cardinal Virtues* in the corners of the chapel on the right of the apse), and – again – Andrea Pozzo (*Events from the Life of St. Ignatius* in the main chapel).

"Rest during the flight into Egypt" by Caravaggio in the Galleria Doria Pamphilj

S. Marcello al Corso* (4 E2). This, the oldest church in the Via del Corso, was rebuilt for the first time in the 12th c. and a second time after 1519 under the supervision of Jacopo Sansovino, and later by Antonio da Sangallo the Younger and Annibale Lippi.

In the handsome travertine facade, which Carlo Fontana designed in 1682-86, bundles of palm fronds replace the volutes. The decoration of the interior, clearly influenced by the style of Sansovino, if not designed by him, has a single nave, with five chapels on either side, and was not completed until the 18th c.; note, to the left of the entrance, the two-fold *monument to the cardinal Giovanni Michiel and his nephew Antonio Orso*, also by Sansovino.

The *baptistery* of the old church, which provides evidence of actual rites of immersion, which are not well documented in Rome, and which can be seen from the main hall of the nearby bank of Banca di Roma, was discovered in 1912: the basin probably dates back to the 8th c., but recent excavations have uncovered a phase that may date back to the 5th c.

S. Maria in Via Lata (3 E-F6). Apparently, Pope Sergius I ordered the foundation of the first church, on structures dating from Roman times, at the end of the 7th c., and it was rebuilt in the 16th c., and completely renovated on the interior on the occasion of the Holy Year of 1650, by Cosimo Fanzago. The facade (Pietro da Cortona, 1658-62) features, in the portico formed by the Corinthian columns, a solution that is not found in any other Baroque church of the time; the campanile is by Martino Longhi the Elder and dates from 1580. The marble and stucco decorations and the paintings on the interior – with a nave and two side-aisles, separated by 12 columns faced in the 17th c. with jasper from Sicily – date from the work done by Fanzago; the *main altar* is attributed to Gian Lorenzo Bernini (1636-43).

Palazzo Doria Pamphilj* (3 F6). This is the most noteworthy of the many palazzi that overlook the Via del Corso – and of those, one of the very few, along with the "Palazzo Massimo alle Colonne," that is still inhabited by the family that ordered its construction; this same family assembled the collection of art on exhibit in the Galleria Doria Pamphilj (see below); it is the result of a great many different phases of construction, which extended from the middle of the 15th c. to the first half of the 18th c. Among those phases, let us specify the facade overlooking the Via del Corso (Gabriele Valvassori, 1731-34), the wing located on the Via del Plebiscito (1739-44), and the main floor, on the Via del Corso (1748-49); the last renovation dates from the 18th c. when, under the supervision of Andrea Busiri Vici, the palazzo was given new elevations overlooking the Vicolo Doria and the Via della Gatta.

The facade* overlooking the Via del Corso (restored in 1991), a masterpiece by Valvassori, is particularly distinctive for the numerous windows in the mezzanine and the ground floor (note the remarkable cornices); also noteworthy is the central portal, where the capitals of the columns, set at the corners, feature the symbol of the lily – the family's heraldic device – in the place of the more usual acanthus leaves; for the side portals, the columns are set at the far sides of the elevation.

Galleria Doria Pamphilj*. This remarkable private collection of more than 400 paintings, largely dating from a period extending from the 16th to the 18th c., was established by Pope Innocent X Pamphilj in 1651, and was subsequently enriched with major new acquisitions; the collection is housed in the splendid halls of the gallery, comprising four separate wings, and still conforms to original arrangement of the artworks on a number of different floors (as many as six in the smaller halls).

The *Salone Aldobrandini*, a great hall that was completed in 1838, contains a number of paintings, of course, but also several commemorative tapestries, sculptures, some of them ancient (the *Laughing Centaur* is taken from a Hellenistic original) and reliefs from the 17th c. (note the *Bacchanal of Putti* by François Duquesnoy).

The visit begins in the reception halls, among which the *Sala dei Velluti* (the Genoan drapes on the walls could be late 18th c.), the *Saletta Verde* in Venetian style, the *Sala da Ballo* redecorated from the end of the 1800's to 1903, and the *Cappella* are of particular interest.

From this point starts the actual gallery. The first section, with Chinese decorations, contains the *Penitent Magdalene Landscape with Escape to Egypt* and *Landscape with the Penitent Magdalene* all by Annibale Carracci; some *Landscapes* by Francesco Albani; and numerous Flemish paintings. At the end you enter a small hall which contains the celebrated *portrait of Pope Innocent X**, by Diego Velázquez (1650), and a *bust of Pope Innocent X* by Gian Lorenzo Bernini.

In the second section, the sculptures belonging to Pamphilj are ancient but were restored in the 17th-18th c.: a couple by Raphael and the portrait of Giovanna d'Aragona. Four smaller halls follow, each dedicated to a different century exhibiting paintings from the family collection chosen to suit modern criteria; in particular: two *Views of Venice* by Gaspar von Wuttel, *Penitent Magdalene* and *A Rest during the Escape to Egypt* by Caravaggio, the *Double Portrait* by Raphael, the portrait of a young gentleman by Tintoretto, *Salomè* by Tiziano, *St. Christopher and John the Baptist* and *St. James the Apostle and St. Anthony the Abbot* by Bicci di Lorenzo, the *Deposition from the Cross* by Hans Memling. In the third section you can find: *St. Jerome* by Lorenzo Lobbo; the *Return of the Prodigal Son*, the *Martyrdom of St. Agnes* and *St. John in the desert* by Guercino; a *Madonna Adoring Her Child* by Guido Reni; the *Bust of Innocent X* by Alessandro Algardi. The *Sala Aldobrandini* was originally the old gallery: as well as canvasses you can admire the ancient statues from the garden of Villa Doria Pamphilj. In the fourth section it is worth stopping a moment infront of: the *Angel with a Tambourine* by Tiziano, *St. John the Baptist* by Mattia Preti, the *Madonna with Child* by Jan Bruegel il Vecchio, the *Bust of Olympia Maidalchini* by Algardi and the *Madonna with Child* by Parmigianino.

Shortly beyond, the Via del Corso opens out into the Piazza Venezia (see page 54).

2 The Historical City

The differences in the origins of the names of the 22 "rioni", or quarters, of modern Rome reveals the clear distinction between the older ones and those created following Italian unification in 1870. The Rione Monti – with a heraldic device consisting of three mountains on a white field, alluding to the three hills it encloses (the Viminal, and part of the Quirinal and the Esquiline) as well as hinting at the age-old distinction between the "montes" (those who lived within the enclosure of the Servian walls) and the "pagi" (residents of the outlying suburbs) – is the first, and one of the very few that tenaciously preserve the ancient Roman traditions. The second is the Rione Trevi; the name is of uncertain origin, and has been transferred to the fountain. The heraldic device consists of three swords. Next, the third one, is the Rione Colonna (the name refers to the column of Marcus Aurelius, making up part of the heraldic crest), which covers a great portion of the enormous area of the classical Campo Marzio and the slopes of the Pincio. The fourth is the Rione Campo Marzio

The immense mole of the Altar of the Fatherland, dedicated to Victor Emmanuel II

(the heraldic crest depicts a crescent moon on a turquoise field), which occupies the "Platea Tiberina," a plain that lies between the hills and the curving banks of the Tiber, consecrated, according to tradition, to the god Mars, following the expulsion of the Tarquins. The fifth one is named the Rione Ponte because it lies close to a bridge, originally called the "Pons Aelius," and now known as the Ponte S. Angelo, which appears naturally enough in the red field of the crest, flanked by statues of St. Peter and St. Paul. The sixth one – in accordance with the traditional sequence – is the Rione Parione, which boasts the Piazza Navona; it is named after an ancient section of the stadium of Domitian (the Latin term "paries" was corrupted in the Middle Ages to "paretone," and finally evolved into the present name); the emblem is a griffin on a silver field. The Rione Regola, the seventh in order, supposedly takes its name from Arenula – which indicates its location on the oxbow curve of the Tiber – and its heraldic crest features a stag on a turquoise field. The eighth "rione," the Rione Sant'Eustachio, has a fairly vague boundary, but abounds in remarkable palazzi and churches (it is therefore also known as the "rione delle cupole," or quarter of cupolas); its heraldic crest refers to the legend of St. Eustachius: it once had as its symbol a stag with the cross between its horns, it now has a bust of the Savior between the horns. The Rione Pigna, named for a pine cone, is the ninth quarter, and is particularly dense with monuments (it encloses the Pantheon, the church of the Gesù, and the churches of S. Maria sopra Minerva and S. Ignazio), features a pine cone on a red field in its heraldic crest; this is a reference to the great pine cone taken from the imperial temple of Isis and Serapis; after decorating the fountain in front of the old St. Peter's (or S. Pietro) for some time, it was moved inside, where it has given its name to one of the courtyards of the Palazzi Vaticani, the Cortile della Pigna. The Rione Campitelli, the tenth quarter, is like some vast outdoor museum – it in fact includes the area of the Fori (Forums), the Campidoglio, and the Palatine hill – and is now more heavily frequented by tourists than by residents; most of the long-time inhabitants were driven out by the demolition required for the construction of the Via dei Fori Imperiali and the Via del Mare; its heraldic crest is a dragon on a white field. The Rione Sant'Angelo, the medieval "rione" which contains the Ghetto, has as its emblem an angel that crushes the devil beneath its feet, while holding a sword and a set of scales. The Rione Ripa, the twelfth, extends from the Isola Tiberina to the Aventine hill, and takes its name – "ripa" means riverbank – from the proximity of the river; the heraldic crest features a wheel on a red field. Trastevere (meaning the "oltre Tevere," or beyond the Tiber) and Borgo ("burg," or quarter, is the name given by the Saxons to the area around the hospital, or Ospedale di S. Spirito in Sassia, that they founded), respectively the thirteenth and the fourteenth, are the most recent of the historical quarters; the former has a lion's head on a field of red as its crest; the latter a composite emblem, a clear indication of its late origins: a lion on a red field standing atop three mountains which are surmounted by a star (the lion is a reference to the Città Leonina, literally "leonine city," or the part of Rome enclosed by the walls of Leo IV). The "rioni" established after Rome was made the capital simply took their names from nearby locations: Esquilino (post 1870), Prati (post 1870), Castro Pretorio (1921), Celio (1921), Ludovisi (1921), Sallustiano (1921), San Saba (1921), Testaccio (1921). The ten tours offered in this chapter run through the areas occupied by the 22 "rioni".

Capital of Christendom ever since the birth of Christianity, Rome features houses of worship in the full succession of styles and architecture that they present throughout history: from the basilican hall to the most daring structures of the 20th c. For centuries writers have marveled over the "tone" and the "color" of the Eternal City – given to other cities by the clothing and hair of the women – but here a result of the various outfits of the clergy; and we can easily believe the elegant travesty of the city offered by Rabelais, who clearly was hinting at Rome in his "île sonnante", with a swipe at the fact that life in the Eternal City had long been regulated by Catholic liturgy and its ineluctable pace.

No matter how many asterisks, different type faces, and bolds and italics we may use, here more than in any other case the guide book shows its inadequacy; which is not so much, or not only, the insufficiency of an author or an expository approach, but far more in general the inadequacy of description itself – as a concept and as a procedure of inevitably simplistic representation – in the face of a reality, of a body of history and art as well as of human endeavor, that dates back – as you may note in many different instances – to places that no description can truly reach: the very roots of our history.

2.1 From Piazza Venezia to Piazza di S. Giovanni in Laterano

This route, setting out as it does from the Piazza Venezia, overlooked by the huge monument raised to commemorate the unification of Italy, leads to places that have long been symbols of the "glory that was Rome" (the Fori Imperiali and the Laterano), for centuries the representative sites of the glory and splendor of ancient Rome and of its rediscovered universal standing in the worldwide body of Roman Catholicism.

From Piazza Venezia, the pedestrian tour runs along the Via dei Fori Imperiali, a long straight avenue embellished by the twin churches of S. Maria di Loreto the SS. Nome di Maria, marked on the left by the structures that are visible of the Fori Imperiali (Trajan's Forum and Trajan's Market are two noteworthy relics of those fora); framed at the end of this road is the vast mass of the

Colosseum, leaving behind on the right, following the entryway to the archeological area of the Foro Romano and the Palatine, brief detours to the Basilica dei Ss. Cosma e Damiano and the church of S. Francesca Romana. Beyond the Piazza del Colosseo, which is overlooked also by the Arch of Constantine and Nero's Domus Aurea – literally, golden home – the straightaway of the "stradone" (literally, "big street"; this is the popular name for the Via di S. Giovanni in Laterano) leads to the Basilica di S. Clemente and the whole complex of S. Giovanni in Laterano, with the basilica and the baptistery of the same name (St. John Lateran).

Piazza Venezia (6 E5; 8 A3). Laid out in its present format by Pope Paul II with a view to the Palazzo di Venezia (see below) and serving as the finish line of the famous horserace called the "Corsa dei Bàrberi" which in Roman Carnevale was run down the Via del Corso, this square represented the first major piece of urban renovation in 16th-c. Rome.

The decision (1882) to erect a monument to Vittorio Emanuele II, first king of Italy, called for a complex rearrangement of the square, in the context of which the Palazzetto Venezia was moved (see page 57) and the erection of the *Palazzo delle Assicurazioni Generali di Venezia* (headquarters of an insurance company; 4 F3; 6 E5; 1902-1906), reflecting in the style of the Venetian Quattrocento the facing Palazzo di Venezia (a plaque on the right side of the building commemorates the Casa di Macel de' Corvi where Michelangelo lived and died).

The inauguration of the monument, on the 50th anniversary of the unification of Italy, and the burial of the Milite Ignoto (Italy's Unknown Soldier) in 1921 reinforced the symbolic character of this square – linked to the Altare della Patria – and when the Palazzo di Venezia became the office of the head of government in 1929, the square was proclaimed the "Foro d'Italia," or Forum of Italy; it is now overwhelmed by heavy traffic.

Palazzo di Venezia* (6 E4-5). This immense building, the first major piece of Renaissance civil architecture in Rome, was begun in 1455-64 by the cardinal Pietro Barbo, as a residence; in 1465-68 he decided to enlarge it, following his election as pope (Paul II), with the new facade of the Basilica di S. Marco and the "viridarium" (the future Palazzetto Venezia), while inside the Sala del Mappamondo was built (1466-67). Following the work done by Pope Paul III, numerous alterations, inside and out, were done over the course of the 18th/19th c., a period during which the palazzo passed from the ownership of the Venetian Republic to that of France in 1797, and in 1814 to Austria; the Italian government confiscated the building in 1916, and largely converted it to the site of the Museo del Palazzo di Venezia (see below).

This building marked the dominance in Rome of the Renaissance model of architecture proclaimed by Leon Battista Alberti: it was built as a block with a rectangular plan and a central courtyard with portico and loggia; in that design the Basilica di S. Marco became the palatine chapel. The influence of Alberti is evident both in the overall design, and in the vault of the entryway onto the square, and in the magnificent fragment of the *courtyard*.

Museo del Palazzo di Venezia*. This museum comprises an exceedingly varied array of collections: a gallery of paintings, including works dating from the 14th to the 17th c., and numerous collections of art objects, ranging from terracotta models to ceramic products, bronze sculptures and an array of fine glass and silver, ivory and silver objects made in Germany (16th and 17th c.) and Venice (16th c.).

The paintings are divided according to their artistic school and chronological order. Of

A fan in the Museo del Palazzo di Venezia

particular interest: *Madonna with Child* by Paolo Veneziano, a *Head of a Young Woman** by Pisanello, the *Head of Redentore* by Benozzo Gozzoli, a *Madonna with Child* by Neri di Bucci. Also noteworthy, the group of canvasses from 16-19th c.

Hall VII, known as the Sala Altoviti because the *stuccoes* and the *frescoes* that adorn it were done by Giorgio Vasari in the Palazzo Altoviti, contains an exceptional array of goldsmithery and religious furnishings, including, a 10th c. rock crystal *Cross*, a coeval ivory *nuptial casket* in Byzantine style, a pair of mid-17th c. tapestries (Games of Putti), 22 paintings (end 18th c. - first half 19th c.) bear witness to the popularity, especially in France, of the so-called pastels; these are accompanied by *fans* and principally 18th-19th c. *miniatures*.

Splendid groups of Italian and European porcelain, dating from the 18th to the 20th c., are arranged in the long collection known as the "Corridoio dei Cardinali" (hall XI); a magnificent collection of small bronzes, largely dating from the Renaissance, and a collection of reliefs, studies, and models, in gesso and terracotta (note the rare collection of *studies* by Alessandro Algardi, Ercole Ferrata, and Gian Lorenzo Bernini) are arranged in halls XVI-XXVI.

The *Sale Studio* house the complete collections of silver and oriental chinaware; the former (ca. 800 pieces, 16th-19th c.) originate from Northern Europe, Russia and Italy where, for example, a service was produced for the Pope, and altar piece with vel-

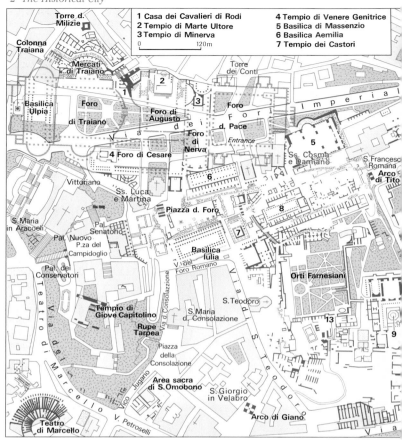

1 Casa dei Cavalieri di Rodi
2 Tempio di Marte Ultore
3 Tempio di Minerva
4 Tempio di Venere Genitrice
5 Basilica di Massenzio
6 Basilica Aemilia
7 Tempio dei Castori

The archeological area of the Fori Imperiali

vet background and a sumptuous table ornament.

The halls of the Appartamento Barbo (undergoing restoration in 1993) contain a major collection of weapons (formerly the Odescalchi collection) and a collection of German, Flemish, and Italian tapestries from the 15th and 16th c.

Also located in the Palazzo di Venezia are the Soprintendenza per i Beni Artistici e Storici di Roma (arts preservation commission) and the *Biblioteca dell'Istituto Nazionale di Archeologia e Storia dell'Arte*, a library with over 300,000 volumes and 15,000 manuscripts, drawings, and prints (note the Fondo Lanciani per l'Archeologia e la Topografia di Roma, a collection concerning archeology and topography of the city).

Basilica di S. Marco* (6 E4), or St. Mark's basilica. Founded by Pope Mark in A.D. 336, this church was rebuilt by Pope Hadrian I in 792, and underwent later renovations (the Romanesque *campanile* dates from the mid-

12th c.) until it was entirely rebuilt under Pope Paul II in the second half of the 15th c. (it was then made the palatine chapel of the neighboring Palazzo di Venezia).

The facade, which dates from the 15th-c. renovation, was largely built with material taken from the Colosseum and the theater of Marcellus: the simple three-arch portico reveals the influence of Leon Battista Alberti; in the atrium, note, among the various architectural fragments, the *funerary plaque by Vannozza Catanei* (d. 1518). The interior shows clear signs of Baroque and 18th-c. transformations, but the handsome coffered *ceiling* dates from the reign of Pope Paul II, and with the ceiling of S. Maria Maggiore is the only 15th-c. ceiling still surviving in Rome; the 17th-c. flooring preserves parts of the Renaissance flooring, while a *well head* dating from the 9th/10th c. standing at the head of the nave, and the apse, decorated with **mosaics** under Pope Gregory IV that date back to 827-844,

Circo Massimo

gressive enclosure of the arches. The handsome interior **courtyard** features, at its center, a *well* carved by Antonio da Brescia.

On the external wall of the "palazzetto," at the corner of the square, note a marble bust depicting Isis, known among the common folk as *Madama Lucrezia*; this is one of the "talking statues" (see page 107).

The Vittoriano (6 E-F5). Known as the Altar of the Fatherland, this enormous monument to Vittorio Emanuele II di Savoia (Victor Emmanuel II of Savoy), the first king of a united Italy, was built from 1885 on to plans by Giuseppe Sacconi. For various reasons, however – not least the very size of the ambitious project – construction was not completed until 1935; the monument itself was completed (though not entirely decorated) in time for the celebration of the half-century anniversary of Italy's unification; the *Altare della Patria*, Altar of the Fatherland, was inaugurated in 1925, following the burial of the Milite Ignoto (Unknown Soldier, 1921). The bronze quadrigae, or four-horse chariots, were set above the propylaea only in 1927.

The overall composition of the Vittoriano hearkens back to Greek and Latin architecture; the Graeco-Latin tradition was held up as the root of an Italian "national" art, still in swaddling clothes. All of the best-known practitioners of academic sculpture in Italy worked on the decoration of the building, producing about a hundred works of sculpture, greatly varying in artistic quality; the frieze with high reliefs (*Triumph of Labor* and *Triumph of Love of Country*) is by Angelo Zanelli.

The interior was decorated by Armando Brasini (1924-35; he also designed the *Crypt of the Unknown Soldier*).

You will now find there: a permanent *exhibition* of documentation and other material concerning the actual construction of the monument (for a tour of it, contact the Soprintendenza per i Beni Ambientali e Architettonici, or commission of art and architecture, of Rome); the *Sacrario delle Bandiere delle Forze Armate*, or sacrarium of the banners of the armed forces; and the *Museo Centrale del Risorgimento*, or central museum of Italy's late-19th-c. unification movement, established in 1906 but only inaugurated in 1970. It has been closed since 1979. Its collections include material dating from the second half of the 18th c. to the outbreak of WWI (of special note: rare documents by the hand of Napoleon Bonaparte and Joaquim Murat; relics of Silvio Pellico, Giuseppe Garibaldi, Giuseppe Mazzini, and Vittorio Emanuele II; documentation con-

both document the medieval origins of the building. In the right aisle, note artworks by Palma the Younger (1st chapel), Carlo Maratta (3rd chapel) and, toward the presbytery, the *tomb of Leonardo Pesaro* by Antonio Canova (1796).

The granite urn in the presbytery contains the bodies of St. Mark (pope) and saints Abdon and Sennen.

The left side-aisle contains, in the Cappella Capranica, three paintings by Pier Francesco Mola. In the sacristy note a *St. Mark Evangelist* by Melozzo da Forlì and *reliefs* on the altar by Mino da Fiesole and Giovanni Dalmata.

Set against the left side of the Palazzo di Venezia, the *Palazzetto Venezia* (6 E4) was reconstructed in 1911-13, with a regularization of the plan; this "viridarium" built at the orders of Pope Paul II in 1464 – as a garden surrounded by a portico, in accordance with the concepts of Leon Battista Alberti – which was enlarged with an upper loggia, in 1466-68, and radically transformed with the pro-

cerning the papacy of Pius IX and the storming of Rome; and eloquent documents and photographic material concerning the Grande Guerra, WWI).

Via dei Fori Imperiali (8 A-B-C3-4-5). This broad boulevard was the result of extensive demolition of the medieval and Renaissance quarters that stood between Piazza Venezia and the Colosseum (its route has cut through the area of the Fori and eradicated – or at least locked underground – an invaluable historical and artistic heritage). The roadway was planned as early as 1925-26, construction began in 1931, and one stretch of the great boulevard was inaugurated (1932) in honor of the tenth anniversary of the Fascist March on Rome. The entire length of roadway was inaugurated on 21 April 1933. Joining Piazza Venezia and the Colosseum, it does, onto Via Cavour, this roadway has become one of Rome's most important traffic arteries: a Sunday ban for cars was experimented with the hypothesis of partly eliminating the thoroughfare to expose the underlying Fori.

The churches of S. Maria di Loreto and the Santissimo Nome di Maria (8 A3). The construction of the church of S. Maria di Loreto began – possibly to plans by Bramante – on behalf of the Confraternita dei Fornari in 1507 and, following the consecration in 1534, the church was completed between 1573 and 1576 – under the supervision of Jacopo Del Duca – with the outsized cupola with an unusual lantern and a campanile; a major restoration was done by Luca Carimini in 1867-73.
The church of the Santissimo Nome di Maria, which is reminiscent of the adjacent church of S. Maria di Loreto, although with adaptations to suit the late-Baroque style, was begun in 1736, on the foundations of the 15th-c. church of S. Bernardo, and was completed around the middle of the century.

Colonna Traiana*, or Trajan's Column (8 A3). One of the very few ancient monuments that survive virtually intact (standing 39.87 m. tall, including the base, and comprising 25 great blocks of marble, each one 3.5 m. in diameter), this column is entirely covered by a spiralling bas-relief frieze, originally brightly painted, that tells of episodes of the Dacian wars (A.D. 101-103 and 107-108); the man who carved these scenes, finely portrayed (there are roughly 2,500 figures) and of exceedingly fine artistic quality, is called the Maestro delle Imprese di Traiano. From the base, which is

decorated with trophaea of barbarian weapons, it is possible to climb a spiral staircase up to the top of the column. Here stands a *statue of St. Peter*, by Tommaso Della Porta and Leonardo Sormani, placed here in 1587, in place of a statue of the emperor.

Foro di Traiano and Mercati di Traiano*, or Trajan's Forum and Trajan's Market (6 E6; 8 A4). This complex, built from A.D. 107 on, to plans by Apollodorus of Damascus, and completed under the reign of Hadrian, demanded immense excavation work; in particular, the engineers had to cut the great saddle that joined the Quirinal with the Campidoglio.
The tour begins with the **market**, which overlooks the Via IV Novembre (present-day entrance) with a great hall, possibly the trading hall; from here you can climb up to the higher floors of the market, to the Torre delle Milizie (see page 35) and to the ruins of the *Castello dei Caetani*, the castle of a powerful family; here, in the Middle Ages, the family built a fortified residence, based on Roman structures.
From the great hall, a stairway leads down to the *Via Biberatica*, which takes its name from the tabernae, or drinks shops and taverns that lined this street; also, you can reach the *hemicycle* of the market. From here you have a fine overall view of the market and forum.
A collection of architectural decorations from the Forums of Augustus and Trajan has been set up in the Markets together with findings from the ex-Antiquarium of the Forum of Augustus.
A passageway runs beneath the modern-day Via Alessandrina and into the **forum**. This forum once comprised the Greek and Roman libraries, the giant temple of Trajan – the size can be guessed at from the surviving sections of shafts of columns, 1.8 m. across, and from the capitals, 2 m. tall – the *Basilica Ulpia*, the largest and most sumptuous Roman basilica (170 x 60 m.; its columns stand in the center of the excavated area). In ancient times, one entered the forum through a triumphal arch, which then led into a square dominated by a statue of Trajan, under whom the Roman empire attained its greatest size.

On the opposite side of Via dei Fori Imperiali, on the SE slopes of the Campidoglio, a bronze copy of a statue of Caesar marks the *Foro di Cesare*, or Forum of Caesar (8 A-B3), begun by Julius Caesar (it was consecrated in 46 B.C.) and completed by Augustus. Excavations begun in 1932 uncovered only about a quarter of the original expanse of the forum. It comprised a rectangular plaza, surrounded by porticoes and closed off to the north by the *temple of Venus Genitrix*; surviving from this structure, note the three raised columns and the crowning trabeation.

Foro di Augusto*, or Forum of Augustus (8 A4). Adjoining Trajan's Market, but emulating in plan the Forum of Caesar (a large portico surrounded a square measuring about 125 x 118 m.), this forum was inaugurated in 2 B.C.; despite a number of archeological campaigns of excavations – especially the digs done in the context of the general plan for exploration and restoration of the Fori, set forth by Corrado Ricci – the front half of the area has yet to be uncovered.

At the center of the forum (to tour it, contact the X Ripartizione del Comune, Rome city government) once stood the *temple of Mars Ultor*, comprising a tufa-stone podium faced with blocks of marble and surrounded by eight columns on each side (one can see the three columns of the right side, 15 m. tall); an apse contained statues of Mars, Venus, and perhaps, of Divus Julius, or Caesar the God.

On the exedra on the left, in the 15th c., the **Casa dei Cavalieri di Rodi**, or house of the Knights of Rhodes (6 E-F6; 8 A4) was built, at one time the priory of the order of the Knights of St. John of Jerusalem (later, the Knights of Rhodes, and then the Knights of Malta, in accordance with a series of westward moves that corresponded to the Turkish expansion throughout the Mediterranean Sea). Its current appearance is largely a result of the work done by Cardinal Barbo, who probably used the same craftsmen and builders that constructed the Palazzo di Venezia.

The facade is adorned with a 15th-c. cross window; the porticoed atrium still features the travertine pillars from the Augustan construction, while the Cappella di S. Giovanni Battista, or chapel of St. John the Baptist, is a 20th-c. adaptation of part of the interior.

On the upper floor, note: the great hall, dominated by a tribune, possibly the meeting hall of the Knights; a loggia with elegant arcades (fine panoramic view*); the Sala Bizantina, or Byzantine hall, in which are assembled fragments of medieval buildings destroyed in the demolition required to build the Via dei Fori Imperiali.

Foro di Nerva, or Forum of Nerva (8 A-B4). Also known as the "Forum Minervae" or "Palladium" – after the temple dedicated here to Minerva, or Pallas Athena – and "Transitorium" or "Pervium" because it was a point of passage between Rome's poorer quarters, or Suburra, and the Roman Forum, this forum adjoined the Forum of Augustus, and was roughly 150 m. in length, but only 45 m. in width. Part of the podium of the *Temple of Minerva* can be seen: the so-called *Colonnacce* (columns, restored 1982-87), which formed a portico, and the attic with a bas-relief frieze set on those columns.

Basilica dei Ss. Cosma e Damiano (8 B-C4). The present-day facade (1947) overlooking the Via dei Fori Imperiali, just after

A detail of the Forum of Nerva

the entrance to the archeological area of the Roman Forum and the Palatine Hill (see page 95), conceals a house of worship created by joining two classical buildings (the library, or Biblioteca del Foro della Pace – see above – and a hall of the temple of Divus Romulus, or the God Romulus, on the Via Sacra – see page 99) donated by Theodoric and Amalasunta to Pope Felix IV, who dedicated them to the two physician brothers who became saints. The present-day appearance of the basilica, on the other hand, is the result of the work done, during the reign of Pope Urban VIII, by Orazio Torriani and Luigi Arrigucci (the floor was raised, concealing in a sort of crypt the Roman interior of the ancient church).

A handsome wooden *ceiling* with paintings spans a hall, frescoed, and with chapels. In the apse, dating from the reign of Felix IV, note the mosaics of the triumphal arch (*Apocalypse* with the *Mystical Lamb Among the Seven Candelabra*) and the vault (*Christ Between St. Peter and St. Paul, Presenting St. Cosma and St. Damian, Accompanied by St. Theodore and Felix IV, with a Model of the Church*); they date from the 6th/7th c. On the main altar, *Virgin Mary with Christ Child*, a 13th-c. painting on panel. In the sacristy and in the lower church (both closed to the public) are a Cosmatesque *ciborium* (13th c.) and an *altar* dating from the 6th/7th c.

S. Francesca Romana (8 C4-5). This church – which can be reached by following a marked route leading here from the Via dei Fori Imperiali, cutting off to the right immediately following the marble *panels* designed by Antonio Muñoz and depicting the expansion of the Roman Empire – was built in the 9th c. and was enlarged in the second half of the 10th c., when it was known as S. Maria Nova to distinguish it from S. Maria Antiqua in the Foro Romano, or Roman Forum; it was dedicated to St. Francesca Romana in the 15th c.

The interior, with a single nave with a handsome coffered ceiling and side chapels, was given its current appearance in the second half of the 17th c. The *confession* beneath the holy arch was built to plans by Gian Lorenzo Bernini (1644-49); in the right transept, behind a grate, are the *Silices Apostolici*, pieces of basalt which refer back to the legend of the fall of Simon Magus; on the main altar, *Virgin Mary with Christ Child*, a 12th-c. panel; the vault of the apse contains a mosaic dating from the same period (*Virgin Mary with Christ Child and Saints*), the 1st chapel on the left contains a *Nativity* by Carlo Maratta.

The exquisite *Madonna Glycophilusa**, an icon dating back to the first half of the 5th c., and formerly housed in the church of S. Maria Antiqua, is now housed in the sacristy, along with a *Virgin Mary Enthroned between St. Benedict and St. Francesca Romana* by Girolamo da Cremona, a *Virgin Mary Enthroned and Saints* by Sinibaldo Ibi, and a canvas (*Pope Paul III and the Cardinal Reginald Pole*) attributed to Perin del Vaga or Sermoneta.

Tempio di Venere e Roma, or Temple of Venus and Roma (8 C5). This building was begun in A.D. 121 by Hadrian, completed by Antoninus Pius, and restored in A.D. 307 by Maxentius; girt by two porticoes, it had a double cella, with opposing apses which contained – in niches – statues of Roma and Venus.

Colosseo*, or Colosseum (8 C-D5-6). Symbol of the city of Rome, the Flavian amphitheater (that is the true name of this world-famous structure) was built in an area occupied by a manmade lake adjoining the Domus Aurea (see page 61), at the behest of Vespasian (the dedication dates from A.D. 79) and was inaugurated in A.D. 80 by Titus with games that are said to have lasted 100 days; it was completed by Domitian and restored by Alexander Severus. In the late Empire it was used for "venationes" (hunting games), while in the Middle Ages, when it was given the name of Colosseum, it was transformed into a fortress, and used by the families of the Frangipane and the Annibaldi. In 1312 it became the property of the senate and people of Rome, it was consecrated to the Passion of Jesus Christ by Pope Benedict XIV, who put an end to the demolition and ransacking of the building (it had become a quarry for building materials).

The facade – made entirely of travertine and split into three registers, each with 80 mighty arches – stands 50 m. tall. The internal elliptical arena (86 x 54 m.) was separated from the "cavea" by a podium, adorned with niches and embellished with marble, where a balustrade separated the members of the imperial family and other notables from the audience at large. The approximately 50,000 spectators that the amphitheater could accommodate entered and left by means of vaulted corridors with stairways leading to the various floors, each with special reserved sections (female spectators were assigned to the upper floors) and, when the sun was bright, an awning – or "velarium" – was spread overhead. In the rooms beneath the arena were tunnels for wild animals and the various stage settings; there were even elevators.

Arco di Costantino*, or arch of Constantine (8 D5). This is the largest and the best preserved of all the ancient arches in Rome; it was built by the senate and the people of Rome in A.D. 315 to honor the tenth anniversary of Constantine's accession to the

The upper story of the Domus Aurea was uncovered during the excavations in the *Parco del Colle Oppio* (9 B-C1-2), which was opened in 1932; inside the park are also the ruins of the *Terme di Traiano*, or baths of Trajan (9 B-C1-2), which Apollodorus of Damascus built in part atop the Domus Aurea (the central wing is enclosed by a wall extending roughly 330 x 315 m., with exedra), and the *Sette Sale* (or seven halls; open: 9-1:30, Sunday 9-1:30, Monday closed; from

The Colosseum, or Flavian amphitheater, the most famous ancient monument in Rome

head of the empire, and to commemorate his victory over Maxentius in 312; in the Middle Ages it was incorporated into the fortifications of the Frangipane clan on the nearby Colosseum; it was restored in the 18th c., but was not freed of the other structures until 1804. In the facade facing the Colosseum and Via di S. Gregorio are *scenes of the return of Marcus Aurelius to Rome* and *scenes of the wars that he waged*, *personifications of rivers*, *Victories* and *Dacian prisoners*, and *deeds of Constantine*. Along the sides *scenes of combat against the Dacians* and *Triumphs of Constantine* and *of his son*. The inscription celebrates the emperor's victory and reunification of the state.
Near the arch, which marked the beginning of the ancient Via dei Trionfi, archeologists have found the remains of the *"Meta Sudans"* (8 C5), an immense fountain – built by Titus, rebuilt by Domitian, and demolished above ground at least in 1936 – from which water seemed to bead out in perspiration.

Domus Aurea* (8 C6). This villa, built by Nero following the great fire of A.D. 64, extended over an area of nearly a square mile. It comprised – beside the princely main building – an immense garden and a man-made lake. The complex is still closed to the public.

1 April until 30 September also open on Tuesday, Thursday, and Saturday afternoons, 4-7 pm), an immense cistern, comprising a number of adjoining rooms, covered with a vault roof, once part of the complex mentioned above.

Basilica di S. Clemente and Convento di S. Clemente* (9 D2). One of the most remarkable and best-preserved architectural palimpsests in all of Rome, this basilica and convent formed around a residential home of the 2nd c. In the following century a Mithraeum was built in the courtyard, and shortly thereafter converted into a Christian church. This building, damaged by the fire caused by the Normans in 1084, was rebuilt by Pope Paschal II, closely adhering to the plan of the previous church. In 1713-19 the church and the bell tower were given their present appearance (restoration 1988-90); the excavation of the structures beneath was undertaken in 1857-60, attaining completion only in 1912-14.
The interior of the **upper basilica** preserves the structure that dates from the beginning of the 12th c.; there is a nave and two aisles, ending in apses and separated by columns, as well as a Cosmatesque floor. In the middle of the nave – adorned in the upper section with frescoes by Pier Leone Ghezzi, Giovanni Odazzi, and Sebastiano

Conca – is the *schola cantorum*, or choir chancel, dating from the 12th c. and incorporating elements that formed part of the lower church; the handsome Cosmatesque *ciborium* in the presbyterium is also from the 12th c., as is the bishop's *throne* in the apse. In the vault of the apse, note the mosaic with the **Triumph of the Cross**, of the Roman school, dating from the first half of the 12th c.: at the center is a *Crucifix with Twelve Doves* (the apostles) *between the Virgin Mary and St. John the Baptist*; on the triumphal arch, note *Christ with the Symbols of the Evangelists, St. Peter and St. Clement with Jeremiah and the City of Jerusalem* (right), and *St. Lawrence and St. Paul with Isaiah and the City of the Bethlehem* (left); in the lower register, note the *Agnus Dei with Twelve Sheep* (the apostles). In the right

Mosaic in the Basilica of S. Giovanni in Laterano

aisle, note the canvases attributed to Conca in the 1st chapel. In the left chapel, note the **frescoes** of the Cappella di S. Caterina, painted by Masolino da Panicale (1428-31), perhaps with assistance from Masaccio or someone else.

From the sacristy, you can descend – along a stairway decorated with fragments from the 4th-c. basilica and from the Mithraeum – to the **lower basilica**, where, in the nave, is a fresco depicting the *Legend of Sisinnio** (the statements and names that adorn the scene are a document of extreme importance to the history of the earliest vernacular Italian); other frescoes dating from the 9th/12th c. adorn the walls of the narthex (*Miracle of St. Clement*) and the nave (*Legend of St. Alessio*).

Take a stairway at the end of the left aisle to descend – beneath the apses of the upper and lower basilicas – to the various Roman structures, and the 3rd-c. *Mithraeum*.

Piazza di S. Giovanni in Laterano, or Square of St. John Lateran (9 E4). This is one of the salient areas in the great project undertaken by Pope Sixtus V of urban renew-

al; it soundly reflects – in the monuments that overlook it (from the Egyptian obelisk to the "novecentista" early-20th-c. style of the Pontificio Ateneo Lateranense, a school) – the Roman architectural culture.

The Lateran, corresponding to the eastern extremity of the Caelian hill, had been the site from the beginning of the Empire of patrician homes: the residence of the Laterani family, confiscated by Nero, was offered to the bishop of Rome and all his successors by Fausta, wife of the emperor Constantine; Pope Melchiades made it the papal residence; the emperor decided to erect the basilica alongside it (approximately 313-318).

It was Pope Sixtus V who decided to reorganize and restructure it (the complex of palace and basilica – locally described as the Patriarchìo – had in fact declined badly following the exile of the papacy to Avignon, in France), under the supervision of Domenico Fontana (1585-89).

The project undertaken by Sixtus was further enriched during the 17th-c. by the new *Ospedale del Salvatore* (9 E3-4), better known today as the hospital of S. Giovanni, and by the *Ospedale delle Donne*, or women's hospital (9 D-E3-4), in the 18th c. (the new facade of the basilica and the reconstruction of the Triclinio Leoniano) and until the last years of papal rule; the urban build-up that followed the unification of Italy on the Esquiline hill meant the rapid disappearance of the villas and gardens that occupied the area around the churches of S. Maria Maggiore and S. Croce in Gerusalemme.

At the center of the square, which – until the exile in Avignon – was the site of the ceremony whereby a newly elected pope took possession of the basilica, stands the *Obelisco Lateranense**, or Lateran obelisk (9 E4) – with the base, it stands 47 m. tall – originally constructed during the reigns of the pharaohs Tuthmosis III and Tuthmosis IV in the 15th c. B.C. and erected before the temple of Amon in Thebes. It was then transported to Rome in A.D. 357 by Constantius II, who ordered it erected in the Circus Maximus; it was knocked down in an earthquake, unearthed in 1587, and placed here by the architect Domenico Fontana.

Palazzo Lateranense (9 E4). Pope Sixtus V commissioned Domenico Fontana (1586-

89) to erect this building to replace the Patriarchìo; with a square plan and three identical elevations and an unusual columned roof terrace surmounting all, the building was first transformed into a hospital, and later into an archives; it was restored under Gregory XVI by Luigi Poletti to contain the Museo Gregoriano Profano (1844), the Museo Pio Cristiano (1854), and the Museo Missionario-Etnologico (1926). In accordance with the Lateran Pact, the building enjoys extraterritoriality; after radical restoration and the transfer of the museums to the Vatican, this has been since 1967 the site of the vicariate of Rome, and since 1987 it has housed the *Museo Storico Vaticano* (you enter it from the portico of the Basilica di S. Giovanni in Laterano), which includes the Papal Apartments and the Historical Museum (Museo Storico) proper.

The **Appartamento Papale**, the official reception area of the pope, in his role as bishop of Rome, occupies 10 lavishly decorated halls, adorned with precious specimens of old weapons; the series of paintings (*Glory of Sixtus V*), conceived by Giovanni Guerra, was executed, before 1589, by such artists as Cesare Nebbia, G.B. Ricci, Andrea Lilio, Paris Nogari, Paul and Matthijs Brill, and Ventura Salimbeni. Note the collection of tapestries (17th/18th c.), in part woven at the manufactory of Gobelins and in part in the Roman manufactories of the Barberini and of S. Michele, and a series of wooden sculptures, dating back to the 13th/15th c.

The **Museo Storico**, or historical museum, enlarged and reinstalled in the loggia on the main floor, comprises three sections – dedicated to the history of the popes, documentation of papal ceremonial, and the history of the papal armed corps – as well as a fine collection of antique armaments from the 16th and 17th c.

The first section, which will be rounded out in time with documents concerning the history of the popes, now comprises an iconographic collection dating from the 16th to the 20th c.; of particular note, as rare objects, are the *portrait of Marcellus II*, by an anonymous artist of the 16th c. and *portrait of Urban VII*, by Jacopino del Conte.

The second section documents the many features no longer used or eliminated from papal ceremonial, through a series of paintings and engravings, as well as objects (gestatorial chairs, flabella, thrones, and thalami) used in papal ceremonies and processions, and the costumes and uniforms of the hereditary offices of the papal family, abolished by Pope Paul VI in 1968.

In the third section, lastly, are memorabilia, uniforms, and banners of the fighting corps of the Church – active until 1870 – and the corps that served in honorary roles in the Vatican.

On the west side of the palazzo note the *Loggia delle Benedizioni* (9 E4), built by Domenico Fontana in 1586, and frescoed by late-Mannerist artists (on the ground floor, note a bronze *statue of Henry IV of France* by Nicolas Cordier, 1608); it is crowned by a balustrade, and by two twin *campaniles* with three-light mullioned windows (13th c.).

To the right of the loggia you may note the baptistery, or **Battistero Lateranense** (9 E4), properly called S. Giovanni in Fonte, and built under Constantine, in the same period as the basilica, upon the foundations of a 1st-c. villa and 2nd-c. baths; modified under Pope Sixtus III, who added the atrium, and under the reigns of the two popes, St. Hilary and John IV, this structure underwent renovation by Francesco Borromini in 1657.

The interior is octagonal: a basalt urn, surrounded by eight columns supporting an architrave which is also octagonal, and is surmounted by an apse, was used for full baptisms; on the walls of the tambour, note frescoes by Carlo Maratta (*Destruction of the Idols*), Giacinto Gimignani, and Andrea Camassei.

Among the fine artworks to be seen in the chapels (for a tour, contact the custodian) we should point out: in the Cappella di S. Rufina a *Crucifix* of the school of Andrea Bregno and a *mosaic* dating from the 5th c. ; in the Cappella di S. Venanzio, aside from the handsome mosaics (7th c.; restored 1826-28) in the apse and in the triumphal arch, and on the *altar* by Carlo Rainaldi, a *plaque* designed by Borromini and the 16th-c. *ceiling*, nicely preserved; in the Cappella di S. Giovanni Evangelista the bronze *doors** of the entrance (late-12th c.), the mosaic vault, dating from the late-5th c., frescoes by Antonio Tempesta and by Ambrogio Buonvicino (late-16th c.) and a *St. John* on the altar, attributed to Taddeo Landini.

Scala Santa, or Holy Staircase (9 E4-5). This building, which was also built at the behest of Sixtus V to contain the private chapel of the popes (the "Sancta Sanctorum") on the second floor of the Patriarchìo, contains the "Scala d'Onore," or ceremonial staircase of the building, which beginning in the mid-15th c. was identified as Praetorium, or governor's residence, of Pontius Pilate, used by Jesus on the occasion of his trial (hence the name). This building is by Domenico Fontana (1589), in plastered brickwork, and it mirrors the layout of the Loggia delle Benedizioni.

The Scala Santa, which one is obliged to climb on one's knees, leads to the Cappella di S. Lorenzo, where the entrance to the "Sancta Sanctorum" is located (the interior can be seen only through grates), named for the relics it contains; its present appearance dates back to the renovation done by the Cosmati in 1278. The frescoes on the vault (*Evangelists*) and in the lunettes date from the 18th c.; dating from the same period is a mosaic with *Christ Pantokrator* in the vault of the presbytery; on the altar, protected behind little doors, an acheropita image (not painted by hand) of the *Savior*, a panel dating from the 5th-6th c., over which a 13th-c. silk image has been overlaid, with a reproduction of the original.

Basilica di S. Giovanni in Laterano*, or St. John Lateran (9 E-F4).

Before this great basilica extends a broad green esplanade; this is the cathedral of Rome, and it is technically named after the SS. Salvatore and the Ss. Giovanni Battista and Giovanni Evangelista (the Most Holy Savior and Saints John the Baptist and John the Evangelist). The basilica that was built under Constantine, which had a layout not unlike that of the original S. Pietro (St. Peter's), was erected between ca. A.D. 313 and 318, on the site of buildings dating from the 1st and 3rd c.; upon those buildings a barracks of the imperial horse guard had already been erected. The basilica was damaged and restored more than once; under Pope Sixtus V the Loggia delle Benedizioni was added, and the transept was decorated under Pope Clement VIII; Francesco Borromini remodeled the nave and aisles for Pope Innocent X.

The spectacular, but frigid **facade** by Alessandro Galilei (1732-35) features a single register of pilaster strips and semi-columns, which support the trabeation with pediment; the balustrade is surmounted by 15 *statues of Christ, Saints John the Baptist and John the Evangelist* and *the Doctors of the Church*.

In the **portico**, the central doorway has bronze *doors** taken from the Curia of the Roman Forum (Foro Romano) and transformed around 1660, while the last door on the right is the *Porta Santa*, opened only during Jubilee years; the *statue of Constantine* on the left comes from the baths built by that emperor on the Quirinal.

The interior, 130 m. in length, includes a nave and four side aisles, which were rebuilt by Borromini in 1646-50 and in 1656-57. The ceiling of the **nave**, possibly designed by Pirro Ligorio, was begun in 1562, completed in 1567 under the reign of Pope Pius V and restored under Pope Pius VI; the flooring is Cosmatesque. In the 12 aedicules, designed by Borromini, note the columns of "verde antico" marble, supporting a pediment adorned by the Colomba Pamphilj (a dove),

and featuring colossal *statues of apostles*, set here prior to 1718; above them, the statues of *prophets*, set in oval cornices, are by such sculptors as Marco Benefial, Pierre Étienne Monnot, Pierre Legros, Sebastiano Conca, Andrea Procaccini, and Pier Leone Ghezzi.

The *tabernacle* at the end of the nave was built, in the pointed-arch style, by Giovanni di Stefano (1367); the *frescoes* in the external panels date from 1367-68 and were retouched by Antoniazzo Romano and Fiorenzo di Lorenzo; silver cases, higher up, enclose relics of the heads of St. Peter and St. Paul, Apostles.

In the upper section of the *papal altar*, where only the pope can say Mass, the old wooden altar is enclosed, which is said to have been used by the first popes. In the confession, below, *tomb of Pope Martin V* by Simone Ghini (1443).

In the **far right side aisle**, between the 2nd and 3rd chapels, note the *statuette of St. James* by Andrea Bregno (1492); further along, Cosmatesque *tomb of the cardinal Casati* (1287) and *tomb of the cardinal Antonio Martino De Chaves* (known as the "Cardinale del Portogallo," or cardinal of Portugal; 1447) with statues by Isaia da Pisa.

In the **intermediate right aisle**, on the 5th pillar, *tomb of the cardinal Ranuccio Farnese* designed by the Vignola, followed by tombs of pope dating from the 11th c.; on the 1st pillar, fragment of a fresco (*Boniface VIII proclaims the Jubilee of 1300*) by Giotto. At the beginning of the **far left side aisle**, *reclining statue of Riccardo degli Annibaldi* by Arnolfo di Cambio; in the Cappella Corsini, which was designed and built by Galilei, the urn and the columns of the *monument to Clement XII* come originally from the atrium of the Pantheon; on the altar of the 3rd chapel (Onorio Longhi, 1600-1610), *Crucifix* attributed to Stefano Maderno.

At the last pillar of the **intermediate left aisle**, *tomb of Elena Savelli* by Jacopo Del Duca (1570).

The **transept** was renovated (1597-1601) in architectural terms by Giacomo Della Porta and in pictorial terms by the Cavalier d'Arpino (who did the *Transfiguration* at the end of the left arm of the transept), who was helped by Paris Nogari, Pomarancio, G.B. Ricci, Cesare Nebbia, Giovanni Baglione, and Bernardino Cesari. An *organ* dating from the end of the 16th c. stands at the end of the right arm of the transept, from which you can enter the *museum* of the basilica (renovated in 1986), with goldsmithery from the 15th c., the

Cross of Constantine (13th/14th c.) and tapestries.

The **apse**, redone in the 19th c. by Francesco Vespignani, is decorated in the semicupola with a **mosaic**, dating from the end of the 13th c., by Jacopo Torriti and Jacopo da Camerino: *Christ, surrounded by angels, atop a hill with the Celestial city of Jerusalem, from which four rivers run down* (the Gospels) *to quench the thirst of the flock* (sheep and deer) *of the faithful.*

The **sacristies** (to tour them, contact the Pontificio Consiglio delle Relazioni Sociali), which you reach by passing beneath the *tomb of Pope Leo XIII* by Giulio Tadolini (1907), contain an *Annunciation*, a panel by Marcello Venusti done to a design by Michelangelo.

The **cloister**, a masterpiece of Cosmatesque art, was built in 1215-32 by the Vassalletto (inscription on the frieze of the portico): the little arches are set on slender columns, sometimes decorated with mosaics, with shapes of all sorts; the vaults of the deambulatories, set on ancient columns adjoining pillars toward the interior, were built later, along with the elevation of the loggia on arches. In the middle of the courtyard, note the 9th-c. *puteal*; along the walls of the cloister, sculptures and ornaments of the ancient basilica, burial slabs, and archeological artifacts, from Roman and early-Christian times.

Porta S. Giovanni (9 E5). The present-day opening, which marks the beginning of the Via Appia Nuova (see page 166), was built in the Mura Aureliane, or Aurelian walls (see page 171) in 1574 by Jacopo Del Duca to replace the gate, or *Porta Asinaria* (9 E5), which can be seen on the right, marked by the semi-cylindrical towers; this gate dates back to the fortifications built under Honorius, as does the counter-gate; this latter, set at a lower level, and sealed off in 1409, was reopened and restored in 1954.

2.2 From Piazza Venezia to the Basilica di S. Pietro

This route runs along a number of streets that bear witness to some of the most profound urban transformations of Rome: Corso Vittorio Emanuele II for those carried out after the unification of Italy and under King Humbert ("umbertina"), Via Giulia for those carried out during the Renaissance, Via della Conciliazione those completed under the Fascist regime. The latter road, moreover, has two further meanings: it links the civil and political center of Rome with the spiritual and religious center across the Tiber, and it follows in theory the route that the papal procession would once take, after the coronation, from S. Giovanni in Laterano (St. John Lateran).

"The Triumph of Baccus" by A. Carracci (Palazzo Farnese)

This tour, a walking tour, leaves Piazza Venezia along the Via del Plebiscito and, after the church of Il Gesù – the prototype of the Counter-Reformation house of worship – passes the Area Sacra dell'Argentina – the largest area dating from the Roman Republic that can now be seen – and continues along the Corso Vittorio Emanuele II, lined by the facades of patrician residences (note the Palazzo Massimo "alle Colonne," Palazzo Braschi, and the Palazzo Farnesina ai Baullari) as well as the remarkable Baroque complex of the Chiesa Nuova with Borromini's Palazzo dei Filippini.

Near the Piazza della Cancelleria, which is dominated by the Palazzo della Cancelleria, you will make your way into the SW section of the "Quartiere del Rinascimento," which abounds in pieces of popular Roman history (Campo de' Fiori) and examples of spectacular architectural genius (Palazzo Farnese and Palazzo Spada) and daring urban planning (Bramante's Via Giulia, punctuated by churches and palazzi).

After you cross the Tiber near Castel S. Angelo, the rigorous view along the Via della Conciliazione finally leads you to the spectacular Piazza S. Pietro.

Il Gesù* (3 F6; 6 E4; 8 A2). This church, more properly known as the church of the Santissimo Nome di Gesù (the Most Holy Name of Jesus), was planned by St. Ignatius Loyola as far back as 1550, but was begun only in 1568, with financing from the cardinal Alessandro Farnese, in accordance with the plans drawn up by the Vignola; Giacomo Della Porta was assigned to design and build the facade; he completed construction of the church and modified the cupola. The building, consecrated in 1584, constituted a model for Roman religious architecture over the century that followed; this paradigm was exported by the Jesuits all over Europe.

The facade, by Giacomo Della Porta (1571-77; restored, 1992), entirely in travertine, has three entrances and two registers of Corinthian pilaster strips, twinned on a line with the nave.

In the layout of the interior, Vignola mingled the new liturgical requirements – which called for a large hall in which attention would be concentrated upon the altar and the pulpit – with an elongated plan: the nave, with a barrel vault, flanked by six chapels, extends into the apsed presbytery, and is intersected by a transept of commensurate width, with a hemispherical cupola set on a cylindrical tambour; in the corners, note four circular chapels.

The array of decorations dates from 1672-85: in the vault, **Triumph of the Name of Jesus**, a fresco by Baciccia (1679), with an original and daring perspectival effect that seems to break out of the limitations of the vault (the gilt cornice, supported by stucco *angels* carved by Ercole Antonio Raggi, was designed by the Baciccia); in the left transept, the *Cappella di S. Ignazio di Loyola**, or chapel of St. Ignatius Loyola, who lies buried here, is a remarkable piece of work by Andrea Pozzo.

Corso Vittorio Emanuele II (maps 3, 6). This thoroughfare, 20 m. across, was begun in 1883 and concluded at the end of the 19th c. as an extension of Via Nazionale towards St. Peter's; runs between the Gesù and the Largo di Torre Argentina along the course of the old Via de' Cesarini – the left side of which survives – and then runs through the so-called "Quartiere del Rinascimento," serving to connect this area with the Vatican, as once did the "Via Papalis" (see page 107) and the "Via Peregrinorum" (see page 69).

Largo di Torre Argentina (3 F5; 6 E3). The name derives from the Latin name for Strasbourg ("Argentoratum"), the birthplace of the bishop Johann Burckhardt, who in 1503 ordered the construction of the *Casa del Burcardo* (note the Italianization of the surname; 3 F4-5; 6 E3; 7 A6); although it was renovated in 1931, it still has the distinctive appearance of a late-medieval German house (the facade overlooking the Via del Sudario is embellished by a loggia with arches). It contains the *Biblioteca* and the *Raccolta Teatrale del Burcardo*, which comprise over 30,000 publications and volumes having to do with the theater and marionettes of the 18th and 19th c., an interesting collection of masks and theatrical figures in painted terracotta, originally the property of Luigi Rasi, and antique costumes and photographs, with which temporary exhibitions on the theme are organised.

Area Sacra dell'Argentina* (6 E3). This sacred area was excavated during the work done in 1926-29 for the expansion of the Largo Argentina, and was given its definitive layout in 1933 by Antonio Muñoz; it is the most extensive sacred area yet excavated, dating back to the Roman republic (to tour it, contact the X Ripartizione del Comune, Rome city government). The circular structure that you can see at the center of the area is the *temple B*, which is considered to be the "Aedes Fortunae Huisce Diei" erected by Quintus Lutacius Catulus in 101 B.C. To the right of it stands the *temple A*, dating from the middle of the 3rd c. B.C., restored under the reign of Domitian; over it, in the 8th c., was built the little church of *S. Nicola de Calcarariis*, named after the craftsmen who made limestone from the marble of ancient monuments during the Middle Ages.

To the left of the circular building are the ruins of the *temple C*, the oldest temple of the four, possibly dedicated to the Italian deity Feronia; it is set on a tufa-stone podium, and has no colonnade on the far side; it too was probably restored during the reign of Domitian, which is when the mosaic floor and the walls of the cella date from.

On the far left of the area you can see the ruins of the *temple D*, which dates from the late-2nd c. B.C., and was rebuilt late in the Republic.

Teatro Argentina (6 E3). Perhaps the most glorious theater of Rome under the popes – and, with the Teatro Valle (see below), the only one still to survive – the Teatro Argentina was built at the behest of Duke Giuseppe Sforza Cesarini and, inaugurated in 1732, it was used for the performance of opera (the triumphant premiere of the "Barber of Seville" was held here in 1816, establishing Rossini as a great composer); it was rebuilt in the late-19th c., and was used for theater in the early-20th c., until it was restored in 1926 by Marcello Piacentini and again in 1967-71 (since then, it has housed the company of the Teatro di Roma).

Palazzo Vidoni (3 F4-5). Now the site of the offices of the Italian prime minister (Presidenza del Consiglio dei Ministri), this building overlooks Corso Vittorio with an elevation built in 1886-87 with the repetition – with occasional variations – of the motifs of the main facade, which overlooks the Via del Sudario built in 1515, and enlarged in the mid-16th c. and again in 1770.

On the opposite side of the "corso" is the 16th-c. *Palazzo Della Valle* (3 F4), which was left unfinished because of the great Sack of Rome in 1527; once attributed to Lorenzetto, it is now thought to have been designed by Andrea Sansovino or Antonio da Sangallo the Younger.

Dating from the 18th c., but restored by Giuseppe Valadier and Giuseppe Camporese in 1820-22, is the *Teatro Valle* (3 F4), with an interior still built of wood.

S. Andrea della Valle* (3 F4). Consecrated only in 1650, this church was built to plans by Carlo Maderno, who worked on them sometime after 1608, basing his work in turn on late-16th-c. plans by Pietro Paolo Olivieri, who conceived the remarkable cupola (1622) – the highest one in Rome, after the dome of St. Peter's (S. Pietro).

The facade, made of travertine, by Carlo Rainaldi and Carlo Fontana, has a single opening in the center, with two large niches on either side, in which stand *statues of St. Andrew, Apostle* and *St. Andrea Avellino* (Ercole Ferrata), *St. Gaetano* and *St. Sebastian* by Domenico Guidi.

Splendid and luminous is the vast Latin-cross interior, organized by Olivieri to resemble the interior of Il Gesù; the decora-

tion of the vault is the result of a restoration done at the turn of the 20th c. The frescoes in the cupola and the apse, the subject of an artistic competition between Giovanni Lanfranco and Domenichino, constitute, with the canvases by Mattia Preti and the paintings by Carlo Cignani, a charming example of Baroque decoration, among the finest in Rome.

The 2nd chapel on the right (Cappella Strozzi) clearly takes inspiration from the work of Michelangelo, as is confirmed by the presence of copies of works by Michelangelo, executed in bronze in 1616. The Cappella di S. Andrea Avellino, a chapel in the right transept, features a *Death of the Saint* by Lanfranco (ca. 1625).

Above the entrance to the left circular chapel, *tomb of Pope Pius II*, completed by a follower of Andrea Bregno (ca. 1470-75). In the 2nd chapel on the left, which dates from the turn of the 17th c., is the tomb of Monsignor Giovanni della Casa, author of "Il Galateo ovvero De' Costumi," a manual of etiquette. In the 1st chapel (Cappella Barberini), which was laid out on the spot where, according to tradition, the body of St. Sebastian was found, and where a small church stood in early Christian times, note the paintings by Passignano, while the side niches contain outstanding statues by Francesco Mochi (*St. Martha*, 1629), Am-

The Palazzo Massimo «alle Colonne»

brogio Buonvicino (*St. John the Evangelist*), Pietro Bernini (*St. John the Baptist*), and Cristoforo Stati (*Mary Magdalene*), while the *putti* above the little arched side doors are by the Bernini, father and son (by Pietro on the right, by Gian Lorenzo on the left).

Set against the exterior left side of the church stands, on a modest pedestal, the *Abate Luigi*, one of the "talking statues" (see page 107).

Palazzo Massimo "alle Colonne"* (3 F4). This is the most noteworthy building in the vast Isolato dei Massimo, or block of the

Massimo, named after one of the oldest families in Rome (the presence of this family in the city has been historically documented as early as the late-10th c.), and set on the medieval "Via Papalis" (see page 107).

Damaged during the great Sack of Rome of 1527, it was rebuilt, at the behest of Pietro Massimo, by Baldassarre Peruzzi, the last building he ever worked on; Peruzzi came up with the idea of a facade in flat rustication to preserve the convex shape of the underlying *Odeon of Domitian* (this structure, capable of accommodating about 10,000 spectators, was closely linked to the stadium of Domitian, or Stadio di Domiziano: for this stadium, see page 106). The palazzo was made particularly monumental by the chiaroscuro effect of the colonnaded portico (hence the name of the palazzo), clearly visible even nowadays, when looking at the building from the Via del Paradiso.

In the portico (restoration, 1990), with a coffered ceiling embellished with stucco decorations in the classical style, there is a splendid *portal* with a rich trabeation set on corbels; the interior (which can be toured with permission from the family, which still resides here) features a first courtyard, studded with sculptures and archeological finds, while the second courtyard, formerly part of the Palazzo Massimo "Istoriato" (see below), is adorned with 17th-c. bas-reliefs and medallions.

The loggia has a wooden *ceiling* with gilt and polychrome coffering (the stuccoes are attributed to Peruzzi or Perin del Vaga); in the large entrance hall, note the frieze (*stories of Fabius Maximus*) by Daniele da Volterra.

The **Palazzo Massimo "Istoriato"**, which overlooks the Piazza de' Massimi, is the oldest building in this block; it was in this building in 1467 that the first printing press in Rome was set up: the paintings on the facade, attributed to the school of Daniele da Volterra, offer a striking example of what most of the palazzi of Rome must have looked like in the Renaissance, since it was then quite common practice to paint the facades of buildings.

The block of the Massimo incorporates the church of *S. Pantaleo* (3 F4), which is documented as far back as the 12th c., and rebuilt before 1689 to plans by Giovanni Antonio de Rossi; the 19th-c. facade by Giuseppe Valadier opens onto Corso Vittorio.

Palazzo Braschi (3 F4). Commissioned by Pope Pius VI for his own family, this building was begun in 1791-96 to plans by Cosimo Morelli and, following the interruption in work due to the French occupation in 1798, continued in 1802 with some assistance from Giuseppe Valadier, and was finally completed in 1811; in 1871 it became property of the Italian state, and was converted into a ministry building; it now houses numerous cultural institutions, including the Museo di Roma (see below).

In the architecture, Morelli hearkened back less to classical examples and more to the classicism of the 16th c.; also unusual for Roman architecture of the period is the large balcony, which extends over the entrance the entire length of the main elevation, and around onto the sides.

The spectecular *stairway** inside is also by Morelli, decorated with 18 ancient columns, originating from the portico of Caligola, and with stuccoes by Luigi Acquisti, while

"The Pope's blessing in St. Peter's square" by Ippolito Caffi (Museo di Roma)

some rooms conserve decorations partly executed by Liborio Coccetti.

Museo di Roma*, or Museum of Rome. First installed in 1952, this museum features paintings, sculpture, and objects of art meant to preserve the historic and cultural memory of Rome, from the Renaissance to the modern age.

It contains artworks by the Baciccia, Pierre Subleyras, Francesco Mochi, Antonio Canova, and Luigi Valadier, *model* and *preparatory works* in terracotta by François Duquesnoy and Domenico Guidi, *scenes of ceremonies* and *scenes of papal processions* from the 17th c., *Roman view paintings* by the Flemish school of the same period, a series of *tapestries* from the French manufactory of Gobelins and the Roman manufactory of S. Michele, *portraits* by Pompeo Batoni, Pietro da Cortona, Giuseppe Chiari, and Andrea Sacchi, a number of marble *busts* and *bas-reliefs* from the 17th c., a series of *views of Rome* and paintings based on Roman costumes and folk festivals, as well as a collection of *majolica* produced locally, and a collection of *men's* and *women's* costumes from the 18th and 19th c., and a substantial array of 19th-c. artworks, by Roman artists and artists of the Roman school.

The Palazzo Braschi also houses the *Gipsoteca Tenerani*, a complete collection of casts of Pietro Tenerani's work, and the *Archivio Fotografico Comunale* and the *Gabinetto Comunale delle Stampe*, Rome's photographic archives and collection of prints and engravings; these two collections constitute a unique source of visual documentation on the development and transformation of Rome and its surrounding territory.

Farnesina ai Baullari* (3 F4). This building, one of the most elegant and exquisite constructions of 16th-c. Rome, is also called – more accurately – Palazzetto Leroy or Palazzetto De Regis, because it was begun in 1522 by the Breton prelate Le Roy, who like to translate his name into Latin as De Regis; the name Farnesina, on the other hand, comes from the lilies of France, which the prelate was authorized to join to his own heraldic device – and which were popularly confused with the lilies of the house of Farnese – while the additional appellation "ai Baullari" was added to distinguish this building from the Villa Farnesina on the Via della Lungara. The most recent studies attribute the building's design to the architect Antonio da Sangallo the Younger, though Baldassarre Peruzzi may also have worked on it.

Museo Barracco*. This exquisite collection of sculpture was assembled by Baron Giovanni Barracco in the late-19th c. The baron's intention was to offer, through a limited number of reasonably representative works, a synthetic look back over the history of ancient sculpture. He donated the collection to the city of Rome in 1904. A library has also occupied the building since 1948.

At the end of the elegant courtyard in Renaissance style, beneath the ancient portico, is a *torso of a seated Apollo*, a marble sculpture from the Hellenistic era; in hall I, with interesting documents and mementos of the founder of the collection, note the headless *funerary statue* (4th c. B.C.) and a Christian *sarcophagus* (4th c. A.D.).

An ancient staircase in travertine, which features a niche containing a fragment of a *Winged Victory* from the Hellenistic era, leads to the second floor.

Here, you should note remarkable relics of *Phoenician art*, a noteworthy group of works of *Egyptian art* dating from 3000 to 30 B.C., *Assyrian reliefs*, *Etruscan artifacts* linked to funerary ceremonies, and a number of specimens of full-relief *Cypriot sculpture* in limestone.

In the halls on the third floor are collections of *Greek statuary*, showing the various styles of the Classical period and the subsequent Hellenistic age, as well as *reliefs*, *busts*, and Roman *statues*.

Palazzo della Cancelleria* (3 F3). The cardinal Raffaele Riario – who in 1483 became titular cardinal of the nearby basilica of S. Lorenzo in Damaso and took possession of the adjoining palazzo – decided to rebuild it and convert it into a home for himself. Work, which began around 1485, continued until the period between 1511 and 1513 (the heraldic devices of Popes Sixtus IV and Julius II, at the corners of the facade, refer to the pontiffs under whose reigns reconstruction was begun and completed); shortly thereafter, the palazzo was confiscated from the Riario family, and was converted into the headquarters of the Cancelleria Apostolica, or Apostolic Chancery.

Over the course of the 16th c., the interior decoration and the Cardinal's Apartment were completed.

From the end of the 18th c. onward the history of the building tends to coincide with the political history of the city of Rome (in 1849, the Roman Republic was proclaimed there); after the unification of Italy in 1870, the privilege of extraterritoriality of the building was preserved, and reiterated in the Lateran Pact (Patti Lateranensi); it now houses numerous cultural institutions of the church, and the Tribunale della Sacra Rota.

It has not yet been determined just who the architect may have been, though the influence of Bramante is quite evident (Vasari documents his participation in the late stages of construction), particularly in the courtyard.

Worthy of mention, in the main facade, is the remarkable horizontal extension and the off-center position of the entrance (portal with granite columns supporting the balcony, and with the heraldic devices of the cardinal Alessandro Peretti) as well as the facing, entirely in travertine. An elegant *balcony** adorns the curvilinear front overlooking Campo de' Fiori and the *Via del*

Pellegrino (3 F2-3; 6 D-E1), part of the ancient *"Via Peregrinorum"*, or route of the pilgrims, extending toward the Vatican (it corresponds to the modern Via dei Banchi Vecchi, Via del Pellegrino, Campo de' Fiori, and Via de' Giubbonari); this area was developed into an urban center between the end of the 15th c. and the end of the 16th c. Of particular note in the complex (closed to the public), we should mention: the **courtyard**, attributed to Bramante; the *Sala Riaria* (or Aula Magna, meaning great hall), decorated under the reign of Pope Clement XI (1718) and restored in 1939; the *Salone dei Cento Giorni*, a large hall with walls decorated with frescoes, set within painted architectural elements designed by Giorgio Vasari; the *Appartamento Cardinalizio*, or cardinal's apartment, where you can admire the Cappella del Pallio, a chapel, and the *Salone di Studio*, a large hall with a vault frescoed by Perin del Vaga.

Campo de' Fiori (6 E1-2). This large square was long one of the most important centers of Rome (horse races, and executions were held here); from 1869 it has been the site of a lively market. According to tradition, its

1st c. B.C. and could seat approximately 18,000 spectators; you can guess its dimensions and note the curve of the "cavea" in the buildings that overlook the nearby Via di Grottapinta; their foundations are based on the structures of the "cavea."

Palazzo Farnese* (6 E-F1). Overlooking the Piazza Farnese – a vast and elegant square adorned by two twin *fountains*, attributed to Girolamo Rainaldi, in which the water jets from Farnese lilies and falls back into basins of Egyptian granite taken from the baths of Caracalla – this palazzo is the largest in terms of sheer volume and the last built of the edifices of the Roman Renaissance. It was begun in 1517, for the cardinal Alessandro Farnese (who later became pope, as Paul III), by Antonio da Sangallo the Younger; when that architect died, it was continued by Michelangelo (1546-49) and Vignola (1569-73), and finally completed by Giacomo Della Porta (1589). Sangallo designed and built the facades on the sides streets and on the square, save for the cornice and the central balcony; these, with part of the second and all of the third register in the courtyard, have been attributed to Michelan-

A lively flower stall in the colorful market of Campo de' Fiori

name comes from Flora, beloved of Pompey, but it is more likely that the name comes from the fact that at the end of the 14th c. the square was for a short time allowed to become a flowering field. At the center stands a *monument to Giordano Bruno* (1887), burnt at the stake here as a heretic on 17 February 1600.

The square occupies what was originally the "platea" of the temple of Venus Victrix, adjoining the *theater of Pompey*, which was built in masonry around the middle of the

gelo; Vignola designed the rear facade, which was completed by Della Porta.

In the majestic elevation, divided horizontally into three floors, or registers, by cornices, note the loggia by Michelangelo, crowned by the heraldic device of the Farnese family; the building is crowned by a splendid **entablature**, likewise decorated with the Farnese lilies.

Inside (it is possible to tour the palazzo, with permission from the French Embassy, which is located here) we should point out:

the magnificent **atrium** by Sangallo, split into a nave and two aisles; the renowned gallery (20 m. long, 6 m. wide), frescoed in 1597-1604 by Annibale Carracci and by Domenichino with the *Triumph of Love over the Universe**, a work that represents the transition from the Mannerist style of decoration to the Baroque style; the *Salone*, or large hall, with a lavish coffered ceiling, *tapestries* that reproduce frescoes by Raphael from the Stanze Vaticane, and, on either side of the monumental fireplace, *Peace* and *Plenty* by Della Porta.

Palazzo Spada* (6 F1-2). This building now houses the Consiglio di Stato, Italy's executive office, and the Galleria Spada (see below), an art gallery; the palazzo was begun in the middle of the 16th c. for cardinal Girolamo Capodiferro, who then sold it to cardinal Bernardino Spada; it was designed and built by Giulio Merisi, Girolamo da Carpi, and Giulio Mazzoni (this latter artist did the lavish decorations of the facade, featuring eight niches with statues of famous Romans), while the later renovation was done by Francesco Borromini.

Mazzoni also did the stuccoes in the courtyard, some of the finest in late Renaissance Rome; from the windows of the library on the left, you can admire the **perspectival gallery** by Borromini, an optical illusion that appears to be much deeper than it is (actual depth, just 9 m.). With authorization from the general secretariat of the Consiglio di Stato it is possible to enter the *Corridoio dei Bassorilievi*, or corridor of bas-reliefs, named for the mythological scenes in marble and plaster relief. Note the interesting *catoptric sundial*, and the *Salone delle Adunanze Generali*, a meeting hall, with noteworthy frescoes dating from 1635.

Galleria Spada. Established in the 17th c. by the cardinal Bernardino Spada, and now a possession of the Italian state, this small collection – which largely comprises works by 16th- and 17th-c. Italian artists and a few excellent copies – is arranged in four large halls, frescoed and furnished with old furniture and marble. It still has the original appearance of a 17th-c. private collection, arranged in two or more rows, in accordance with purely decorative criteria.

Hall I contains busts from Roman times, set on 18th-c. consoles, as well as a curious wooden, bronze, and alabaster *pendulum-clock*; on the walls, note the *portraits of the cardinal Bernardino Spada* by Guido Reni and the Guercino, *Landscapes* by Domenichino, and paintings by Gaspard

Dughet and Giuseppe Chiari.

In the next hall (II), we particularly recommend – aside from the gilt carved wooden *tabernacle* (1636-39) with the 16th-c. bas-relief of the *Annunciation* – the two fragments of a decorative frieze painted in tempera by Perin del Vaga, intended to cover the wall beneath Michelangelo's Last Judgment in the Sistine Chapel; among the many paintings, we should point out the *St. Christopher and St. Luke* by Amico Aspertini, the *Portraits* by Domenico Tintoretto and Hans Dürer, the *Botanist* by Bartolomeo Passarotti, three *Heads* by Parmigianino and a *Portrait of Pope Paul III*, 16th-c. copy of a Titian.

A doorway flanked by marble columns leads into the hall III, an immense room with two splendid *lamps* made of Murano glass (17th and 18th c.) and a decorated ceiling (1699); in the center, in a wooden cradle, *Sleep*, a 17th-c. work of the Roman school, and *celestial globe* (1616) and *terrestrial globe* (1622); on consoles and benches, busts and sculptures from Roman times; on the walls, *Seascapes* by Nicolò dell'Abate, *Allegories* by Carlo Cignani and Sebastiano Conca, *Portraits* by Peter Paul Rubens and Marco Benefial, *Death of Dido* by the Guercino, a sketch by the Baciccia for the fresco in the cupola of the church of the Gesù, *Intimate Celebration of Mark Antony and Cleopatra* by Francesco Trevisani and artworks by Antonio Carracci, Francesco Solimena, and Pier Francesco Mola.

In the last hall (IV) are canvases by Artemisia Gentileschi, Michelangelo Cerquozzi, Orazio Borgianni, Mattia Preti, and Orazio Gentileschi.

Via Giulia* (6 E-F1). Built at the behest of Pope Julius II (Giulio in Italian, hence the name), as a parallel and counterweight to Via della Lungara (see page 139) on the far bank of the Tiber and as the site of the most important buildings of the Papal State (the Palazzo dei Tribunali was one of its strongpoints), this street was opened by Bramante at the turn of the 16th c., and it still constitutes a long straight road, only partly altered by the demolitions and destruction of the Fascist era (there were plans for a connection between the Lungotevere and the Chiesa Nuova).

If you turn to the left in the Via di S. Eligio, and enquire at n. 9, you can tour the church of **S. Eligio degli Orefici** (7 A4), designed by Raphael – under the influence of Bramante – and built in 1509-75. The interior, built to a Greek-cross plan, with a hemispherical cupola with a lantern, is decorated with *frescoes* by Matteo da Lecce and Taddeo Zuccari.

Carceri Nuove (3 F2). This prison was commissioned by Pope Innocent X on the site of the Palazzo dei Tribunali, begun by Bramante on behalf of Pope Julius II but left unfinished; parts of the rusticated basement with projecting benches survive (the so-called "Sofas of Via Giulia").

Next door, dating from the turn of the 19th c., is the stern facade of the *Prigioni*, a former prison building that now houses the *Museo di Criminologia*, a museum of criminology.

Chiesa Nuova* (3 E3). The "new church" was built from 1575 on over the foundations of the older church of S. Maria in Vallicella, by Matteo da Città di Castello and Martino Longhi the Elder (the facade, which is derivative of the facade of the church of the Gesù, was built in the early-17th c.) and is bound up with the life of Filippo Neri (St. Philip Neri), who founded the oratory (Oratorio) in 1551, recognized as a congregation by Pope Gregory XIII (the so-called Filippini). Longhi, on the other hand, endowed the building with a dome that had no tambour; the dome opens directly upon an interior space that is lavishly decorated in a triumphant Baroque style. In the ceiling, note the major *frescoes** by Pietro da Cortona, who also designed the stuccoes.

In the **presbytery** note the altar piece (*Virgin Mary with the Christ Child*), which covers a fresco with the same subject, from the earlier church, and the two sides, perhaps the masterpiece of the Roman sojourn (1606-1608) of Peter Paul Rubens. The Cappella Spada or Cappella di S. Carlo Borromeo, to the right of the presbytery, is adorned with lavish marble facing and paintings by Carlo Maratta (*Virgin Mary with the Christ Child, and St. Charles Borromeo and St. Ignatius Loyola*). To the left of the presbytery is the *Cappella di S. Filippo Neri*, a chapel designed by Onorio Longhi and built by Paolo Marucelli (1600-1604), embellished with exquisite carved marble, inserts of mother-of-pearl and semi-precious stones: the *Deeds of the Saint* are by Pomarancio.

Adorning the chapel of the **left transept** is a *Presentation of the Virgin Mary in the Temple* by Federico Barocci; on either side are statues by Valsoldo.

In the **sacristy** note a marble group (*St. Philip and an Angel*; 1640) by Alessandro Algardi and, in the vault, *Angels with the Instruments of the Passion* by Pietro da Cortona (1633-34).

Only on the occasion of the feast of St. Philip (25 May in the afternoon, and 26 May) is it possible to enter the **Santuario**

Terreno, or ground-floor sanctuary, comprising a chamber with the burial urn, upon which stands a silver *bust of the saint* by Algardi and a chapel with a handsome painting of *St. Philip and the Angel* by Guercino. The **Santuario Superiore** or upper sanctuary, which also comprises an antechamber (note the famous *St. Philip and the Virgin Mary* by Guido Reni) and the private chapel of the saint (reconstruction, 1635), contains a Florentine *bas-relief* from the early-16th c., a late-Byzantine *triptych*, an exquisite *Nativity* of the school of Jacopo Bassano, a *Virgin Mary with Christ Child and St. Martina* by Pietro da Cortona and a *St. Philip in the Catacombs* by Pomarancio.

The **chapels on the left** stand out for the *Annunciation* by Passignano (5th chapel), the *female saints* by Pomarancio (vault of the 3rd chapel) and the *Presentation in the Temple* by the Cavalier d'Arpino (1st chapel).

Palazzo dei Filippini (3 E2-3). The Chiesa Nuova forms part of this large palazzo, by Francesco Borromini, who succeeded in merging with a harmonious design the numerous challenges of volumetric composition. We have fine examples of his work in the *Torre dell'Orologio**, or clock tower, set in the elevation of the palazzo that overlooks the Via del Governo Vecchio (see page 107) and shaped with concave and convex surfaces, and, on the interior, the *Oratorio**, or oratory – one of the masterpieces of Borromini's architecture – a vast hall used both for the delivery of holy sermons and the execution of polyphonic music (it was in this room that the musical form developed that was later known as the oratorio).

Among the numerous institutions that have their offices in the palazzo (the Filippini now only occupy the side on the Via della Chiesa Nuova) we should mention: the *Biblioteca Vallicelliana*, the oldest public library in Rome (just under 120,000 volumes, nearly 500 incunabula, 7,000 16th-c. books, and 2,500 manuscripts); the reading room and even the book shelves were designed by Borromini; the *Emeroteca Romana*, an archives that contains nearly all the newspapers printed in Rome from the 18th c. to the modern day.

S. Giovanni dei Fiorentini* (3 E1). Built at the behest of Pope Leo X, who commissioned designs from Antonio da Sangallo the Younger, Baldassarre Peruzzi, Michelangelo, Raphael, and Jacopo Sansovino, this church was begun by Jacopo Sansovino in 1519; Carlo Maderno (1602-1620) designed and built the cupola and the transept, while the facade was done by A. Galilei (1734).

The interior has a nave and two aisles, separated by a massive order of pillars, with five chapels on each side; this is an unusual translation into architectural terms of the austere atmosphere that came on the heels of the Council of Trent, modified by decorations from the age of Baroque.
In this church, both Maderno and Borromini lie buried: a tomb stone in the nave, beneath the majestic cupola, commemorates Maderno; a plaque that is cemented into the 3rd pillar on the left commemorates Borromini.

If you walk along a short stretch of Corso Vittorio toward the center of town, you can see the *Palazzo del Banco di S. Spirito* (3 E2), which overlooks the Largo Tassoni; built by Antonio da Sangallo

emperor Hadrian as a tomb for himself and for his successors; it was begun around A.D. 123 (for ease of access, the emperor built the bridge over the Tiber known as the "Pons Aelius," later known as Ponte S. Angelo: see page 148) and was completed under the reign of Antoninus Pius; the remains of members of the royal family were laid to rest here up to the reign of Caracalla. It comprised a square base that supported a cylindrical construction; inside, there were three huge halls, stacked one over the other, which are intact; here were the imperial tombs and a double spiral staircase; you can still climb the first length of that staircase.
The emperor Aurelian made the mausoleum

An array of stone angels on the approach to Castel S. Angelo

the Younger in 1521-24; this was the site of the Zecca Pontificia, or papal mint, in which the "paolo" was coined, a gold coin with a closely controlled weight that circulated throughout Italy between the 16th and 18th c., along with the Venetian "zecchino" and the Florentine florin, or "fiorino."

Piazza di Ponte S. Angelo (3 D2). This square was both the site of public executions (not far off was the prison of Tor di Nona) but also of a thriving marketplace; it has lost its old function as the entranceway to Ponte S. Angelo (see page 148) following the construction of the riverfront boulevards, the Lungotevere.

Castel S. Angelo* (3 B-C1-2). This building has become a symbol of Rome; it commands a magnificent position along the Tiber, and it is in a sense the heir to the stupendous *"Hadrianeum"* (plan), built at the orders of – and probably designed by – the

a fortified outpost forming part of the defenses of the city, girding it with walls and towers; the gate that opened into this walled perimeter was later known as the Porta S. Pietro, and was joined to the basilica through the "Portica," used by the pilgrims on their way to the tomb of the apostle Peter. During the Gothic wars – as had been the case under Theodoric and as was the case in the centuries that followed – it served as both a prison and as a fortress, and with the transfer to Rome of papal temporal authority, it became a defensive outwork. Assigned to a French garrison upon the occasion of the return of Pope Urban V from the papal exile in Avignon, it was retaken and occupied in 1379 by the populace of Rome in an uprising; Boniface IX transformed it once again into an unassailable stronghold of the authority of the popes (from the bastions of the castle, which was the rallying point of resistance and struggle at the time of the sack of Rome in 1527, Cellini boasts that he fired the shot that killed the commander of the troops of the Holy Roman Emperor): Pope Nicholas V was responsible for the construction of three of the corner bastions, Pope Alexander VI added the fourth. The modern-day configuration of the complex is the result of restorations begun at the end of the 19th c., while later came the restoration (1933-34) of the moats and bastions, with the new layout as a garden.

The fortress now appears as an enclosure wall, square at the base, reinforced at the corners by the bastions, or Bastioni di S. Giovanni (right) and the Bastioni di S. Matteo (left; on the opposite corners are the Bastioni di S. Marco and the Bastioni di S. Luca – they are named after the four Evangelists); along the curtain wall between the Bastioni di S. Giovanni and the Bastioni di S. Luca, the old entry portal of the castle has been reconstructed. The ancient Roman cylindrical structure is surmounted by the square tower, upon which stands the papal apartment, dating from the Renaissance and overlooking the Tiber; on the large terrace, note the statue of the Archangel Michael, sheathing his sword.

Museo Nazionale di Castel S. Angelo*. This museum contains an exquisite collection of ceramics and an interesting collection of antique weapons, furnishings, and Renaissance paintings.

Beyond the **Cortile del Salvatore**, the broad **Ambulacro di Bonifacio IX**, or deambulatory of Boniface IX, which works its way between the cylindrical keep and the square walled perimeter of the castle, features the surviving fragments of the marble decoration dating from the time of Hadrian.

At the end of the **dromos**, which contains five models illustrating the historical and architectural development of the mausoleum, the old **spiral ramp** climbs up to the right of the **diametrical ramp** which, built at the orders of Pope Alexander VI, leads to the left into the **Cortile d'Onore**, or courtyard of honor: at the center stands the *statue of the Archangel Michael*, carved by Raffaello da Montelupo in 1544; on the right side of the courtyard is the entrance to the **Armeria**, or armory, which contains an array of ancient and antique weapons and military memorabilia, dating from prehistoric times up to the 19th c.; on the left side, you enter the **Sale di Clemente VIII**, or halls of Clement VIII, used often to hold temporary shows (the *Sala della Giustizia* was the site of the Roman tribunal in the 16th and 17th

c.; the *Sala d'Apollo* was decorated in grotesques by Perin del Vaga and students; the Cappella di Leone X features a lovely marble relief dating from the 16th c., depicting the *Virgin Mary with Christ Child*).

The adjoining halls, known as the **Sale di Clemente VII**, feature handsome friezes and decorated ceilings; the walls bear numerous paintings, including a *St. Sebastian* and *St. John the Baptist* by Niccolò di Liberatore, the *Savior* and *St. Onofrio* by Carlo Crivelli, *Virgin Mary with Christ Child and Saints* by Luca Signorelli.

From the **Cortile del Pozzo**, named after an old 15th-c. well (a stairway leads to the **bath rooms**, with refined decorations attributed to Giovanni da Udine), you can enter the **Prigioni Storiche**, or prisons, or else climb up to the elegant **loggia of Paul III**, decorated in grotesques (1543) and attributed to Antonio da Sangallo the Younger; from here, the **"giretto" of Pius IV** (panoramic view*) leads you to the **loggia of Julius II**, attributed to Giuliano da Sangallo.

You then enter into the elegant rooms of the **Appartamento di Paolo III**, decorated between 1542 and 1549 to plans by Perin del Vaga. It comprises the *Sala Paolina*, entirely decorated with stuccoes by G. Della Porta and frescoes of the school of Perin del Vaga; the *Camera del Perseo*, or chamber of Perseus, which takes its name from the handsome frieze (*stories of Perseus and Andromeda*) done by Perin del Vaga and whose walls are adorned with 17th-c. Flemish *tapestries*; the Camera di Amore e Psiche, with *Virgin Mary* by B. Montagna.

A passageway decorated with grotesques leads to the **Sala della Biblioteca**, with the ceiling frescoed by Luzio Luzi and furnishings from the 15th c.; on the right, the **Camera dei Festoni**, or hall of festoons, contains the deeply felt painting of *St. Jerome* by Lorenzo Lotto; on the left, the **Camera dell'Adrianeo** displays artworks by Dosso Dossi, Giovanni Baglione, and Nicolas Poussin; from the Camera dei Festoni you can climb up to the **Sala Cagliostra** (the notorious adventurer Cagliostro was held prisoner here), which now contains a collection of majolica (12th/18th c.).

From the Sala della Biblioteca, or library, you can enter the **Camera del Tesoro**, literally the treasure chamber, a large round room characterized by a series of Renaissance armoirs (built to contain the Archivio Segreto di Paolo III, the secret archive of Paul III) and by the Forziere di Giulio II and the Forziere di Sisto V, the strongrooms of Julius II and Sixtus V, in which the treasure of the Church was stored.

From the vestibule of this area, a narrow stairway dating back to Roman times leads past the Sala Rotonda, to the **Sala delle Colonne**, or room of columns, which – like the two adjoining rooms – contains medieval, Renaissance, and Baroque sculptures.

From the Sala Rotonda, or round room, you can climb up all the way to the large **terrace** atop the castle, from which you can enjoy a splendid panoramic view (note the bronze *Archangel Michael* by Pieter Antoon Verschaffelt, set here in 1752 to replace the marble Archangel Michael by Raffaello da Montelupo, and the *Campana della Misericordia*, literally the bell of mercy, which pealed to announce executions) or else you can climb down to the **Appartamento del Vicecastellano**, comprising three 18th-c. rooms containing paintings depicting the complex throughout history.

Via della Conciliazione (2 C-D5-6). Framed toward the Tiber and toward the city by two symmetrical fore-buildings and closed off at the far end by the facade of S. Pietro (see page 76), this great avenue was designed, in a chilly monumental style, by Marcello Piacentini and Attilio Spaccarelli, and built following the demolition of the buildings that ran between Borgo Vecchio and Borgo Nuovo, narrow lanes that constituted the so-called "spina dei borghi." The demolition of this "spina" – which opened out about midway across Piazza Scossacavalli, allowing visitors to have only a sudden view of the facade of the Basilica Vaticana and the cupola by Michelangelo – and the subsequent reconstruction of part of the buildings, meant to overlook the new road, began in the mid-1930s, but the thoroughfare was not completed until 1950, with the installation of high sidewalks and streetlamps, with structures reminiscent of the obelisk set on a line with the vanishing point.

The **Via Traspontina** (2 C6), which runs off to the right from the Via della Conciliazione, leads to the **Mura Leonine**, walls built by Leo IV in A.D. 847-852, over which runs a narrow covered passageway, known as the *"Passetto"* or *"Corridoio"*, added by Pope Nicholas III to allow the pope to flee from the Vatican into the fortress of Castel S. Angelo; the walls bear many signs of the work done over the centuries.

On the *Via dei Corridori* (2 C5), which takes its name from the passageway mentioned above, you can see, at n. 14, the *Palazzo di Jacopo da Brescia*, attributed to Raphael, and completed prior to 1520, the facade, rebuilt here, overlooked the Borgo Nuovo.

Palazzo Torlonia* (2 C5). Bramante may have produced the first design of the building, which was finally built (ca. 1500-1520) to plans, apparently, by Andrea Bregno; it became property of King Henry VIII (it was the residence of the English ambassador), and was then purchased by the Torlonia family, who had the rear wing constructed, but only in 1820. The facade is similar to that of the Palazzo della Cancelleria; the porticoed courtyard is adorned with fountains.

View of Castel S. Angelo in a drawing of 1806

Palazzo dei Penitenzieri (2 D5). The facade is reminiscent of the facade of Palazzo di Venezia: the construction dates back to ca. 1480, when it was begun for the cardinal Domenico Della Rovere, probably to plans by Baccio Pontelli, and the name derives from the transfer here, just after 1650, of a congregation, the Congregazione dei Penitenzieri; it is now the headquarters of the Ordine Equestre del S. Sepolcro di Gerusalemme, and part is used as a hotel. The two little fountains on either side of the base date from the reign of Pope Paul V, and bear the dragon of the crest of the Borghese family; a large hall on the main floor (to tour the building, contact the Governatore Generale of the order) features in the ceiling *mythological scenes* attributed to Pinturicchio.

After you have passed the two tall *propylaea* designed by Marcello Piacentini and Attilio Spaccarelli as an announcement of the colonnade by Bernini, you are in Piazza S. Pietro (see below).

2.3 The Basilica di S. Pietro and the Città del Vaticano

No visit to Rome would be complete without at least a quick trip to the foremost church of all Christendom, and to the remarkable museums to be found in the Città del Vaticano, or Vatican City. The Basilica di S. Pietro, or St. Peter's, itself a giant museum, is the largest Catholic church on earth (the vast size is hard to grasp or notice, even for the sharpest-eyed visitors); with the complex of the Palazzi Vaticani, it offers a balanced synthesis of the art and architecture of many different centuries – and of much more.

This tour, which of course is a walking tour, begins at Piazza S. Pietro and runs first past the Basilica di S. Pietro, or St. Peter's cathedral, shifting then into the complex of the Musei Vaticani, and coming to a pleasant conclusion in the Città del Vaticano, or Vatican City. The exceptional number and remarkable quality of the art works found here suggest that you make two separate visits of the church and the museums.

Piazza S. Pietro* (2 C-D4). This, St. Peter's Square, was at the time of the original basilica occupied in part by churches and oratories that merged into the dense fabric of the "borghi," or medieval quarters; the spectacular open space now presented, which measures 240 m. along the line of the fountains, and 196 m. in length, is enclosed by the grandiose *colonnade* built by Gian Lorenzo Bernini on behalf of Pope Alexander VII. The ellipse, at the center of which stands the Obelisco Vaticano (see below) and which has as a backdrop the basilica crowned by the great cupola by Michelangelo (see further below), was built in 1656-67 with a four-fold row of columns – for a total of 284, with 88 pillars – in a slightly converging arrangement toward the point of view, and if you occupy the central focal point, the columns of each colonnade will appear perfectly lined up behind the columns of the first row. No fewer than 140 statues of saints (many carved after wax models by Bernini) surmount the portico; at the end of the portico on the right is the famous Portone di Bronzo (bronze door) of the Palazzo Vaticano.

Obelisco Vaticano, or Vatican obelisk (2 C-D4). Towering at the center of the square (measuring from the ground to the tip of the cross is approx. 41 m.; the obelisk itself stands 25.5 m. tall), this obelisk even in ancient times stood near the basilica: Caligula had ordered it transported from Alexandria in Egypt, where it decorated the "Forum Iulii", in A.D. 37 to adorn the circus later known as the Circo di Nerone, where the apostle Peter was martyred and where the first basilica of Constantine was built. In the place of the globe is a cross that contains a fragment of the Holy Cross; the bronze *lions* are by Prospero Antichi, who created them at the same time that the the obelisk was being set into its present location, at the behest of Sixtus V and directed by Domenico Fontana.

The *fountains* on either side of the obelisk are by Carlo Maderno (right; 1613) and Carlo Fontana (left; 1677).

Basilica di S. Pietro*, or St. Peter's cathedral (2 C-D3-4). The first basilica built under

The faithful gather to receive the blessing of the Pope every Sunday in Piazza S. Pietro

Constantine was begun around A.D. 320, consecrated by Pope Sylvester I in 326, and completed in 349. An immense and magnificent structure with a nave and four aisles, divided by columns, it was preceded by a vast atrium in the form of a quadriporticus, with a basin in which to perform ablutions ("cantharus") in the which water poured down from the pine cone ("pigna") that now adorns the courtyard after which it is named ("Cortile della Pigna").

At the middle of the 15th c., all the same, it became clear that the cathedral required a radical renovation, and the decision to carry that renovation out was made by Pope Nicholas V at the advice of Leon Battista Alberti, and the job was entrusted to Bernardo Rossellino (1452). It was, however, Pope Julius II who decided actually to start work, and in 1506 he hired Bramante, who was succeeded by other designers, who wavered back and forth between the ideas of a basilica with a Greek-cross plan or one with a with a Latin-cross plan: Bramante began with a Greek-cross plan; Raphael conceived the building on a Latin-cross plan; Baldassarre Peruzzi wanted to return to the Greek-cross plan, Antonio da Sangallo the Younger to the Latin-cross plan; Michelangelo, returning to Bramante's idea, crowned the church with a vast cupola, imagining it isolated and looming at the center of a great square; upon the death of Michelangelo, work was carried on by Vignola, Pirro Ligorio, Giacomo Della Porta, and Domenico Fontana.

Pope Paul V imposed the Latin-cross plan, and hired Carlo Maderno to extend the church forward, lengthening it; with the addition of three chapels on either side, he finished this phase of work in 1614 (even though 1612 is inscribed on the frieze): on 18 November 1626, on the 1,300th anniversary of the first consecration, it was opened for worship by Pope Urban VIII. Gian Lorenzo Bernini, who had succeeded Maderno, wished to complete the facade with two great bell towers, but problems of all sorts – including structural problems – prevented the completion of that project.

S. Pietro is 186 m. long (218 m., including the portico); the diameter of the cupola by Michelangelo is 42 m,; the maximum height, from the ground to the cross at the top of the cupola, is 136 m.; the total covered area is 22,067 sq. m.

The broad **staircase** on three levels before the facade is by Gian Lorenzo Bernini and is flanked by the large *statues of St. Peter* (left; Giuseppe De Fabris) and *St. Paul* (right; Adamo Tadolini).

The creation of Carlo Maderno, the **facade**, crowned at the center by a pediment, and punctuated by eight columns with lateral pillars, is occupied in the lower section by a central portico (see below) and by two arches at the extremities (the arch on the left leads into the Vatican City, or Città del Vaticano); in the upper section there is a series of nine balconies: the central one is called the *Loggia delle Benedizioni*, in that it is from here that the pope blesses the city, but also because this is where the announcement is made of the election of a new pope. It is crowned by a balustrade upon which stands 13 statues of the Savior, John the Baptist, and the Apostles (reduced to just 11, because St. Peter is missing); the two great clocks were added by Giuseppe Valadier.

The **cupola***, conceived by Michelangelo, who also supervised its construction as high as the tambour, features a base with 16 ramparts, embellished with Corinthian columns; the double-shell dome, divided by ribbing into 16 gores, was the work of Giacomo Della Porta and Domenico Fontana (1588-89). The side cupolas, created by Vignola, are merely decorative.

In the **portico**, beyond the door on the right that leads into the vestibule, or Vestibolo della Scala Regia, you can see the *equestrian statue of Constantine* by Bernini (1670). The last of the five doors on the right is the *Porta Santa*, opened only during Jubilee years; note on high the original inscription with the bull with which Pope Boniface VIII promulgated the first Jubilee in 1300. The bronze *doors** of the central portal (plan, 1) were cast by Filarete (1439-45), at the behest of Pope Eugene IV, for the old cathedral. Above the central entrance of the portico is the *Mosaico della Navicella*, a mosaic executed by Giotto in 1298 but entirely redone in the 17th c. The other three bronze doors are modern: the doors in the last portal on the left (*Porta della Morte*) are by Giacomo Manzù.

The interior is dominated by the bronze baldachin by Bernini, at the center of the cross vault, crowning the papal altar: if you consider that it is the same height as Palazzo Farnese (29 m.), you get a better idea of the harmonious proportions of the structure, fooling the onlooker as to the actual enormous size of the building. Between the massive pillars are arches, 13 m. wide and 23 m. tall.

In the pavement of the **nave**, near the door, is a large *disk* of porphyry upon which, the night of Christmas, A.D. 800, Charlemagne kneeled to receive from Pope Leo III the consecration and imperial crown. On the last pillar on the right, on a marble throne, is a bronze *statue of St. Peter** (2), once thought to date from the 5th c., but more likely dating from the 13th c. – and possibly by Arnolfo di Cambio.

The **cupola** is surprising for its vast size, set as it is on five piers with a pentagonal section, and with a perimeter of 71 m., supporting the vaults of four grand arches; in the tambour there are 16 windows between pairs of pilaster strips supporting the final cornice, upon which rises the cupola, divided by 16 enormous ribbings. The mosaic decoration, done to cartoons by the Cavalier d'Arpino that were executed in 1605, occupies six registers. At the base of the

piers supporting the cupola, note the four large statues built at the orders of Urban VIII: *St. Longinus* (3; 1639) by Bernini; *St. Helena* (4; 1646); *St. Veronica* (5) by Francesco Mochi (1632); *St. Andrew* (6) by François Duquesnoy (1640). Above them, four balconies by Bernini display particularly precious relics.

To cast the **baldachin**, begun by Bernini prior to 1624 – with the assistance of Duquesnoy, Giuliano Finelli and, for the architectural aspect, Francesco Borromini – and inaugurated by Pope Urban VIII Barberini in 1633, it was popular belief that the bronzes from the pronaos of the Pantheon had been melted down (and there is a notorious

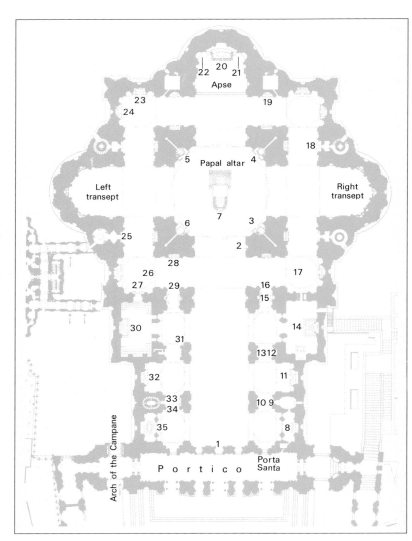

The Basilica di S. Pietro: plan

Pasquinade: "Quod non fecerunt barbari, fecerunt Barberini," i.e., what the barbarians missed, the Barberini destroyed): among the vines of the spiral columns, note the bees of the Barberini crest, while on high, where four angels support great festoons, four volutes converge to support a gilt globe with a cross.

In the **confession** (7) below that, designed and built by Carlo Maderno, 99 perennial lamps light the "tomb of St. Peter."

The decorative array of the chapels in the **right aisle**, like those in the left aisle and in the transept, includes 18th-c. mosaic copies of 16th-/17th-c. artworks, since moved to S. Maria degli Angeli. On the altar of the first chapel (Cappella della Pietà; 8), behind protective glass, the **Pietà***, a marble group executed in 1498-99 for the cardinal Jean de Bilhères de Lagraulas, legate of Charles VIII in Rome, by Michelangelo (signature on the band across the breast of the Virgin Mary); this work clearly marks that artist's transition to expressive maturity; in the vault, *Triumph of the Cross* by Giovanni Lanfranco. In the 1st passageway, on the right (9), beneath the *statue of Leo XII* (Giuseppe De Fabris, 1836), is Bernini's *Cappella delle Reliquie*, also known as the Cappella del Crocifisso for the precious wooden Crucifix, attributed to Pietro Cavallini. On the left (10), *funerary monument of Kristina of Sweden* by Carlo Fontana. In the 2nd chapel (Cappella di S. Sebastiano; 11), on the left, *monument of Pius XII* by Francesco Messina. In the 2nd passageway, on the right (12) *tomb of Innocent XII*, designed by Ferdinando Fuga. On the left (13), *monument of the Countess Mathilda of Canossa* designed by Bernini. The large Cappella del SS. Sacramento (14), a chapel decorated with gilt stuccoes and enclosed by a *grate* designed by Francesco Borromini, features on the altar a *ciborium* made of gilt bronze, executed by Bernini in 1674; he took his inspiration from the little temple built by Bramante in S. Pietro in Montorio. In the 3rd passageway, on the right (15) *monument of Gregory XIII* by Camillo Rusconi (1720-23). On the left (16) *tomb of Gregory XIV* (d. 1591; the *statues of Religion* and *Justice* are by Prospero Antichi). Now you are in Michelangelo's deambulatory, which forms a square running around the piers supporting the cupola; at the cor-

ners are four chapels covered by cupolas (note, in the passageways on the sides of the altars, the columns from the earlier basilica). On the altar of the *Cappella Gregoriana* (17), the work of Giacomo Della Porta in 1583, note the *Madonna del Soccorso* (11th c.) once in the earlier basilica. In the niches of the **right transept**, statues of the founders of religious orders. In the passageway to the Cappella di S. Michele, on the right (18), *monument of Clement XIII**, one of the best known works by Antonio Canova (1784-92). In the passageway toward the apse, on the right (19), *tomb of Clement X* designed in 1684 by Mattia De Rossi.

The "Pietà" by Michelangelo in St. Peter's cathedral

The **apse**, or tribune, serves as a backdrop to the triumphal **Cattedra di S. Pietro**, or throne of St. Peter (20), a Baroque "macchina" in gilt bronze, conceived by Bernini to complete the symbolic and theatrical effect of the baldachin: the ancient wooden throne (this is actually thought to be a throne of Charles the Bald, dating from the 9th c., and not the throne of St. Peter at all) is enclosed in the throne by Bernini, supported by *statues of the Fathers of the Church*; a "gloria" in gilt stucco, with angels and putti amidst the clouds, highlighting the symbol of the Holy Ghost. The niches on the sides contain two great papal tombs: the *monument of Urban VIII** by Bernini (21; 1627-47) and the *monument of Paul III** by Guglielmo Della Porta (22; 1551-75).

In the Cappella della Colonna, on the right (23), altar with the relics of St. Leo the Great, dominated by the marble altarpiece by Alessandro Algardi (1646-50) depicting *St. Leo the Great meeting with Attila*. On the facing altar (24), *Virgin Mary*, possibly from the 15th c.

Beyond the **left transept** and the entrance to the sacristy (25; see below), you will see the *Cappella Clementina* (26), completed by Giacomo Della Porta, where, beneath the altar, rest the remains of St. Gregory the Great. Facing it, *tomb of Pope Pius VII* (27; 1823), done by Bertel Thorvaldsen at the behest of the cardinal Consalvi, the only work by a Protestant artist in S. Pietro.

In the **left aisle**, on the left, against the pier of the cupola (28), there is a mosaic copy of Raphael's Transfiguration. In the passageway, on the right, *monument of Leo XI* (29; 1634-52) by Algardi. The exceedingly lavish chapel, or *Cappella del Coro* (30) was designed by Carlo Maderno; the gilt stuccoes of the vault are attributed to Carlo Maratta. In the next passageway, on the left, note the gilt bronze **tomb of Innocent VIII** by Pollaiolo (31; 1498), moved from the old basilica in 1621 (on that occasion, the relationship between the two depictions of the pope was inverted). The Cappella della Presentazione (32) features on the right the *monument of Pope John XXIII* by Emilio Greco, on the left the *monument of Pope Benedict XV* by Pietro Canonica. In the passageway to the 1st chapel, on the right (33) note the *monument to Marie Clementine Sobieski*, wife of James III Stuart, designed by Filippo Barigioni; on the left (34), *monument of the last Stuarts*, executed by Canova in the form of stelae (1817-19). Next comes the baptistery (35), with a basin formed by the cover of an ancient porphyry sarcophagus, that probably came from the tomb of Hadrian (Sepolcro di Adriano), later the tomb of Otto II.

The **sacristy**, which you enter from the left transept, was built by Carlo Marchionni (1776-84). In the vestibule, on the left, 16th-c. *statue of St. Andrew*. The Sagrestia dei Canonici (a splendid *Glory of Saints* by Federico Zuccari adorns the entrance to this sacristy) adjoins a chapel that features on its altar a canvas by Giovanni Francesco Penni and, directly across, a *Virgin Mary with Christ Child and John the Baptist* by Giulio Romano.

Museo Storico Artistico-Tesoro di S. Pietro. This museum of art history and treasure of St. Peter's can be reached from the corridor of the sacristy, and is open from 9 am to 6

pm, with entrance allowed until 5:30 (in the summer, from 9 am until 7 pm, with entrance allowed until 6:30), and it contains all that survives of the original treasury, plundered a first time by the Saracens in A.D. 846, a second time in 1527, and a third time by Napoleon.

Among the priceless objects still in the treasure let us mention: in hall I, the *Colonna Santa*, or Holy Column, said to be the column against which Christ leaned in the temple of Solomon, though it dates in fact from the 4th c.; in hall II, the *dalmatic said to have belonged to Charlemagne*, though it is in reality Byzantine; and the famous *Crux Vaticana*, or Vatican Cross, a gift from the Eastern Emperor Justin II to the city of Rome (6th c.); in hall III, the **monument to Sixtus IV**, a masterpiece signed by the Pollaiolo and dating from 1493; in hall V, two *chandeliers* traditionally said to be by Benvenuto Cellini; in hall IX the *sarcophagus of Giuno Basso**, prefect of Rome in A.D. 359, with *scenes from the Old and New Testament*.

Sacre Grotte Vaticane. With access through a passageway at the base of the Pilastro di S. Longino della cupola, these grottoes comprise two sections: the "Grotte Nuove" and the "Grotte Vecchie," or new and old grottoes. The new grottoes were created when the floors were raised for the new building: these grottoes are arranged in a semicircle, with the Cappella di S. Pietro, or chapel of St. Peter, at the center, built atop the grave of the apostle; dating from a slightly later period is the ring of corridors that lead to the oratories set at the bases of the piers of the cupola and the five chapels. The old grottoes were created in 1606, when Pope Paul V ordered the demolition of the forward section of the ancient basilica: they are made up of three aisles with depressed vaults set on massive pillars, which extend some 50 m. under the nave. The excavations done at the behest of Pope Pius XII showed that the basilica of Constantine was not built on the structure of the Circus of Nero, but rather upon cemetery structures dating from the 1st to 4th c.

The tour first runs through the **"Grotte Nuove"**, where, in the Cappella dei Patroni d'Europa which lies to the right of the downward ramp, you can see a handsome *Virgin Mary Enthroned, with Angels* from the late-13th c., formerly in the old basilica. Just before the Cappella di S. Elena is a *head of St. Andrew* by Isaia da Pisa (1463), while the Cappella di S. Pietro or Cappella di Clementina, roughly midway along the circular corridor, features a malachite altar (this is the closest altar to the "tomb of Peter") which incorporates an altar dating from the 6th c.; above the sacellum that lies opposite, with the sepulcher of Pope Pius XII, *Virgin Mary with Christ Child*, a 15th-c. fresco. The Cappella di S. Maria de Porticu, which lies beyond the Cappella di S. Veronica, has a fresco by Pietro Cavallini on the altar.

You then enter the **"Grotte Vecchie"**, the left aisle of which is closed to the public; at the beginning of the right aisle, in a small circular chapel that opens off to the left, is the tomb of Pope John XXIII, flanked by the tombs of queen Kristina of Sweden and the queen of Cyprus. Also on the left you can enter the Sala delle Iscrizioni, or hall of inscriptions, where there is a collection of epigraphs from pagan and early Christian times, up to the 14th c. At the end of the aisle are the *tomb of Boniface VIII*, partly built by Arnolfo di Cambio, and the *tomb of Nicholas III*, which re-used an early Christian sarcophagus. In the nave, note the *monument to Pope Pius VI, shown praying*, the last work of Antonio Canova, finished by Adamo Tadolini nel 1821-22.

The lantern atop the dome of St. Peter's

If you make reservations at the Ufficio Scavi della Fabbrica di S. Pietro, you can visit the **Necropoli Precostantiniana**, or Pre-Constantinian Necropolis, thus completing the tour of the Sacre Grotte Vaticane; here six halls contain tomb stones, funerary monuments, and reliefs, by – among others – Giovanni Dalmata, Paolo Taccone, and Paolo da Siena.

The necropolis, with both pagan and Christian tombs, extends along a little lane, lined with mausoleums – each of which attributed to a specific family, often noted in a plaque above the entrance – inside of which are niches for cinerary urns and fine works of painting. On a line with the confessional altar on the upper floor of the basilica, note a modest monument, composed of two stacked niches, that indicates the original burial site of the apostle Peter.

Ascent to the dome of St. Peter's (Cupola di S. Pietro). An elevator, which stops at the outer right flank of the basilica, will take you up to the terrace, from which you can enjoy

a splendid view* of the city and the square below. From the terrace, a fairly accessible stairway (330 steps) leads up along an interior circular corridor, which allows you to have a fairly close view of the mosaics in the dome (see page 77). Lastly, a final stairway leads up (far harder to climb) to the top of the lantern: a narrow spiral staircase leads to the exceedingly panoramic external gallery, from which the view* extends far beyond the outskirts of the city. An elevator descends inside the chruch near the monument to Maria Clementina Sobieski.

In the so-called "octagons" above the transept, the *Archivio della Fabbrica*, or archive of construction, has been installed (special permission required), but there are plans to install the most exquisite items from the Museo Petriano, including the *ciborium** created at the wishes of Pope Pius II and the **monument to Paul II** by Giovanni Dalmata and Mino da Fiesole.

The Palazzi Vaticani and the Musei Vaticani

In medieval times, when the popes lived in the Palazzo del Laterano, near St. Peter's there existed a residence dating back as far as Pope Symmachus; here resided the Holy Roman Emperors Charlemagne and Otto I. It was Pope Innocent III who decided to make the building the permanent seat of the papacy, a decision that was made official by the fact that the first conclave following the Great Western Schism was held here. In

1450 Pope Nicholas V began to warm to the idea of a Palazzo Vaticano, or Vatican palace, centered around the courtyard, or Cortile del Pappagallo, a building that Bramante joined with the little palace of Innocent VIII, or Palazzetto di Innocenzo VIII, at the behest of Julius II, by means of a series of stacked and arched corridors (part of those structures now surround the Cortile del Belvedere); Pope Leo X – with his architect Bramante – was responsible for the construction of the Logge di S. Damaso (one of these loggias was called the Loggia di Raffaello because Raphael completed it); Paul III had the Cappella Paolina and the Sala Regia built; Sixtus V – and his architect Domenico Fontana – built the wings that overlook the ancient thoroughfares; Urban VIII built the Scala Regia.

The Palazzi Vaticani now house the Musei Vaticani, or Vatican Museums, a unique set of collections of remarkable importance – both for the beauty of the settings and for the immense value of the artworks assembled there. It was not until the end of the 18th c., that popes Clement XIV and Pius VI began establishing the papal collections in proper museums; till that period they had been arranged in accordance with the Renaissance style, in the two courtyards – Cortile Ottagono and Cortile del Belvedere, as well as in the Casina di Pio IV. Adjoining the Palazzetto di Innocenzo VIII is the Braccio Nuovo, built at the behest of Pius VII, while Gregory XVI was responsible for the foundation of the Museo Egizio and the Museo Etrusco, Pius IX built the Scala Pia, a stairway, and Leo XIII opened to the public the Appartamento Borgia, and Pius XI built the Palazzo della Pinacoteca, while John XXIII and Paul VI constructed the building for the museums that were formerly at the Palazzo Lateranense.

A shuttle bus service takes you to the Information Office, to the left of the courtyard of the church, at the entrance of the Viale Vaticano.

Cortile delle Corazze. To reach it, you follow a covered passageway; at the center, it is adorned by the *base of the column honoring Antoninus Pius* (161); it joins the atrium of the Quattro Cancelli, or four gates (2).

Museo Gregoriano Egizio*. Founded by Pope Gregory XVI in 1839, and in 1989 reorganized by the Egyptologist Jean-Luc Grenier, with a view to putting the artifacts in context, in accordance with the succession of Egyptian dynasties, this museum has a collection of epigraphs dating from 2600 B.C. to the 6th c., as well as numerous specimens of sculpture, sarcophagi and funerary steles, documents and artifacts linked to the funerary rites, and artworks from the Roman era, inspired by Egyptian art (the sculptures in hall III come from the Villa Adriana – or Hadrian's Villa – at Tivoli).

Cortile della Pigna. The bronze *"pigna,"* or pine cone, which is set on a landing of the

double stairway in front of the *niche of Bramante*; in the Middle Ages this sculpture gave the quarter its name; it was made in Roman times, probably to crown a fountain near the Iseo Campense, and it was then set in the atrium of the first church of St. Peter's to feed the "cantharus" (baptismal font).

This courtyard is part of the much larger Cortile del Belvedere, designed by Bramante to connect the Palazzetto di Innocenzo VIII with the Palazzo Vaticano (the structure was enclosed with linking galleries, with terraces), and broken up in 1587-88 by Domenico Fontana, with the erection of a wing of the library; Raffaele Stern built the Braccio Nuovo, which split the original space up into three parts.

Museo Chiaramonti. Ordered by Pius VII and set up under the supervision of Antonio Canova, this museum contains a vast and varied collection of ancient statuary and a rich collection of inscriptions.

The **Museo Chiaramonti** proper – which occupies about half of the gallery (300 m. in length) and was built by Bramante – contains Roman artifacts, based on Greek originals, and original works (note, in section XIX, the *bust of a Roman Man*, which dates from the second half of the 1st c. B.C.).

The **Galleria Lapidaria**, or Lapidarian Gallery (to visit this gallery, contact the Direzione Generale, or head office, of the museum), which occupies the rest of the gallery, contains about 4,000 pagan and Christian inscriptions; they were assembled at the initial behest of Pope Clement XIV, while the collection was further enriched by popes Pius VI and Pius VII.

In the **Braccio Nuovo**, or new wing, note the 2nd-c. mosaics* set in the flooring, as well as numerous busts on brackets and columns, and statues set in niches. Of special note are: 14, **statue of Augusto di Prima Porta**, found in 1863 in the Villa "ad Gallinas Albas"; 23, the so-called statue of *Modesty*, a Roman sculpture of the 2nd c.; at the far end of the gallery, note the *bust of Pius VII* by Antonio Canova; 67, *Wounded Amazon*, a Roman replica from a Greek original (the arms and legs were added by Bertel Thorvaldsen); 106, *The Nile**, a 1st-c. Roman sculpture; 111, the *Athena Giustiniani*, a marble sculpture from an original Greek bronze; 117, a *satyr at rest*, from the renowned work by Praxiteles; 123, **Doriforo**, a Roman replica from the original by Polycletus.

Museo Pio-Clementino*. This museum, named for two popes, was inaugurated in

771; its namesakes were Clement XIV and Pius VI, who enriched the collections of Greek and Roman sculpture that had existed in the Vatican as early as the 16th c. From the square vestibule, which you enter by a stairway at the beginning of the Museo Chiaramonti, and which conserves the decorations by Daniele da Volterra as well as the *sarcophagus of Lucius Cornelius Scipio Barbatus* (turn of the 3rd c. B.C.), you pass, through the round vestibule (note, from the balcony, the remarkable *Fontana della Galera* – 6 – a fountain in the shape of a 17th-c. galleon), into the cabinet named after the renowned **Apoxyomenos***, a Roman replica (the only one known) of the original bronze by Lysippus (4th c.).

Special mention should be made of the stairway, or *Scala di Bramante** (it can be seen from the room behind the Gabinetto dell'Apoxyomenos), a spiral structure with granite columns in the four registers, built in the first decade of the 16th c.

From the round vestibule, you emerge, on the left into the Cortile Ottagono (5), an eight-sided courtyard designed by Bramante and renovated in the 18th c., which features remarkable works of art, set inside the cabinets at the four corners of the portico. In the 1st cabinet on the left, note the remarkable **Apollo del Belvedere***, or Belvedere Apollo, copied during the Empire from a 4th-c. original attributed to Leochares, discovered at the end of the 15th c. near the church of S. Pietro in Vincoli. The next cabinet takes its name from the celebrated **Laocoon***, a copy, carved in Greek marble by Agesandro and by his sons Polydorus and Athenodorus in the 1st c., from a Hellenistic original; the group was rediscovered in the Domus Aurea in 1506, and exerted considerable influence upon Michelangelo and on Renaissance art. The **Hermes**, too, which was originally believed to be Antinous, in the 3rd cabinet, is a copy from the reign of Hadrian taken from a Greek original. By Antonio Canova, in the 4th cabinet, is the **Perseus**.

The next hall, the Sala degli Animali, features sculptures with groups and figures of animals, extensively restored by Francesco

Antonio Franzoni and, in the floor, 4th-c. mosaics; note: in the left wing, a *statue of Meleager*, a copy done in Roman times (ca. 150) from an original by Skopas, and in the right wing, two small *mosaics* from the Villa Adriana, or Hadrian's Villa.

The Galleria delle Statue, or gallery of statues, is decorated with frescoes from the school of Pinturicchio and embellished by: 85, *Eros di Centocelle*, also known as the *Genio del Vaticano*, a Roman copy from a Greek original; 80, *bust of a triton*, a piece of Greek art from the 2nd c. B.C.; 62, **Apollo Sauroctono**, a Roman replica of a bronze by Praxiteles; between the splendid *Candelabri Barberini** (10 and 13; 2nd c.), 11,

The Laocoon (Musei Vaticani)

Sleeping Ariadne, from a Hellenistic original dating from the 2nd c. B.C.

Adjoining the gallery are the Sala dei Busti, with busts of Roman emperors and deities, and the Gabinetto delle Maschere, with ancient polychrome mosaics set in the floor and, at the center, 37, the lovely *Venus of Cnidus**, a refined replica of the statue by Praxiteles.

The following hall, the Sala delle Muse, contains numerous Roman copies of portraits of philosophers and poets, and the renowned **Torso del Belvedere**, signed by Apollonios of Nestor (1st c. B.C.); the work, uncovered in the early-15th c., influenced the artists of the Renaissance and, in particular, inspired Michelangelo for his figures of "ignudi" in the Cappella Sistina.

After the round hall – where you can admire: 3, the *Jove of Otrìcoli**, 1st-c. copy from a Greek original of the 4th c. B.C.; 8, colossal *statue of Hercules* in gilt bronze, a Roman work from the 2nd c., based on Greek models from the 4th c. B.C. – you reach the Greek-cross hall, dominated by two large 4th-c. *sarcophagi*, in red porphyry: on the right is the *sarcophagus of Constantina**, from the Mausoleo di S. Costanza, on the left is the *sarcophagus of St. Helena**.

Museo Gregoriano Etrusco. Founded in 1837 by Gregory XVI, this collection includes Etruscan artifacts found largely during digs done in Latium in the first half of the 19th c., and a substantial collection of Greek and Italic vases.

After the 1st hall, which is devoted to the early Etruscan-Latial Iron Age (9th/8th c. B.C.), you enter the 2nd hall, which contains the material found in the tomb, or **Tomba Regolini-Galassi** (ca. 650 B.C.), discovered intact at Cervèteri in 1836 and abounding in furniture and precious objects in a Eastern style, resulting from three separate burials; also worthy of note is the *Urna Calabresi*, a cinerary urn dating back to the second half of the 7th c. B.C. The Sala dei Bronzi (3rd hall), or hall of bronzes, contains the famed *Marte di Todi**, a bronze statue of Mars from the end of the 5th c. B.C.; the 4th hall is devoted to stone monuments, the 5th hall to the collection of Benedetto Guglielmi, who donated to Pope Pius XI in 1937 his collection of materials from the necropolis of Vulci, dating back to the 7th/5th c. B.C. (the renovation should result in the unification of the Guglielmi collection, which is now in part on display in the Appartamento di S. Pio V: see below). In the hall of jewels (6th hall) note the remarkable collection of goldsmithery, while in the succeeding halls (7th-18th halls) is a series of Roman antiquities, the Falcioni collection (Etruscan and Roman objects from the area around Viterbo) and the collection of ceramics donated by Mario Astarita to Pope Paul VI in 1967, with interesting specimens of Greek ceramic production.

Sala della Biga. This splendid "hall of the chariot" has a circular plan, in Carrara marble (Giuseppe Camporese), and takes its name from the *biga*, or chariot, in the center, reassembled by Francesco Antonio Franzoni in 1788 with pieces dating back to Roman times, including a chest from the 1st c. used as a bishop's throne in the church of S. Marco.

Galleria dei Candelabri. About 80 m. long, this gallery is named after the pairs of marble candelabra beneath each arch; the vaults were frescoed in 1883-87. The materials found here date from classical times.

Galleria degli Arazzi and Galleria delle Carte Geografiche. The former takes its name from the *tapestries* ("arazzi," in Italian), woven in the 16th c. in Brussels by Pieter van Aelst, which replaced the tapestries by Raphael, now in the picture gallery. The latter gallery is adorned by *maps*, frescoed in 1580-83; note the vault, decorated with stuccoes and paintings by Girolamo Muziano and Cesare Nebbia.

Appartamento di S. Pio V. Comprising the Galleria di S. Pio V, two small halls, and the Cappella di S. Pio V, this suite of rooms temporarily houses the *Giacinto Guglielmi Collection**, which features artifacts made by Etruscans, and a set of Attic ceramics.

Stanze di Raffaello. Part of the Appartamento di Niccolò V, these rooms feature the splendid decorative arrays – among the most noted and significant in the history of Italian art – commissioned by Julius II from the young Raphael in 1508, and by him completed, with assistants, between 1508 and 1525.

The **Sala di Costantino**, or hall of Constantine, was completed in 1525 by Giulio Romano, Raffaellino del Colle, and Giovanni Francesco Penni, in accordance with drawings and instructions left by the late Raphael. On the wall facing the windows, note the *Victory of Constantine over Maxentius* by Giulio Romano; continuing clockwise amidst figures of pontiffs enthroned and virtues, note the *Baptism of Constantine* and *Donation of Constantine* by Penni, and *Apparition of the Cross to Constantine* by Giulio Romano.

With special permission from the from the head office, or Direzione, you can enter the **Loggia di Raffaello**, begun by Bramante and completed by Raphael (1512-18) who entrusted its direction to his pupils, including Giovanni da Udine, Giulio Romano, Polidoro da Caravaggio, and Perin del Vaga. Of the 13 bays, 12 are decorated with *episodes from the Old Testament*, the last one with *scenes from the New Testament*; set upon pilaster strips and pillars, on the other hand, is a minute decoration made up of grotesques, interweaving fantastic, naturalistic, and architectural motifs, as well as small mythological figures and festoons.

From the Sala di Costantino you pass into the **Sala dei Palafrenieri**, also known as the

Sala dei Chiaroscuri, a vast room with apostles and saints, by Federico and Taddeo Zuccari.

The **Cappella di Niccolò V**, which features frescoes of the *stories of the martyrs Stephen and Lawrence** executed by Fra Angelico between 1448 and 1450, marks the beginning

Portrait of Pope Alexander VI (Pinacoteca Vaticana)

of one of the oldest areas in the papal palace.

A short passageway leads to the **Stanza di Eliodoro**, which was frescoed by Raphael, between 1512 and 1514, in accordance with an iconographic program designed to glorify the church, and probably developed by Pope Julius II. On the wall dividing this room from the Stanza della Segnatura, note the *Meeting of St. Leo the Great and Attila**; if you continue counterclockwise, you can see the *Mass of Bolsena**, dramatic and powerful, the *Expulsion of Heliodorus**, executed with the collaboration of Giulio Romano and Giovanni da Udine, and the *Liberation of St. Peter**, with innovative light effects.

Next is the **Stanza della Segnatura** (the name refers to the fact that important official documents were signed in this room), which – with the exception of a number of decorations in the vault, by Sodoma and Bramantino – was entirely painted by Raphael between 1509 and 1511; the frescoes, in which the ideals of Humanistic culture linked to the classical tradition converged with the results of research into perspective during the 15th c., are considered among Raphael's absolute master-

pieces. Proceeding to the left, from the wall closest to the Stanza dell'Incendio di Borgo, you will find the famous *Disputation of the Sacrament**; on either side of the window, *Gregory IX Approves the Decrees** and *Justinian Consigns the Pandects to Tribonianus* (in the lunette around the window, *Strength*, *Prudence*, and *Temperance*); on the wall facing the Disputation, note the renowned *School of Athens** (a number of the figures bear the features of famous men of the time: the figure with the compass bears a resemblance to Bramante, while the seated figure with its head on its arm has the features of Michelangelo); on the wall with the window overlooking the Cortile del Belvedere, note *Mt. Parnassus**, completed in 1511. The chiaroscuro paintings on the socle that runs around the walls were executed to replace the wooden facing, by Perin del Vaga; the depictions of the Sciences and the Arts in the vault, on the other hand, were done by Raphael.

In the **Stanza dell'Incendio**, completed during the papacy of Leo X, the frescoes on the walls were for the most part done by pupils, to cartoons and drawings by Raphael, in accordance with a program based on episodes concerning other popes named Leo: on the facing wall, the *Fire in Borgo** which was put out by Leo IV making the sign of the cross; on the right wall, the *Coronation of Charlemagne by Leo III*; on the left wall, the *Victory of Leo IV over the Saracens*; on the wall with the window, note the *Oath of Leo III*. The paintings in the vault are by Perugino.

Appartamento Borgia. Set beyond the Cappella di Urbano VIII, which features frescoes by Pietro da Cortona and rough models by Antonio Canova, this apartment was splendidly frescoed by Pinturicchio and assistants, commissioned by Alexander VI Borgia, between 1492 and 1495 (note the remarkable wealth of decoration in hall V, known as the Sala dei Santi, which may be the artist's greatest work).

This apartment contains part of the vast *Collezione d'Arte Religiosa Moderna*, a collection of modern religious art, inaugurated by Pope Paul VI in 1973, and comprising a vast array of sculptures, paintings, and drawings (ca. 800), by Giacomo Manzù, Auguste Rodin, Henry Matisse, Felice Casorati, Giorgio Morandi, Emilio Greco, Carlo Carrà, Marino Marini, Georges Rouault, Vasily Kandinsky, Otto Dix, Umberto Boccioni, Giorgio De Chirico, Oskar Kokoschka, Ottone Rosai, Paul Klee, Georges Braque, Pablo Picasso, Giuseppe Capogrossi, and Renato Guttuso, among others.

Cappella Sistina*, or Sistine Chapel. One of the most noteworthy works of Renaissance art, this chapel was built at the behest of Sixtus IV between 1475 and 1481. It is a rectangular room lit by six large windows on each long side, and covered by a depressed barrel-vault; the 15th-c. floor is made of

"Transfiguration" by Raphael

polychrome marble; an elegant marble *screen*, by Mino da Fiesole, Andrea Bregno, and Giovanni Dalmata (they also designed and executed the balustrade of the *choir chancel*) divides the room into two parts. Between 1481 and 1483 Sixtus IV commissioned several of the best-known artists of the time – including Sandro Botticelli, Luca Signorelli, Piero di Cosimo, Perugino, Domenico Ghirlandaio, and Pinturicchio – to do the frescoes on the side walls and the walls facing the altar; in 1506 Pope Julius II continued the project of decorating the chapel, assigning the task to Michelangelo who, between 1508 and 1512, frescoed the vault and, under the papacy of Paul III, the far wall.
Frescoes on the side walls and the walls facing the altar. In the lower area, there are fake draperies, upon which were applied the tapestries by Raphael, now in the picture gallery. In the central area, on the right, note the *episodes of the life of Moses*; in particular,

note the second panel which depicts *The Burning Bush, Moses Killing the Egyptian and Chases the Madyanites from the Fountain, The Daughters of Jethro*, and a fifth panel with *The Punishment of Kore, Dathan, and Abiron*, both by Sandro Botticelli; on the left *episodes from the life of Christ*, and among them in particular note the second (*Purification of the Leper* and *Temptation of Christ*) by Domenico Ghirlandaio, and the fifth (*Handing Over the Keys*), one of Perugino's greatest masterpieces. In the upper area of the side facing the altar, between the windows, note 2 portraits of popes.
Frescoes of the vault. This enormous pictorial series, restored between 1981 and 1994, occupies the entire surface, in a remarkable fusion of architectural elements and plastic depictions, underscored by brilliant colors. The immense composition is organized into three stacked registers: in the central area are nine stories from Genesis*, illustrating from the panel of the altar: the *separation of light from darkness*, the *creation of the stars*, the *separation of the waters*, the magnificent *Creation of Adam*, the *creation of Eve*, the *original sin*, the *sacrifice of Noah*, the *universal deluge*, and the *drunkenness of Noah*; between the panels, in a marble structure, are depicted pairs of **"ignudi***," or nudes bearing large medallions. The register below that contains the powerful *figures of sibyls and prophets*, enthroned. In the triangular gores and the corners of the vault in the lower register other *Bible stories* are portrayed, while in the webs and the lunettes above the windows, note the *ancestors of Christ*.

Frescoes on the far wall (restored in 1993). Between 1536 and 1541, transcending the iconographic ideals and the perspectival relationships of Renaissance art, Michelangelo portrayed the magnificent and appalling **Last Judgment*** as a vast scene in movement in a limitless space. Dominating it all is the majestic and implacable figure of *Christ the Supreme Judge*, with, seated next to him, the *Virgin Mary*, and, all around them, *saints*, *patriarchs*, and *martyrs* crowding into Paradise; on the right the blessed souls ascend to heaven, and on the left the damned souls are hurled down into Hell, where they are welcomed by Charon and Minos. At the bottom is depicted: on the left, the *Resurrection of the Dead*, at the center, the *angels sounding the Last Trump*, and, on high, in the spaces of the lunettes, *angels with the symbols of the Passion* (the figures, originally nude, were covered with bits of cloth in 1564 by Daniele da Volterra because Pope Pius IV judged them to be scandalous).

Special permission is required in order to tour the *Cappella Paolina*, by Antonio da Sangallo the Younger; this chapel contains the last frescoes painted by Michelangelo (*Conversion of St. Paul* and *Crucifixion of St. Peter*).

Sala delle Nozze Aldobrandine. Beyond the Sala degli Indirizzi di Pio IX, which contains religious artistic objects in ivory and metal, and a collection of Roman glass, this room takes its name from a splendid *fresco**, probably dating from the reign of Augustus, and depicting the preparations for the wedding of Alexander the Great and Roxana, discovered in 1605 near the arch of Gallienus. The frescoes on the ceiling are by Guido Reni.

A single room, set directly after the Sala dei Papiri, constitutes the *Museo Sacro*, founded by Benedict XIV to contain precious Christian antiquities (note the Byzantine mosaic with *St. Theodore*, dating from the mid-14th c.).

Biblioteca Apostolica Vaticana. Established by Sixtus IV in 1475 (already, however, Pope Nicholas V had selected the site, on the ground floor of his own palazzo), this library has accumulated manuscripts and printed texts over time; it now possesses 75,000 manuscript volumes and 70,000 archive volumes, more than 100,000 separate hand-written texts, and about 800,000 printed volumes. The rooms that make up the long gallery are: the Galleria di Urbano VIII (the *planispheres* date from 1529); the Sale Sistine; the Biblioteca di Sisto V (small gallery), in which the largest and the smallest codex from the library are on display; periodically materials of the institution are put on exhibition; the splendid *Salone Sistino**, by Domenico Fontana in 1587-89, lavishly decorated under the supervision of Giovanni Guerra and Cesare Nebbia.

From the Albani and Carpegna collections, and, in part, from excavations done between 1809 and 1815, come the materials from Etruscan, Roman, and medieval times found in the *Museo Profano*.

Pinacoteca Vaticana*. This remarkable collection of paintings was inaugurated by Pius VI in 1816, after Antonio Canova had recovered 77 works of art that had been given to France with the treaty of Tolentino; it was later expanded with specimens of various origin. Beyond the vestibule and hall I (Sala dei Primitivi; note the *St. Francis of Assisi* signed by Margaritone d'Arezzo), hall II features work by Giotto and his followers: at the center, note the **Stefaneschi polyptych**, painted in Rome by Giotto and his assistants, and intended for the Basilica di S. Pietro; on the walls, note works by Pietro Lorenzetti, Simone Martini, Gentile da Fabriano, and Sassetta.

In hall III, you can admire works by Filippo Lippi, Benozzo Gozzoli and Fra Angelico, in hall IV, note two masterpieces by Melozzo da Forlì: the fragments of the fresco depicting the *Ascension** and a large fresco of *Sixtus IV Appointing the Prefect of the Biblioteca Vaticana** (1477). Next come: hall V, with the *Miracles of St. Vincent Ferrer* by Ercole de Roberti, and the *Pietà* by Lucas Cranach the Elder Vecchio; hall VI, dedicated to polyptychs (note the *Pietà* by Carlo Crivelli); and hall VII, devoted to the 15th-c. Umbrian school.

Hall VIII is one of the most sumptuous and interesting in the picture gallery; in it, aside from the 10 **tapestries** commissioned from Raphael by Pope Leo X for the Cappella Sistina, or Sistine Chapel (1515-16), are: the **Transfiguration**, assigned to Raphael in 1517 but completed by Giulio Romano and Giovanni Francesco Penni, the splendid **Madonna di Foligno**, painted by Raphael between 1512 and 1513, and the *Coronation of the Virgin Mary*, the first large composition by Raphael (1503).

After you cross hall IX, note the **St. Jerome** by Leonardo da Vinci (ca. 1480), you enter halls X and XI, which contain artworks from the 16th c.: note the magnificent *Madonna dei Frari* (1528) and the *portrait of the doge Nicolò Marcello* by Titian, the *Sacrifice of Isaac*, attributed to Ludovico Carracci, and the *Annunciation*, signed by the Cavalier d'Arpino (1606). Of special interest, in the hall XII, is the *Deposition** by Caravaggio (1602-1604), the *Communion of St. Jerome* by Domenichino (signature; 1614) and the *Crucifixion of St. Peter* by Guido Reni.

The 17th and 18th c. are represented in halls XIII (note the *St. Francis Saverio* by Antonie Van Dyck and the *David and Goliath* by Pietro da Cortona), XIV, and XV, which feature works by Carlo Maratta and Sebastiano Conca, as well as portraits.

Halls XVI, XVII, and XVIII conserved models by Gian Lorenzo Bernini and specimens of Byzantine, Greek, and Russian religious art.

Museo Gregoriano Profano*. This museum was established by Gregory XVI in 1844 in the Palazzo Lateranense, while the transfer to the current site dates from 1970; the rich series of pagan epigraphs became part of the collection at the end of the 19th c., while the Greek and Roman artifacts come from excavations done in the papal state.

Of the four sections into which the museum is split up, the first is dedicated to Greek originals, represented here by the *Stele del Palestrita**, an Attic relief dating from the middle of the 5th c. B.C., by **fragments of sculptures from the Parthenon** and by a *head of Athena**, in the style of Magna Graecia (mid-5th c. B.C.).

The second section concentrates on Roman copies and variations on Greek originals: one important example is the *Niobide Chiaramonti**, probably derived from a group done by Skopas or Praxiteles. The *Tomb of Vicovaro*, on the other hand, probably dates back to about A.D. 30/40.

A relief with personifications of the Etruscan cities of *Tarquinia*, *Vulci*, and *Vetulonia* documents, in the third section, Roman sculpture of the 1st and 2nd c., which has two other noteworthy instances in the relief of the altar, or *Ara dei Vicomagistri** (ca. A.D. 30-40) and in the 39 *fragments** of the tomb of the Haterii.

The fourth section is devoted to sarcophagi; and the fifth is dedicated to Roman sculp-

ture of the 2nd and 3rd c.; note in particula the torso of a *loricate statue*, possibly o Trajan or Hadrian.

Museo Pio Cristiano. This museum wa founded by Pope Pius IX in the Palazzo La teranense to contain the material found i catacombs and in the earliest churches o Rome; it was transferred to its present lo cation in 1963, and it preserves architec tural and sculptural elements (note th fragment of the *inscription of the Cippus o Abercio* dating from the reign of Marcu Aurelius) as well as mosaics; the adjoinin section of inscriptions can be toured by requesting permission in the head museun office (Direzione).

Museo Missionario-Etnologico. Objects o the applied arts and documents concernin non-European civilizations come in par from the Missionary Exhibition assemblec in the Jubilee Year of 1925 (the institutior was founded in 1926 in the Palazzo Latera nense), to which the donations of congre gations and private individuals have beer added over the years.

Museo Storico Vaticano. This is a detached section located in the Palazzo Lateranense (see page 62); it comprises a collection o the various means of transport used by the popes over the centuries.

Vatican City

Following the signature of the Patti Lateranensi, or Lateran Pact, the Città del Vaticano became an independent state, extending over an area of 0.44 sq. km. (the city/state comprises, aside from the territory enclosed by the Mura Vaticane, or Vatican walls, three patriarchal basilicas, the Palazzo del Laterano, Palazzo della Cancelleria, and Palazzo di Propaganda Fide, the Ospedale del Bambin Gesù, a hospital, and the Palazzo Pontificio di Castel Gandolfo, with Villa Cybo and Villa Barberini), with a population of 550; this state issues its own stamps and coins its own money, as well as transmitting radio programs and publishing a daily newspaper ("L'Osservatore Romano"); it also has its own police force, which includes the Swiss Guard (the uniforms that these soldiers wear even now were supposedly designed by Michelangelo).

The pontiff concentrates in his person all the legislative, executive, and judicial powers of the Vatican state – powers that are then in turn exercised through the appropriate agencies – and represents the Vatican

state internationally, through the cardinal named as Secretary of State; he is also the Bishop of Rome and the head of the Roman Apostolic Catholic Church. In governing the Church, the pope is assisted by the Sacred College of Cardinals (Sacro Collegio dei Cardinali) and by the Roman Curia.

When a pope dies, the cardinals gather in a conclave (from "cum" = with & "clavis" = key, i.e., a place locked with a key), usually in the Sistine Chapel, or Cappella Sistina, to elect a successor: if the successor has been elected, then an announcement is made by burning the ballots, producing a white cloud of smoke; if no decision has been reached, then a cloud of black smoke is released, by burning damp straw along with the ballots of that vote.

Sacred ever since the foundation of Rome, the territory upon which the Città del Vaticano now stands had considerable political importance at least as far back as the time of Charlemagne, who, by having himself crowned in the basilica by Pope Leo III, not only restored the imperial myth in the west, but laid the foundations for mporal power. It was not until A.D. 847-855 that ... e city was enclosed within a walled perimeter ... he Mura Leonine, or walls of Leo), and during ... e Middle Ages Rome increasingly took on the ... ppearance of a fortified citadel, and with the end ... the Western Schism it became the definitive ... te of the Holy See.

he golden age of the temporal power of the pa... acy began with Pope Nicholas V; this pope not ... nly was the first to conceive ... e idea of a new Basilica di S. ...etro, or St. Peter's cathe-... ral, but he also aspired to ... edesign the entire city of ... ome as the capital of a mod-... n state; his indications were ... ken up by his successors, ... nd culminated – following ... e sack of Rome in 1527, ... hich pushed Pius IV to en-... rge the Leonine City with ... e Borgo Pio – in the great ... rban projects undertaken by ... ope Sixtus V and the com-... letion of the Basilica di S. ...etro. The later architectural ... rojects undertaken in the Cit-... del Vaticano was designed ... hiefly to gather, preserve, ... nd optimize the immense art ... ollections, adapting sections ... f the historic buildings, and, ... more recent eras, building ... ew ones.

he Città del Vaticano, or ... atican City, can be toured ... nly by a request with the ... fficio Informazioni Pelle-... rini e Turisti (in Piazza S. ... ietro, to the left of the ... reat church courtyard, or ... sagrato"): from March to ...)ctober, Tuesday, Friday,

Swiss guards

nd Saturday, 10 am (with the addition of the ... istine Chapel, Monday and Thursday, 10 ... m); from November to February, Satur-... lay, 10 am.

.mong the many buildings to be admired in ... he Vatican City, we should point out the ... ula delle Udienze Pontificie*, or papal au-... ience hall, set behind the Collegio Teu-... onico (Teutonic college), built by Pier Lui-... i Nervi with a daring seashell-shaped struc-

ture, capable of accommodating 12,000. Beyond the *Palazzo del Governatorato* (1931) extend the splendid *Giardini Vaticani**, or Vatican gardens, laid out in the Italian style (in many areas according to the original designs of the 16th c.). These gardens contain the **Casina di Pio IV**, a little mansion that was begun under Pope Paul IV who ordered it built by Pirro Ligorio in 1558; the building was completed in 1561, and comprises two separate structures and two side pavillions: the smaller structure, with a fountain before it, is adorned by mosaics in the base and by a loggia higher up; the larger structure has stucco decorations and, inside, frescoes by Federico Barocci, Santi di Tito, and Federico Zuccari.

2.4 The Campidoglio, the Foro Romano and the Palatine

his tour, which runs through many of the ... nost famous monumental and archeologi-... al zones of the city – and on earth – allows ... he sightseer to form a clear idea of the ... vay that artists and architects, from the Re-... naissance onward, revitalized the decora-... ive style of antiquity in this city. The re-

markable tour of the Foro Romano and the Palatine allows a visitor to imagine the grandeur and ancient splendor of the buildings of Rome – despite the fact that they have gradually been stripped to make way for other, newer builings, especially in this area; often the new buildings have inherited a considerable portion of the older ones' enduring charm.

The walking tour runs, to the west of the Vittoriano and Piazza Venezia, through the Piazza d'Aracoeli, from which two stairways run up the slopes of the Campidoglio to the church of S. Maria in Aracoeli, founded in exceedingly early times, and the Piazza del Campidoglio by Michelangelo, orchestrated around the Palazzo Senatorio (site of public power in the city) and around the Palazzo dei Conservatori and the Palazzo Nuovo, now occupied by the Musei Capitolini (the oldest museum collections on earth), which still stand high on the Capitoline hill, which still preserves traces of buildings from the classical era (temple of Jove and the Tabularium).

After Pietro da Cortona's church of the Santi Luca e Martina and the Carcere Mamertino, in which – according to a medieval legend – St. Peter was imprisoned, the archeological area of the Foro Romano and of the Palatine immerse you in the glorious past of classical Rome, with an assembly of archeological monuments that range from the earliest necropolises dating from the Iron Age to the late Basilica of Maxentius, and including true masterpieces of architecture (arches of Septimius Severus and Titus) and painting (houses of Livia and of Augustus).

S. Maria in Aracoeli* (8 B3). The ancient church of S. Maria in Capitolio, named after a Benedictine monastery that had formerly been occupied by Greek monks, took on it present title in the 14th c., following the re construction done in 1285-87, at the behes of the Franciscans, and possibly built t plans by Arnolfo di Cambio; the stairway which Lorenzo di Simone Andreozzi bui leading up to the image of the *Virgin Mar with Christ Child* (10th/11th c.), now set o the main altar, in thanksgiving for the en of the Black Death of 1348, was inaugurate in that year by Cola di Rienzo. Further im provements were carried out under Pop Pius IV, and in the 17th c., when the nav was redecorated; it was deconsecrated du ing the French occupation (it was used a sta ble). The church now appears with th 13th-c. brick facade, with three portals su mounted by as many windows; standin before that facade, in the church cour yard, is the tomb stone of the Humanis Flavio Biondo.

The interior has a nave and two side aisles divided by columns, with a handsome Cos matesque floor and a coffered *ceiling* (157 75), built by the Roman Senato in thanks giving for the victory of Lèpanto; it is a re markable document of art in Rome betwee the end of the 13th c. and the late 18th c Even the counter-facade, with the *funerar monument of the cardinal Ludovico d'Albre* (to the right of the central portal) by Andre Bregno, and the *tomb stone of Giovann Crivelli* (wall) by Donatello, is an indicato of what a treasure chest this church really is; among the artists who actually worke on site, or for the church indirectly, ther

The Palazzo Senatorio in the Campidoglio area, built to plans by Michelangelo

are Pinturicchio (the famous series of **stories of St. Bernardino** in the 1st chapel on the right), the Pomarancio (*stories of the Passion* in the 2nd on the right), Francesco Cavallini (the stuccoes in the 6th and 8th), Michelangelo (the *tomb of Cecchino Bracci*, in the space of the right side door, was built by Francesco Amadori to a design by him), Arnolfo di Cambio (*tomb of Luca Savelli* on the left wall of the right transept), Lorenzo and Jacopo di Cosma (they signed the two *pulpits* near the terminal pillars in the nave), Pietro Cavallini (fresco of the *Virgin Mary with Christ Child, Enthroned, and Saint Matthew and Saint John* in the Gothic aedicue of the Cosmatesque *monument to the cardinal Matteo d'Acquasparta* in the left transept), again Pomarancio (frescoes and stuccoes in the 5th chapel on the left) and Benozzo Gozzoli (*St. Anthony of Padua and two donors*, the sole remaining fresco, from the series that once decorated the 3rd chapel).

From the right side portal, set in the base of the Romanesque *campanile* (of which only two stories survive), you can climb down to the *portico*, which may have been built by Nanni di Baccio Bigio in 1554.

Piazza del Campidoglio* (8 B3). Trapezoidal in shape, this square was designed by Michelangelo, who also designed the Palazzo dei Conservatori and Palazzo Nuovo, which respectively close off the square to the right and the left (for both, see page 92), the *"cordonata"*, or graded ramp, which was later modified by Giacomo Della Porta and was cut at the base in 1929, runs up to the square, and is enclosed by the balustrade, modified by Della Porta in 1585, which rings this square, overlooking the city.
Embellishing the splendid setting are the *Dioscuri* on the balustrade, dating from the late empire, placed there by Della Porta to replace the statues designed for that site by Michelangelo, now in Piazza del Quirinale, the *trophies of Marius* from the age of Domitian, the *statues of Constantine* and *Costans II* from the baths of Constantine, and milestone columns; at the center of the square, on the pedestal designed by Michelangelo, as was the paving, stood until 1981 the equestrian statue of Marcus Aurelius, now on the ground floor of the Museo Capitolino (a copy will be set on the pedestal).

This square occupies one of the peaks of the Campidoglio, the site of one of the earliest settlements in the territory that is now occupied by Rome. Some 50 m. tall and in an ideal position to command the Tiber, between the Forum and the Campo Marzio, this hill was accessible in historical times only along a single road (the "Clivus Capitolinus") and two stairways; enclosed by fortifications linked to the walls of the city, it soon became a place of worship: Romulus supposedly built the first sanctuary here, dedicating it to Jove Pheretrius, while the age of the Tarquins – although the temple was only consecrated in 509 B.C. after the expulsion of those kings and the proclamation of the republic – saw the construction of the *temple of Capitoline Jove*, also known as the temple of the Capitoline triad, inasmuch as it was also dedicated to Juno and Minerva; for centuries this was the official temple of Rome.
After the great fire of 83 B.C., the Campidoglio was partly rebuilt by Sulla (this reconstruction included the building of the Tabularium: see below) and again by Domitian. When the empire collapsed, the hill was gradually abandoned until it reverted to pasturage, and other buildings were erected on the ruins (the Fortress of the Corsi rose on the site of the Tabularium, the first nucleus of the Palazzo Senatorio; on the site of the temple of Juno Moneta rose the church of S. Maria in Aracoeli), until the accession of Michelangelo who modified its orientation for Pope Paul III, opening it toward the modern city.

Palazzo Senatorio (8 B3). Placed here to close off the square in the direction of the Fori, this building had a turreted medieval appearance until the 16th c., while the current facade is the result of an adaptation (Giacomo Della Porta and Girolamo Rainaldi, 1582-1605) of the original design by Michelangelo, of which the *scalea* survives. In the niche, Matteo da Città di Castello placed a *statue of Minerva seated*, dating from the age of Domitian when in 1588-89 the fountain was added; the great *statues of the Tiber* (right; it was actually the Tigris) and *the Nile* (left) come from the baths of Constantine. The tower, on the summit of which stands an ancient cross and a *statue of Minerva-the goddess Roma*, was built by Martino Longhi the Elder, in the place of the existing medieval structure, in 1578-82; the bells date from the 19th c., when the clock that adorns the facade of Aracoeli was installed.
This building is now the site of the city administration, and is therefore not open to the public; we would point out in particular the Aula Consiliare, or council hall, adorned with a *statue of Julius Caesar* and a *statue of a Roman admiral* (age of Trajan).

To the right of the Palazzo Senatorio, a stairway allows you to enter the *Protomoteca Capitolina*, a collection of busts that was begun in the Pantheon by Antonio Canova (who carved the busts of *Pope Pius VII* and *Domenico Cimarosa*, 1807-1808).

If you hug the right side of the building, you will come to a terrace with a panoramic view (remarkable vantage point over the Foro Romano), that offers a fine perspective on the rear elevation of the Palazzo Senatorio, which incorporated 11 original arches of the **Tabularium**, the state archive of ancient Rome, built by Quintus Lutatius Catulus, consul in 78 B.C.; it was used in the Middle Ages as a storehouse and as a prison: behind the large portico, which served as a background to the Forum, there were various vaulted chambers, on several levels, connected by stairways.

Palazzo dei Conservatori (8 B2-3). The site of the ancient elective magistrates of the city, after whom it is named, this building stands on the site of an earlier structure, possibly dating back to the 12th c., rebuilt a first time in the 15th c., and a second time in 1563-68 based on the designs done by Michelangelo for the facade, the portico overlooking the courtyard, and the stairway.

The courtyard features a giant *head of Constantine*, part of a single monument, formerly in the basilica of Maxentius, which comprised also the fragments of arm, leg, hand, and feet; in the portico at the far end is a large *statue of Roma* (age of Trajan) between *statues of captured barbarian kings* (2nd c.), a group that once belonged to Federico Cesi, and a colossal *head of Constantius II*; on the left wall of the courtyard, note the reliefs and trophies formerly in the cella of the temple of Hadrian. Opposite from the Palazzo dei Conservatori is the *Palazzo Nuovo* (8 B3), built at the behest of Pope Innocent X by Girolamo and Carlo Rainaldi (1655) in harmony with Michelangelo's plans and designs.

Musei Capitolini*. The collections are located in the Palazzo dei Conservatori, where it is possible to tour the Appartamento dei Conservatori, the Museo del Palazzo dei Conservatori, and the Pinacoteca Capitolina, and in the Palazzo Nuovo, entirely occupied by the Museo Capitolino.

The **Appartamento dei Conservatori**, a suite of rooms that can be reached from the atrium of the Palazzo dei Conservatori (the documents assembled here illustrate the history of the museum) along a stairway – with stuccoes by Luzio Luzi (1576) and, in the panels, historic reliefs taken from the monument honoring Marcus Aurelius and from the so-called Arco di Portogallo, or arch of Portugal (the *statue of Charles of Anjou* was attributed to Arnolfo di Cambio) – comprises a series of rooms now used as official settings by the city government.

Once the site of sessions of the public council, the *Sala degli Orazi e Curiazi* contains a *marble statue of Urban VIII**, executed by Gian Lorenzo Bernini and assistants (1635-39), as well as the bronze *statue of Innocent X** by Alessandro Algardi (1645-50), while the walls are covered with

A giant head of Constantine

frescoes that imitate tapestries, by the Cavalier d'Arpino (1595-1638).

After you pass the Sala dei Capitani, literally the hall of the captains, with frescoes by Tommaso Laureti (1587-94) and five marble statues of Captains of the Church (16th and 17th c.), you will reach the Sala dei Trionfi, or hall of triumphs, where, among various masterpieces of ancient sculpture, you can admire the renowned *Spinario (or boy removing a thorn from his foot)**, an elegant bronze specimen of Hellenistic art (1st c. B.C.).

You will then enter the Sala della Lupa, or hall of the she-wolf, at the center of which you may admire the famed **Lupa Capitolina**, or Capitoline she-wolf, here since the mid-16th c., a symbol of Rome, executed in bronze at the turn of the 5th c. B.C. (the twins, attributed to Pollaiolo, were added in the 15th c.); on the far wall, note the fragments of the *Fasti Consolari* and *Fasti Trionfali*, literally consular and triumphal splendors, taken from the Arch of Augustus, in the Roman Forum, now destroyed.

In the adjoining Sala delle Oche, or hall of the geese, you may observe the *Medusa's*

Head by Bernini (1630) and, at the center, the magnificent *dog*, in serpentine, a decorative sculpture after a Greek original dating from the 4th c. B.C.

Beyond the little Sala delle Aquile, or hall of eagles, the Sala degli Arazzi, or hall of tapestries, takes its name from the *tapestries* on the walls, tapestries that were executed in Rome between 1764 and 1768. Through the *Cappella Nuova*, or new chapel, inaugurated in 1960, you will reach the *Sala delle Guerre Puniche**, or hall of the Punic wars, the only room to preserve virtually intact its 16th-c. decoration, by Jacopo Ripanda and collaborators.

After you pass through the Cappella Vecchia, or old chapel, with stuccoes and frescoes dating from the 16th and 17th c., you will emerge into the passageway that leads to the Museo del Palazzo dei Conservatori, a museum which features a series of *Views of Rome* by Gaspare Vanvitelli.

The **Museo del Palazzo dei Conservatori** houses material from various origins and eras: inscriptions with the lists of Roman magistrates from 1640 on; a series of sculptures discovered on the Esquiline; you should note: a *Seated Girl*, a refined Hellenistic sculpture dating from the 2nd c. B.C.; a *bust of Commodus**, depicted with the attributes of Hercules, 2nd c.; and the *Esquiline Venus**, a delightful work from the 1st c. B.C.; steles, reliefs, and statues dating from the 6th and 5th c. B.C.; a number of Egyptian works; Christian epigraphs and reliefs; a rich collection of Greek, Etruscan, and Italic vases belonging to the Castellani collection, donated to the city in 1867: note the interesting *Tensa Capitolina*, a reconstruction of a 4th-c. chariot, used in sacred processions, and the **krater of Aristonothos**, signed by the potter, and dating from the end of the 7th c. B.C.; the colossal *head of Constantine II* (4th c.); the splendid *funerary bed* (1st c. B.C.); a *litter* dating from the 1st c. A.D.; the sculptures from the gardens of Maecenas on the Esquiline, including a *Hercules in Combat*, after a 3rd-c. B.C. original, and a relief of a *dancing maenad*, a splendid Roman copy from an original by Callimachus.

The **Braccio Nuovo** largely contains sculptures found during the most recent excavations (the tufa-stone structures that are visible belong to the temple of Capitoline Jove: see page 91), and the **Museo Nuovo**, dedicated to the finds from the excavations done after 1870. Among the materials displayed there are the famous bronze *horse*, a Greek original from the school of Lysippus, discovered in the 19th c. in

Trastevere, and the *sculptures of the pediment* of the temple of Apollo Sosiano, along with other finds which serve to illustrate the various artistic and historical phases of Roman monumental construction. A selection of this material in on display in the ex Montemartini industrial centre in Via Ostiense (see p.40).

The **Pinacoteca Capitolina**, or Capitoline art gallery, was founded by Pope Benedict XIV in 1748 with the acquisition of the Sacchetti collection and the Pio di Savoia collection; it comprises noteworthy examples of Italian and European art, from the Middle Ages to the 18th c.

From hall I, which contains works by the Emilian and Ferrarese schools of the 16th c. (in particular, the *Sacred Family* by Dosso Dossi) you enter hall II, with major Venetian works from the 15th and 16th c., including a *Baptism of Jesus*, a youthful work by Titian (ca. 1512), the unfinished *Christ and the Adulteress* by Palma the Elder, the *Portrait of a woman with the appearance of St. Margherita* by Giovanni Girolamo Savoldo and the *Portrait of an archer* by Lorenzo Lotto. In hall III, note also the *Romulus and Remus suckled by the she-wolf* by Pieter Paul Rubens (1617-18),

The Lupa Capitolina, a symbol of Rome

the *portrait of Gian Lorenzo Bernini* by Diego Velázquez (1630) and the portraits of *the painters Lucas* and *Cornelio de Wael* by Antonie Van Dyck; in hall IV the panel paintings, dating from the 14th to the 15th c., that document the styles of the Umbrian, Tuscan, and Emilian schools (in particular, a *St. Bartholomew* attributed to Maestro della Dormitio di Terni – 14th c. – and a *Magdalene* and *St. Bartholomew* by pupils of Pietro Lorenzetti).

After you cross through hall V, which contains an exquisite *collection of porcelain* (18th c.) donated by Francesco Cini in 1881, and *St. John the Baptist* by Caravaggio, you will reach the Sala dell'Ercole (VI), named after the colossal *Hercules* in gilt bronze, a Roman copy after an original from the 2nd c. B.C.; also note the artworks by Pietro da Cortona. In hall VII, known as the Sala di S. Petronilla, there are artworks by Giovanni Lanfranco, Domenichino, Guido Reni, and Ludovico Carracci, as well as the *Burial and Glory of St. Petronilla*, one of the most famous paintings by Guercino (1623), and *La Buona Ventura*, or the Fortune-Teller, by Caravaggio

"La Buona Ventura", or the Fortune-Teller, by Caravaggio (Pinacoteca Capitolina)

(ca. 1595). The Sala Nuova and the passageway contain other works from the 16th and 17th c.

In the exedra at the end of the courtyard of the **Museo Capitolino** is the fountain known as the *Fontana di Marforio*, from the name commonly given to the colossal river god that lies there (1st c.), one of the "talking statues" (see page 107). In a room on the right of the courtyard stands, following the demanding series of restorations done in 1981-90, the celebrated **equestrian statue of Marcus Aurelius**, which had adorned the Piazza del Campidoglio as far back as 1538, when it was moved there from St. John Lateran: the splendid group, which was mistakenly thought to be of Constantine – which assured its survival in the Middle Ages – and long a model for other similar works, depicts the emperor as he is about to address the populace after a victorious campaign, while the horse is about to place its right hoof on the head a vanquished enemy; there are still signs of the ancient gilding, which is thought to be of great supernatural importance according to popular superstition.

The Stanze Terrene, or ground floor rooms, on the left, display statues, reliefs, and inscriptions linked to the eastern cults of Mithras, Isis, and Serapis, widespread in the west during the imperial era; the Stanze

Terrene, or ground floor rooms, on the right, contain statues, busts, and sarcophagi (including the celebrated *Amendola sarcophagus with combat between Greeks and Galatians**, a Roman artwork from the 2nd c.).

The Galleria on the second floor features a noteworthy collection of Hellenistic sculptures and Roman copies after Greek originals; in particular, the *Drunken Old Woman* from an original dating back to the 3rd c. B.C., *Athena* from a 5th-c. B.C. bronze original, a *statue of a fighting warrior* reassembled in the 17th c., with the torso of the Discus-Thrower, by Myron, l'*Hercules killing the Hydra*, a 2nd-c. work restored by Alessandro Algardi in the 17th c.

The Sala delle Colombe, or hall of doves, is noteworthy for the refined mosaic from the Villa Adriana, or Hadrian's Villa, depicting *four doves drinking from a vase*, as well as for the *statuette of a little girl defending a dove*, a Roman copy after a Hellenistic original (3rd/2nd c. B.C.). The Gabinetto della Venere, or cabinet of Venus, takes its name from the renowned *Venere Capitolina**, or Capitoline Venus, a Roman replica of the Venus of Cnidus.

The Sala degli Imperatori, or hall of emperors, contains, arranged in chronological order, 65 *busts of Roman emperors*, one of the richest collections of its sort, and interesting from both a historical and an artistic point of view. The adjoining Sala dei Filosofi, or hall of philosophers, contains 79 *busts of philosophers*, *poets*, *physicians*, some Greek and some Latin, and not all identified; on the walls are Greek *votive bas-reliefs* and a *fragment of a sarcophagus*, which probably served as an iconographic model of the Deposition by Raphael.

Among the numerous sculptures located in this vast Salone, or hall, one should particularly note: the *statue of a Young Centaur* (known as the Laughing Centaur) and a *statue of an Old Centaur* (known as the Weeping Centaur), signed by Aristeas and Papias (2nd c.); a *statue of an amazed old woman*, a wonderfully effective work of Hellenistic art; the celebrated *wounded Amazon*, an excellent copy after a Greek original of the 5th c. B.C.

The Sala del Fauno (this hall is named for the *Laughing Faun* in rosso antico marble, a

Roman copy after a Hellenistic original in bronze) is preparatory for the Sala del Galata Morente, which contains works that were returned by France in 1816: at the center dominates the **Dying Galatian**, one of the most remarkable creations of ancient sculpture, unearthed in the 16th c. in the grounds of the Villa Ludovisi; near it, among other tems, are the *Amor and Psyche*, after a Hellenistic work dating from the 3rd/2nd c. 3.C.,and the *sleeping satyr*, one of the best known sculptures of antiquity.

s. Luca e Martina (8 B3). Conceded by Pope Sixtus V in 1588 to the Accademia di S. Luca; the pope added the name of St. Luke to the original title of the church (S. Martina), which belonged to the church built by Pope Honorius I in the Foro di Cesare; the reconstruction to its present-day appearance was done by Pietro da Cortona, in the years 1635-64.

The elegant facade presents a strong sense of verticality, accentuated by the central convex shape. The interior is organized according to a plan based on the Greek cross, surmounted by a cupola with a small lantern. In the floor is the tomb stone of Pietro da Cortona.

Carcere Mamertino (8 B3). This, the state penitentiary of Rome (it is the ancient "Tullanum," in which – according to a legend that has absolutely no historical foundation St. Peter was supposedly imprisoned, and baptized his fellow prisoners with water that bubbled up from an underground stream), was given its modern name during the Middle Ages, and was consecrated to S. Pietro in Carcere – St. Peter in Prison – in 1726.

The travertine facade, which dates from 4 B.C. and is preceded by a portico, conceals the older facade made of tufa stone, a material that was also used in the construction of the interior (open, 9-12 and 30-5), which dates back to the 2nd c. A.D.; the interior is linked by an aperture with a room below, into which the condemned men were dropped and then strangled.

Archeological area of the Foro Romano and the Palatino*, or the Roman Forum and the Palatine (8 B-C-D-E3-4-5). This archeological site, located between the Campidoglio, the Palatine hill, and the Via dei Fori Imperiali – which broke up the continuity between the Roman Forum and the Imperial Fora – is one of the most important archeological sites on earth.

Tradition indicates the Palatine hill as the place in which Rome was founded (the hill was nicely located to control the fords of the Tiber on a line with the Isola Tiberina and the meeting place and market that had risen near those fords, on the left bank of the river), and legend speaks of an earlier occupation of the hill by the Greeks who came from Arcadia with the king Evander and his son Pallas. Linked to the tradition of the city's origins were the cults typical of the Palatine, including that of the "Lupercalia," rites which were celebrated near the "Lupercal," a grotto at the foot of the hill where the She-Wolf supposedly suckled Romulus and Remus.

Throughout the republican age, this hill was in particular the residential quarter of the nobility and the ruling class: among the many illustrious figures who lived here were Cicero, Mark Antony, and Augustus; the latter was interested in linking his image to that of the the mythical founder of Rome; the choice of the first emperor was imitated by his successors (the palaces of Tiberius, Caligula, and Nero were all built on the Palatine), but it was especially under Domitian and Septimius Severus that the Palatine hill was transformed into the immense monumental complex of the "Palatium" (hence the name that has since come to be used for all aristocratic residences).

The decline and eventual abandonment of the Palatine, which occurred in parallel with that of the Campidoglio, dragged out from the decline and fall of Rome to the mid-16th c., when the cardinal Alessandro Farnese renovated it, converting it into his own villa (the Orti Farnesiani); excavations, which began in the late-18th c. and continue to the present day, with major finds in some cases (the discovery of the house of Augustus), have led to the almost total dismantling of that lavish Farnese estate.

The valley enclosed by the Palatine, the Campidoglio, and the Quirinal was soon the site of the growing commercial activity that spilled over from the Foro Boario and the Foro Olitorio, and by the end of the 7th c. B.C. it had become the focus of city life. The great sewer, the Cloaca Maxima, which flowed down to the Tiber, helped to drain the marshy land, reclaiming it for use in political functions ("Comitium"; the royal house that was first the site of the king and later of the pontifex maximus) as well as religious ones (cult of Vesta), so that the area was finally transformed, in the center-most area, into the Roman "piazza" par excellence: the Forum.

The final version of this zone came under

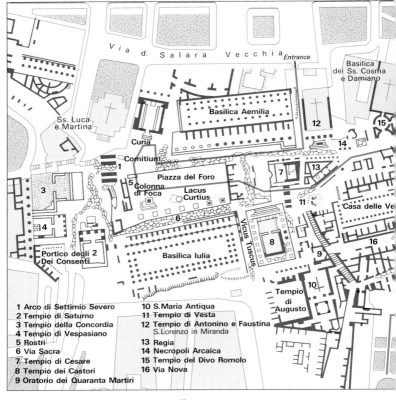

V i a d. S a l a r a V e c c h i a *Entrance*

Basilica dei Ss. Cosma e Damiano

Ss. Luca e Martina

Basilica Aemilia

Curia

Comitium

Piazza del Foro

Colonna di Foca

Lacus Curtius

Portico degli Dei Consenti

Basilica Iulia

Vicus Tuscus

Casa delle Ve

Tempio di Augusto

1 Arco di Settimio Severo
2 Tempio di Saturno
3 Tempio della Concordia
4 Tempio di Vespasiano
5 Rostri
6 Via Sacra
7 Tempio di Cesare
8 Tempio dei Castori
9 Oratorio dei Quaranta Martiri
10 S.Maria Antiqua
11 Tempio di Vesta
12 Tempio di Antonino e Faustina
    S.Lorenzo in Miranda
13 Regia
14 Necropoli Arcaica
15 Tempio del Divo Romolo
16 Via Nova

The archeological area of the Roman Forum

Caesar and Augustus (suppression of the "Comitium"), while with the construction of the Foro di Cesare and the Foro di Augusto (the forums of Caesar and Augustus) – followed by the other "imperial forums, or fora" – this area was transformed into a monumental official reception area, and preserved its structure unchanged for centuries. During the imperial age, aside from the various restorations and the construction of the temple of Antoninus and Faustina, there were only a few occasional "intrusions," in particular, the various honorary monuments (arch of Septimius Severus).

The erection in A.D. 608 of the column honoring Phocas was the last new construction in the Foro Romano, or Roman forum; the monuments were in time converted into Christian houses of worship, while the area progressively went to pasture as it was slowly silted over (Campo Vaccino).

In the Renaissance, just as studies of the ancient world were first being undertaken, the area became a remarkable quarry for building materials of every sort. Systematic excavations were undertaken at the turn of the 19th c., and they have never reall ceased since.

A tour of the archeological area begins wit the **Foro Romano**, or Roman Forum (pla above), to which you walk down from Larg Romolo e Remo along a ramp that skirts t the left the temple of Antoninus and Faust na (see page 98) and on the right the rui of the *Basilica Aemilia*, founded in 179 B.C whose name derives from the "Gens Ae milia," the clan that decorated it in the 1s c. B.C.; it was rebuilt under Augustus (th ruins that can be seen today date from tha period), and was then once again deva tated by fire, possibly during the sack c Rome by Alaric (410).

Beyond the temple of Caesar (see page 98 and, on the right, the ruins of the foundatio of the circular *aedicule of the Cloacir Venus*, stands the facade of the *Curia* which is supposed by tradition to hav been founded by Tullus Hostilius; it w rebuilt around 80 B.C. by Sulla, and the again by Caesar who had it moved to its pr sent location, and, after the great fire c 283, by Diocletian (the ruins visible da back to this period), while the modern e

Basilica di Massenzio

Antiquarium Forense

S.Francesca Romana

Arco di Tito

16

Clivus Palatinus

Uccelliere

Orti

rnesiani

N

0   25   50 m

the *"Lapis Niger,"* or black stone, that indicates what was thought to be the burial site of Romulus; as you climb down the stairway, you can see a cippus with the inscription of a "lex sacra," or holy law (the earliest example of boustrophedon in Latin: 6th c. B.C.).

The **Arch of Septimius Severus** was erected on the 10th anniversary of the ascent to the throne of that emperor; in the Middle Ages it was incorporated into other buildings. With three fornices, both sides of its attic bear a celebratory inscription that hails the victories won by the emperor and by his two sons, Caracalla and Geta, over the Parthians, the Arabs, and the Adiabeni; above the smaller openings are depictions of *episodes from the wars waged by Septimius Severus against the Parthians*; in the frieze below, note the *triumphal procession*. To the left of the arch, the *Rostri* constituted the tribune for orators, which Caesar ordered moved here from the "Comitium" during his renovation of the Forum; the platform, of exceedingly ancient origin – 3 m. tall, 24 m. long, and 12 m. wide – was decorated in 338 B.C. with the beaks of warships ("rostri") captured at Anzio.

In the area beind the Arch of Septimius Severus and the Rostra stand – aside from a circular base that once supported the "Umbilicus urbis" (the symbolic center of Rome) and the site of the "Miliarum aureum" (a column that marked the point of departure of all the imperial roads leading away from Rome) – the ruins of various ancient houses of worship.
The eight granite columns with architrave belonged to the *temple of Saturn**, one of the most highly venerated monuments in Republican Rome, which was inaugurated in 497 B.C.
On the slopes of the Campidoglio you will see the *temple of Concordia*, a reconstruction done under Tiberius of the sanctuary built by Furius Camillus in 367 B.C. to celebrate the reconciliation between patricians and plebeians, after the secession of the Aventine, the *temple of Vespasian**, built by Domitian in A.D. 81 in honor of his father and of his brother Titus, was restored by Septimius Severus and Caracalla and unearthed in 1811 by Giuseppe Valadier (three Corinthian columns remain), and the *Portico degli Dei Consenti**, probably the last major monument dedicated in Rome to pagan worship; it is structured with two wings that meet at an angle.

loration of this complex began in 1900 nd ended in 1937. It was here that the Roman senate met; along the long side of the ectangular inner room, note the three low edges, faced with marble, upon which sat he roughly 300 senators (the vote "per sessionem" entailed having those favorable on one side, and those opposed on he other); on the podium, at the end, a tatue of Victory once stood; in its place is ow a statue of a Roman in toga (possibly rajan) from the time of the empire. This is lso the temporary site of the so-called *utei of Trajan**: on the faces of the two arble parapets is a relief depiction of *sacficial victims* (boar, ram, bull), the *distribtion of food by the emperor* and the *deruction of the rolls of back taxes*.

he square just before the Curia was occupied y the *"Comitium,"* where the assemblies of the eople were held until the time of Julius Caesar, ho moved them to the Campo Marzio. eneath the level of the "platea," or plaza, are the uins of the exceedingly ancient *Santuario di ulcano*, a sanctuary of Vulcan, or "Volcanal"). art of this complex, on the surface, was the quare area paved with black marble: this was

Before the Rostri extends the *Piazza del Foro**, a large plaza with a rectangular shape (ca. 120 x 50 m.), enclosed in the distance by the temple of Caesar (see below) and bounded to the right by the *Via Sacra* – the name comes from the processions to the sanctuaries erected along its route – whose distinctive polygonal paving still survives.

Built on the site of an ancient marsh (a puteal commemorates the "Lacus Curtius"), of the many monuments that adorned it (there is documentary evidence of the equestrian statues of Domitian and Constantine) we can form some idea from the *column of Phocas*, the last honorary monument erected in the Forum, dedicated in A.D. 608 by the hexarch of Italy, Smaragdo, to the emperor of the Eastern Empire, Phocas, who had donated the Pantheon to the pope; set on a stepped base, it was once surmounted by a great bronze statue.

Beyond the Via Sacra extends the *Basilica Iulia*, in which the tribunal of the centumviri met; it was erected by Caesar in the place of the Sempronia, and was completed by Augustus; rectangular in shape (49 x 101 m.) and faced in marble, it comprises a central hall surrounded by a gallery with pillars; carved into the pavement are a number of gaming boards ("tabulae lusoriae").

The *temple of Caesar* was dedicated to the Divus Julius by Octavian Augustus in 29 B.C. (i.e., to Julius Caesar Deified) on the spot where Caesar's body had been cremated. Before the pronaos stood a terrace, partly restored in 1933, that was called the "Rostra ad Divi Julii," because it was adorned with the beaks of Egyptian warships captured at Actium in 31 B.C.

The nearby *temple of the Castori** *, also known as the Dioscuri (Castor and Pollux), was built in 484 B.C. by the son of the dictator Aulus Postumius, to fulfill the vow taken by his father during the battle of the Lacus Regillus (499 B.C.); it was rebuilt repeatedly (the three fluted columns date from the restoration done by Tiberius).

Located here is the church of **S. Maria Antiqua**, the most important – and the oldest – house of Christian worship in the Forum (it was consecrated to the Virgin Mary in the 6th c.), which was built on the site and using some of the materials of one of the rooms of the vestibule of the Imperial Palaces on the Palatine. Restored and embellished by popes John VII, Zacharias, Paul I, and Adrian I, it was abandoned following a series of earthquakes, and in the 13th c. the church of S. Maria Liberatrice was built here, and was demolished in 1900 to restore the previously existing building.

This church contains a remarkable array of wall paintings, beginning with the fresco in the right side aisle, which was originally in the atrium, depicting the *Virgin Mary as Queen, Enthroned, among Angels and Saints* (Pope Adrian I, the client, is shown with a square halo); in the left aisle, note the pagan and Christian sarcophagi (note the one with *stories of Jonah*), on the walls are *stories from the Old Testament* (upper band) and *the Savior* and *saints of the Greek and Latin*

Church (lower band); in the apse, with a handsome floor with geometric designs, note the *Christ Giving a Benediction and the Virgin Mary Presenting Pope Paul I* (with the square halo); in the chapel to the left of the apse, frescoes dating from the reign of Pope Zacharias: in the rectangular niche at the end *Crucifixion**.

To the right of the church is the so-called *temple of Augustus*, which features a hall – rebuilt at the end of the 1st c. – in which ruins have surfaced possibly parts of commercial structures dating back to the 1st c. B.C.

Skirting the right side of the temple of Caesar, you may note the circular base and a number of fragments from the *temple of Vesta**, rebuilt once again under the reign of Septimius Severus, which contained the fatal objects which were thought to have determined the fortune of Rome.

The *Casa delle Vestali*, or house of the Vestals, was the site of a female priesthood said to have been founded by Numa Pompilius to guard a sacred flame; this edifice was rebuilt by Nero after the great fire of A.D. 64, and restored and enlarged repeatedly thereafter: it comprised a large rectangular atrium, surrounded by a two-story portico; the rooms on the sides of the great hall at the end were used as warehouses for the sacred furnishings, while the long sides were lined with the sleeping quarters of the priestesses and other rooms.

Lying before the temple of Vesta are the foundations of the *Regia*, traditionally said to have been the home of Numa Pompilius which was the home of the first priest of Rome and the site of the sacrarium of Mars as well as of the altar upon which sacrifices were made to Jove, Juno, and Janus the structures that can be seen nowadays date from the 6th c. B.C.

Dedicated by the Roman Senate to the deified wife of Antoninus Pius and, after his death, also dedicated to that emperor, the *temple of Antoninus and Faustina**, once included the columns made of cipollino in the pronaos, which stand 17 m. tall; the building, of which the podium has survived intact (the steps are almost entirely the result of reconstruction) was transformed into the church of S. Lorenzo in Miranda in the 7th/8th c.

To the right of the temple, grassy beds mark out the tombs of the *archaic necropolis*, excavated in 1902 (the materials are now housed in the Antiquarium Forense) the burial sites used by the earliest inhabitants of the Palatine, between the end of the 10th c. and the 8th c. B.C.

The successive structure, the *temple of the God Romulus** was begun at the behest of Maxentius in honor of his son, and was completed under Constantine; the facade features a portal, originally part of an older building, with the original bronze *door* (the keyhole is one of the oldest on earth). In the rear hall, during the 6th to 7th c., the basilica of Ss. Cosma e Damiano was installed (see page 59).

The immense ruins that you can see on your left as you continue to climb belong to the **basilica of Maxentius**, which was also begun under Maxentius in A.D. 308 and was completed by Constantine (hence the other name by which it is known). Set upon a platform measuring 100 x 65 m., the interior was divided up into three aisles; the central aisle, or nave (80 x 25 m., with a height of 35 m.) was covered with a cross vault while the side aisles were covered with barrel vaults; the ruins that can be seen belonged to the right aisle, where you can see the apse added by Constantine near the new entrance giving onto the Via Sacra (the original entrance overlooked the Colosseum). The exceedingly lavish marble decoration and the slabs of gilt bronze that

The House of the Vestals, in the Roman Forum

covered the roof were all removed; the slabs of gilt bronze were used by Pope Honorius I in 626 to cover the first St. Peter's. After you have reached the top, on your right you will see the arch of Titus (see below), and on the left the former monastery of S. Francesca Romana (the church of the same name is described at page 60), where

the *Antiquarium Forense* is located, a museum containing material found in the area of the Roman Forum. In hall I, at the center, is a model of the archaic necropolis of the Forum; in the display windows, *pottery and earthenware* and *furnishings* of the tombs, both crematory and ditch (9th/8th c. B.C.), and small *vases* with relief decorations; on the walls, drawings and photographs of the excavations. In halls II-V, a reconstruction of the *burial tombs* for children, made out of tree trunks and dating back to the 8th/7th c. B.C.; imported *Greek ceramics* and materials from the excavations in the area of the temple of Vesta; *votive statuettes* made of bronze, *architectural terracotta* and a mould of the archaic inscription of the "Lapis Niger." The halls VI-IX feature archaic *antefixes*, *inscriptions*, and fragments of *Greek ceramics* dating back to the 6th or 5th c. B.C.; *imperial busts*, a fragment of a frieze with the *myth of Aeneas and of the origins of Rome* taken from the Basilica Aemilia, a *torso of Victory* from the Basilica Iulia, the *group of the Dioscuri* and the *statue of Apollo* taken from the Fonte di Giuturna, and a series of medieval *paintings*, detached from the walls of the churches of S. Adriano and S. Maria Antiqua. In the cloister, there are architectural and decorative fragments, inscriptions, and capitals.

To commemorate the victories of Vespasian and Titus over the Jews, victories which included the taking of Jerusalem and the destruction of the Temple, Domitian ordered the construction of the **Arch of Titus**, with a single fornix, with fluted columns faced in marble, incorporated during the Middle Ages into the fortified constructions erected by the clan of the Frangipane and liberated from those structures only in 1821 by Giuseppe Valadier, who supplied the missing section. In the decorative apparatus, note the reliefs in the arch, depicting the *triumphal procession leading the way for the emperor, and bearing, as booty of war, the wealth of the temple of Solomon* (right) and the *imperial quadriga bearing Titus, accompanied by Victory, shown crowning him* (left), and, in the middle of the coffered vault, the *Apotheosis of Titus*.

A marked itinerary takes you along the "Clivus Palatinus" in the archeological area of the **Palatine** (plan page 100-101), which was occupied in the mid-16th c. by the Orti Farnesiani, or Farnese gardens, built at the behest of Pope Paul III, on behalf of the cardinal Alessandro Farnese by Vignola, at first, and later by Jacopo Del Duca and Girolamo Rainaldi. Closed off toward the Forum by a retaining wall, and accessible through a portal, that has since been moved to the Via di S. Gregorio, one once entered these gardens through a system of ramps that, beyond the two stacked fountains, ran up to the upper terrace (a splendid view of the excavations), where the *Uccelliere*, or aviary, still stands, one of the few 16th-c. structure spared during the archeological excavations.

The garden in the rear (the complex has contained since 1625 the first botanical garden on earth) conceals the *Domus Tiberiana*, an imperial residence which was built on houses dating from the late republic, and which was later incorporated into the Domus Aurea.

At the western end of the terrace, a stairway descends to one of the most significant areas of the dig. The podium on the right belongs to the *temple of the Magna Mater*, erected to Cybele in 204 B.C. and, after the restoration done at the end of the 2nd c. B.C., rebuilt again by Augustus in 3; the black stone was kept here, symbol of the goddess. Not far away, archeologists have also unearthed the *temple of Victory*, built in 294 B.C. and restored in the 1st c. B.C.; at the end of the 1940s, archeologists found three *huts** here, dating from the early Iron Age, which are evidence of the first settlement of future Rome right on the Palatine, thus confirming the legend that the house of Romulus was here.

Also of special note is the so-called **Casa di Livia**, celebrated for the splendid paintings that adorn the triclinium (*false windows with views*) and the dining room (*mythological scenes* in the Pompeiian style and, on the right, *Mercury preparing to liberate Io from the captivity of Argus*).

Because of its elegance and the beauty of the ornamentation, this was long thought to be the **house of Augustus**, which however was later recognized as having been in a nearby structure, on two floors, part of a complex of constructions – which also include the Greek and Latin libraries, a temple of Apollo, and a series of porticoes – built around 36 B.C. This "domus," too, was later incorporated into constructions of the Flavian age, and is rich in paintings of exceedingly high artistic quality, which can be admired in the so-called Stanza delle Maschere, or room of masks (decorations linked to theatrical settings) and in the Stanza delle Prospettive and the Studiolo. Just prior to the beginning of the *cryptoporticus of Nero*, a subterranean passage that linked the imperial buildings, you can climb up to the floor of the Imperial Palace,

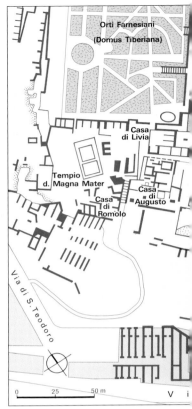

The archeological area of the Palatine

comprising the Domus Flavia, the Domus Augustana, and the Stadium Palatinum.

The *Palazzo dei Flavi**, or palace of the Flavians, was the true imperial palace of Rome in the sense that it was the center of the various official functions of the state: in the three-aisle *Basilica*, the emperor listened to the debating of lawsuits (keep in mind that it was possible to appeal directly to the emperor from the earliest years of the Roman empire), the *Aula Regia* was used for imperial audiences, and the *Lararium* served as a private chapel.

A very large peristyle separates the three reception rooms, from the imperial *triclinium*, and the dining room; note the luxury indicated by the remains of the marble floor in the left side of the hall and in the raised apse.

In the 16th c., upon the ruins of the Domus Flavia, the Villa Stati Mattei was built, and then enlarged by Virginio Vespignani in 1855. All that survived the demolition of the complex was the so-called *Loggetta Mat-*

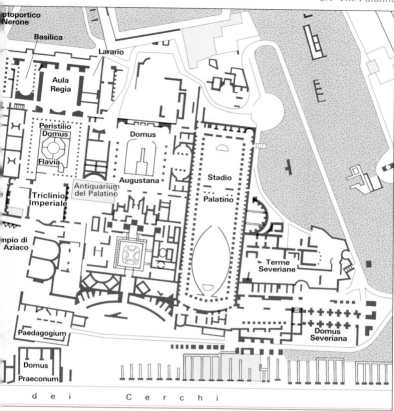

tei, with frescoes attributed to Baldassarre Peruzzi or his school, and the 19th-c. building that is now the site of the *Antiquarium del Palatino*, which contains sculptures uncovered on the Palatine from 1870 to the modern day, and a series of stuccoes and frescoes, from the reign of Augustus right up to late antiquity. Among the most noteworthy artworks, we should point out: bas-reliefs with Egyptian carvings, executed in marble at Rome; fragments of frescoes with *the figure of Apollo* and *small putti riding rams* (1st c.); an exquisite *Leda and the Swan* of clear Hellenistic inspiration; two *heads of Attis* and two ideal *heads*, Roman copies after Greek originals from the 5th c. B.C.; a *statue of a young boy* in green basalt; a *head of Athena Promachos** (late-6th c. B.C.); a *bust of a man* from the reign of Augustus, and a *torso of Mercury*, a Roman work inspired by a Greek original from the 5th c. B.C.

Adjoining the Domus Flavia is the *Domus Augustana*, part of the imperial residence until the capital was moved.

If you skirt the peristyle while heading to-

ward the Circus Maximus, you can see from on high (the "domus" occupied two or three floors) the *"Paedagogium"*, site of the college of the imperiale pages, built during the reign of Domitian, and the *Domus Praeconum*, a wing of the Imperial Palace.

The *Stadium Palatinum*, ordered built by Domitian and restored under Septimius Severus, was surrounded on the interior with a two-story portico, in which the imperial tribune stood, at the center of the east side; the oval enclosure was built in the high Middle Ages, possibly by Theodoric. Lastly, the ruins of the *Domus Severiana**, an expansion of the Domus Augustana ordered by Septimius Severus (panoramic view*); this palace was built with the bath facilities whose ruins can be seen near the curve of the Stadium.

Set on the southern slopes of the Palatine hill was the Settizodio, a monumental nymphaeum commissioned by Septimius Severus and demolished at the end of the 16th c. by Pope Sixtus V, who re-used a number of parts of it in his Cappella Sistina, or Sistine Chapel, in the basilica of S. Maria Maggiore.

2.5 From Piazza Venezia to the Trinità dei Monti

This route runs through the most charming area in Rome, punctuated by landmarks and pieces of architecture that extend over the historic lifespan of the city. Streets, monuments, and urban spaces of all sorts underscore the remarkable stratification that is the result of centuries of occupation of this area, where one can witness the succession – at times, harmonious; in all cases, noteworthy – of various functions linked to the city's immense political history. We should not overlook the remarkable urbanistic quality of this area, the result of a steady process of reclamation that, in terms of the scope and the quality of the projects, is perhaps unrivalled in all of Italy.

Carriage in Piazza di Spagna

After taking the Via del Corso from Piazza Venezia as far as the church of S. Maria in Via Lata, and after turning off to the left and following the brief Via Lata, the walking tour sets off from Piazza del Collegio Romano, and is punctuated in the first section by several of the most important complexes in Rome (church of S. Maria sopra Minerva, the Pantheon, church of S. Luigi dei Francesi), set in an urban context that in more than one point still has an ancient feeling.

Beyond the "political focal point" of Palazzo Madama, the church of S. Ivo alla Sapienza is a bellwether of the artistic battles between Borromini and Bernini, which, in the neighboring and renowned Piazza Navona – one of the most remarkable urban landscapes in Rome – left evident traces in the fountain, or Fontana dei Fiumi and in the church of S. Agnese in Agone, while Pietro da Cortona was the architect of the elegant Baroque setting of Piazza di S. Maria della Pace, where the church of S. Maria della Pace contains masterpieces by Raphael,

and the first Roman project by Bramante; there are also splendid artworks by the Sansovino, Raphael, and Caravaggio in the church of S. Agostino.

The tour then penetrates into the Rione Campo Marzio, running along the famous Via dei Condotti, and culminating in the Baroque festivity of the Spanish Steps, or Scalinata di Trinità dei Monti, heralded by Bernini's fountain, or Fontana della Barcaccia and by Borromini's Palazzo di Propaganda Fide.

Collegio Romano (6 D4). Built at the behest of St. Ignatius Loyola for those who wished to become members of the Company of Jesus, and inaugurated on 28 October 1584 (and now attributed to the architect Giuseppe Valeriano), this complex – which covers an area of 13,400 sq. m. including the church of S. Ignazio (see page 50) – once contained the library which served as the original core of the Biblioteca Nazionale Centrale "Vittorio Emanuele II" (see page 32), the Museo Kircheriano, the Spezieria, and the Osservatorio Astronomico, an astronomical observatory; after it became property of the government, part of the school was set aside for the Liceo-Ginnasio "Ennio Quirino Visconti" – the first high school in the capital – while the rest of the building was occupied by the Museo Nazionale Preistorico-Etnografico "Luigi Pigorini" (a museum, now at EUR: see page 177), and from 1975 on, by the Ministero per i Beni Culturali e Ambientali, or ministry for culture and the environment.

Atop the central wing of the facade is a clock, to which all other clocks in Rome were set; on the right is a tower for astronomical observations, built in 1787.

S. Maria sopra Minerva* (6 D3-4). This church is named after the temple of Minerva Calcidica, upon the ruins of which it stands. It belonged to the Greek nuns of Campo Marzio and, later, to the Dominican order – who have occupied the convent since the 13th c. – and it was rebuilt beginning in 1280 and opened for worship in the mid-14th c. Nearly a century later, Cardinal

Giovanni Torquemada had the nave covered with a vault, reducing its height. In the 16th c., Giuliano da Sangallo made changes on the area around the choir, while in the 17th c., Carlo Maderno enlarged the apse, modified the triumphal arch, redecorated the interior in accordance with the Baroque style, and modified the facade. The unsuccessful attempt to restore the original Gothic forms of the interior dates from 1848-55.

The front (restored in 1992) is punctuated by three portals: the side portals feature frescoed lunettes, while the central portal – with pediment – is attributed to Meo del Caprino; set into it are inscriptions, heraldic crests, and, near the right corner, plaques concerning the floods of the Tiber from 1422 until 1870.

The interior is split up into a nave and two aisles, with a cross vault, a transept, and two chapels on either side of the presbytery; the *holy-water stoups* with putti date from 1638; to the right of the central portal is the *funerary monument to Diotisalvi Neroni* (1482) of the school of Andrea Bregno.

The 2nd chapel (Cappella Caffarelli) in the right aisle is noteworthy for the *S. Luigi Bertrando* by Baciccia on the altar, and, above it, a *St. Dominick* attributed to the Cavalier d'Arpino. In the 7th chapel, on the right wall, is the *sepulcher of the bishop Giovanni de Coca* (1477) by Andrea Bregno (the fresco with *Christ as Judge, between Two Angels* is attributed to Melozzo da Forlì and Antoniazzo Romano); on the left is the *sepulcher of the bishop Benedetto Soranzo* (1495) of the school of Bregno.

In the right transept, the *Cappella Carafa* * (restored, 1989-91), with an entrance arch attributed to Mino da Fiesole, Verrocchio, and Giuliano da Maiano (the figures of the young boys are attributed to Luigi Capponi), preserves a *frescoed decoration* * by Filippino Lippi (1488-93); on the left wall, note the *sepulcher of Pope Paul IV* (1559) designed by Pirro Ligorio. Alongside it is the *funerary chapel of the cardinal*, also decorate by Lippi, together with Raffaellino del Garbo. To the left of the Cappella Carafa, note the *sepulcher of Guglielmo Durand* (1296) by Giovanni di Cosma (signed). In the next chapel, the Cappella Altieri, *St. Peter Presents Five Blessed to the Virgin Mary* by Carlo Maratta, and, in the lunette on the far end, *Glory of the Holy Trinity*, a fresco by Baciccia (1671-72).

Against the pillar to the left of the presbytery, **statue of Christ Risen** by Michelangelo (1519-20). Beneath the main altar, note the *sarcophagus of St. Catherine of Siena* at-

tributed to Isaia da Pisa. The Gothic choir was transformed in 1536 to contain the *funerary monuments of Pope Clement VII** and *Pope Leo X** by Antonio da Sangallo the Younger (1536-41): on an elegantly decorated base, four fluted columns surround three entrances with statues, while above the trabeation is a high tripartite attic, decorated with reliefs; the *statue of Clement VII* is by Nanni di Baccio Bigio, while the *statue of Leo X* is by Raffaello da Montelupo, and the *prophets* and high reliefs are by Baccio Bandinelli.

In the vestibule of the left transept, note the *tomb of the cardinal Matteo Orsini* (1340), the *tomb of the cardinal Domenico Pimentel*, designed by Gian Lorenzo Bernini and executed by Ercole Ferrata, and the *burial slab of Fra Angelico* (1455; restored 1975) by Isaia da Pisa. In the Cappella Frangipane, and chapel formerly known as the Cappella Maddaleni Capiferro, *Virgin Mary with Christ Child* from the workshop of Fra Angelico; on the left, *sepulcher of Giovanni Alberini*, attributed either to Agostino di Duccio or Mino da Fiesole, incorporating a Roman sarcophagus depicting Hercules wrestling the lion. In the chamber, or *Camera di S. Caterina* (1637), note the detached *frescoes* by Antoniazzo Romano (1482-83). On the wall right at the beginning of the left aisle, note the *Virgin Mary with Christ Child, and the Two Young Saints John*, a remarkable group dating from 1670. On the 2nd pillar, *funerary monument of Maria Raggi* by Bernini (1643), which also contains the *tomb of Giovanni Vigevano* (1630) between the 4th and 3rd chapels. Near the left door of the church, note the *tomb of Francesco Tornabuoni** (1480), one of Mino da Fiesole's finest works; above it is the *tomb of the cardinal Tebaldi* by Bregno and Giovanni Dalmata (1466).

The adjoining cloister features frescoes from the early-17th c. and noteworthy 15th-c. *tombs*, including the tomb of the *Cardinal Pietro Ferricci* attributed to Mino da Fiesole. Since 1725 the convent has housed the *Biblioteca Casanatense*, a library specializing in Church history.

At the center of the square that stands before the church is the *"Pulcin della Minerva"* – "Pulcin" meaning "chickadee" – an Egyptian obelisk dating from the 6th c. B.C., unearthed in 1665 in the area of the Iseo Campense; it stands on the back of a marble elephant designed by Bernini and carved in 1667 by Ercole Ferrata.

Piazza della Rotonda (6 C-D3). Dominated by the cylindrical mass of the Pantheon (see below) – hence the other name, of

Piazza del Pantheon, by which this square is known – it is characterized by the 18th-c. facade of palazzi which in part reflect the porticoed area which stood before the temple in antiquity.

The *fountain*, designed by Giacomo Della Porta and carved by Leonardo Sormani by 1575, was "completed" in 1711, at the behest of Pope Clement XI, with the *obelisk of Rameses II*, taken from the Iseo Campense.

Pantheon * (6 D3). One of the most renowned monuments of ancient Rome, due to its state of preservation, vast size, and skillful construction, this temple stands out for the remarkably stylistic typology, whereby the round cella with a thermal type cupola or dome is contaminated with the traditional pedimented pronaos, typical of normal temples.

The building was erected in 27 B.C. by Marcus Vipsanius Agrippa, son-in-law of Augustus; following the restorations completed by Domitian and Trajan, it was rebuilt entirely in A.D. 118-125 by Hadrian (the fact that the inscription from the original temple was set on the pediment of the new building long confused attempts to establish the correct age of the building), and was finally completed under Antoninus Pius; restored in 202 by Septimius Severus and Caracalla but then abandoned, the Pantheon was ceded in A.D. 608 by Phocas, the emperor of Byzantium, to Pope Boniface IV, who dedicated it to the Virgin Mary and all the martyrs. In the Middle Ages, it was used as a fortress, while in 1625, at the orders of Urban VIII Barberini, the bronze sheating of the beams of the portico was removed to cast 80 cannon for Castel S. Angelo and the four tortile columns of the baldachin of St. Peter's (hence the renowned pasquinade, "Quod non fecerunt barbari, fecerunt Barberini," i.e., 'what the barbarians didn't destroy, the Barberini did...'); in 1870 the Pantheon was made the sacrarium of the kings of Italy, and was restored with the elimination of the gates of the pronaos (they had been installed to prevent the market which was held on the square from extending all the way to the temple) and the demolition of the bell towers by Bernini (the so-called "orecchie d'asino," or donkey's ears).

The pronaos, 33 m. in width and 16 m. in depth, features 16 monolithic columns (eight on the front and the other arranged to form three aisles) made of grey and pink granite, 13 m. tall; the bronze doors of the portal date back to a reconstruction done during the time of Pope Pius Pio IV; on either side of the portal are two niches, probably intended for the statues of Augustus and Agrippa. The rotunda has brick walls 6.2 m. thick; the dome, 43.3 m. in diameter is made of concrete.

The interior is made up of seven semicircular and rectangular niches, with two monolithic fluted marble columns on the front, each 8.9 m. tall, while the far niche is surmounted by an arch, symmetical with the arch over the entrance; in the space between the niches are eight aedicules with small columns that support pediments. In the vault, decorated with five registers of coffers, there is an oculus, about 9 m. across, and bordered with bronze. This is the only high opening in the building; the marble floor, with inscribed squares and circles, is largely original.

In the 1st chapel on the right, *Annunciation*, a fresco attributed to Melozzo da Forlì. In the 2nd chapel, *tomb of Vittorio Emanuele II* first king of Italy (d. 1878), designed by Manfredo Manfredi. In the aedicule between the 5th and 6th chapels, *tomb of Raphael*, an ancient sarcophagus made of Greek marble, with a well known Latin couplet composed by Bembo engraved on the front: "Ille hic est Raphael timuit quo sospite vinci, rerum magna parens et moriente mori" (here lies that Raphael by whom, when he was alive, nature, the great mother of all things, feared being bested; when he died, nature feared death); above, *Madonna del Sasso* *, sculpture by Lorenzetto (1520) commissioned by Raphael for his own tomb. In the 6th chapel, *tombs of Umberto I* (1900; Giuseppe Sacconi) and Margherita di Savoia. In the 7th chapel (Cappella dei Virtuosi del Pantheon) *funerary epigraphs of the "virtuosi" Flaminio Vacca* (1605), *Taddeo Zuccari* (1566) and *Perin del Vaga* (1547).

The Via del Pantheon, which runs off from the north side of the Piazza della Rotonda, leads to the Piazza della Maddalena, overlooked by the church of **S. Maria Maddalena** (6 C3), one of the most representative pieces of late-Baroque Roman architecture, originally built around a 14th c. chapel that was entrusted in 1586 to St. Camillo de Lellis as the center of the Ministri degli Infermi, a charitable organization; the so-called Minsters of the Infirm decided to rebuild it in 1621. The lively facade (restored, 1987), added in 1735 by Giuseppe Sardi, is the most noteworthy piece of Rococo architecture in Rome. The interior – with an elliptical nave with chapels along the sides, a transept, and a cupola – is a notable blend of a longitudinal plan with a central plan.

Following the right side of the church, in the Via delle Colonnelle, you will reach the Piazza

Night-time view of Piazza della Rotonda with the Pantheon

apranica, named after the stern *Palazzo Capra-ica** (6 C3), a typical example of a building rom the early Roman Renaissance. Built in 1451 with the incorporation of existing houses and the Cappella di S. Agnese – a chapel that still hous-s the noteworthy panel of the *Virgin Mary En-throned, with the Christ Child, Two Saints, and the ardinals Capranica* by Antoniazzo Romano (c. 451) – this building was the site of the Collegio apranica, founded in 1456 by Cardinal Domeni-o as a place to educate young people pursuing n ecclesiastic career (it was the first school of :s sort in Rome), it is now mostly occupied by he *Cinema Capranica*, one of the oldest movie ouses in Rome.

. Luigi dei Francesi (6 C2). The church was egun in 1518 for the future Clement VII nd was completed in 1589 by Domenico ontana to plans by Giacomo Della Porta. he broad facade, made of travertine, fea-ures two registers of differing sizes; it is di-ided into five bays: in the lower register here are three portals and two niches, con-aining *statues of Charlemagne* and *St. Louis* y Pierre l'Estache (1746); in the upper reg-ster, with a central balcony, the niches ontain *statues of St. Clotilde* and *St. Joan of alois*, also by L'Estache.

nside, the nave and two side aisles are unctuated by pillars, the rich marble and tucco decoration was designed by Antoine)érizet (1756-64); at the center of the vault, *)eath and apotheosis of St. Louis* (1756). In he 2nd chapel on the right, *St. Cecilia, St. 'aul, St. John the Evangelist, St. Augustine, nd St. Mary Magdalene*, a copy by Guido Leni of the original by Raphael in the Pina-oteca Nazionale of Bologna, an art gallery; he frescoed decoration (*stories of St. Ce-ilia*) is a masterpiece by Domenichino

(1616-17). In the 5th chapel on the left (Cap-pella Contarelli): **St. Matthew and the Angel** (altar), **Martyrdom of St. Matthew** (right wall) and **Vocation of St. Matthew** (left wall), masterpieces* by Caravaggio (1597-1602); in the vault, frescoes by the Cavalier d'Arpino.

The Via della Dogana Vecchia runs south from the square that lies before the church, skirting to the left along the *Palazzo Giustiniani* (6 C-D3), be-gun by Giovanni and Domenico Fontana in 1585-87 and completed in 1678, possibly by Francesco Borromini; it was in this building in 1947 that the Constitution of the Italian Republic was signed (the palazzo is now the residence of the Presi-dent of the Senato).
The square that lies a little further along takes its name from the church of *S. Eustachio* (6 D3), founded, according to legend, by Constantine on the site in which that saint was martyred, and re-stored in 1196; the *campanile* dates back to the 12th c., and has twin-light mullioned windows, now partly walled up; the 18th-c. renovation re-sulted in the bronze and polychrome-marble *main altar* (Nicola Salvi, 1739), surmounted by *baldachin* by Ferdinando Fuga (1746).

Palazzo Madama (6 C-D2). The name of this palazzo comes from Madama Margheri-ta d'Austria, the widow of Alessandro de' Medici; the palazzo was built in 1503 by Giovanni de' Medici on a 15th-c. core struc-ture, and was enlarged in 1512; its present-day appearance was the work of Paolo Marucelli (1637-42), although it did under-go further transformations during the reigns of popes Benedict XIV and Pius IX. Since 1871 it has housed the Italian Senato, or sen-ate; it presents a sumptuous facade (re-stored in 1991) with a portal set on columns, surmounted by a balcony, windows with lavish cornices, an entablature with a frieze studded with putti, and remarkable chimneys. The Sala d'Onore (to visit, contact the office of the Questura del Senato) is decorated with frescoes (in the vault *Italia tricolore*, on the walls *episodes of the Senate of ancient Rome*) by Cesare Maccari (1880).

Palazzo della Sapienza (6 D2). The venerable Università Romana, or university of Rome – based here from the reign of Eugene IV (1431-47) until 1935, when the Città Universitaria was inaugurated (see page 164) – was founded by Pope Boniface VIII in 1303, but the complex (now the site of the *Archivio di Stato di Roma*, or state archives of Rome; documents of the Papal State from the 9th to the 19th c.), was begun in the 16th c., to plans by Guidetto Guidetti, under the supervision of Pirro Ligorio and, after further work by Giacomo Della Porta, was completed in the early-17th c.; beginning in 1632 more work was done by Francesco Borromini, who built the facade overlooking the Piazza di S. Eustachio, with an elegant portal surmounted by a balcony and arched window, and, at the end of the courtyard, with two orders of arches (restored in 1992), the church of **S. Ivo** (1642-50), perhaps his masterpiece, and one of the best known and loved creations of Roman Baroque. The church is a complete synthesis of the rhythms and proportions of the courtyard, which are further expressed and resolved in the spiraling cupola and in the cusped little lantern. On the main altar, designed by G.B. Contini (1684), *Saints Ivo, Leo, Pantaleone, Luke, and Catherine of Alexandria in glory of angels*, a canvas by Pietro da Cortona (1661).

Piazza Navona* (6 C-D2). Extraordinary urbanistic complex created in Baroque Rome – and one of the most spectacular and popular sites in the city – Piazza Navona takes its unusual shape and size from the underlying *stadium of Domitian*, built prior to A.D. 86 (it was 275 m. in length, 106 m. in width, and could accommodate about 30,000 spectators) on land which, during the reigns of Caesar and Augustus, had contained a wooden enclosure, and where Nero had ordered the construction of an amphitheater for the "ludi quinquennali," or five-year games. On the site of the stadium – some ruins of which can be seen in a palazzo in Piazza di Tor Sanguigna, while others are visible in the underground rooms of S. Agnese in Agone (see below) – rose, from the 13th c. on, houses and towers, and in the Renaissance, churches and palazzi, while the market of the Campidoglio was moved to the square in 1477.

The name is a corruption of the work for the games that were held here (the succession was "agone," "nagone," "navone," and "navona"), but – since the name "navona" also seems to describe a large ship in Italian – the form probably stuck in part as well because it was common practice to flood the square for the processions by boat of prelates and princes in August; decorated carriages were also paraded through the square for Roman Carnevale.

A popular tourist attraction and meeting spot, when the weather is fine, the square maintains an old tradition, into the small hours: that of the stalls that sell sweets and toys, from the beginning of December until the day of Epiphany.

Fontana dei Fiumi* (6 D2). Of Rome's three renowned fountain sites, arranged along the central line of the square and fed by the *Acqua Vergine*, or Aqua Virgo, this one is

The Fontana dei Fiumi in Piazza Navona

certainly the most famous and the loveliest. Gian Lorenzo Bernini designed it in 1651 for Innocent X as a rock-like base with a lion and a horse drinking deeply: at the corners sit the colossal personifications of the *Nile* (Giacomo Antonio Fancelli), the *Ganges* (Claude Poussin), the *Danube* (Antonio Raggi), and the *Rio Plata* (Francesco Baratta), which according to popular tradition express the rivalry between Bernini and Borromini; the *obelisk* atop the fountain dates from the time of Domitian, and came originally from the circus of Maxentius.

Also based on a design by Bernini is the *Fontana del Moro* (6 D2), a fountain named for the Ethiopian depicted struggling with a dolphin, carved by Giovanni Antonio Mari. Symmetrical to this fountain is the *Fontana del Nettuno* (6 C2), designed by Giacomo Della Porta (1576), and adorned with sculptures only in 1878.

S. Agnese in Agone* (6 D2).

Built between the 8th c. and 1123 on the site on which, according to tradition, St. Agnes was pilloried nude, only to be later miraculously covered by her hair (the miracle is depicted in a marble relief by Alessandro Algardi set on an altar in one of the rooms beneath), this church was given its modern appearance by Girolamo and Carlo Rainaldi in 1652, and was completed by Francesco Borromini in 1653-57 (hence, it is said, the expressions of fear and disdain on the faces of the personifications of the world's rivers in the fountain by Bernini, Borromini's rival), who designed the concave facade with a single register of pillars and columns, surmounted by a dome, as well as the twin bell towers.

The interior still conserves – of the original plan by Rainaldi – the Greek cross and the niches on the cross vault. The cupola, supported by eight columns, was frescoed (*Glory of Paradise*) by Ciro Ferri in 1689, while the spandrels were frescoed (*Cardinal Virtues*) by Baciccia in 1665. On the altars, from the right, works by Giovanni Francesco Rossi, Ercole Ferrata, Domenico Guidi, Antonio Raggi, and Melchiorre Caffà. Above the entrance, *monument to Innocent X*, a pope who is buried, with other members of the Pamphilj family, in a crypt to the left of the main altar, by G.B. Maini (1730).

In the underground chambers, which you enter through a door set in the right wall of the second altar, you can see ruins of the circus of Domitian (see page 106), a Roman mosaic floor, and, on the wall, medieval frescoes.

To the left of the church is the broad flat facade of *Palazzo Pamphilj* (6 D2), built by Girolamo Rainaldi in 1644-50 and now the site of the Brazilian embassy, the Casa del Brasile (Brazilian House), and the Centro di Cultura Italo-Brasiliano (Italian/Brazilian cultural center).

Opposite the palazzo is the church of *Nostra Signora del Sacro Cuore* (6 D2), formerly the church of S. Giacomo degli Spagnoli, built – possibly by Bernardo Rossellino – on occasion of the Jubilee year of 1450

The interior, modelled after the German Hallenkirche," has a nave and two aisles, with a cross vault, punctuated by lobate pillars. In the 3rd bay, note the Renaissance *choir chancel* in polychrome marble by Pietro Torrigiani. Behind the main altar, note the tripartite marble *backdrop* * to the serlian window by Pietro and Domenico Rosselli (turn of the 16th c.). The 2nd *chapel* on the left (*Cappella di S. Giacomo*), by Antonio da Sangallo the Younger, features side frescoes by Pellegrino da Modena.

Pasquino and the "talking statues" (6 D2).

Set against the rear elevation of the Palazzo Braschi (see page 68) is all that survives of a Hellenistic torso (the group it belonged to depicted Menelaus supporting Patroclus), that was admired by Michelangelo.

It is said that, following the death of Pasquino, a talented master tailor of Rome who was famous for his biting comments on the powerful, on the wrongs and injustices of the authorities, around 1500, a statue was unearthed on the spot where Pasquino's house had stood; the statue had previously been buried three-quarters of the way, and the part that emerged was used as a mud-scraper: the torso of that statue was mounted on a pedestal.

Following the style and the example of the late Pasquino, anonymous authors of satires, epigrams, and denunciations against corruption and high-handed abuses of power – these were often learned men of the cloth, who would hold debates, in the so-called "congresso degli arguti," or congress of wits – would attach their little libels to the pedestal of this statue, known throughout Rome as the Pasquino: and those epigrams were called "pasquinades."

Quite soon Pasquino had someone to talk to, as it were, in the statue of Marforio (see page 94), who received the replies to the pasquinades.

In time, their numbers multiplied, with Madama Lucrezia (see page 57), the Abate Luigi (see page 67), the Facchino, and the Babuino (see page 48).

Via del Governo Vecchio (6 C-D1).

This street, once the site of papal processions – inasmuch as it was part of the medieval *"Via Papalis"* between St. Peter's and St. John Lateran, corresponding to the Via dei Banchi Nuovi, Via del Governo Vecchio, Via di S. Pantaleo, and Via di Torre Argentina – is renowned for its antique shops. The *Palazzo del Governo Vecchio* (6 C-D1) from which the street takes its name, stands at n. 39, and has been allowed to deteriorate shockingly; it was built in 1473-77 by the Milanese cardinal Stefano Nardini (and the building is sometimes called the Palazzo Nardini), who was made governor of Rome by Pope Paul II; the palazzo was used from 1624 as the headquarters of the governor. The facade, dating from the Renaissance but somewhat remodelled since, features on the second floor a set of architraved windows, with the name Nardini and the date 1477; the marble portal bears a frieze with little palm motifs.

S. Maria della Pace* (6 C1). Rebuilt beginning in 1482, possibly by Baccio Pontelli, this church was restored in 1656, at the behest of Pope Alexander VII, by Pietro da Cortona, who added the convex Baroque facade, preceded by a semicircular pronaos with twin Doric columns, serving as a sort of theatrical backdrop for the Piazza di S. Maria della Pace.

The interior comprises a short nave with two bays and cross vaults, which still maintains its 15th-c. structure, and by a dome tribune. In the **nave**, the 1st *chapel* on the right (*Cappella Chigi*), by Raphael, features

The Church of S. Maria della Pace

a bronze high relief (*Christ Transported by Angels*) by Cosimo Fancelli and, on either side, marble sculptures (*St. Catherine* and *St. Bernardino*) by Fancelli and by Ercole Ferrata. Above the arch of the chapel, *Sibyls** (from left, the *Cumaean Sibyl*, *Persian Sibyl*, *Phrygian Sibyl*, and *Tiburtine Sibyl*), painted in 1514 on behalf of Agostino Chigi by Raphael, who was influenced here by the frescoes by Michelangelo in the Cappella Sistina, or Sistine Chapel; in the lunette above, *prophets* by Timoteo Viti, also designed by Raphael. The first chapel on the left (Cappella Ponzetti) features, on the al-

tar, a *Virgin Mary with St. Bridget and St. Catherine and the Cardinal Ponzetti*, a fresco by Baldassarre Peruzzi (1516; he did the *stories from the Old and New Testaments* in the vault of the apse). The 2nd chapel on the right (Cappella Cesi) was designed by Antonio da Sangallo the Younger (1525).

The octagonal **tribune** has a cupola, designed by Sangallo and decorated in stucco to designs by Pietro da Cortona; in the tambour are a *Visitation* by Carlo Maratta (1655), a *Presentation in the Temple* by Peruzzi (1524), a *Birth of the Virgin Mary* by Raffaele Vanni, and a *Transit of the Virgin Mary* by Giovanni Maria Morandi. The *choir* and the *main altar*, which features a 15th-c. image of the *Madonna della Pace*, or, Our Lady of Peace (it is traditionally said that the statue was hit by a rock and bled, and the church was built to house the statue,) are by Carlo Maderno (1611), while the statues in the pediment are by Stefano Maderno (1616). In the chapel to the left of the main altar, note a handsome wooden *Crucifix* from the 15th c.

The adjoining **cloister** (open: 10-12 and 4-6, Sundays and holidays 10-12; closed Monday) is the earliest work by Bramante in Rome (1500-1504): it has survived intact, and it is surrounded by a portico with arches set on pillars; in the upper loggia, it is surmounted by large bracket cornice; note the alternating pillars and columns.

To the right of the church, you may note the vast bulk of *S. Maria dell'Anima* (6 C1-2), erected on the site of a chapel of the hospice for German, Dutch, and Flemish pilgrims, and rebuilt in 1500-1523, possibly by Giuliano da Sangallo. The Renaissance facade, which overlooks the Via di S. Maria dell'Anima, features three portals in the classical style, now attributed to Andrea Sansovino (he did the group of the *Virgin Mary between Two Souls in Purgatory* in the pediment over the central portal); the elegant *campanile* (1502) with twin-light mullioned windows is crowned by large cornices and by a conical cusp, faced with majolica of various colors.

Via dei Coronari (6 C1-2). This street is named for the vendors of holy wreaths ("corone sacre," hence "coronari," once very numerous here; nowadays the street is better known for its antiques shops. It has almost entirely preserved its Renaissance and Baroque appearance (the squares along its length, however, are the result of demolition done in 1939), though nowadays many of the buildings along this street are badly in need of care.

Among the numerous buildings, special note should be paid to the *Palazzo Lancellotti* (6 C1), rebuilt for the Cardinal Scipione to plans by Francesco da Volterra, and completed by Carlo Maderno; the elegant portal, with columns and surmounted by a balcony, was designed by Domenichino, while the interior features halls with vaults decorated by frescoes by Guercino and Agostino Tassi.

Piazza di Tor Sanguigna (6 C2). The family that gave this square its name once had a fortress here; all that survives is the *torre*, or tower, incorporatated in the modern structure on one side of the large open area, marked by alternating layers of fine tufa stone and bricks.

The adjoining square, on the other hand, takes its name from the *Palazzetto delle Cinque Lune* (6 C2), attributed to Antonio da Sangallo the Younger; the building was moved to its present site following the opening of the Corso del Rinascimento.

The Via di S. Agostino, which runs off from the east side of the Piazza delle Cinque Lune – literally the Square of Five Moons – leads to the church of **S. Agostino** (6 C2), founded in 1420, enlarged in 1479-83 by Giacomo da Pietrasanta and Sebastiano Fiorentino, transformed inside by Luigi Vanvitelli in 1756-61, and finally decorated by Pietro Gagliardi in 1856. A set of stairs extends in front of the facade, which is a typical facade of the early Roman Renaissance; it is tripartite and has three portals, with the central portal crowned by a pediment, and framed by exquisite candelabra. The interior, split into three aisles by pillars made of polychrome marble, features five apsed chapels on each side; at the intersecion with the transept, Vanvitelli replaced the original hemispherical cupola with a bowl-shaped done. To the right of the central portal, note the *Madonna del Parto* * by Jacopo Sansovino (1521). On the 3rd pillar on the left side of the nave, note the *Isaiah the Prophet* * by Raphael (1512); below it is *St. Ann and the Virgin Mary with Christ Child* *, a sculptural group by Andrea Sansovino (1512). In the pediment of the 4th chapel in the right aisle, *God the Father*, a panel of the 15th-c. Umbrian school. On the main altar, which was designed by Gian Lorenzo Bernini (1627), is a Byzantine *Madonna*. In the 1st chapel of the left aisle is the *Madonna dei Pellegrini* *, an altar piece by Caravaggio (1605).

Beside the church stands the *Biblioteca Angelica*, the first public library in Rome, founded by Angelo Rocca in 1614 and specializing in literature and philology.

Palazzo Altemps (6 B-C2). Built after 1471 on the site of medieval houses and buildings (the *altana*, or roof terrace, that crowns the building is by Martino Longhi the Elder, and dates from 1585), this palazzo was restored by Virginio Vespignani in 1837, by Antonio Muñoz in 1949, and – after being purchased by the Italian state as a separate branch of the Museo Nazionale Romano (for the historical context, see page 32) – it was again restored after 1984. The *courtyard*, attributed to Antonio da Sangallo the Elder and Baldassarre Peruzzi, was completed by Longhi; in the halls, works by Melozzo da Forlì, Polidoro da Caravaggio, and others have been uncovered.

The renowned **Ludovisi collection** of ancient art was assembled in 1621-23, in accordance with the antiquarian tastes of the period, by the cardinal Ludovico Ludovisi, nephew of Pope Gregory XV. Among the artworks, many of which were heavily restored (a number of them were restored by Alessandro Algardi or Gian Lorenzo Bernini), we should mention: the *Athena Parthenos*, signed by Antiochos Metiochos; the *Hermes Ludovisi*, from a 5th-c. B.C. Greek original, restored by Algardi; the *Galatian Killing Himself with His Wife* *, renowned for its intensity of expression and anatomical precision; the large *mosaic of Castel Porziano* dating from the 2nd c.; the colossal *head of a goddess* from the 5th c. B.C.; the *Ares Ludovisi* *; the *Aphrodite of Cnidus*, a copy taken from Praxiteles; the *sarcophagus with a battle between Romans and barbarians* * (around A.D. 250); the controversial *Ludovisi throne* * (5th c. B.C.) almost certainly originating from the "Locri Epizephiri" (Magna Grecia, Calabria). There are also the ancient sculptures from the Mattei, Del Drago, Brancaccio and Egyptian collections, the latter consisting of items originating from the Temple of Iside and Serapide in the Campo Marzio.

Palazzo Primoli (6 B2). Built in the 16th c. but radically transformed – at the behest of Giuseppe Primoli – by Raffaele Ojetti, who added the new facade overlooking the Lungotevere in 1909, this palazzo houses the *Museo Napoleonico*, a museum of Napoleon, donated to the city in 1927 by the count Giuseppe Primoli, son of Pietro Primoli and Carlotta Bonaparte. The 15 halls (each of which is devoted to a celebrated individual or a specific period of history) are richly furnished with period furniture, and contain artworks, authentic letters, various memorabilia, jewelry, costumes, and objects linked to the history of the Bonaparte family; of special note, aside from the satirical drawings and caricatures, is the *portrait of Napoleon* by Joseph Chabord (hall I), *Luciano Bonaparte* by François-Xavier Fabre (hall II), a marble *bust of Paolina Bonaparte* by Antonio Canova (hall VI), the *portraits of Zenaide and Carlotta* by Jacques-Louis David (hall IX), and *Carlotta dressed as a peasant woman* by Wicar (hall XI).

Also housed in this building are: the *Praz collection*, which belonged to the art critic Mario Praz and was purchased by the Galleria Nazionale d'Arte Moderna in 1986, comprising more than 1,200 objects from the Neoclassical period.

Via dell'Orso (6 B2). The name of this "street of the bear" comes from a fragment of sarcophagus with a lion mauling a wild boar, set at the corner with the Via dei Soldati; the street is lined with shops of craftsmen and antiques dealers, as well as the *albergo dell'Orso*, which may date from as early as the late-15th c. and occupies a little palazzo from that period; the facade, with loggias and porticoes, restored in 1935-37, features handsome terracotta decorations.

The church of *S. Antonio dei Portoghesi* (6 B2), whose curious facade dominates the Via dei Portoghesi (a continuation of the Via dell'Orso), was rebuilt by Martino Longhi the Younger (1630-38) on a place of worship dating from the 15th c., and in an area inhabited by a colony of Portuguese settlers in Rome.

Inside, lavishly decorated with polychrome marble, note the depressed-arch cupola (1674-76) by Carlo Rainaldi; also note the *monument to Alessandro de Souza* by Antonio Canova (1808).

Palazzo Borghese (6 A3). Built by the Della Genga family, possibly to plans by the Vignola, and completed for the cardinal Camillo Borghese by Flaminio Ponzio between 1605 and 1614, this building, known as the "harpsichord" for its unusual floor plan, is one of the most impressive palazzi of all Rome. Set on Piazza Borghese, the elevation comprises three full floors and two mezzanines, with two portals, surmounted by balconies and rich heraldic crests; on the nearby Via di Ripetta note the famous "keyboard" by Ponzio (1612-14).

A short detour along the Vicolo del Divino Amore, which runs off from the southern side of the Piazza Borghese, and along the Via dei Prefetti (along the right-hand segment of this street), will take you to the *Palazzo di Firenze* (6 B3), built for Jacopo Cardelli in 1516-30, heavily renovated by Pope Julius III, and from 1561 onward the property of the Florentine banking family of the Medici (whence its current name). The harmonious inner courtyard, with a portico on three sides, is overlooked by the brick elevation by Bartolomeo Ammannati; the loggia overlooking the garden, known as the "Atrio del Primaticcio,"

can be toured by contacting the Società Dante Alighieri, which has had offices in this palazzo since 1926; the loggia has frescoes and stuccoes (1553-55) by Prospero Fontana, who – with Jacopo Zucchi – also did the frescoes in the rooms of the palazzo.

Via dei Condotti (6 A4-5). Literally, the "street of the conduits" – the conduits in question are those that carried the water of the Aqua Virgo, or Acqua Vergine, but the street itself dates back only to the 16th c., when it constituted the main thoroughfare of the "Via Trinitatis," running from the Pincio to the Tiber, along with the Via della Fontanella di Borghese and the Via del Clementino.

Along this street – lined by the display windows of internationally famous shops and boutiques – note the numerous aristocratic homes dating from the 17th and 18th c., the church of the *Santissima Trinità degli Spagnoli* (6 A4), built in 1741-46 by Emanuel Rodriguez dos Santos, and frescoes in the vault of the apse and in the dome by Antonio Velázquez (he also did the canvases hanging on the walls of the main chapel), and the *Caffè Greco* (6 A5), a cafe named for the merchant who opened it in 1760, popular with artists, litterati, and adventurers (among other famous clients, let us mention Goethe, Stendhal, and Casanova). Some of the furnishings are original.

Piazza di Spagna* (4 B- C2-3). This is one of the most famous open-air spaces on earth, and one of the most monumental squares in Rome; it attained its present-day appearance between the end of the 15th c. and the end of the 19th c. Until the 17th c. it was called the "Platea Trinitatis," with reference to the church that looms high above it; thereafter it was called the Piazza di Spagna – actually the section before the home of the Spanish ambassador was called that, while the section toward the Via del Babuino was called the Piazza di Francia. Typical of the 17th and 18th c. in appearance, and with the distinctive shape of two triangles with a joint apex, this square – from the 16th c. onward – was the cultural and sightseeing center of Rome (it was soon festooned with hotels, taverns, and magnificent homes), while in the 19th c. it was crowded with antiquarians and photographers.

The Barcaccia* (4 B3). At the foot of the Scalinata della Trinità dei Monti (or Spanish Steps; see below), this fountain-qua-sculpture of a boat was commissioned, in commemoration of the great flood of 1598, by Pope Urban VIII (the sun and the bees are symbols of the Barberini family) in 1629 and assigned to Pietro Bernini, who completed it with the assistance of his son Gian Lorenzo; the invention of the sinking boat – which gave the fountain its name – was a way of concealing the technical problems of low water pressure.

Scalinata della Trinità dei Monti*, or Spanish Steps (4 B3). One of the most spectacular urban settings of the Baroque period, this stairway was built at the wishes of Pope Innocent XIII by Francesco De Sanctis in 1723-26. When flowers bloom in the spring, it is bedecked with large vases of azaleas.

The *Casina Rossa*, or little red house, to the right of the stairway, where John Keats lived, dying in 1821, has housed since the turn of the century the *Keats-Shelley Memo-*

dell'Immacolata Concezione, or column of the Immaculate Conception (4 C3), discovered in 1777 in the monastery of S. Maria della Concezione in Campo Marzio, and erected here by Luigi Poletti in 1856 in commemoration of a dogma proclaimed by Pope Pius IX (the bronze *statue of the Virgin Mary* is by Giuseppe Obici); nearby is the terminus of the procession led by the pope on 8 December, for the feast of the Immaculate Conception; at n. 57 is the *Palazzo di Spagna* (4 C3), formerly Palazzo Monaldeschi and since 1647 the site of the Spanish embassy to the Holy See; it was transformed in 1647-55 by Antonio Del Grande and in 1815 (note in particular the *Damned Soul* and the *Blessed Soul* by Gian Lorenzo Bernini, 1620).

Running along the right side of the Palazzo di Propaganda Fide along the Via di Propaganda you

The spectacular Piazza di Spagna with the Spanish Steps

rial Foundation. Round the corner is *Babington's*, the first Roman tea house.

Palazzo di Propaganda Fide* (4 C3). This building houses the Congregation of Propaganda Fide, established by Pope Gregory XV in 1622, and was built at the wishes of Monsignor Bartolomeo Ferratini (1586) and donated to the congregation in 1626. In 1639-45, Gaspare De Vecchi built the wing on the Via Due Macelli; the facade overlooking the square was modified in 1644 by Gian Lorenzo Bernini, while Francesco Borromini built the two wings on the Via di Capo le Case and the Via di Propaganda – the latter features a remarkable elevation*. Completing the SE "triangle" of Piazza di Spagna are: at the center, the *Colonna*

will reach Borromini's church of **S. Andrea delle Fratte** (4 C3), which in the 12th c. was called "S. Andrea de Hortis" because it is outside of the residential center; the reconstruction of the church, begun in 1604-1612, was continued from 1653 by Francesco Borromini until his death (he built the apse, the tambour of the dome, and the campanile), and finally completed by Mattia de Rossi (1691). The *campanile* has a square plan, and numerous registers; inside, the single nave has three chapels on each side. Note the exceedingly high dome; also of note are the marble *angels* (Gian Lorenzo Bernini, 1668-69) on either side of the presbytery.

Church of the Trinità dei Monti (4 B3). Begun in 1502 by Louis XII, king of France, this church was consecrated in 1585 by Pope Sixtus V and restored in 1816 at the behest of Louis XVIII. A stairway with two different flights, built by Domenico Fontana in 1587, extends before the facade, in a single register with pilaster strips, a portal and columns and attic, with a thermal window in the center. The interior, with a single nave divided by a gate (normally closed) at the height of the 3rd chapel, still shows elements of late-Gothic architecture in the triumphal arch, the presbytery, and the transept; note the

decorated the interior, with the assistance of his brother Taddeo; at n. 30 in the Via Gregoriana you should note a curious portal and windows in the form of infernal mouths. Inside is the *Biblioteca Hertziana*, founded by Enrichetta Hertz in 1900 and specializing in the history of Italian art (ca. 170,000 volumes).

To the left of the church, on the other hand, in an exceedingly panoramic location overlooking the

The Garden of Villa Medici

frescoes by Daniele da Volterra and assistants in the Cappella Della Rovere (3rd on the right), the artwork by Perin del Vaga in the Cappella Pucci (7th on the left) and the Cappella Massimo (5th), with decorations by Perin del Vaga (1537), completed by Taddeo and Federico Zuccari.

In the square lying before the church, the Piazza della Trinità de' Monti (panoramic view*) looms the *Obelisco Sallustiano* (4 B3), an obelisk taken from the "Horti Sallustiani" erected here by Giovanni Antinori at the behest of Pope Pius VI in 1789; the hieroglyphics are a Roman imitation of the hieroglyphics of the Obelisco Flaminio, or Flaminian obelisk.

To the right of the church, the area between the Via Sistina and the Via Gregoriana is occupied by the *Palazzetto Zuccari* (4 B3), erected in 1592 by Federico Zuccari in order to accommodate an academy of painting; Zuccari himself

Pincio, is the **Villa Medici** (4 A3), the result of a transformation of a building owned by the Crescenzi family, done in 1564-75 by Nanni di Baccio Bigio and Annibale Lippi at the behest of the cardinal Giovanni Ricci; it was purchased and enlarged by Ferdinando dei Medici, and then from 1804 it became the site of the *Accademia di Francia*, founded in 1666 by Louis XIV in order to allow young Frenchmen to study in Rome (it still contains a lavish library of art, architecture, and music).

The austere external facade contrasts with the *elevation* overlooking the garden, which features two side forewings with turrets and porticoed central wing – attributed to Bartolomeo Ammannati – with a central Serlian window. The rich stucco decorations, the festoons (several of which taken from the Ara Pacis Augustae), bas-reliefs, and statues make it one of the finest examples of the Roman antiquarian style of the late-16th c.

The vast *garden** still preserves its original design, and includes a "pomarium" with straight paths and hedges.

2.6 From Piazza Venezia to Via Veneto

This route runs through or past some of the most carefully structured areas designed by the architects of the age of Pope Sixtus; these architects made certain thoroughfares the centerpieces of their overall designs made up of roads and squares, with widely visible monuments. The Strada Felice is one of the finest examples of the reorganization of the road system in the 16th

c., which – although not completed – left a noteworthy imprint.

Of the two quarters ("rioni") through which this route runs, the Rione Trevi extends toward the summit of the Quirinal hill; construction went on particularly in the 17th c., when the area was gradually renovated, especially the older section – just behind the Via del Corso – with the construction of very fine palazzi. At the end of the 19th c., the Rione Ludovisi was intensely built up; here the development and speculation that followed the unification of Italy resulted in the destruction of one of Rome's most elegant villas.

From Piazza Venezia, the walking tour runs to the church and square of the Santissimi Apostoli, linked to the memory of the Colonna family (the Galleria Colonna is one of the most important private art galleries in Rome), which serve as an entrance to the Rione Trevi, embellished by the famous Trevi fountain (Fontana di Trevi).

Beyond Piazza Barberini – which is adorned by Bernini's fountain, the Fontana del Tritone, at its center, with, off to the right, Palazzo Barberini, which contains the Galleria Nazionale d'Arte Antica, another major Roman art collection – the tour continues through the Rione Ludovisi along the Via Veneto, once a world-renowned part of Rome, lined with large shady trees and handsome palazzi dating from the end of the 19th c. and the turn of the 20th c. At the end of this street is the gate, or Porta Pinciana.

Piazza dei Santissimi Apostoli (4 F3). In the area now occupied by this square – reorganized under Pope Paul III and once adorned with a large marble basin (possibly dating from the reign of Constantine) set on a stepped pedestal from which Arnaldo da Brescia is said to have harangued the people of Rome – long ago the goldsmiths and jewelers of Rome had their shops; today the square features the Palazzo Colonna, on the right, with the complex of the Santissimi Apostoli (for both, see below); on the left are aristocratic 17th-c. buildings (note in particular at n. 80 the *Palazzo Odescalchi* – 4 F2-3; 6 D5 – begun by Carlo Maderno and given the façade overlooking the square by Gian Lorenzo Bernini in 1664).

Palazzo Colonna (4 F3). Built at the wishes of Pope Martin V on the site of a castle dating back to before the year 1000, this palazzo was partly rebuilt in 1730 by Nicola Michetti; the elevation overlooking the square dates back to the 18th c., and features shops at its base, as well as two portals, and is further embellished by two side pavilions with a loggia and large windows. The elevation overlooking the Via IV Novembre dates back only to 1879.

The corner pavilion on the Via IV Novembre houses the *Museo delle Cere*, or wax museum, and was once the Coffee-Haus; on the third floor it features a handsome hall with a vault frescoed by Francesco Mancini (*Fa-*

ble of Amor and Psyche); in the large inner courtyard stands the palazzo proper, which was built in 1484 for the cardinal Giuliano Della Rovere and incorporated into the 18th-c. construction; here the Galleria Colonna is housed (see below).

The layout of the gardens of the *Villa Colonna* (4 E-F3-4) dates from 1611-25; villa and palazzo are joined by arches that run over the Via della Pilotta; in the garden are the ruins of the *temple of Serapis*, built at the order of Caracalla.

Galleria Colonna*. This, the most important private collection in Rome – along with the Doria Pamphilj collection – was established by the cardinal Girolamo Colonna in 1654-65 and later enlarged by Lorenzo Onofrio and Fabrizio Colonna; reduced sadly in 1798 by the forced sale of a great number of exquisite items, it was once again enriched in the 19th c. with a number of 14th- and 15th-c. Italian paintings. Thanks to these additions – and other more recent acquisitions – the collection has regained its former splendor. Set in the sumptuous 17th-c. rooms of the palazzo, the collection comprises a solid and spectacular group of paintings extending from the 14th to the 18th c., as well as numerous Roman statues. You will pass through a small entrance, with portraits of historical characters, and a vestibule, in which the *Christ Crowned with Thorns* by Francesco Trevisani is displayed, among other artworks; from here you will enter the *Sala della Colonna Bellica*, a hall named after the column in marble of rosso antico hue (symbol of the family) that stands at its center; in the vault note the fresco (*Apotheosis of Marcantonio II Colonna*) by Giuseppe Bartolomeo Chiari (1689-1702), and on the walls, paintings by Scipione Pulzone, Dosso Dossi, Palma il Vecchio, Bronzino (*Venus, Cupid, and Satyr*), and Jacopo Tintoretto (*Narcissus at the Spring*).

Seven steps lead up to the Sala Grande*, or great hall, which is decorated with stuccoes, large mirrors (the flowers and putti were painted by Carlo Maratta and Mario de' Fiori) and frescoes (*episodes from the life of Marcantonio II Colonna*) executed by Giovanni Paolo Schor, Giovanni Coli and Filippo Gherardi; note the canvases by Guercino (*Martyrdom of St. Emerenziana*), Niccolò di Liberatore (*Madonna del Soccorso*), Giovanni Lanfranco (*Mary Magdalene in Glory*), and Francesco Albani (*Ecce Homo, with Two Angels*).

Beyond the Sala dei Paesaggi, or hall of landscapes, which contains two remarkable *cases* (the first is made of sandalwood and semiprecious stones; the second is made of ebony and small panels of carved ivory) and French and Flemish *landscape paintings* from the 17th c., you enter the Sala dell'Apoteosi di Martino V (or hall of the apotheosis of Martin V, after the painting of that subject in the center of the ceiling, by Benedetto Luti); in this hall, you can admire the celebrated painting, the *Mangiafagioli*, or Bean-Eater, by Annibale Carracci and the *Portrait of a Gentleman* by Paolo Veronese, as well as paintings by Paris Bordon, by Scarsellino, and by Francesco Salviati; following that is the *Sala del Trono*, or throne room, meant for the use of the pontiff, which leads into the Sala dei Primitivi, with artworks by Bartolomeo Vivarini, Jacopo Avanzi, Pietro da Cortona, and Bernardino Luini.

Basilica dei Santissimi Apostoli (4 F3). Built under the reign of Constantine, as you can see from an inscription in the entry portico, which attributes the foundation to St. Julius I, and rebuilt by Pelagius I – in honor of the apostles Philip and James and in commemoration of the victories of Narses against the Goths – and completed under John III in A.D. 570; at the end of the 15th c., Sixtus IV completed the general renovation undertaken by Martin V by adding the portico, even though the general appearance of the church dates back to a reconstruction done during the reign of Clement XI, and largely overseen by Carlo Fontana (1702-1714); this reconstruction led to the destruction of most of the frescoes by Melozzo da Forlì on the tribune.

The Neoclassical facade, built to plans by Giuseppe Valadier (1827), features a large rectangular window in the middle. The portico, attributed to Baccio Pontelli, is oblique with respect to the main axis of the church, and comprises nine arches; the balustrade above it with *statues of Christ* and *the apostles* was added by Carlo Rainaldi.

Under the portico note: a *lion* with the signature of a certain Vassalletto (13th c.); on the left wall, *funerary stele of Giovanni Volpato* by Antonio Canova (1807).

The interior, dating from the 18th c., has a nave and two aisles, divided by pillars; on the vault, note the *Triumph of the Franciscan Order*, a fresco by Baciccia. The wall behind the altar of the 3rd chapel on the right features the surviving 15th-c. **frescoes** (restored, 1989; to see them, enquire in the sacristy) of the Confession of St. Eugenia, done at the behest of the cardinal Bessarion. Among the most noteworthy *funerary mon-*

uments, we should mention that of the *cardinal Pietro Riario* (left wall of the apse), by Andrea Bregno, and that of *Clement XIV* (to the left of the apse), the first Roman project entrusted to Canova (1789), with *Allegories of Meekness* and *Modesty* at the base.

The adjoining *Palazzo dei Santissimi Apostoli* was built by Giuliano da Sangallo (1478-80), with a corner tower and marble windows, adorned with heraldic crests, for the cardinal Giuliano Della Rovere. The two interior *cloisters* date from the end of the 15th c. and the turn of the 16th c.; the first has arches set on columns, while the second contains the *funerary monument of the cardinal Bessarion* (d. 1472) and a *cenotaph of Michelangelo*, set here before the remains of the artist were moved to Florence.

Oratorio del Crocifisso (4 E2). Built by Giacomo Della Porta, this oratory features a Mannerist facade (1568) and, inside, a charming rectangular hall, frescoed with some expressive freedom and brilliant late-16th-c. color, by Paris Nogari and Baldassarre Croce (right side of the counter-facade), Pomarancio (left side of the counter-facade), by Giovanni De Vecchi and Nicolò Circignani (right wall), Cesare Nebbia and again Circignani (left wall), with subjects linked to the True Cross.

Piazza di Trevi* (4 D3). The name of this square – and of the quarter, or Rione Trevi, and, of course, the fountain – come from the "trivium," or three-way crossroads, in Piazza dei Crociferi.

This elegant space, dominated by the Trevi Fountain (see below), is embellished by the facade – with columns (hence the folk name of "canneto," or reedbed) and adorned on high by the heraldic crest of the cardinal Giulio Mazzarino (or Mazarin) – of the church of the *Santi Vincenzo e Anastasio* (4 E3; 6 C5), which was renovated in 1640-46 da Martino Longhi the Younger; it is the parish church of the nearby Palazzo del Quirinale, and was for centuries the papal residence; this explains why the relics of nearly all the popes that ever lived here are conserved in the building.

Fontana di Trevi* (4 D3). This fountain displays a remarkable blend of classical rigor in the architectural elements and theatrical flair in the setting and placement of the Baroque sculptures; it was undertaken in 1732, under the reign of Clement XII, by Nicola Salvi, and it was finally inaugurated in 1762 under Clement XIII. It features a large attic, with balustrade, allegorical figures, and the heraldic crest of Clement XII:

The theatrical setting of the Fontana di Trevi

emerging from the large central niche is the large *statue of Ocean*, riding a chariot shaped like a seashell, drawn by seahorses; before them splash tritons (Pietro Bracci, 1759-62); in the side niches – on the right, note *Health* (Filippo Della Valle), and above that, the *Virgin Mary Pointing Out the Freshwater Spring to the Soldiers* (Andrea Bergondì); on the left, *Plenty*, also by Della Valle, and above it *Agrippa Approving the Plans for the Aqueduct*. The entire decoration was clearly designed with Bernini's work in mind: the basin (it is a folk belief that tossing a coin into this fountain ensures that one will return to Rome) represents the sea, and the statues follow the same theme.

The fountain is set against one of the shorter sides of the *Palazzo Poli*; this building has become an integral part of the Trevi complex, soon to be converted into a museum of engraving and printing instruments, under the auspices of the Istituto Nazionale per la Grafica.

Under the auspices of the same institution are the Gabinetto Nazionale delle Stampe a national collection of prints (see page 141) and the *Calcografia Nazionale, a collection of engravings*, which occupies the small Neoclassical palazzo at n. 6 in the Via della Stamperia; the latter was founded in 1738 by Clement XII. Among the more-than-23,000 engravings in this collection, we should mention those by G.B. Piranesi, Salvator Rosa, Francesco Bartolozzi, Giorgio Morandi, and Carlo Carrà; also worthy of note is the collection of photographs (plates and prints from the 19th c.) and engravings taken from works by Italy's greatest painters.

Palazzo Carpegna (4 D3). This building is the result of the reconstruction – done for the Carpegna family by Francesco Borromini in 1643-47 – of a 16th-c. building (the architect built the internal *oval ramp* and the loggia on the ground floor); since 1932 it has housed the *Accademia Nazionale di S. Luca*, which holds the collection originally belonging to the Università dei Pittori (literally, university of painters) once housed in the church of Santi Luca e Martina in the Roman Forum, or Foro Romano, and the **Galleria dell'Accademia di S. Luca**, which features a lavish array of paintings, chiefly from the 17th to 19th c.

The collections include: the *Bacchus and Ariadne* by Guido Reni, a *Harbor* by Antonio Tempesta, an interesting copy of Raphael's *Galatea*, by Pietro da Cortona, and a *bust of Napoleon* sculpted by Antonio Canova, a splendid copy of Titian's *Triumph of Bacchus* by Nicolas Poussin, a *portrait of Clement XI* by Baciccia, a fragment of a fresco by Raphael, with a *Putto Bearing a Festoon**, the *Annunciation to the shepherds* by Jacopo Bassano, numerous *portraits* by Titian, Alessandro Allori, Frans (II) Pourbus, Federico Zuccari, and Andrea Appiani, *landscapes* from the 18th c. (note those by Jan Frans van Bloemen), *genre scenes* by Anthonie Palamedesz and Michiel Sweerts, *rural scenes* by Monsù Stendardo and by Sweerts, the *sculptural group of Ganymede and the Eagle* by Bertel Thorvaldsen, *Roman Ruins* by Giovanni Paolo Pannini, *Veduta*

115

prospettica by Canaletto, *Virgin Mary with the Christ Child and Angels Making Music* by Antonie Van Dyck, and a small panel by Pieter Paul Rubens depicting the *Coronation of Pomona*, a *River-Figure* in terracotta, attributed to the Tribolo, a *Flagellation* by Francesco Trevisani, a *Battles* by Borgognone, a *Self-Portrait* (1724), the *Dinner at Emmaus* (1707), and *Mary Magdalene* – all by Benedetto Luti, a *Venus and Amor* by Guercino, and *seascapes* by Claude-Joseph Vernet. The last two halls (VII e VIII) contain works by Salvator Rosa, Ludovico Gimignani, the Sassoferrato, Jean François De Troy, and Guido Reni, and terracotta bas-reliefs that were submitted to the academic competitions of the 18th c. (note in particular the terracotta model for the bas-relief of the monument to Leo XI in the Vatican, depicting the *Pope Receiving the Abjuration of Henry IV* by Alessandro Algardi).

In the sale accademiche, open on request to the Direction, are the portraits of the members of the academy, the canvases that placed first in the various competitions, and a *Virgin Mary with St. Luke* begun by Raphael.
Adjoining the gallery are a noteworthy specialized *library* (since 1877 it has also possessed the collection donated by the architect Antonio Sarti) and the *Archivio dell'Accademia*, an archive established in the 17th c.

The Museo delle Paste Alimentari (6 C6) is the only one of its kind (created from the collections of Vincenzo Agnesi) document the value, even cultural, of this food.

Via del Tritone (4 C-D2-3-4). This busy shopping street takes its name from the triton created by Bernini in Piazza Barberini (see below), and is distinguished by the "Humbertine" palazzi that line it (the street was widened, in fact, between 1885 and 1925, during the reign of King Humbert, or Umberto).

Piazza Barberini (4 C4-5). At the center of the wide sidewalk, isolated from its original context, is the **Fontana del Tritone**, or fountain of the triton, designed in 1642-43 by Gian Lorenzo Bernini on behalf of Pope Urban VIII (the bees, heraldic symbol of the Barberini family, form part of the lavish allegorical design, made up of four dolphins whose tails support a sea shell, from which the triton, a sea divinity, emerges). Bernini also designed the *Fontana delle Api*, literally fountain of the bees, also dedicated to the Barberini family (1644), and now at the corner of the Via Veneto.

Via delle Quattro Fontane (4 C-D-E4-5-6). This street is only a part of the long straight boulevard, the *Strada Felice*, planned by Pope Sixtus V to link the Trinità dei Monti with the church of S. Croce in Gerusalemme; together with the *Via Sistina* (4 B-C3-4), which runs down from the Pincio to converge upon Piazza Barberini, this street offers an idea of the majestic route, overlooked by gardens and aristocratic villas, replaced in the 17th c. by patrician palazzi, joined during the 19th c. by a dense network of residential buildings.

Palazzo Barberini* (4 C-D5). Heralded on the Via delle Quattro Fontane by a large 19th-c. *gate* fashioned by Francesco Azzurri, this building – purchased by the Italian state in 1949 to be used as the location of the Galleria Nazionale di Arte Antica (see below) but still partly occupied by the officer's club of the Italian army (Esercito) – was designed and built by Carlo Maderno. On a site already occupied by a villa that had been the property of the cardinal Francesco Barberini since 1625, Maderno planned a daringly innovative structure, with broad open wings, that successfully blended the shapes of the traditional aristocratic urban palazzo with those of the villa with garden. Gian Lorenzo Bernini, who showed great respect for Maderno's design, impressed his mark with the glassed-in loggia and the famous *stairway with a square stairwell*, leading up to the Galleria, while Francesco Borromini developed the concept of the *spiral staircase* with twin columns, on the right side of the elevation.

Galleria Nazionale d'Arte Antica*, or national gallery of ancient art. Established in 1895 and formerly housed in the Palazzo Corsini alla Lungara – where the collection of that name is still on exhibit – this gallery has been housed here since 1949; the major collection of works, dating back from the 12th to the 18th c., is the result of the combination of collections of aristocratic Roman families (Torlonia, Chigi, Sciarra, Barberini, et al.), as well as purchases and bequests. The *bust of Urban VIII*, a marble sculpture by Bernini (1637-38), and the *Virgin Mary with Christ*, considered to be miraculous and dating from the second half of the 12th c., are arranged in the small antechamber and the passageway leading to hall I, frescoed like the next three halls by Antonio Viviani; hall I contains works by artists from the school of Rimini, clearly inspired by the work of Giotto (14th c.), and Venetian and Tuscan paintings from the 15th c., while hall II contains the lovely *Virgin Mary with Christ Child** by Filippo Lippi (1437); Lippi also did the later panel of the *Annunciation*.Beyond hall III, with more works from the Tuscan school of the 15th c. (note the *Mary Magdalene* by Piero di Cosimo and the model for the *Pietà* by Francesco di Giorgio Martini), hall IV contains paintings by Perugino, Antoniazzo Romano, and Lorenzo da Viterbo, while in the next hall (V) note the *Holy Family* by Andrea del Sarto and the unfinished *Virgin Mary with Christ Child* by Domenico Beccafumi.

Among the paintings in hall VI, chiefly from the milieu of Raphael, we should make special mention of the renowned *Fornarina** by Raphael – said to be the artist's beloved, the *Virgin Mary with Christ Child* by Giulio Romano (ca. 1525) and the *portrait of Stefano Colonna* by Bronzino (1546); in hall VII, which still features a splendid frescoed vault (*Triumph of Divine Wisdom*) by Andrea Sacchi in 1629, note the *Adulteress*, a youthful work by Jacopo Tintoretto (1546-48), and *Venus and Adonis* by Titian, while the adjacent small chapel (hall VIII) was frescoed by Pietro da Cortona and Giovanni Francesco Romanelli.

Hall IX, which contains the remarkable sketches (*Adoration of the Shepherds* and *Baptism of Christ*) by El Greco (ca. 1596-1600), is followed by hall X, in which artworks from the school of late Roman Mannerism are on exhibit; then comes hall XI, decorated with *putti bearing a heraldic crest* by Pietro da Cortona and his school, and hall XII, dedicated to the landscape painting of the 17th c.; after hall XIII, hall XIV features two renowned paintings by Caravaggio (*Judith and Holofernes**, 1599-1600; *Narcissus**) and a number of interesting works by followers of Caravaggio; the work of those follwers makes up the bulk of the halls XV and XVI.

Major works of 17th-c. Neapolitan painting are on display in hall XVII (note the *Resurrection of Lazarus* by Mattia Preti, ca. 1650), while in hall XVIII note the *Penitent Mary Magdalene* by Guido Reni (1610-15) and *Et in Arcadia Ego* by Guercino (1618; he also painted the *Flagellation of Christ*). Among the 15th- and 16th-c. Flemish works in hall XIX we should also mention the splendid *portrait of Henry VIII* by Hans Holbein and *portrait of Erasmus of Rotterdam* by Quentin Metsys; in hall XX are works by Baciccia and the Sassoferrato and two youthful paintings by Gian Lorenzo Bernini (*portrait of Pope Urban VIII*, ca. 1624; *Self-Portrait as David*, ca. 1625). The tour of the second floor ends with the immense hall known

as the Salone Pietro da Cortona, with the spectacular fresco (**Triumph of Divine Providence**, 1633-39) considered to be the artist's masterpiece.

On the upper floor is a noteworthy collection of paintings from the 18th c. (including works by Gaspare Vanvitelli, G.B. Tiepolo, Francesco Trevisani, Luigi Garzi, Marco Benefial, and Pompeo Batoni); the splendid halls known as the Sale dell'Appartamento contain furnishings, glass, majolica, and 18th-c. costumes.

Via Veneto* (4 A-B-C4-5). The full name is actually Via Vittorio Veneto, and this street was built in 1886-89 as a row of luxury ho-

A scene from the film "La Dolce Vita" by Federico Fellini

tels; it became world famous in the Fifties and Sixties as one of the main centers of Rome's "Dolce Vita"; it is renowned for its hotels, cafes, and luxury boutiques, and is also particularly pleasant for its width and greenery.

Among the architecture that is particularly worthy of note is the *Palazzo del Ministero dell'Industria, Commercio e Artigianato*, a government building (4 B-C4-5), by Marcello Piacentini and Giuseppe Vaccaro (1928-32), and the *Palazzo Boncompagni* (4 B5), known also as the Palazzo Margherita because it was the residence of the queen of Italy, Margherita di Savoia; it is now the site of the embassy of the United States of America; the architect Gaetano Koch who built it in 1886-90 took his inspiration from the Roman palazzi of the 16th c.

S. Maria della Concezione (4 C4-5). Also known as the church of the Cappuccini, it was built between 1626 and 1630 to plans by Antonio Casoni but it has lost the context in which it stood as a majestic structure, because of the construction of Via Veneto.

The interior, with a single nave, has five chapels on each side, and features: a *St. Michael Archangel* by Guido Reni (ca. 1635) and a *Christ Derided* by Gherardo Delle Notti in the 1st chapel on the right; *St. Francis Receives his Stigmata* by Domenichino in the 3rd chapel; the *tomb stone of the cardinal Antonio Barberini* (the inscription reads "hic iacet pulvis, cinis et nihil": here lies dust, ashes, and nothing more) before the main altar; the *monument to Alexander Sobieski* by Camillo Rusconi, to the left of the main altar; a *Madonna* of the Umbrian and Marche school from the first half of the 15th c. and a *St. Francis* * by Caravaggio in the sacristy.

Many visitors also tour the adjacent *Cimitero dei Cappuccini*, literally, cemetery of the Capuchin monks, in which the walls of the five chapels contain the bones and skulls of about 4,000 monks (the floor is scattered with dirt taken from the holy sites of Palestine).

Casino dell'Aurora * (4 B4). Sole surviving remains of the Villa Ludovisi, which developed during the 17th c. on the site of the Roman "Horti Sallustiani" and which was sacrificed to make way for the enormous real estate development that followed the unification of Italy; the Casino dell'Aurora is a 16th-c. mansion, with a cross plan; a forward wing was added in 1858.

Inside (to tour it, ask for permission from the Amministrazione Boncompagni at n. 44 in Via Ludovisi) there are remarkable works of art. The *Sala dell'Aurora* is one of the masterpieces of Guercino, who painted, in tempera, the *Allegory of the Day* (left lunette) and the *Allegory of the Night* (right lunette); in the Sala del Camino or Sala dei Paesi you should note the *Landscapes* by Guercino (right), Paul Brill (wall opposite the entrance), and Domenichino (over the entrance), and, at the center of the ceiling, the *Dance of the Putti*, attributed to Pomarancio. On the second floor, the little hall immediately following the entrance features, on the ceiling, an oil painting directly on the surface (*The Elements and the Universe, with Zodiacal Signs*) possibly by Caravaggio (ca. 1597); the nearby hall is known as the Sala della Fama, literally hall of fame, after the painting on the ceiling by Guercino and Agostino Tassi.

Porta Pinciana (4 A4). This so-called gate is actually just an arch made of travertine, which was flanked in the 6th c. by two cylindrical keeps: the other five fornices, or openings, are modern.

Beyond the gate is one of the entrances of the Villa Borghese (see page 152).

2.7 From Piazza Venezia to Porta Pia

As far back as the 17th c., with the gradual completion of the buildings on the Quirinal, used as the papal residence and headquarters of the organs of government of the papal state, the figurative center of gravity of the Rione Trevi shifted from the area around the Acqua Vergine, or Aqua Virgo, toward the "monte." This section remained the most important and prestigious area of Rome, and the victorious entry of the Bersaglieri, the Italian brigade of sharpshooters, and the transfer of the capital here gave it a further push; when the complex of the Quirinal became the royal residence, the new ministerial buildings were arrayed along the line of the Strada Pia, which was renamed Via XX Settembre, inasmuch as it ran toward the area of the wall that was stormed on that date (20 September).

From Piazza Venezia, this walking tour – after following the Via Battisti and the Via IV Novembre – climbs up along the Via XXIV Maggio to the Piazza del Quirinale, one of the political "poles" of the Italian state, where the Fontana di Monte Cavallo, a fountain, is a reminder of the ancient name of this square, and the Palazzo della Consulta offers mute testimony to the artistic flair of Ferdinando Fuga.

The straight line of the Strada Pia, renamed the Via del Quirinale and Via XX Settembre and designed at the end of the 19th c. as an executive office center of Rome (note the ministerial buildings along the street, after the crossroads of the Quattro Fontane), leads past the churches of S. Andrea al Quirinale and S. Carlo alle Quattro Fontane – on which both Gian Lorenzo Bernini and Francesco Borromini worked – and the "twin" churches of S. Susanna and S. Maria della Vittoria, and to the Porta Pia, by Michelangelo, which looms large in the history of the final campaign for Italian unity.

The Porta Pia, the monumental gate designed by Michelangelo

Via XXIV Maggio (4 E-F4). This road, which runs straight from Largo Magnanapoli to the Piazza del Quirinale, was opened in 1877 at the time of the definitive renovation of the Via Nazionale.

Dating from that same project is the unassuming facade of the church of *S. Silvestro al Quirinale* (4 F4), whose interior, with its single nave, with cupola and a deep presbytery, was shorn of its first two chapels. The noteworthy ceiling was painted (*Delivery of the Keys* and *Virgin Mary with Christ Child*) in the 16th c.; the panels (insignia of Leo X) in the floor of the 1st chapel on the left are by Luca Della Robbia (1525-27; Raphael also used them in the Logge Vaticane); the *Cappella Bandini**, at the end of the left transept, has an octagonal plan, a cupola, and a small lantern: it is the work of Ottaviano Mascherino (1580-85), while the tondoes in the corbels of the cupola were frescoed (*Biblical scenes*) by Domenichino in 1628 and the stucco sculptures in the corner niches were created by Alessandro Algardi and Francesco Mochi.

Palazzo Pallavicini Rospigliosi (4 F4). This great aristocratic building, which occupies the site of the *baths of Constantine*, was begun by Flaminio Ponzio in 1605 for the cardinal Scipione Borghese and completed by Carlo Maderno in 1616; it later belonged to the cardinal Giulio Mazzarino and to the Pallavicini Rospigliosi family, which still lives here. To the left of the portal onto the street is the *Casino Pallavicini* (open: the 1st of every month, 10-12 and 3-5), which features in the ceiling of the central salon,

or great hall, the famous *Aurora** painted by Guido Reni in 1614 and, on the walls, paintings by Antonio Tempesta and Paul Brill. On the second floor of this palazzo is the **Galleria Pallavicini**, an art gallery established by Nicolò Pallavicini with his son, the cardinal Lazzaro Pallavicini, and expanded further following the marriage of Maria Camilla Pallavicini with G.B. Rospigliosi (1670) and the fusion of the art collections of the two families; despite a partial dispersal in the 20th c. of works from the Rospigliosi collection, the Galleria Pallavicini was enriched during the same century with works from the collections of the Medici del Vascello.

In the collection of Italian and European paintings, we should mention in particular: *Landscapes* by Paul Brill and Jan Frans van Bloemen; the *Rest on the Flight into Egypt* by Pietro da Cortona; the *Virgin Mary with Christ Child and Young St. John* by Guercino; *Portraits* by Antonie Van Dyck; *Lust Driven Out by Chastity* by Lorenzo Lotto; the *Conversion of Saul* and the *Judgement of Paris* by Luca Giordano; *Perseus and Andromeda* by Guido Reni; *St. John in the Desert* by Pomarancio; the *Virgin Mary with Christ Child* by Giampietrino; a *Portrait of Hélène Fourment* by Peter Paul Rubens; *Ferdinando II de' Medici* by Justus Sustermans; *Portrait of Primo Lechi* by Tintoretto; the *Brawl in Front of the Embassy of Spain* by Diego Velázquez; and *Original Sin* by Domenichino.

Piazza del Quirinale* (4 E4). Overlooking one of the finest views in Rome, this square stands atop the Quirinal hill, supposedly

119

named after a place of worship of Quirinus, or after the city of "Curii," whence the Sabines of Tazio supposedly originated, before settling on this hill.

The ancient name of Monte Cavallo that applies to this area is taken from the Dioscuri, Roman copies from the imperial age of original Greek statues dating from the 5th c. B.C.; these statues were found in the baths of Constantine, and now stand upon the monumental fountain, or **Fontana di Monte Cavallo** which adorns the square. The "mostra d'acqua," or fountain at the end of an aqueduct, over which the two statues loom – they are 5.6 m. tall – depicting the two heroes in the act of halting the horses, is the result of projects set afoot by

and the *great tower* to the left of the facade date respectively from 1638 and 1626).

A long period of construction was also required for the so-called *Manica Lunga*, or long sleeve, the right side of the palazzo, which creates a remarkable foreshortening effect along the Via del Quirinale (see below; the total length is about 360 m.).

Once the residence of the kings of Italy, and ever since 1947 the home of the president of the Italian Republic, this palazzo is open to the public on Sundays, 9-12 am. The inner *courtyard*, porticoed on the left, was the reception area for heads of state and heads of government; the *palazzetto* at the far end is a creation of Mascherino and features an elegant double loggia with arches, while the majestic *Scalone d'Onore* or

A mounted presidential guard in front of the Palazzo del Quirinale

Pope Pius VI (who in 1786 ordered Giovanni Antinori to erect the obelisk here that had originally stood at the mausoleum of Augustus) and Pius VII, who had Raffaele Stern add the vast basin in 1818.

Palazzo del Quirinale* (4 D-E3-4-5). This impressive complex, which was restored to its original color scheme by the work done in1987, was erected as the summer residence of the popes, on a site once occupied by a villa that belonged to the cardinal Ippolito d'Este, and before him to the family of the Carafa. The project was entrusted to Martino Longhi the Elder in 1573, and was carried on by Ottaviano Mascherino (1578), Domenico Fontana, Flaminio Ponzio, Carlo Maderno (*portal*), and finally by Gian Lorenzo Bernini (the *Loggia delle Benedizioni*

staircase of honor, was built by Ponzio (1611-12); the *Cappella Paolina* on the other hand was built by Maderno (1617) to the exact shape and size of the Cappella Sistina.

The halls contain masterpieces by Botticelli, Claude Lorrain, Lorenzo Lotto, and Melozzo da Forlì (the *Christ in Glory* that adorns the great staircase, or Scalone d'Onore, comes from the Basilica dei Ss. Apostoli); Guido Reni worked in the *Cappella dell'Annunciata*, a chapel built in 1610 to plans by Ponzio, Pietro da Cortona worked in the Sala del Balcone, Antonio Carracci in the Sala del Diluvio, Giovanni Lanfranco and Agostino Tassi (1616) in the Sala Regia.

In the back, in the vast *gardens*, where the head of the Italian state holds a reception to commemorate the anniversary of the Italian Republic, you can still see the 16th-c. layout of the gardens of the villa of the Cardinal d'Este; the *Coffee House* was built by Ferdinando Fuga on behalf of Pope Benedict XIV.

Palazzo della Consulta* (4 E4). Built by Ferdinando Fuga in 1732-34 (the elegant facade has recovered its original colors, following the restoration of 1988-91), it was the site of an administrative court, the Tribunale della Consulta e della Segnatura dei Brevi; from 1955 it has housed the Corte Costituzionale, Italy's constitutional court.

Via del Quirinale (4 D-E4-5). This street runs along the first stretch of the *Strada Pia*, and was built around 1560 by Pius IV – following a Roman road – in the context of the project to improve the structures of the Quirinal hill; the segment beyond the crossroads of the Quattro Fontane, or four fountains, was renamed Via XX Settembre (see below). The urban development that followed led to the construction – in the segment extending to Piazza di S. Bernardo – of the Palazzo del Quirinale and of several religious complexes, while the next segment remained undeveloped until the second half of the 19th c.

S. Andrea al Quirinale* (4 E5). One of the masterpieces of the artistic maturity of Gian Lorenzo Bernini – as well as a centerpiece of the religious architecture of the Baroque era – this church was commissioned by the cardinal Camillo Pamphilj (1658); the architect developed an unusual elliptical plan, in which the main facade is on the smaller side. The location of the **altar**, designed by Bernini and preceded by an aedicule, is enhanced by the cupola (the figures in stucco are by Antonio Raggi) and by a daring lantern; in the four chapels, note the canvases by Baciccia in the 1st chapel on the right, and the *Virgin Mary with Christ Child and St. Stanislaus Kostka* by Carlo Maratta in the 2nd chapel on the left.

S. Carlo alle Quattro Fontane* (4 D5). The construction of this church was one of the longest tasks in the architectural career of Francesco Borromini, who began work on it in 1638, leaving the church unfinished upon his death (1667): the interior (plan) is one of his first creations; the facade – which features a *statue of St. Charles Borromeo* by Antonio Raggi in the niche over the portal; to the left of that is the distinctive campanile – was the last. Just slightly prior to his work is the adjoining *cloister* with an octagonal plan.

The nearby **Quadrivio delle Quattro Fontane**, literally the crossroads of the four fountains, is adorned with four elegant fountains set in the large niches; the fountains feature *statues of the Tiber, the Arno, Diana,* and *Juno* (1588-93).

Via XX Settembre (5 A-B-C1-2-3). Formerly part of the Strada Pia, this street was renamed in the late-19th c. – after the 20th of September – to commemorate the day of the historic breach in the walls of Rome; the street has been much developed, with office buildings that have incorporated existing churches.

S. Susanna (5 C1). This is the American national Catholic church, and was rebuilt by Sixtus IV on the ruins of buildings dating from the 2nd to 4th c., and modified in 1595 by Carlo Maderno, who built the handsome facade (1603) and simplified the interior to a single apsed nave with two chapels on each side (the frescoes, with *scenes from the life of St. Susanna and Susanna the Jewess* were executed by Baldassarre Croce in 1595).

Opposite this church, and in a secluded location, is the church of *S. Bernardo alle Terme* (5 C1), a late-16th-c. adaptation of one of the corner towers of the baths of Diocletian (see page 34); the interior, built to a circular plan, with a large coffered dome reminiscent of the dome of the Pantheon, features niches with *statues of saints* by Camillo Mariani (ca. 1600), while the choir has the *Vergine lauretana*, from the same period, by Carlo Saraceni.

Fontana del Mosè* (5 C1), or fountain of Moses. It was designed, in the form of a nymphaeum, by Domenico Fontana in 1587; the water pours out of large niches and splatters into basins adorned with Egyptian lions (the originals are in the Musei Vaticani); the large *statue of Moses* at the center is by Leonardo Sormani and Prospero Bresciano (1588).

S. Maria della Vittoria (5 C1). Built upon a prior house of worship consecrated to St. Paul, this church was built at the behest of the cardinal Scipione Borghese by Carlo Maderno (1608-1620), the name comes from an image of the Virgin Mary to which was attributed the victory of the Catholic armies over Protestant Prague in 1620 (memorabilia of the battle can be seen in the sacristy).

The interior, where the weight of Baroque decoration is alleviated by fine polychrome marble elements, has a single nave, with three connected chapels on either side. The *Triumph of the Virgin Mary over Heresies* and the *Fall of the Rebellious Angels* in the vault, and the *Our Lady of the Assumption in Glory* in the cupola were painted by Giovanni Domenico Cerrini in 1675, while the fairly theatrical arrangement of the organ over the entryway was implemented by Mattia de Rossi (1680). The 2nd chapel on the right features paintings by Domenichino (those on the side walls are his last Roman works, 1630); in the choir behind the altar is the *Elevation of St. Paul to the Third Heaven* by Gherardo delle Notti (1620). The church is particularly famous for the presence, in the Cappella Cornaro, which opens into the left transept, of the **Statue of St. Theresa Pierced by the Love of God**, a masterpiece by Gian Lorenzo Bernini (1646), who also did – with his assistants – the *statues of the members of the Cornaro family.*

Palazzo dei Ministeri del Tesoro e del Bilancio (5 B-C1-2). This large building, which houses the Italian ministries of the treasury and the budget, was the first new building designed for public offices in Rome, the new capital; it was designed in 1872-78 as the office building of the Ministero delle Finanze, or ministry of finance.

In the austere interior, since 1961, the *Museo Numismatico della Zecca Italiana*, a numismatic museum of the mint, is located. Unique in its kind, it features a selection of about 150 medallions created between the 19th and 20th c. (note the two *medallions* designed by Giacomo Manzù), the papal medals created between the 15th and 20th c., and the exceedingly interesting collection of coins (more than 7,000 specimens) designed for the Kingdom of Italy and for the Italian Republic, for the Vatican City, for the Republic of San Marino, and for other countries throughout Europe and the world. There is a section that illustrates the processes used to make coins and medals.

Palazzo dell'Ambasciata di Gran Bretagna, or building of the embassy of Great Britain (5 A3). A daring piece of modern architecture, built in 1968-71.

The wall on the side opposite the road encloses the *Villa Bonaparte* (5 A2-3), also known as Villa Paolina after the sister of Napoleon who lived there, and now the site of the French embassy to the Holy See, a 16th-c. building transformed around the middle of the 18th c. (the decorations by Giovanni Paolo Pannini in the "casino," or lodge, date from that period as well).

Porta Pia* (5 A3). This is the only gate of the Mura Aureliane, or Aurelian walls (see page 171) that has its main facade looking inward, as was ordered by Pope Pius IV as a backdrop for the Strada Pia (see page 121); it was designed by Michelangelo (1561-64) with an allusive decoration (the Medici "palle," or balls, paterae with dangling ribbons, and the squared-off block of white marble at the center, were immediately thought to be references to the basin, soap, and towels used by barbers, which it is said was the first profession of the Medici family). The outer facade, on the other hand, is by Virginio Vespignani.

To the military corps of the Bersaglieri, who made the historic "breach" in the walls of Rome (a *commemorative column* erected in 1895 and surmounted by a statue of *Victory* marks the spot, to the left of the gate in the outer wall of the perimeter, now covered with marble inscriptions), is dedicated the interior, adorned by busts of heroes and a monument to Enrico Toti. The *Museo Storico dei Bersaglieri* – a military museum – contains memorabilia and documentation concerning the Bersaglieri; founded in 1932.

Beyond the gate is the beginning of the Via Nomentana (see page 161).

2.8 From Piazza Venezia to S. Croce in Gerusalemme

Along this route you can observe some of the most interesting structures marking the seams between the Rome of the 16th and 17th c. and the Rome that arose in the 19th c. and following the unification of Italy; along this harmonious transition area there are also relics of the medieval city, here and there echoed in the 19th-c. buildings.

From Piazza Venezia, this tour – a walking tour despite the considerable length – follows the Via dei Fori Imperiali as far as the mouth of the Via Cavour, which was cut at the end of the 19th c. through the Rione

Monti (the short detours through this quarter to the church of the Madonna dei Monti and the Basilica di S. Pietro in Vincoli allow the sightseer to get a sense of the welter of exceedingly old buildings); along this thoroughfare, you climb the westernmost slopes of the Esquiline hill, which are dotted with towers and ancient churches (in particular, note the Basilica di S. Prassede). After you have visited the basilica of S. Maria Maggiore – a central feature of this route – you will walk back down the slopes of the Esquiline hill along the Via Merulana, which dates back to the end of the 16th c., and you will then begin to make your way into the quarter, or Rione Esquilino – after passing Palazzo Brancaccio, site of the Museo Nazionale d'Arte Orientale, a museum of Oriental art – with particular focus on the Piazza Vittorio Emanuele II; this quarter is characterized by a dense network of structures in the Turinese style, though some older structures have survived (arch of Gallienus, auditorium of Maecenas).

The architectural debut of Bernini (church of S. Bibiana) and the so-called temple of Minerva Medica serve as prelude to the Roman Porta Maggiore (in particular, note the descent into the nearby neo–Pythagorean basilica of the same name); from there, you will continue on to S. Croce in Gerusalemme, a basilica that preserves what are said to be relics of the passion of Christ.

Torre dei Conti (8 B4). This tower, built in 1203 under Pope Innocent III, incorporates in its base an exedra from the adjoining Foro della Pace (see page 60), over which lie alternating layers of flint and marble.

S. Pietro in Vincoli* (8 B6). Accessible via a stairway that runs off to the right from the Via Cavour, passing under the so-called Palazzo dei Borgia, this church in named after the miracle of the chains with which St. Peter was bound in Jerusalem; Eudoxia Minor, the wife of the emperor Valentinian III, gave these chains to St. Leo I Magnus; when the chains were laid close to the chains supposedly worn by the apostle when imprisoned in Rome, it is said that they miraculously fused into one set of chains (now preserved in the church).

The first building, erected in the 3rd c., survives only in the ruins found beneath the basilica; it was replaced in the 4th c. by a church dedicated to the apostles. This place of worship was rebuilt during the lifetime of Eudoxia Minor, and consecrated during the reign of Sixtus III, in A.D. 439; it was further renovated in the second half of the 15th c., at the turn of the 18th c., and finally in the second half of the 19th c.

Through the 15th-c. *portico*, with arches set on octagonal stone pillars, and through a marble portal from the same period, you can enter the church itself; the interior is impressive, with 20 columns made of ancient marble (the bases date from the 18th c.); the nave, which culminates in a triumphal arch set on two ancient granite columns, was modified in 1705-1706 by Francesco Fontana, who added the heavy depressed-arch wood-vault, with coffering. To the left of the entrance, note the *monument to Antonio and Piero del Pollaiolo* with busts of the two brothers, by Luigi Capponi (turn of the 16th c.). On the 1st altar of the right aisle, *St. Augustine* by Guercino; attributed to Domenichino are the two oil *portraits* in the monuments to the cardinal Girolamo Agucchi and to Lanfranco Margotti, on either side of the 2nd altar. The right transept is occupied by the **mausoleum of Julius II**, a smaller version of the enormous project assigned by Pope Julius II to Michelangelo in 1513 (Michelangelo worked on it for three years, until he

Moses, detail in the Mausoleum of Julius II, by Michelangelo

was taken off the project by Leo X): the seated figure toward the bottom is *Moses** (1514-16), the figures in the niches are *Leah* and *Rachel*, begun by Michelangelo and completed by Raffaello da Montelupo (1542-45); the other sections of the monument are by their students. The ante-sacristy, which you enter through a carved wooden *door* dating from the first half of the 16th c., contains a *Liberation of St. Peter* by Domenichino (1604) and a *St. Augustine* by Pier Francesco Mola. In the chapel to the right of the tribune, note the *St. Margaret* by Guercino. The confession underneath the main altar (the *baldachin* is by Virginio Vespignani, 1876) contains in its altar two small doors made of gilt bronze, decorated with *scenes from the life of St. Peter* in bas-relief, attributed to Caradosso (1477); behind the doors is an urn made of gilt bronze (1856) containing the supposed chains of St. Peter. In the crypt beneath the altar, note the early-Christian *sarcophagus* with what were once believed to be the relics of the Maccabees. The 2nd altar in the left aisle is adorned by a

Byzantine mosaic (*Bearded St. Sebastian*; ca. A.D. 680); to the left of the first aisle is the *tomb of Nicholas of Cusa* (d. 1464), with a bas-relief attributed to Andrea Bregno.

Basilica di S. Martino ai Monti (9 A-B2). Dedicated by Pope Symmachus to Saint Sylvester and Saint Martin, and rebuilt under Pope Sergius II, the present appearance of this basilica dates back to the 17th-c. restoration. Inside (the entrance is on the Viale del Monte Oppio) there is a nave and two aisles (the side aisles have handsome

Mosaic in the Cappella di S. Zenone

wooden ceilings dating from the 17th c.), and are separated by ancient columns. The central stairway leads down to the crypt from which, if you enquire in the sacristy, you can enter a hall that dates back to the 3rd c., part of the "Titulus Equitii" upon which this house of worship was originally founded: in it, you can observe Roman and medieval architectural fragments, the remains of frescoes dating from the 9th c., and a Cosmatesque ciborium.

Basilica di S. Prassede* (9 A2). As early as A.D. 489 a house of worship stood on this site, and was rebuilt under Pope Paschal I (this pope had the relics of some 2,000 martyrs transferred here from the catacombs), and then restored twice over the following centuries.

A courtyard, which features ruins of the early-Christian colonnade on the left, extends before the facade, which dates from the reign of Paschal I; in the facade note the 16th-c. portal. The three-aisle interior, divided by granite columns (you normally enter from the right side of the church), still features part of the 9th-c. structure; at the center of the pavement, note the porphyry disk which covers the well in which St.

Prassede supposedly found placed the remains of the martyrs (inscription).

The **Cappella di S. Zenone** in the right aisle – the most important Byzantine monument in the city of Rome – was built by Paschal I as a mausoleum for his mother, Theodora; there is clear classical influence in the cross-plan, with corner columns and a cross-vault; the entry portal in part comprises re-used material, and is surmounted by a large mosaic lunette; the *pavement*, a splendid example of "opus sectile" in polychrome marble, is ancient; the mosaics (heavily restored) depict: in the vault, the *Savior*, set in a medallion borne aloft by four angels, in the large lunette on the right, *male saints*, in the lunette below, *Christ, Between St. Paschal I and Valentinian*, in the niche on the altar, *Virgin Mary with Christ Child, Enthroned* and *female saints*; in the large lunette on the left, *female saints*, in the niche below, *Theodora episcopa*, *Virgin Mary* and *female saints*; in the room to the right of the entrance is the *Column of the Flagellation*, brought here from Jerusalem in 1223 and said to be the pillar against which Christ was bound during the Flagellation.

On the 3rd pillar of the nave, note the *bust of the bishop G.B. Santoni*, a youthful work by Gian Lorenzo Bernini.

The triumphal arch is decorated with *mosaics** dating from the reign of Pope Paschal I (within the walls of Jerusalem, *Jesus Between Two Angels* and, at the bottom, the *apostles with St. Paul, John the Baptist, and the Virgin Mary*; on either side, *Moses and Elijah*). *Mosaics**, possibly from the same period, can be seen in the apse; they depict: in the center, *Christ Giving a Benediction*, on the left, the *Saints Paul and Prassede* and *St. Paschal I Offering the Church*, and, on the right, the *Saints Peter, Pudenziana* and *Zeno*, beneath the *River Jordan*, the *Agnus Dei* (the Savior) and *the sheep* (the disciples), *Jerusalem* and *Bethlehem* (the cities of gold) and the dedicatory inscription.

Piazza di S. Maria Maggiore (5 F2). This square is adorned in the center by a Corinthian *column* that originally stood in the basilica of Maxentius, but was moved here by Carlo Maderno in 1614, as a "counterweight" to the Obelisco Lateranense, or

Lateran obelisk, at the end of Via Merulana. Sixtus V, on the other hand, was responsible for the placement of the small *obelisk*, a Roman imitation of an Egyptian obelisk, taken from the mausoleum of Augustus, in the center of the Piazza dell'Esquilino before the rear elevation of the Basilica of S. Maria Maggiore and on a line with the Strada Felice (see page 116),

Basilica di S. Maria Maggiore* (5 F2). This basilica, built according to legend on the site of a miraculous snowfall by Pope Liberius (for this reason, it is also known as the Basilica Liberiana or the basilica of S. Maria ad Nives), actually dates back no further than the reign of Sixtus III, according to excavations; in the 5th c., it had a nave and two aisles, no transept, and a central apse. During the reign of Pope Nicholas IV the apse was rebuilt, further back, a transept was added, as were the mosaics in the apse and on the facade; in the 16th c. the chapels were added; Pope Paul V built the palazzo to the right of the facade (1605), Clement XI began the palazzo on the left, which was completed by Ferdinando Fuga, who also ordered the restoration of the interior.

In the new **facade** – which replaced the original facade in 1741-43 while preserving the mosaics, and from which juts up the Romanesque *campanile* built in 1375-76 on a base dating back to the 11th/12th c., and completed in the second half of the 15th c. – Fuga placed a triple-arch loggia above the architraved portico; the rear elevation was built by Carlo Rainaldi (1669-75).

In the **portico** you should note the bronze *statue of Philip IV of Spain* (1692) and, on the left, the *Porta Santa*, or Holy Door.

The decoration of the **loggia**, to which you climb up along a stairway on the left, comprises two series of *mosaics** by Filippo Rusuti (signed; late-18th c.), heavily restored.

Among the patriarchal basilicas of Rome, S. Maria Maggiore is the only one to have maintained an interior appearance similar to its original aspect, despite the fact that the apse was rebuilt far to the rear of its original site, and the interruption of the colonnades with arches on a line with the Cappella Sistina (Sistine Chapel) and the Cappella Paolina; when Fuga worked on this area (1746-50), he limited himself to concealing various irregularities and asymmetrical forms. The enormous space (length roughly 85 m.) is subdivided into a nave and two aisles, by 36 monolithic columns which support the trabeation, which is adorned by a mosaic frieze dating

from the 5th c.; the floor is, in part, the work of Cosmatesque masters; the handsome coffered *ceiling*, attributed to Giuliano da Sangallo, is said to have been gilded with the first gold to arrive from America.

Along the side walls of the **nave**, above the trabeation, one should admire the 36 *mosaic panels** dating from the time of Sixtus III but restored in 1593, an exquisite document of the art of the late Empire; dating from the same period is the *mosaic** in the triumphal arch. The *confession* was redone by Virginio Vespignani in 1862-64 in order to house a silver urn (Luigi Valadier) that in turn contained the relics of the cradle of Bethlehem.

In the **apse**, note the exquisite *mosaic**, signed by Jacopo Torriti (1295); it depicts the *Coronation of the Virgin Mary, Between the Cardinal Giacomo Colonna and Pope Niccolò IV, Flanked by Two Rows of Angels and by St. John the Baptist, St. James, St. Anthony, and St. Peter, St. Paul, St. Francis*. In 1931, the transept of Nicholas IV was partly uncovered, with frescoes of *prophets** attributed to Pietro Cavallini, Cimabue, or a youthful Giotto.

In the **right aisle**, the Cappella dei Ss. Michele e Pietro in Vincoli – which you enter from the left side of the baptistery – still preserves paintings (there are gaps; *evangelists*) attributed by modern critics to Piero della Francesca; in the adjoining courtyard stands a column, shaped like a cannon and surmounted by a Crucifix, commemorating the abjuration of Henry IV of France (1596). Beyond the *Cappella delle Reliquie*, or chapel of relics, rebuilt by Fuga in 1750, lies the **Cappella Sistina** or Cappella del SS. Sacramento (Sistine Chapel), designed by Domenico Fontana at the wishes of Pope Sixtus V (1584-87), with a Greek-cross plan, enclosed by a dome and faced with marble taken from the Settizodio; this chapel was frescoed under the supervision of Cesare Nebbia and Giovanni Guerra (1587-89; restored 1871): the *ciborium*, shaped like a small temple (Ludovico Del Duca, 1590), is borne aloft by four *angels* by Sebastiano Torrigiani; from there, a small stairway leads up to the *Oratorio del Presepio* or oratory of the manger, an exceedingly old chapel renovated by Arnolfo di Cambio (ca. 1290; Arnolfo did the *David* and *Isaiah* in the spandrels of the entrance arch, the altar frontal, the mosaic floor, and – behind the altar – the *Three Magi, St. Joseph*, the *ox* and the *ass*); on the right wall of the chapel is a *monument to Sixtus V* (1588-90) designed by Fontana (the *saints* on either side are by Flaminio Vacca and Pietro Paolo

125

Olivieri); on the left wall, note *monument to St. Pius V* (1586-88), likewise by Fontana (the *saints* flanking it are by Valsoldo and G.B. Della Porta). In the sacristy adjoining the chapel, set in the pavement is the *burial stone of the Bernini family* (Gian Lorenzo Bernini is buried here as well). On the right wall at the end of the nave is the Gothic *tomb of the cardinal Consalvo Rodriguez* by Giovanni di Cosma (signed).

At the beginning of the **left aisle** is the **Cappella Paolina** or Cappella Borghese, built at the orders by Pope Paul V by Flaminio Ponzio (1605-1611); this chapel copies with even greater splendor the layout used by Fontana in the facing chapel, the Cappella Sistina: the frescoes in the spandrels of the cupola and the large lunette above the altar are by the Cavalier d'Arpino, the *Virgin Mary and the Apostles* in the dome, by Cigoli (1612); the exceedingly handsome *altar* (1613) was the work of Pompeo Targoni; on the frontispiece, note a relief in marble and gilt bronze (*Pope Liberius Traces the Plan of the Basilica*) by Stefano Maderno; on the right wall is the *tomb of Pope Clement VIII* by Ponzio (the *frescoes* in the large lunette under the arch are by Guido Reni, 1613), who also built the *tomb of Pope Paul V* on the opposite wall (the *frescoes* in the large lunette and in the "sottarco" are, once again, by Reni, 1613). The next chapel, the *Cappella Sforza*, built by Tiberio Calcagni and Giacomo Della Porta (1564-73) to plans by Michelangelo, features an *Our Lady of the Assumption* by Sermoneta.

Above the interior face of the Porta Santa, or holy door, note the *tombs of the cardinals Filippo and Eustachio De Levis* (1489), in the style of Giovanni Dalmata.

We recommend a short detour to the church of *S. Pudenziana* (5 F1), which was originally founded as the "titulus Pudentis" (hence the corruption into the name Pudenziana), and built upon the structure of a Roman house, transformed in the 2nd c. into a bath house, and in the 4th c. into a basilica with nave and two side aisles. The Romanesque *campanile* with five registers dates back to the turn of the 13th c.; the facade was redone in 1870. The interior was transformed in 1588 by Francesco da Volterra into a nave alone (the cupola, also by Francesco da Volterra, was frescoed by Nicolò Circignani), but it still contains a *mosaic* in the apse, dating from the end of the 4th c.; Francesco da Volterra also began work, on the left side of the nave, on the *Cappella Caetani*, a chapel that was completed by Carlo Maderno (the mosaics are by Paolo Rossetti and designed by Federico Zuccari).

Via Merulana (9 A-B-C-E2-3-4). This thoroughfare runs from S. Maria Maggiore to S. Giovanni in Laterano (St. John Lateran), and was built, along the course of a street of the same name, dating back to classical times (the name is taken from the landholdings of the family of the Meruli), for the most part at the behest of Pope Gregory XIII on the occasion of the Jubilee year of 1575 and completed by Pope Sixtus V; after the unification of Italy, it became one of the main thoroughfares of the Quartiere dell'Esquilino.

Palazzo Brancaccio (9 A-B2-3). This was

The Basilica of S. Maria Maggiore

the last aristocratic palazzo to be built in Rome in the true monumental style, and it is certainly the most impressive project ever completed by Luca Carimini, who began work on it in 1886, but did not complete it until 1912.

It is now the headquarters of the *Istituto Italiano per il Medio e l'Estremo Oriente* (Is-MEO, or Italian institute for the Middle East and the Far East; the library contains over 53,000 volumes and a rare collection of Tibetan manuscripts) and of the **Museo Nazionale d'Arte Orientale**, or national museum of Oriental art, founded in 1957; this museum documents the cultural history and the artistic production of the territory extending from Iran to Japan; the material, partly owned by the state and in part the fruit of archeological campaigns conducted in Iran, Pakistan, and Afghanistan by IsMEO, comprises artifacts which date from the earliest period of prohistory to the modern era.

The Iranian section (4th millennium B.C. - 8th c. A.D.) features – aside from the material (3200-1800 B.C.) unearthed during the excavations of the ancient trading town of *Shahr-i Sokhta* (the Iranian Sistan region), bronzes, terracotta statuettes, glass, and goldsmithery; following that is the Islamic section, devoted to Iranian, Turkish, and Hispano-Moorish ceramics; in particular, note the material (ceramics, bronzes, architectural fragments) from the *Palace of Ghaznī* (11th/12th c.), unearthed in Afghanistan in 1957-66. Of special interest, in the Indian section that follows, is the array of sculptures in green schist and in stucco, known as *art of Gandhāra* and based upon Buddhist doctrine. If you continue past the numismatic collection (Iranian, Indo-Greek, and Indian medallions and coins), you will reach the Southeast Asian collection, including scroll-paintings and sculptures in materials of all sorts, from Thailand, Cambodia, Burma, Indonesia, Nepal, and Tibet. The tour ends with the section devoted to the Far East, with artworks from China, Japan, and Korea.

Auditorium di Mecenate* (9 B3). This last rectangular hall with large niches on the walls and an apse with stairway and niches (open: 9-1:30, Sunday 9-1, Monday closed; from 1 April until 30 September, Tuesday, Thursday, and Saturday, also 4-7) was discovered in 1874. Probably, it was a summer nymphaeum that formed part of the "Horti Maecenatiani"; note the remains of the wall paintings dating from the 1st c.

If you turn to the left from Via Merulana into the Via Aleardi you can tour (Tuesday and Thursday, open 9-12 and 4-7, Sunday, 10-12) the **Casino Massimo Lancellotti** (9 D4), a 17th-c. guest lodge, attributed to Carlo Lambardi, and part of the larger villa destroyed during the rapid buildup of Rome following the unification of Italy (since 1948 it has been the headquarters of the Francescani di Terra Santa, or Franciscans of the Holy Land); in it is the most important Roman work by the Nazarenes, painters from the German culture who took inspiration from the Italian Renaissance. The three rooms overlooking the garden were frescoed with scenes taken from the great poems of Italian literature.

On the Via Tasso, behind, is the *Museo Storico della Lotta di Liberazione di Roma* (9 D4), commemorating the struggle for the liberation of Rome against Nazi occupation late in WWII; the museum was established in 1957 in the building that was the headquarters of the head office of the SS; in 1944 it became a prison for political prisoners.

Piazza Vittorio Emanuele II (9 A-B3-4). Lined on two sides by buildings with colonnaded porticoes (1882-87) and the site of the busiest marketplace in the city, this square is heart of the "Quartiere Piemontese," pride of the urban planners of the reign of King Humbert (Umberto), and is the largest square in Rome (316 x 174 m.).

S. Bibiana* (9 A5). Now in a heavily degraded urban setting, this church was founded as a small early-Christian basilica and was rebuilt by Honorius III, and once again in 1624-26 by Gian Lorenzo Bernini (this was his architectural debut); on the interior, with a nave and two aisles, divided by columns, he designed the two chapels on either side of the apsidal area, which he rebuilt, as well as the main altar (this incorporates an alabaster basin dating from the reign of Constantine, with relics of the three martyrs), and the *statue of S. Bibiana* in the aedicule. The *episodes from the life of the saint* on the walls of the nave are by Agostino Ciampelli (right; he did the altarpiece with *St. Demetria* in the chapel to the left of the apse) and by Pietro da Cortona (left; he did the altarpiece with *St. Dafrosa* in the chapel to the right of the apse).

Temple of Minerva Medica* (9 B6). Of uncertain origin (it formed part of the "Horti Liciniani"), this temple takes its name from a statue, found nearby and now in the collections of the Musei Vaticani, in which the goddess Minerva was depicted with a serpent. It consists of a great ten-sided hall, with niches, above which are arched windows, once sheathed in marble and mosaics. The structure, which dates from the 4th c., was one of the great models of Renaissance and Baroque architecture.

Porta Maggiore* (14 E3). Originally there were two apertures in the Mura Aureliane, or Aurelian walls (see page 171), because this marked the beginning of two main roads, the *Via Prenestina* (an exceedingly ancient road that the Romans re-used to travel from Rome to "Praeneste," modern-day Palestrina) and the *Via Casilina* (the ancient Via Labicana, renamed the Via Casilina after "Casilinum," as modern Capua was then called, and where this road ended); these two openings occupied two arches of the *Claudian aqueduct* and the aqueduct known as the *"Anio Novus"*,, which were first begun by Caligula in A.D. 38 and were completed by Claudius in A.D. 52. The massive architecture, with two fornices flanked by aedicules, and rendered lighter by a large attic. In this attic, on the side overlooking the Piazzale Labicano, are carved inscriptions commemorating the work of Claudius and the restorations of the aqueducts carried out under Vespasian in A.D. 71 and under Titus in 81.

In 1838, near the central aedicule, the *tomb of Eurisace** was unearthed, a funerary monument from the late republic, built by a baker in memory of himself and his wife Atinia; it is made of travertine, and on it you can see as a decorative motif sacks, jars, and, in the frieze, scenes from the cycle of production and sale of bread.

The roadbed of the Rome-Naples train line conceals the underground **Basilica di Porta Maggiore** (to tour it, contact the Soprintendenza Archeologica, or archeological commission of Rome), discovered in 1917; it is thought that it belonged to a Neo-Pythagoran sect, because of the mythological subjects depicted (first half of the 1st c.) inside; note the decoration in the apse, with *Sappho throwing herself into the sea from the crag of Leucas*, probably symbolic of the purification of the soul from the weight of material existence.

Aqueduct of Nero (14 E-F2-3). A branch of the Claudian aqueduct (see above) built by Nero to supply water to his great mansion, the Domus Aurea, and extended by Domitian as far as the Palatine, this aqueduct runs along the Via Statilia and, after the intersection with the Via di S. Croce in Gerusalemme, continues on into the gardens of *Villa Wolkonsky* (9 D5-6; 14 E-F2-3), an elegant villa dating from the Romantic period, built by the Russian princess Zenaide, and now the residence of the ambassador of Great Britain.

S. Croce in Gerusalemme* (14 F3-4). On the site of the present-day basilica, in the first half of the 3rd c., there stood a villa where the empress Helena, mother of Constantine, had a private residence: probably from that time there has been a Christian church here, rebuilt by Pope Lucius II (1144-45) in a basilican form and, after the work done in the 15th and 16th c., renovated in 1743 by Domenico Gregorini and Pietro Passalacqua, who transformed the nave and replaced the previous narthex with an atrium. The facade, slightly concavo-convex, echoes the style of Borromini, and is one of the highest achievements of Roman "barocchetto," or late-Baroque.

The interior, with a nave and two side-aisles separated by colossal granite columns, partly incorporated in the pillars added in the 18th c., preserves a Cosmatesque *floor*, restored in 1933; in the apse, note the *tomb of the cardinal Francesco Quiñones* by Jacopo

The Basilica of S. Croce in Gerusalemme

Sansovino (1536); in the apsidal vault, note the fresco (*Discovery of the True Cross by St Helena and its Recovery by Heracleius* and *Christ Giving a Benediction, among Cherubs*) attributed to Antoniazzo Romano; in the Cappella di S. Elena, to which you can climb down along a late-15th-c. graded ramp, and under the floor of which it is said that there is earth from Mt. Calvary, brought by the saint to Rome, with relics of the Passion of Christ (for this reason, the church is known as S. Croce in Gerusalemme, or the True Cross in Jerusalem), the vault is decorated

with a *mosaic**, attributed to Melozzo da Forlì or Baldassarre Peruzzi, a copy of the original from the time of Valentinian III; in the
Cappella delle Reliquie (to tour it, enquire in
the sacristy) a reliquary by Giuseppe Valadier contains the *relics of the True Cross*; in
an adjoining room, you can see a *Crucifixion*
by the school of Giotto and two *statuettes of
St. Peter and St. Paul*, of the 14th-c. French
school.

The adjoining convent was built in the 10th c.,
in part upon the *Castrense amphitheater* (14 F3),
one of the most notable buildings to be incorporated into the Mura Aureliane, or Aurelian

walls (see page 171; you can see it as you pass
through the walls to the right of the basilica and
turn left onto the Viale Castrense); it was built
by Heliogabalus and Alexander Severus for court
spectacles; its size (88 x 75 m.) testifies to the importance that the "Sessorium," the ancient imperial residence, had taken on by the 3rd c.

The area to the left of the basilica is the site of the
Museo degli Strumenti Musicali, a museum of
musical instruments opened in 1974; it contains
a collection of about 3,000 instruments, dating
from antiquity to the 20th c.: note the harpsichord built in Leipzig in 1537 by Hans Müller, the
splendid *Barberini harp*, and the *pianoforte* built
in 1722 by Bartolomeo Cristofori.

2.9 From Piazza Venezia to the Aventine and the Celian Hills

This route leads to the two hills that were
set aside for sites of worship and prestigious homes ever since the earliest times;
the two hills have maintained – until recent years – a secluded character with respect to the intense urbanization of the
city center, to which they already belong by
right. The Aventine, a hill that was originally
plebeian, and later patrician, and which
was in the Middle Ages the site of monastic
orders, was built up with elegant little villas
during the first decades of the 20th c.; it has
now become the most luxurious quarter
of Rome, thanks to its low population density and the ideal relationship between
built-up spaces and green area.
The ancient "Caelius" was never heavily
settled, but the buildings that were built upon it were prestigious, and were either religious, residential, or public, especially in
connection with the games in the nearby
Colosseum. Abandoned after the fall of the
empire, the hill was transformed into an
area of villas and vineyards (patrician country residences and agricultural estates),
conserving a rural appearance until the
unification of Italy, when it was decided to
urbanize it, in consideration of its fairly
central location.
From Piazza Venezia, following the walking
tour (buses may be used to get from the
Teatro di Marcello, or theater of Marcellus to
Piazzale Ugo La Malfa) you will first penetrate
into the Rione Sant'Angelo, the Roman *Ghetto* where from 1555 to 1848 the Jews were
confined; it is characterized by an intricate
network of buildings, comprising noble
palazzi (especially the "Isola dei Mattei" and
the "Isola dei Cenci Bolognetti"), impressive
churches, and noteworthy pieces of architecture from Roman times (Portico of Octavia) and the Middle Ages (Casa dei Vallati).

Beyond Piazza della Bocca della Verità begins the tour of the Rione Aventino, a quarter that features the ancient basilicas of S.
Sabina, S. Prisca, S. Saba, and S. Balbina.
The Rione Celio is still characterized by
early-Christian houses of worship (church
of S. Gregorio Magno, basilica of the Santi
Giovanni e Paolo, S. Stefano Rotondo, with
its complex plan and impressive frescoes);
here the Parco Celio and the Parco di Villa
Celimontana are two of the few green
spaces to serve the immense surge in construction in Rome that followed the unification of Italy, while the area that is occupied by the Ospedale Militare del Celio, a
military hospital, features notable relics
from classical times.

S. Maria in Campitelli* (8 B1-2). Built on an
existing building to fulfill a vow taken during the plague of 1656 and to recover the
miraculous image of S. Maria in Portico,
this church was begun by Carlo Rainaldi in
1662 but was not consecrated until the turn
of the 18th c. Late-Baroque in design, the interior features an unusual hybrid between
longitudinal and central floor plan. The
baptistery features two 15th-c. *tabernacles*,
and in the 2nd chapel on the right *St. Ann,
St. Joaquin, and St. Mary* by Luca Giordano.

S. Caterina dei Funari (8 A-B1). The long
restoration done on this church, which was
originally built by Guidetto Guidetti in 1560-
64 (dating from the same period is the campanile, built upon an existing tower), yielded the handsome travertine facade, inspired
by the facade of the church of S. Spirito in
Sassia. Particularly noteworthy inside are
the paintings by Annibale Carracci (*Coronation of the Virgin Mary*, ca. 1600) in the 1st
chapel on the right.

"Isola" dei Mattei (8 A-B1). This is a complex of buildings – enclosed by Via Caetani, Via delle Botteghe Oscure, Via Paganica, and Via de' Funari – that the family descended from Giacomo Mattei gradually purchased and enlarged, beginning in the 15th c.

Standing at the corner of the Via de' Funari and the Via Caetani is the **Palazzo Mattei di Giove**, built by Carlo Maderno in 1598 and completed in 1618; this is the site of the Discoteca di Stato, or state archive of recordings, the *Biblioteca di Storia Moderna e Contemporanea*, a library of modern history

The Palazzo Mattei di Giove

with more than 300,000 volumes, the Centro Italiano di Studi Americani, an institute of American studies, and the Istituto Storico Italiano per l'Età Moderna e Contemporanea, another historical institute. The inner elevation of the building overlooks a *courtyard* (entrance at n. 32 in Via Caetani) that is one of the loveliest in the city: the niches contain statues and busts, while from stucco cornices dangle ornamental festoons. A staircase embellished with ancient sculptures leads up to the majestic loggia, which is also lavishly decorated with 16th-c. *busts of emperors*. Many rooms in this building feature paintings by Pietro da Cortona, Domenichino, Pomarancio, Giovanni Lanfranco, and others.

At numbers 17-19 in Piazza Mattei you will find the *Palazzo di Giacomo Mattei*, originally built in the 15th c., and enlarged in the next century, possibly by Nanni di Baccio Bigio.

If you turn to the right in Via Paganica you will reach, at n. 4 in Piazza dell'Enciclopedia Italiana, the *Palazzo Mattei di Paganica*, built for Ludovico Mattei, beginning in 1541, possibly by Nanni di Baccio Bigio, and the site of the offices of the Istituto dell'Enciclopedia Italiana, the leading Italian encyclopedia.

Fontana delle Tartarughe* (8 B2). Literally the fountain of the turtles, it was de-

signed in 1581-84 by Giacomo Della Porta; the bronzes are by Taddeo Landini, the turtles appear to have been added in 1658 by Gian Lorenzo Bernini.

Closing the Piazza Mattei, at n. 10, is the *Palazzo Costaguti*, built in the mid-16th c.; inside, though it is closed to the public, are remarkable frescoes and canvases from the 16th and 17th c.

Via del Portico d'Ottavia (8 B-C1). This street is named after the Roman structure that can be seen at the end of the street (see below), and it once marked one of the boundaries of the Ghetto, established in 1555 by Pope Paul IV on the model of the Ghetto of Venice; in the Roman Ghetto Rome's Jews, who had already begun to move to the area as early as the end of the Middle Ages, were forced to reside until 1870, in conditions of squalor and overcrowding. The walls had already been demolished and the Ghetto had definitively been opened by Pope Pius IX in 1848.

In the line of buildings along the left side of the street note the celebrated *Casa de Manili*, upon which is the inscription that it was rebuilt in the year 2221 after the foundation of Rome – i.e., in 1468; a demonstration of the interest in the classics on the part of the Humanist Lorenzo Manili can be seen in the Roman high reliefs (particularly famous is the *lion devouring a fawn*) and the Greek stele set in the facade, the inscriptions, and the name of the owner, in Latin and in Greek.

The west side of the nearby Piazza delle Cinque Scole is blocked off by the **Isola Cenci Bolognetti** (8 B1), a complex of buildings arrayed around a small hill – the Monte dei Cenci, created by the covering over of Roman ruins – and belonged to the Cenci family as far back as the end of the 15th c.; this family was already well known in Rome in the Middle Ages.

The *Palazzo Cenci Bolognetti*, at n. 23 in this square, dates from the 16th c.; during that century the chapel of *S. Tommaso ai Cenci* was renovated; it stands on a cross-street, the Via Monte de' Cenci, and features a Roman funerary urn, set between the two portals, belonging to a certain Marcus Cincius Theophilus, set here for the similarity of the name to that of the family (Cenci). Overlooking the adjoining Piazza Cenci is, at n. 56, the *Palazzetto Cenci*, built by Martino Longhi the Elder in 1579-84, to the right of which stands the arch, or *Arco dei Cenci*.

Portico di Ottavia*, or Portico of Octavia (8 B1). Over 130 m. in length, and just under 120 m. in width, this portico was built in 14 B.C. by Quintus Cecilius Metellus; the name it now bears dates from the renovation done at the behest of Augustus, who in 23 B.C. dedicated it to his sister Octavia. From the Middle Ages until the demolition of the walls of the Ghetto, the portico was a thriving fish market; a plaque commemorates an odd privilege that fell to the Conservatori, magistrates of the city: they were entitled to the heads of all fishes that were larger than a certain given size.

The portico now serves as the entrance of the church of *S. Angelo in Pescheria* which gave the "rione" its name, and was founded in the mid-8th c. but has been restored repeatedly since; inside, the 15th-c. interior with a nave and two side aisles features, in the 2nd chapel on the left, a *fresco* attributed to Benozzo Gozzoli (1450).

To the right of the portico stands the *Casa dei Vallati*, a house first built in the 14th c. but heavily renovated during the project to isolate the theater of Marcellus (Teatro di Marcello; see page 44).

Sinagoga Nuova, or New Synagogue (8 B-C1). This Jewish house of worship, built between 1899 and 1904, is arranged inside in three orthogonal arms, surmounted by "matronei", while the fourth arm contains the edicola dell'Arca Santa.

In a separate section of the building is a small exhibition, or *Mostra della Comunità Ebraica di Roma*, with notable archeological finds, taken from the catacombs, prints, silver work, and religious accessories.

Piazzale Ugo La Malfa (8 E-F3). Beyond the Piazza della Bocca della Verità (the temples and the church of S. Maria in Cosmedin are described on page 42), this square offers the finest view of the excavations of the Palatine (in the foreground, you can recognize the Domus Augustana: see page 101) and the Circus Maximus (see page 42); it is embellished by the *monument to Giuseppe Mazzini* (Ettore Ferrari), set here on the centennial of the Repubblica Romana, behind which extends the *Roseto Comunale*, or city rose garden (to visit it, telephone 5746810).

From the *Parco Savello* (8 E-F2), a park named after a fortress that stood here around the year 1000, and also known as the "Giardino degli Aranci," or orange grove, there is a splendid panoramic view of Trastevere, the Vatican, and the "Quartiere del Rinascimento."

S. Sabina* (10 A4). This basilica, founded in A.D. 425 on the site of the "titulus Sabinae," received, from Pope Eugene II in A.D. 824 the iconostasis, the ambos, and the ciborium,

while the campanile and the cloisters date from the 13th c. – when Pope Honorius III gave it to St. Dominick, who according to legend planted the first orange tree in Rome in the nearby garden. The restoration of the original arrangement of the interior was done, on the other hand, by Antonio Muñoz, who largely eliminated the work done by Domenico Fontana (1587) and Francesco Borromini (1643).

In the atrium, whose arches are supported upon ancient columns, the portal, with a marble cornice, features wooden **doors**, dating from the original basilica, with panels depicting *scenes from the Old and the New Testaments*; of considerable historic importance for the parallel structure between the scenes from the two major sections of the Bible.

The interior has a nave and two aisles, modelled after the churches of Ravenna, and above the door is a mosaic fragment with an *inscription* in golden letters, attributed to Paolino da Nola, commemorating Pietro d'Illiria, builder of the first church here, Pope Celestine I, and the Council of

The New Synagogue

Ephesus of A.D. 431. In the nave, above the arches, note the *frieze* with red and green marble, dating from the 5th/6th c.; the *episcopal throne* was assembed with fragments dating from the 5th to 9th c., while the apsidal vault features a fresco by Taddeo Zuccari (1560), heavily restored by Vincenzo Camuccini in 1836, with little more than the subject of the ancient mosaic. The Cappella di S. Giacinto (or chapel of St. Hyacinth) in the right side-aisle, contains a canvas (*Virgin Mary and St. Hyacinth*, 1600) by Lavinia Fontana and frescoes by Federico Zuccari. In the Cappella d'Elci in the left side-aisle, note the *Madonna del Rosario* by Sassoferrato.

Complex of the order of the Cavalieri di Malta*, or Knights of Malta (10 A-B3-4). At the end of the 10th c., a Benedictine monastery stood here; in the middle of the 12th c. it passed into the hands of the Knights Templar; these were replaced in time by the Knights Hospitaller of Jerusalem, and their priory was here until the end of the 14th c. The elevation overlooking the square and the 17th-c. renovation of the complex was the work of G.B. Piranesi (this is the only actual architecture that he practiced): obelisks, aedicules, and emblems of the cardinal G.B. Rezzonico, for whom Piranesi worked – all adorn the enclosure wall and the friezes of the portal; an opening in the portal provides a perfect frame for the dome of St. Peter's.

Also part of the complex (for a tour, contact the Sovrano Ordine di Malta, Via dei Condotti n. 68) is the church of **S. Maria del Priorato**, the facade of which was designed by Piranesi in the context of the surrounding environment, and decorated with stuccoes like the interior (note the throne of the Grand Master of the order and a 9th-c. *altar*) and the *Villa dell'Ordine*, which features portraits of all the Grand Masters, and is surrounded by a handsome garden, also designed by Piranesi.

S. Prisca (10 A-B5). It is said that this church was built on the ruins of the house of St. Prisca, a Roman martyr who was beheaded under the emperor Claudius; dating from the period from the 3rd to the 5th c. were the earliest houses of worship, incorporated into the structure under popes Hadrian I (772) and Paschal II. The work done in 1456 under Pope Callixtus III gave the church its present-day appearance.

Of particular interest is the underground **mithraeum of St. Prisca** (to tour it, contact the Soprintendenza Archeologica di Roma, the agency in charge of archeological sites in the city); here you can see the ruins of a 1st-c. house, a nymphaeum from the age of Trajan, a building from the 2nd c., and a number of rooms adapted in that same period for the worship of Mithras; note in particular the cella of the sanctuary, at the far end of which is an aedicule with *Mithras Killing a Bull* and *Saturn Lying Down,* while the frescoes on the walls illustrate the *Seven Degrees of the Initiation* (right) and a *Procession in Honor of Mithras and the Sun* (left).

S. Saba* (10 C-D6). Dedicated to the head of Eastern monasticism, this church was built on the summit of the "Piccolo Aventino," or Little Aventine Hill (Piazza Albania and the Viale Aventino are described on page 42) by an early Christian settlement; it was assigned to Cluniac monks in the 13th c., then to the Cistercian monks and later, under Pope Gregory XIII, to the Collegio Germani-

The Church of S. Maria del Priorato

co Ungarico, directed by Jesuits. It was restored in 1932-33.

Standing before the facade overlooking the courtyard are a portico and a galleria, dating back to 1463; note the archeological fragments and a handsome relief with a *Horseman with Falcon*, dating from the 8th c. You can enter the church itself through a marble *portal* with mosaic decorations, signed by Jacopo di Lorenzo di Cosma and dated 1205; inside, note the nave and two side-aisles, divided by 14 ancient columns, with Cosmatesque flooring dating from the 13th c. and apsidal frescoes done for the Jubilee year of 1575, based on previous decorations; above the bishop's throne is a *Crucifixion*, dating from the 14th c., though heavily repainted. The odd, third side-aisle, on the left, was in all probability originally a portico, and it bears on the walls major *frescoes* dating from the late-13th/early-14th c. In the corridor toward the sacristy, note the fragments of votive panels, from the Benedictine period (12th c.).

S. Balbina (11 C2). This ancient building (the "titulus Sanctae Balbinae" dates back

A.D. 595) appears as it was renovated in
927-30 by Antonio Muñoz, during which
eriod the facade was also restored to its
riginal form.

he interior (you enter on the right, through
ie cloisters of the convent) comprises a
rge apsed hall with side niches, adorned
ith fragments of the old church, which
as renovated in the 8th c., again during the
enaissance, and in the 19th c. The schola
antorum was reassembled by Muñoz; note
ie remarkable Cosmatesque *funerary mon-
ment of Stefano de Surdis* on the entrance
all on the right (14th c.), originally in the
ld St. Peter's (S. Pietro); the *Crucifixion* in
ie 4th niche on the right was probably by
ino da Fiesole; the frescoes in the vault of
ie apse are by Anastasio Fontebuoni
599), while the *throne* is Cosmatesque
3th c.); the frescoes in the 3rd niche on
ie left are attributed, at least the most re-
ent layer (*Virgin Mary, Christ Child, and
postles* and *Image of Christ*), to the school
Pietro Cavallini.

Gregorio Magno (11 A2). Built in the
liddle Ages on the site of a monastery
rected by St. Gregory the Great, this
urch today has the appearance given it
y G.B. Soria in 1629-33 in the facade –
hich emulates the model of the church of
Luigi dei Francesi, and is preceded by a
road portico – and by Francesco Ferrari in
725-34 on the interior, which is divided
y ancient columns and pillars; the fresco
the vault dates from the 18th c. (*Triumph
Faith*, Placido Costanzi). Note, at the end
the right aisle, the altar of S. Gregorio
agno (St. Gregory the Great), in which
ie bas-reliefs of the altar frontal (Luigi
apponi) depict the *30 Masses of the Saint*;
so note the paintings, of the Umbrian
chool, and, dating from the same period, in
ie predella: *St. Michael Archangel Subju-
iting Lucifer, apostles,* and *St. Anthony, Ab-
t, and St. Sebastian*. The stone *statuettes of
Andrew and St. Gregory the Great* that
and before the main altar also date from
ie 15th c. The *Cappella Salviati* (to tour this
iapel, contact the monastery) was de-
gned by Francesco da Volterra and com-
eted by Carlo Maderno (1600): according
tradition, the fresco of the *Virgin Mary
id the Christ Child* on the right wall sup-
osedly spoke to St. Gregory the Great;
ie marble *altar* on the left chapel is by An-
rea Bregno.

handsome little square on the left of the
pectacular stairway of the church con-
ins three oratories, established here at the
rn of the 17th c. by the cardinal Cesare Ba-

ronio (to tour them, contact the Capitolo in
the Basilica di S. Maria Maggiore).

With a small portico extending before it, the
Oratorio di S. Andrea, or oratory of St. Andrew – restored for the cardinal Scipione
Borghese by Flaminio Ponzio in 1607-1608 –
is a real treasure chest of paintings by Guido Reni (*St. Andrew being led to his martyrdom*, left), Domenichino (*Flagellation of St.
Andrew*), Pomarancio (the *Virgin Mary and
St. Andrew and St. Gregory*, altar), and Giovanni Lanfranco (*St. Sylvia and St. Gregory*,
counterfacade).

The oratory, or *Oratorio di S. Silvia*, set to
the right and dedicated to the mother of St.
Gregory the Great, has a handsome wood-
en ceiling, and, in the dome of the apse, a
Concert of Angels (1608-1609) by Guido Reni
and Sisto Badalocchio.

On the left is the oratory, or *Oratorio di S.
Barbara*, frescoed by Antonio Viviani (1602),
which features a marble *counter* dating from
the 3rd c.

Basilica dei Ss. Giovanni e Paolo (8 E5-6),
or basilica of saints John and Paul. This
church dates back to the 4th c. and was
heavily damaged by the Normans in 1084,
thereafter it was rebuilt by Pope Paschal II;
the campanile was completed at the end of
the 12th c., when the original narthex was
opened to make a portico. Around 1950
Francis Cardinal Spellman commissioned
a restoration of the church, arranging for
work to save the bell tower and to return
the church's facade to its early-Christian
appearance. A Cosmatesque portal leads
inside, where there is a nave and two side-
aisles, divided by columns flanked with
pillars; here it is still possible to see the
work done in 1715-18 (note the 18th-c. canvas by Marco Benefial, on the 1st altar on
the right, with *St. Saturnine Destroying an
Idol*); dating from 1588 is the fresco (*Christ
in Glory*) by Pomarancio in the apse; and
dating from the 13th c. is the fresco of
Christ Enthroned Between Six Apostles in a
room adjoining the church (to see it, enquire with the priests); lastly, note the
panel in the sacristy, by Antoniazzo Romano.

The underground chambers of the church
(to tour them, contact the Soprintendenza
Archeologica di Roma) preserve the ruins
of a complex of buildings from the classical
era, partly re-utilized by an early Christian
community in the 2nd c. The nymphaeum
preserves a notable fresco from the 3rd c.,
the medieval oratory features paintings
from the 9th/12th c., and the "Confessio"
has 4th-c. paintings.

Arco di Dolabella (8 E6). The fornix of this arch seems to be a relic of the Porta Celimontana, a gate cut through the Servian walls (see page 32), and was also later reused in the aqueduct of Nero (see page 128).

The wall that runs to the right of the gate encloses a splendid 13th-c. **portal**, built by Jacopo and Cosma dei Cosmati, and surmounted by an aedicule with a mosaic (*Jesus Between Two Freed Slaves*).

S. Maria in Domnica (9 F1). The 16th-c. reconstruction of this church, once thought to have been the work of Raphael (interior) and Baldassarre Peruzzi (elegant portico, with five arches), is now attributed to Andrea Sansovino, who worked on the structures built in the 9th c. by Pope Paschal I, in turn upon the site of an existing place of worship ("dominicum," hence the name that the church still bears).

Inside, the church still maintains the basilican form of the 9th c., with a nave and two side aisles (the aisles end in small chapels with apses), divided by columns in grey granite. Under the 16th-c. coffered ceiling runs a frieze by Perin del Vaga, designed by Giulio Romano; the triumphal arch and the apse are decorated by handsome *mosaics* * dating from the time of Paschal I (restored in 1985).

The adjoining *Park of Villa Celimontana* (8 F5-6) was created in 1928 on the site of the 16th-c. Villa Celimontana, which belonged to the Mattei family. In the *"casino,"* or lodge, built for Ciriaco Mattei to plans by Jacopo Del Duca (1581-86), the *Società Geografica Italiana* has had its head-

quarters since 1926; the library is the largest in the sector in Italy (about 250,000 volumes); the *museum* contains souvenirs and artifacts from the travels of Italian explorers, as well as cartographic and ethnographic documents.

S. Stefano Rotondo * (9 F1). This is the oldest church with a circular plan in Rome (it dates back to the 5th c.), although the original structure – with two concentric circular colonnades, in which was inscribed a Greek cross – was modified by the addition of a portico in the 12th c. and by the elimination (under the supervision of Bernardo Rossellino, in the middle of the 15th c.) of the outermost circular colonnade and of three arms of the Greek cross. The columns of the surviving interior deambulatory enclose a central area, punctuated in turn by columns upon which the architrave supporting the masonry section of the apse is set; the exterior wall is frescoed with 3¢ scenes of *Martirologio* or history of the martyrs, by Pomarancio, Antonio Tempesta and assistants.

Parco del Celio (8 D-E5-6). Opened at the turn of the 19th c. on the site of the 16th-c. Vigna Cornovaglia and on the platea of the *temple of the Divus Claudius*, or the God Claudius, dedicated by Agrippina to her husband in A.D. 54, and transformed by Nero into a nymphaeum adjoining his Domus Aurea, this park is one of the loveliest green areas in all Rome.

Just a little further along, you will come out into the Piazza del Colosseo (see page 60).

2.10 From Piazza Venezia to the Trastevere and to the Gianicolo

The route runs through the "trans Tiberim," literally, area beyond the Tiber, which had already been partly built up prior to the age of Augustus, in particular with buildings used for storage and the flourishing commercial activity linked to the Roman river port.

It was precisely because of the flourishing trade in this area that, ever since ancient times, the area was a popular residence for outsiders; the first Jewish community of Rome settled here, and numerous synagogues were built (the ruins of one synagogue have been found in the Vicolo dell'Atleta); the community remained here until the 13th c., when the Jews began to move to the Campo Marzio and the Suburra, "preliminary" moves to being segregated into the Ghetto (1555).

It was under Pope Sixtus IV that the Trastevere, established as a "rione" at the end of the 13th c., was equipped with an entirely new bridge (specifically, the Ponte Sisto); this project was linked up with another one encouraged by Pope Julius II – and supervised by Bramante – that called for two roads running along the banks of the Tiber (the Via Giulia and the Via della Lungara). Just prior to the middle of the 17th c., Pope Urban VIII built the walls that were named after him, designed to defend the city from the Janiculum side – the sack of Rome in 1527 had made it painfully clear how necessary this was – and to link up the fortifications of Borgo and the Vatican with the Aurelian walls; this decision led to a considerable enlargement of the area of the "rione"; the quarter underwent a rapid subsequent urbanization, in the context of which the hospital, or Ospedale dei Ss. Maria e Gallicano and the giant complex of S. Michele were built.

Under Pope Pius IX the "rione" was given its definitive appearance and layout which finally put an end to the centuries of flooding, and allowed the construction of new

Viale di Trastevere – linked to early Christian worship (church of S. Crisogono and church of S. Cecilia in Trastevere), the nearby river port on the Tiber (Ospedale di S. Giovanni Battista dei Genovesi), and the 19th-c. "Quartiere Mastai."

Beyond the area of S. Maria in Trastevere, heart of the "rione," the Porta Settimiana, a

The Villa Doria Pamphilj, the largest public park in Rome

bridges, specifically the Ponte Mazzini, the Ponte Garibaldi, and the Ponte Palatino – there was a definitive break in the economic and spiritual identity of river and "rione"; on a line with the Ponte Garibaldi, the Viale di Trastevere was opened, running down toward the railroad station, or Stazione di Trastevere.

The slow but inexorable transformation of the population has meant that Trastevere has lost its population of proletarians and craftsmen, and in their place a population of the middle class and civil servants has risen. This transition has influenced the personality of the various festivals (especially the Festa de' Noantri) and the markets especially the famous Mercato di Porta Portese), although the character and "color" of Papal Rome has not vanished entirely.

This tour, which is a walking tour despite its length (short stretches can however be traveled by bus; the buses are particularly frequent on the Via Arenula and the Viale di Trastevere), runs from Piazza Venezia and then heads toward the river, along the Via delle Botteghe Oscure and the Via Arenula, streets that are overlooked by the 17th-c. church of S. Carlo ai Catinari and the 20th-c. Palazzo del Ministero di Grazia e Giustizia. Ponte Garibaldi marks the beginning of Trastevere, a quarter rich in historical legacies – especially in the area to the SE of the

gate in the Aurelian walls, marks the beginning of the Via della Lungara, punctuated on the left by major buildings (suffice it merely to mention the Palazzo Corsini, site of the Galleria Corsini) and on the right by the 16th-c. Villa Farnesina, and closed off at the end by the facade of the hospital, or Ospedale di S. Spirito in Sassia, the oldest in Rome.

The climb up to the Janiculum (Gianicolo), echoing with the memories of the Roman Republic, along the late-19th-c. scenic promenade and past the church of S. Pietro in Montorio, with the adjoining small temple by Bramante, marks the end of this walking tour.

Palazzo Caetani (6 E-F3). Formerly Palazzo Mattei, this palazzo stands at n. 32 of Via delle Botteghe Oscure and since 1963 has housed the Fondazione Caetani; it may have been built by Nanni di Baccio Bigio in 1564 and decorated by Taddeo and Federico Zuccari.

S. Carlo ai Catinari* (6 F2). This church – named for the shops of basin-makers ("botteghe di catini") that were once numerous in the area – was built in honor of St. Charles ("S. Carlo") Borromeo by Rosato Rosati in 1612-20 (who also designed the dome*); the travertine facade was added, being completed by G.B. Soria in 1638. The interior, restored by Virginio Vespignani in 1857-61, is particularly noteworthy for the frescoes by Mattia Preti on the counterfacade; for the *Cardinal Virtues* by Domenichino (1627-30) in the spandrels of the dome; for the *main altar*, executed by Martino Longhi the Younger, which features an altar piece (*St. Charles Borromeo Carries the Holy Nail in Procession*) by Pietro da Cortona (1650); for the *Glory of St. Charles* by Giovanni Lanfranco in the vault of the apse; and for a *St. Charles Borromeo in Prayer* by Guido Reni, in the choir.

To the left of the facade begins the *Via de' Giubbonari* (6 E-F2), part of the old "Via Peregrinorum," or pilgrims' way (see page 69), in which modern clothing shops have taken the place of the old workshops where jackets were made.

Palazzo del Ministero di Grazia e Giustizia, or justice department building (6 F2). Among the buildings erected under the reign of Humbert I (in a style known as "umbertino") which now line the Via Arenula, this is certainly the largest and the most noteworthy (it was designed and built by Pio Piacentini in 1913-32).

The church behind that building, **S. Maria in Monticelli** (6 F2), with an 18th-c. facade but dating back much earlier (the first restoration dates from 1101), contains a *Flagellation* by Antonio Carracci (2nd chapel on the right), a fragment of 12th-c. mosaic (apse) and a 14th-c. *Crucifix* (2nd chapel on the left).

S. Crisogono* (7 D5). The simple facade, now overlooking the Viale di Trastevere (see below), tells little of this building's long history; it dates from a 5th-c. basilica – upon which the original church of S. Crisogono was built in 1123-29 – and restored by G.B. Soria in 1620-26. Inside, the nave and two side-aisles are separated by 22 re-used granite columns and by the noteworthy 13th-c. Cosmatesque *flooring*, the triumphal arch is set on large porphyry columns; the *Cappella del Santissimo Sacramento* (in the right side-aisle) is attributed to Gian Lorenzo Bernini; the *baldachin* by Soria in the presbytery is supported by four alabaster columns; the *Blessed Virgin Mary* in its ceiling is by Cavalier d'Arpino; the late-13th-c. mosaic in the vault of the apse is attributed to the school of Pietro Cavallini.

Viale di Trastevere (7 D-E-F4-5). This tree-lined boulevard was designed with its Parisian counterparts in mind; it was built in 1888 to run toward the new train station, Stazione di Trastevere, which was opened in 1889; it is nowadays a crowded and noisy thoroughfare linking up with the quarters known as Gianicolense and Portuense.

Along this road – or immediately nearby – there are a number of interesting building complexes.

The 18th-c. complex of the hospital, of *Ospedale dei Ss. Maria e Gallicano* (7 C-D5) incorporates the *church of Ss. Maria e Gallicano*, built to a Greek-cross plan with four apses (from two of those apses the patient could attend services while still remaining in the hospital proper). The entire complex was designed by Filippo Raguzzini; in 1826 Pope Leo XII made a gift to the hospital of an *anatomical theater*, comprising two hemicycles, with a cupola and a stucco frieze.

The *Piazza Mastai* (7 D-E5), scarred by the construction of the great boulevard (or "viale"), was once the center of the *"quartiere"*, or quarter of Mastai, which was renovated under the supervision of Andrea Busiri Vici (1863-75) around the building of the former *Manifattura dei Tabacchi*, or tobacco factory (7 D-E5-6), built by Antonio Sarti in 1860-63 and deprived of its side wings in 1958.

Another hospital marks the subsequent stretch on the right of the Viale di Trastevere: the *Ospedale Nuovo Regina Margherita* (7 D-E4-5), built in the structures of the former Benedictine *monastery of S. Cosimato*; this monastery, built in the 10th c., had a handsome Romanesque cloister added in the middle of the 13th c., and another cloister was added during the reign of Pope Sixtus IV; during the same period the adjoining *church* was also rebuilt. It overlooks the Via Roma Libera with a 12th-c. porch, while the carved portico dates from the 15th c., and is set in a Renaissance facade.

Immediately behond this, on the Viale di Trastevere, note the facade of the *Palazzo del Ministero della Pubblica Istruzione* (Ministry of Education; 7 E-F4), designed and built by Cesare Bazzani in 1914-28.

The **Villa Sciarra** (7 F2-3), which you can enter from Via Calandrelli, was given to the state in 1930, after which it was converted into a public garden, maintaining the romantic drives, the fountains, and the fake ruins; the "casino," or lodge, damaged in the uprising of 1849 and restored in 1932, contains the *Istituto Italiano di Studi di Germanici*, with a lavish specialized library

Via dei Genovesi (7 D6). It was the fleet of Genoa, which had an active colony on the banks of the Tiber, that gave the name to this street. The *Vicolo dell'Atleta* took its name from a statue of an athlete uncovered here in 1844 and now on display in the Musei Vaticani; the medieval *house* at n. 14 has been identified as the only ancient synagogue still surviving in Rome (note the Hebrew inscription on the central column).

Basilica di S. Cecilia in Trastevere* (7 D6). An entrance, thought to have been designed by Ferdinando Fuga, leads into an immense courtyard with a garden, extending before the church, which was built by Paschal I at the beginning of the 9th c., upon the structure of a 5th-c. "titulus," and was embellished by the addition of the campanile and the right wing of the convent with a cloister between the 12th and 13th c.; the many restorations (the first was done in 1540, the most recent one was completed in 1981), and in particular, the restorations done in the 18th c., have altered the general structure of the building.
The portico that extends before the facade still has, on the architrave, a 12th-c. mosaic frieze. Inside, in the nave and two aisles, a vestibule has, on the left wall, the *monument to the cardinal Nicolò Forteguerri*, attributed to Mino da Fiesole and reassembled in 1895. In the vault over the nave, note the *Apotheosis of St. Cecilia* by Sebastiano Conca (ca. 1727). From the right aisle, through a frescoed corridor, you can reach a room that is thought to have been the "calidarium," where it is believed that the saint was exposed for three days to hot vapours before being martyred; on the altar, note the *Decapitation of St. Cecilia* by Guido Reni. The Cappella dei Ponziani and the Cappella delle Reliquie, also in the right aisle, contain noteworthy paintings, respectively by Antonio del Massaro and by Luigi Vanvitelli. At the center of the presbytery is the celebrated *ciborium** by Arnolfo di Cambio, signed and dated, 1293; beneath the altar, *St. Cecilia** by Stefano Maderno (1600), which depicts the body of the saint as it appeared when examined in 1599. In the vault of the apse, a mosaic depicts the *Savior, Giving a Benediction, with St. Paul, St. Cecilia, St. Paschal I, St. Peter, St. Valerian and St. Agatha** (ca. 820).
It is possible to visit the *cloister* (12th c.) and from here, you can enter the choir of the nuns, in which you can admire the remains of the **Last Judgement**, a large fresco by Pietro Cavallini (1289-93; restored in 1980), and the most notable work of Roman painting prior to Giotto.

S. Maria dell'Orto (7 E5-6). The original Greek-cross plan, by Giulio Romano or an artist influenced by Bramante, was transformed into a basilican plan around the mid-16th c., while Vignola (in the lower section) and Francesco da Volterra (in the upper section) built the facade. Frescoes by Taddeo and Federico Zuccari adorn the 1st chapel in the right aisle and the apse; the venerated painting *Virgin Mary with Christ Child* dates from the mid-15th c., and was originally painted on the wall of a garden, and now adorns the main altar; note canvases and frescoes by Giovanni Baglione in the 3rd and 1st chapel on the left.

S. Francesco a Ripa (7 E5). Along with the adjoining convent, where St. Francis is said to have stayed once, and which is now undergoing restoration, after having served for a time as a military barracks, this church existed as early as the 10th c., with the name of S. Biagio, but its present-day appearance

A typical scene in the characteristic Trastevere quarter

dates from the renovation done by Mattia de Rossi (1681-85); the architect rebuilt the church almost entirely, saving only the 16th-c. chapels on the left. The interior, with a nave and two aisles set on pillars, features a masterpiece by Gian Lorenzo Bernini in the left transept, the *Blessed Ludovica Albertoni* *; the *St. Ann and the Virgin Mary*, behind the statue, is by Baciccia.

Behind the church is the Piazzale di Porta Portese, named after the gate of *Porta Portese* (7 F5), built in travertine, with Tuscan-order columns flanking the fornix, in the walls built under Pope Urban VIII (see page 142) by Marcantonio de Rossi in 1644; this is the starting point of the Via Portuense, which runs toward Fiumicino.

The gate also marks the southern edge of the vast area – enclosed between the Via Portuense and the Viale di Trastevere – where every Sunday morning there is an immense and crowded market of clothing, low-end antiques, and used things of all sorts.

Via di S. Francesco a Ripa (7 D-E4-5). This road was built under Pope Paul V in 1610-11 between the church of S. Francesco a Ripa (see above) and the church of S. Maria in Trastevere (see below), and cuts at an angle across the renowned Viale di Trastevere (see page 136).

Basilica di S. Maria in Trastevere * (7 C4). The present-day church was built, with material taken from the Baths of Caracalla, under the reign of Pope Innocent II (1138-48), but we know that there was a house of worship here as far back as Pope Julius I (roughly the middle of the 4th c.); the subsequent work (in particular, the modification of the facade and the reconstruction of the portico in 1702 to plans by Carlo Fontana, as well as a restoration done by Virginio Vespignani on behalf of Pope Pius IX) did little to alter the substance of the building's structure; note the 13th c. mosaic, on the facade, depicting the *Virgin Mary Enthroned, with Two Donors* and two *processions of women* (the mosaic of the *Virgin Mary with Christ Child* in the aedicule of the Romanesque campanile dates from the 17th c.). The portico contains marble objects, sculptures, and inscriptions taken from the interior of the basilica or from the catacombs, and placed here in the 18th c.; the cornices of the three doors (the side doors are surmounted by little 14th-c. statuettes) date back to the Roman empire.

Inside, 22 ancient columns divide the nave and aisles; the triumphal arch is supported by two granite columns; the transept is raised; the ceiling was designed by Domenichino.

In the right transept, near the *cenotaph of the cardinal Francesco Armellini*, possibly by Andrea Sansovino, is the Cappella del Coro d'Inverno, built to plans drawn up by Domenichino: on the altar, *Madonna di Strada Cupa*, attributed to Perin del Vaga.

In the presbytery, the *"fons olei"* marks the spot where, in 38 B.C., legend has it that oil spurted out of the ground, a prodigious occurrence that was later interepreted as having been a sign of the impending coming of the Messiah; the *paschal candelabrum* is from the workshop of the Vassalletto family. The celebrated **mosaics** in the apse, done after 1143, depict: in the vault, on the left, *Pope Innocent II with a Model of the Basilica*; on the arch, note the *prophets Jeremiah and Isaiah, symbols of the evangelists* and the *Candelabra of the Apocalypse*; at the center of the half-dome, note the *Christ Crowning the Virgin Mary*; up high, above the *saints* and the *Pavillion of the Empyrean, with the hand of the Eternal Father Crowning the Son*; beneath that is the *Mystical Lamb* (the 12 little sheep are the apostles, and the holy cities symbolize the Church). The other major series of mosaics, on a line with the windows, is by Pietro Cavallini and depicts *stories of the Virgin Mary*. The marble *throne* with an unusual disk-shaped backrest dates from the 12th c.

To the left of the apse, note the renowned *Cappella Altemps* (Martino Longhi the Elder, 1584-85); on the altar is the *Madonna della Clemenza* *, literally Our Lady of Mercy, an encaustic panel, Roman art, dating from the 6th or 7th c.

In the left aisle is the *Cappella Avila*, a chapel, with a cupola by Antonio Gherardi (1680).

Museo del Folklore e dei Poeti Romaneschi (7 C4). Established in 1976 on the second floor of the former convent of S. Egidio, this museum features documentation concerning the history of folkways and customs in 18th- and 19th-c. Rome, a series of views documenting the transformation of the city after 1870, and a section dedicated to the "poeti romaneschi," or Roman dialect poets, with special reference to Trilussa. Aside from the abundance of visual material – including a series of English engravings from the 18th c., watercolors by Franz Ettore Roesler, drawings by Bartolomeo Pinelli and paintings by Plinio Nomellini – we would point out the lively and thorough reconstructions of a number of characteristic Roman shop rooms, such as an "osteria," or tavern; a pharmacy, and the shop of a public scribe; also note the moulds of the famous "talking statues."

S. Maria della Scala (7 C3-4). Begun in 1593 and completed in 1610, this church was restored in 1851. The *Cappella di S. Teresa d'Avila* (right transept) was designed by Giovanni Paolo Pannini; beside works by Carlo Rainaldi (main altar), the Cavalier d'Arpino (the vault of the presbytery), Alessandro Algardi (altar of the Cappella della Madonna della Scala, which contains the miraculous image to which the church was dedicated, in the left transept), Pomarancio (1st chapel on the left), left us point out the *Decapitation of St. John the Baptist* (1619; 1st chapel on the right), a

The Basilica of S. Maria in Trastevere

masterpiece by Gherardo delle Notti. On the third floor of the adjoining 17th-c. convent, which includes two *cloisters* (the larger of the two is by Matteo da Città di Castello), is the old *pharmacy*, with the furnishings and instruments used in the 17th c.

Porta Settimiana (7 B3). At the end of the 15th c., Alexander VI Borgia had this gate built, in the place of the postern gate cut through the Aurelian walls (see page 171), with a single fornix, crenelated; the restoration carried out under Pius VI (1798) did nothing to alter the structure. On the right (numbers 19A-20) is the *Casa della Fornarina*, a house that belonged to the woman who is thought to be portrayed in Raphael's renowned portrait of the Fornarina.

Via della Lungara (7 A-B3). Also known as the Via Santa for the flow of pilgrims heading for St. Peter's, and designed by Bramante, along with the parallel Via Giulia (see page 71), this road – until the construction of the embankment walls and the building of the Lungotevere, which destroyed the section overlooking the river – boasted one of the finest views in Rome, marked by an almost uninterrupted succession of 16th- and 17th-c. villas and palazzi.

Immediately to the left, beyond the Porta Settimiana, is *Palazzo Torlonia* (7 B3), whose 16th-c. structure has been badly cut away by the construction of apartment blocks; the Museo Torlonia which once occupied the palazzo – the collection is now in storage – is rich in remarkable items from the classical era, including 107 busts of emperors.

At the end of Via Corsini, which skirts the right side of the palazzo, you can enter the **Orto Botanico**, or botanical garden (7 B2-3; open: winter 9-5:30; summer 9-6:30; closed on Sunday and August), founded long ago, and since 1883 part of the gardens of Palazzo Corsini (see below). In it, environments typical of specific climates have been reconstructed, while a little manmade lake allows the development of aquatic species; note the 19th-c. greenhouses for orchids and succulents.

Palazzo Corsini (7 A-B3). Erected by the cardinal Raffaele Riario (1510-12), this building was the home in the 17th c. of queen Kristina of Sweden, who organized a circle of artists, which in time developed into the Accademia dell'Arcadia; Kristina died here (her room is one of the very few to survive intact from the original building); the facade by Ferdinando Fuga, perhaps the finest piece of architecture along this street, was built after the Corsini family purchased the building in 1736 in order to install the Galleria Corsini in it (see below).

The heritage of the academic life that existed in this palazzo continues nowadays in the *Biblioteca Corsiniana*, a library founded in 1754 and renowned for its exquisite collections of incunabula and manuscripts, in the *Biblioteca dell'Accademia* (1848), but especially in the *Accademia Nazionale dei Lincei*, the oldest academy in existence, and a leading cultural and academic institution in Italy, founded by the prince Federico Cesi in 1603.

Galleria Corsini*. This unique 18th-c. Roman collection has survived intact, and was begun in the 18th c. by the cardinal Neri

Maria Corsini and donated to the Italian state in 1883; recently reassembled in the original rooms, it offers an overview of Italian schools in the 16th and 17th c., and features a sizable collection of non-Italian artwork.

After crossing the immense atrium and climbing the stairway, decorated with ancient marble, you reach the vestibule, which features some ancient sculptures as well as the dancing *Fauno* and the *Cleopatra* by Pietro Paolo Olivieri. In hall I, where the *Vision of St. Catherine of Genoa* by Marco Benefial, the *Adoration of the Magi* by Sebastiano Conca, and artworks by Pompeo

Fresco by Raphael depicting Galatea (Villa Farnesina)

Batoni, Francesco Trevisani, and Giovanni Paolo Pannini are all on display, you will then enter hall II, which contains a series of Italian and non-Italian portraits, a *St. Sebastian Cared for by Angels* by Peter Paul Rubens, a *Virgin Mary with Christ Child* by Murillo, the *Madonna della Paglia* by Antonie Van Dyck, a *triptych* by Fra Angelico, a small *altarpiece* by Giovanni da Milano, the *Holy Family* by Fra Bartolomeo and the *Baptism of Jesus*, a bronze statuette by Alessandro Algardi.

Of particular interest, in hall III, is the *St. John the Baptist** by Caravaggio, the *Virgin Mary with Christ Child* by Orazio Gentileschi, and artworks by Michelangelo Cerquozzi, Simon Vouet, and Philips Wouwerman, in the

display case, *Coppa Corsini* (a goblet from the 1st c. B.C.). Hall IV features – alongside the *Landscapes* and *Genre Scenes* by Jan Frans van Bloemen, Josse de Momper, and Aert van der Neer – the *Erminia and Tancredi** by Gaspard Dughet (17th c.).

The next hall (V), known as the Sala della Regina Cristina di Svezia, after queen Kristina, features frescoes in the vault from the school of the Zuccari and, on the walls, a number of *Still Lifes* by Christian Berentz, among the numerous small bronzes, note the *Time Ravishing Youth* by G.B. Foggini. At the center of hall VI – which contains works by Nicolas Poussin and Carlo Maratta, the *Judith* by G.B. Piazzetta, and four lovely pastels by Rosalba Carriera – note the *Trono Corsini* (a throne from the 1st c. B.C.).

In hall VII note the *Holy Family* by Simone Cantarini, a *Virgin Mary* by Sassoferrato, *Tamar and Giuda* by Giovanni Lanfranco, and *Salome with the Head of John the Baptist* by Guido Reni; in hall VIII, dedicated chiefly to the Neapolitan school, note works by Spagnoletto, Massimo Stanzione, Mattia Preti, Luca Giordano, and Salvator Rosa.

Villa Farnesina* (7 A-B3). Built on behalf of Agostino Chigi by Baldassarre Peruzzi (1506-1510), this villa became the property of the Farnese family in 1590 (hence the name); in 1714 it passed to the Bourbon dynasty of Naples. It was restored in 1863 and in various phases over the course of the 20th c. (the last major restoration was completed in 1983); the splendid gardens sloping down to the banks of the Tiber, the original setting for the building, were eliminated in 1884, along with the loggia overlooking the river, said to have been designed and built by Raphael, as a result of the construction of the Lungotevere.

It is embellished with a loggia with five arches, set between two foreparts, that is now enclosed in glass in order to provide protection for the frescoes; it is surmounted by a carved frieze with festoons and putti.

From the 19th-c. atrium (open: weekdays, 9-1) you will reach the **Loggia di Psiche** named for the frescoes of the story of Psyche done to cartoons by Raphael, executed before 1517 by Giulio Romano, Giovanni da Udine, Giovanni Francesco Penni, and Raffaellino del Colle; the mythological depictions in the nearby Sala del Fregio are by Baldassarre Peruzzi. The *Sala di Galatea**, whose ceiling – by Peruzzi – features a number of panels, broken up by painted architecture (mythological and astrological themes make up the horoscope of Agostino Chigi), and takes its name from the famous *Galatea** painted by Raphael on the main wall (1513-14); on the left, the *Polyphemus* by Sebastiano del Piombo (1512-13) contrasts – with its hues typical of Venetian painting – with the style of Raphael. The Salone delle Prospettive, formerly frescoed by Peruzzi and repainted shortly after the middle of the 19th c., was restored during the most recent project. The adjoining bedroom, frescoed by Sodoma in 1517 and retouched by Carlo Maratta, is a reference to the wedding of Agostino Chigi.

Besides housing the offices of the nearby Accademia Nazionale dei Lincei, the villa is the site of the *Gabinetto Nazionale delle Stampe*, founded in 1895 for the preservation of the drawings and prints of the Biblioteca Corsiniana and including, when the Corsini donation was made, nearly 6,400 drawings, and 60,000 prints, now amounting respectively to about 21,000 and 110,000 (some of the largest collections in Italy); the drawings are for the most part Italian (Florentine and Roman schools), while the prints are also by non-Italian artists, many of which depict Rome and its topography.

Adjoining the outer enclosure wall, you can still see part of the foundation of the *Scuderie Chigi*, stables attributed to Raphael and demolished in 1808.

Palazzo Salviati (2 E-F6). Believed to have been a youthful work by Giulio Romano (1520-27) who built a *chapel* inside, in the style of Bramante (to tour it, contact the Stato Maggiore della Difesa at the Ministero della Difesa), this palazzo was completed in its present-day form by Nanni di Baccio Bigio at the behest of Cardinal Salviati; in 1794 it became the property of the Borghese family, in 1840 it passed to the Papal government, and since 1870 it has belonged to city, and contains military offices and agencies.

Porta S. Spirito (2 D5). The construction of this gate, as a sort of conclusion to the Via della Lungara (the opening of the piazza Delle Rovere to the front has, however, interrupted the ancient outlook), was marked by conflicts between Antonio da Sangallo the Younger – who began it in 1543 in a classical style, with four giant columns and two side niches with a large central arch – and Michelangelo.

Ospedale di S. Spirito in Sassia* (2 D-E5-6). This is the oldest hospital in Rome (it dates back to the time of the foundation of the Rione Borgo). It was built at the behest of Pope Innocent III on an existing structure, and began to function as a hospital at the turn of the 13th c.; it was entrusted to the order of S. Spirito. Aside from caring for the sick and infirm, this hospital served as a haven for abandoned or poverty-stricken children, and as early as the 13th c., it had numerous branches throughout Europe. Sixtus IV (1473-78) had it rebuilt entirely, while his successors – Alexander VII, Benedict XIV, and Pius VI – added more wings and buildings; in the years 1927-33 the structures visible beside Porta S. Spirito were built, and extend onto the nearby Lungotevere in Sassia.

The complex, which enjoyed total independence and, quite early, considerable wealth, due to the profits from the Banco di S. Spirito, a bank that was founded in 1605, was a place of teaching and research, as one can tell from the *Museo Storico Nazionale dell'Arte Sanitaria*, museum of medical art, which contains anatomical paintings, wax models, gynecological and surgical instruments (Arabic and ancient Roman, as well) and a handsome collection of pharmacy vases, with an adjoining specialized library.

The interior of the hospital is of special interest, where there are some remarkable examples of Renaissance civil architecture, such as the *Corsia Sistina*, a ward – possibly by Baccio Pontelli (1473-78) – and the *Sala Baglivi* and the *Sala Lancisi*, adorned with some 1,000 m. of 15th-c. frescoes by various artists, clearly of Umbrian origin. Among the frescoed walls of the vestibule of the Corsia Sistina, note the *baldachin* of the Altare di S. Giobbe, attributed to Palladio (ca. 1546). The arch of the entrance in Borgo S. Spirito n. 2, by Gian Lorenzo Bernini, conceals the original *portal** (late-15th c.), attributed to Andrea Bregno.

The huge block of the hospital contains – beyond Porta S. Spirito – the church of **S. Spirito in Sassia** (2 D5), dedicated to the Virgin Mary in the 8th c. and rebuilt a first time in the 13th c., and a second time, along with the hospital, for the Jubilee year of 1475 (on that occasion, the *campanile* with four registers of twin-light mullioned windows, was built, possibly by Baccio Pontelli); Pope Paul III commissioned Antonio da Sangallo the Younger to renovate it once again, while Sixtus V assigned Ottaviano Mascherino to complete the facade. Inside, in the single nave with five apsed chapels on each side, there are frescoes in the apse by Jacopo and Francesco Zucchi (1583), and in the 3rd chapel on the left, in the tomb of Antonio Foderato, a *Pietà* by Jacopo Del Duca, possibly designed by Michelangelo.

Linked to the church, by a wall with an elegant Serlian window, is the *Palazzo del Commendatore* (named after the office of director of the hospital), begun in 1567, possibly to plans by Nanni di Baccio Bigio.

Gianicolo, or Janiculum. It was the cult of Janus, practiced here, that gave this hill its name; it rises high over the Trastevere and looks eastward over the city.

In just two years (1642-44) it was enclosed within the *walls of Urban VIII*, which ran from Porta Cavalleggeri until they joined the Aurelian walls on a line with Porta S. Pancrazio (see below); from there these walls ran down to the river at Ripa Grande (the Porta Portese was built at the juncture with the older walled perimeter). These walls were the scene of furious fighting in 1849 between troops led by Garibaldi and the French troops, commanded by General Nicolas Charles Victor Oudinot.

The slopes are dotted with buildings dating from the 19th and 20th c., along with religious institutions of considerable cultural importance.

Church of S. Onofrio al Gianicolo (2 F5). Begun in 1439, this church was not completed until the 16th c., and was restored, along with the cloister, in 1946. Under the Renaissance portico that bounds the church courtyard, note the three lunettes by Domenichino that depict *stories of the life of St. Jerome*, while the Cappella della Madonna del Rosario, a chapel opening off on the right, has a richly adorned Baroque facade. Inside, with only a nave with five side chapels and a polygonal apse, there is an *Annunciation* by Antoniazzo Romano, and a tondo (*Eternal Father*) believed to be by Baldassarre Peruzzi in the 1st chapel on the right, a series of frescoes that may be a youthful work of Peruzzi in the apse, and the *funerary monument to the cardinal Filippo Sega*, with a portrait of Domenichino, in the 3rd chapel on the left. In the handsome 15th-c. *cloister*, note the lunettes with *stories of St. Onofrio* in part by the Cavalier d'Arpino.

In the adjoining convent, where the poet Torquato Tasso died on 25 April 1595, there is a handsome *Museo Tassiano*, devoted to the poet; it contains manuscripts and early editions of the poet's work, as well as a lovely lunette (*Virgin Mary and Christ Child with a Donor*), set on a false mosaic background, and attributed to Giovanni Antonio Boltraffio.

Passeggiata di Gianicolo* (7 A-B-C-D1-2). This promenade was built in the late-19th c. atop the bastions of the walls of Pope Urban VIII (Mura di Urbano VIII; see above) and punctuated on either side by busts of soldiers who fought under Garibaldi, and it offers remarkable panoramic views of the city. One of the highest points is marked by a *lighthouse* (7 A1), designed by Manfredo Manfredi in 1911 and donated to Rome by the Italians of Argentina, while nearby is the *equestrian monument to Anita Garibaldi* (7 B1; 1932); the large plaza just beyond is dominated by the *equestrian monument to Giuseppe Garibaldi* (7 B1) by Emilio Gallori (1895).

On the slope that descends toward the river, a remarkable loggia-belvedere looks out over the city – with three Serlian arches set on columns and pilaster strips at the ends – and forms part of the splendid *Villa Lante** (7 B1), built by Giulio Romano (1518-27), who erected it on the ruins of the Villa of Martial, now the site of the embassy of Finland (which has owned the building since 1950) to the Holy See, and of the *Istituto Romano di Finlandia*, a cultural institute with a specialized antiquarian library.

Porta S. Pancrazio (7 D1-2). The modern-day structure (Virginio Vespignani) represents the partial reconstruction of the gate built here during the reign of Urban VIII, damaged by the fighting in 1849.

It contains the *Museo Garibaldino*, which features documentation of the events of the Repubblica Romana, or Roman republic.

The 17th-c. gate replaced the ancient Porta Aurelia, which marked the beginning in the Aurelian walls (see page 171) of the *Via Aurelia*, built around the middle of the 3rd c. B.C. toward southern Etruria, and extended as far as Luni in the 1st c B.C. by the censor Marcus Aemilius Scaurus; it was not until imperial times that the route, which ran as far as what is now the city of Arles, was named the Via Aurelia; during the Middle Ages it was largely abandoned because of the prevalence of malaria.

From Piazzale Aurelio and out the Porta S. Pancrazio, a brief detour along the Via di S. Pancrazio leads you, near the beginning of the Via Aurelia Antica, to the entrance to **Villa Doria Pamphilj**, the largest public park in Rome (9.5 km. around the perimeter), which features a number of reminders of the luxurious life of leisure and hunting led by the Doria and the Corsini families, the owners in the 18th c. The renovation done by Alessandro Algardi was vast in its scope; it involved the two handsome fountains, the *Fontana della Lumaca* (the sculptural group is reminiscent of an original work by Gian Lorenzo Bernini) and the *Fontana del Giglio*, but focused especially on the *Casino di Allegrezze**, a lodge that was also known as the Casino del Bel Respiro, or even the Casino delle Statue (this is now a reception area of the Italian government), with rich decoration in ancient marble carvings on the facade, and a secret garden, adorned with statues and bas-reliefs.

The park contains a stretch of the *Acquedotto Paolo*, an aqueduct built by Pope Paul V (1609-1612), in part by restoring the aqueduct built by Trajan in A.D. 109, to bring to Rome, and particularly to Trastevere, water from the area around the lake of Bracciano.

If you continue along the Via di S. Pancrazio, which runs along the left, skirting the enclosure wall of the villa, you will reach, at the end of a short tree-lined avenue, the basilica of *S. Pancrazio*, which dates back to the 5th c. but which was rebuilt in the 17th c., with further work done in the 19th c.; the 15th-c. facade, and, in the left aisle, the remains of the Cosmatesque ambos are all that survives of the ancient structure; in the chapel to the left of the presbytery, *St. Theresa of the Infant Jesus* by Jacopo Palma the Younger.

Fontana dell'Acqua Paola (7 D2). This fountain, set on a panoramic terrace, was built by Flaminio Ponzio and Giovanni Fontana at the behest of Pope Paul V (1608-1612); in the form of a triumphal arch, it is surmounted by dragons, symbols of the Borghese family, while figures of monsters, housed in the side niches against a handsome natural backdrop, spurt water.

Via Garibaldi (7 B-C-D2-3). This main throughfare runs from Porta S. Pancrazio down along the Gianicolo (Janiculum) toward Trastevere and the Lungotevere, and was opened in 1867. On the right side, note the white mass of the *Mausoleo Ossario Gianicolense* (7 D3), a mausuleum dedicated in 1941 to those who fell fighting to make Rome part of Italy.

S. Pietro in Montorio* (7 D3). The ancient name of the Janiculum ("Mons Aureus") survives in the name of this church, which may have been founded in the 9th c. but was rebuilt in its modern-day form in the last 20 years of the 15th c., to plans by Baccio Pontelli and restored following the fighting of 1849. The facade has a noteworthy Gothic *rose window*; inside, with a single nave with three bays and two main chapels that form a transept, we would point out: the *Flagellation of Jesus** by Sebastiano del Piombo in the 1st chapel on the right, the *Madonna della Lettera* attributed to G.B. Lombardelli in the 2nd chapel on the right, the *Conversion of St. Paul* by Giorgio Vasari – who depicted himself in the figure in black on the left edge of the painting – and the balustrade with put-

Portrait of Giuseppe Garibaldi

ti by Bartolomeo Ammannati (who also did the *Justice* and *Religion* in the funerary monuments to the side) in the 4th chapel on the right, built by Vasari, and lastly the *St. Francis Transported by Angels* by Francesco Baratta on the altar of the 2nd chapel on the left, by Gian Lorenzo Bernini.

At the center of the cloister to the right of the church stands the little temple, or **Tempietto di Bramante***, with a circular cella, surrounded by a deambulatory with 16 Tuscan-order columns in granite, enclosed by a light and elegant ribbed cupola, supported by a tambour with seashell niches; among the masterpieces of Renaissance Rome – and perhaps one of the finest interpretations of classical forms of the early-16th c. – it was built (1508-1512) on the site where St. Peter was thought to have been crucified.

3 The Lungotevere

Guidebooks to Rome and histories of ancient Rome almost never speak of the Tiber ("to speak of the Tiber," according to the street guide by Blasi, "would be to recount the history of Rome itself"), so greatly is the image of the city bound up with that of the watercourse along which its entire history has unfolded.

This river, the largest on the Italian peninsula, rises at an altitude of 1,268 m. in the Tuscan-Emilian Apennines (Monte Fumaiolo); about half of its total length of about 400 km. runs through Latium, and it receives the waters of the tributary river Aniene just outside of Rome; after running through the capital, it divides at Capo Due Rami: on the left, the Fiumara Grande constitutes the Tiber's true mouth, on the right the river feeds the Canale di Fiumicino.

One of the pre-Roman names of the Tiber (the Etruscan "Rumon") may have been the source of the name Romulus, and of the name of the city itself; Rome developed in all likelihood due to the presence of a natural ford on a line with the Isola Tiberina, an ideal crossroad of the roads that ran from the interior to the sea and from Etruria to Campania; on a line with the ford was a livestock market (Foro Boario) and a vegetable market (Foro Olitorio). The watercourse, navigable only in the last 34 km., was for centuries Rome's main source of supplies, and it was watched over during the reign of Augustus by special magistrates ("Curatores Alvei Tiberis") and, later on, by the "Comites Riparum et Alvei Tiberis."

The construction housing the Istituto Storico e di Cultura dell'Arma del Genio on the Tiber

Despite the fact that there have been officials in charge of the river banks throughout the history of Rome, the banks were always cluttered with houses, floating mills (the so-called "passonate" served to direct water onto the blades of these floating mills), detritus, fish weirs, and other solid structures; from time to time, a great flood of the Tiber – many of them recorded on plaques set on walls throughout the city – would rise and sweep it all away; the ancient bridges, which were gradually abandoned, beginning as early as the high Middle Ages, were replaced entirely by ferryboats for centuries.

The "muraglioni," or embankments, erected after the terrible flood of 1870, created a sharp division between Rome and its river, putting an end to age-old cusoms (and even professions, such as the trade of the "acquaroli" or "facchini," who delivered Tiber river water to the doorstep; the river water was believed to be particularly health-giving; more recently pollution has gradually put an end to river bathing, which was usually done from special rafts and barges, which were once abundant along the river banks.

Although a number of stretches both outside of the city (toward Ostia) and inside the city (between the Foro Italico and the Isola Tiberina) are served during the fine weather by reg ular boat lines, the route we suggest here is a driving tour, and winds, along the tree-lined riverfront boulevards, or Lungotevere, along the right bank of the river, between the Ponte Milvio, built to bridge the Tiber for the Via Flaminia and for many centuries the first indication of one's entrance into Rome, and the modern bridge, or Ponte Sublicio on a line with the Rione Testaccio, punctuated by relics of the Fascist era (complex of the Foro Italico), the late-19th c. (Rione Prati and Palazzo di Giustizia), and early-20th c. (Quartiere della Vittoria); strictly walking tours along the opposite banks (note in particular the excursion through the area of the 18th-c. river port, or Porto di Ripetta, where the Mausoleo di Augusto and the Ara Pacis Augustae now stand) and the tour of the Isola Tiberina. The numerous and charming panoramic views (let us mention only the one near the Castel S. Angelo) also suggest the possibility – despite the heavy traffic along the riverfront boulevards, or Lungotevere – of a stroll from Ponte S. Angelo and the Isola Tiberina.

From Ponte Milvio to Ponte Sublicio

Ponte Milvio* (12 B3). As early as the 3rd c. B.C. there was a wooden bridge here; in 109 B.C. the censor Marcus Aemilius Scaurus rebuilt the bridge in tufa-stone, with four arches and two large towers on either end (the tower on the right, toward the Piazzale di Ponte Milvio, was fortified by Belisarius in 537 and later enlarged). The current appearance of the bridge is the work of Giuseppe Valadier (1805), who transformed the fortified tower into a gate, and adorned with statues the end on the banks toward the Piazzale Cardinal Consalvi. During the defense of Rome at the time of the Repubblica Romana, this bridge was demolished at the orders of Garibaldi in an attempt to slow the advance of the French troops. The common name "Ponte Molle" derives from an age-old corruption of the ancient name "Mulvius."

Just upstream from this bridge is the *Ponte Flaminio* (Flaminian bridge; 12 B4), designed by Armando Brasini in 1938-43 and finally completed in 1951.

Casa Internazionale dello Studente, or international house of the student (12 B2). Designed by Enrico Del Debbio and Piero Maria Lugli (1960), this building is crossed by a broad street called the *Viale del Ministero per gli Affari Esteri* (12 A-B2), containing the offices of the ministry of foreign affairs, a building that is known as La Farnesina from the name of this quarter, which belonged to the Farnese family: the building was designed by Del Debbio, with Arnaldo Foschini and Vittorio Ballio Morpurgo, and begun in 1938 as the Fascist Palazzo del Littorio; it was completed only in 1956.

Foro Italico* (12 B-C-D1-2-3). This great complex of sports facilities, reception halls, and places of study, was built to plans by Enrico Del Debbio in 1928-32; revised in 1936 by Luigi Moretti, it well represents

the Fascist idea of a link between ideological and athletic training.

The Foro Italico was divided in style between Rationalist and classical motifs, and before it stood the *obelisk* dedicated to Mussolini, which stood more than 17 m. tall, made entirely of Carrara marble; this obelisk still stands at the center of Piazza De Bosis; note the array of buildings, now the *Palazzo dell'ISEF* (12 C2), which also houses the Auditorium of RAI state television, and the *headquarters of CONI* (12 C2); the compex was completed by a series of sports facilities, among which we should mention the **Stadio dei Marmi** (12 B1-2; Enrico Del Debbio, 1932), a stadium studded with more than 60 larger-than-life-size statues; dating from the end of the 1930s are the *mosaics* – done to cartoons by Gino Severini, among others, that adorn the *Viale del Foro Italico* (12 C2), the central thoroughfare of this complex.

Later additions include the *Stadio Olimpico* (12 B-C1), built in the 1950s, and enlarged and partially roofed over for the World Cup soccer games in 1990, and the *Stadio Olimpico del Nuoto* (swimming; 12 C-D2), built for the 1960 Olympics.

Ponte del Foro Italico (12 C2). Once known as the Ponte del Duca d'Aosta, this bridge was built by Vincenzo Fasolo, in a rhetorical and monumental style, in 1936-39.

Casa delle Armi (12 D1-2). Also known as the Casa della Scherma, this building was designed and erected by Luigi Moretti (1935-36) as a place in which to engage in sports and in study, in two separate wings, linked by a hanging walkway; in recent years it has been used as a courtroom.

Behind the Casa delle Armi rise the slopes of the *Monte Mario*, 139 m. tall, and the meridian geodetic point of Rome.

This villa, which Mario Mellini built here in the

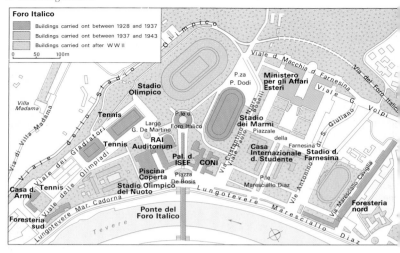

Foro Italico

Buildings carried ont between 1928 and 1937
Buildings carried ont between 1937 and 1943
Buildings carried ont after W W II

0   50   100m

late-15th c., has been the site since 1935 of the *Osservatorio astronomico e meteorologico*, or astronomical and meteorological observatory (12 E1; 13 A1), the sliding dome of which can be seen from the Lungotevere, as well as the *Museo Astronomico e Copernicano*, or museum of astronomy and Copernicus, which has collections of old sextants, eyeglasses, telescopes, sundials, and armillary spheres; it also has one of the most noteworthy collections on earth of globes, and a library of more than 20,000 volumes. Fine view from the terrace.

On the slopes of Monte Mario – but visible from the Piazzale Maresciallo Giardino – is **Villa Madama** (12 D1), which takes its name from Madama Margherita di Parma, wife of Alessandro de' Medici; it was designed by Raphael at the behest of the cardinal Giulio de' Medici (1518); work was continued by Antonio da Sangallo the Younger and by Giulio Romano. Restored in 1913 by Pio Piacentini, it has been since 1940 the official reception site of the Ministero per gli Affari Esteri, or foreign ministry; contact that office for authorization to tour the building.

Istituto Storico e di Cultura dell'Arma del Genio, or historical institute of the Italian army engineering corps (12 E2; 13 A3). Founded in 1906 at the behest of King Vittorio Emanuele III and merged in 1933 with the Istituto di Architettura Militare, or institute of military architecture, this historical institute was moved here from Castel S. Angelo in 1940; it comprises an historical and visual archive (20,000 maps and prints), an historical and documentary archive (15,000 documents, dating back to the 18th c.) and a specialized library with 24,000 volumes dating back to the 17th c. The adjoining *Museo Storico dell'Arma del Genio* documents the social goals pursued by the Genio, or engineering corps, and its tasks in wartime; among the

exhibits, note the *Bleriot XI monoplane*, one of the earliest Italian reconnaissance aircraft. The *Museo dell'Architettura Militare* traces the evolution of fortifications and sieges using models from ancient times till present day.

Ponte del Risorgimento (12 F4; 13 B5). This bridge was designed to connect the Viale delle Belle Arti (see page 156) with the Quartiere della Vittoria (see below), involved in the International Exposition of 1911; it was the first bridge in Rome made of reinforced concrete.

The *Viale Mazzini* (13 B-C2-3-4), which runs off to the right, is the main thoroughfare of the **Quartiere della Vittoria** – also known as the Quartiere Mazzini, after the Piazza Mazzini, around which it is laid-out in a giant star-shaped plan.

On the occasion of the Exposition of 1911, small villas and residential homes were built here for an international architectural competition.

Along Viale Mazzini stand: at n. 14, the *Palazzo della Direzione Generale della RAI*, the offices of Italy's national tv corporation (13 B4; 1963-65), "heralded" by the famous *Dying Horse* by Francesco Messina (1966); a little further along, the *church of Cristo Re* (13 B4; Marcello Piacentini, 1924-34).

Ponte Matteotti (13 C5). Built in 1924-29 as the Ponte Littorio, like ancient Roman buildings with the use of tufa-stone faced with brick and travertine, this bridge is famous because not far from here, in 1924, the Socialist member of the Italian parliament, Giacomo Matteotti, was kidnapped and later killed; the site is now indicated by a stela; on a line with that monument, on the riverfront, is the *Scalo Francesco De Pinedo* (13 C5), site of the landing by the aviator of that name in a seaplane, in 1925.

Upstream from the bridge is the massive *Palazzo del Ministero della Marina* (Italian navy; 13 B-C5), designed in the Neo-Baroque style in 1912 but completed only in 1928; the elevation is adorned by the enormous anchors of the Austrian cruisers "Viribus Unitis" and "Tegetthoff."

Ponte Pietro Nenni (13 C-D5). This exceedingly modern bridge, over which the 'A' line of the Rome Metropolitana, or subway, runs over the Tiber, was designed and built by Luigi Moretti in 1965-72, entirely in reinforced concrete.

Ponte Regina Margherita (13 D5). This bridge was built by Angelo Vescovali (1886-91), and links the Pincio to the Vatican; it has three arches in masonry, faced with travertine.

On a line with the bridge, running off from Piazza della Libertà, to the west, is the *Via Cola di Rienzo* (2 A-B5-6; 3 A1-2-3; 13 D-E3-4-5), one of the chief thoroughfares of the **Rione Prati**, the only quarter of Rome located outside of the Mura Aureliane (Aurelian walls; see page 171). The name Prati was used to indicate, between the 17th and 19th c., all of those sites in the Tiber valley in which the river, running slowly and winding considerably, deposited rich silt in considerable amounts; here there were plenty of vineyards and cheerful open-air taverns. The construction of the Prati di Castello, named after the nearby Castel S. Angelo, was accelerated following the unification of Italy, to provide housing for the new corps of Italian civil servants; this gave the quarter considerable homogeneity in the style, quality, and typology of buildings. This quarter still has much of the flavor that the well-read visitor may recall from the works of Pirandello, many of which are set here.

Ponte Cavour (13 E5). This bridge, part of the overall project of urbanization of the Rione Prati, and built by Angelo Vescovali nel 1896-1901, replaced the Ponte di Ripetta – in reality little more than an iron walkway, which had in turn replaced a ferry used by groups of holiday-makers who were heading for the taverns of the Prati di Castello – for which a toll was charged up until 1883.

Near the eastern end of the Ponte Cavour lay, until the construction of the embank-

ments ("muraglioni"), the Porto di Ripetta, a river port built in ancient times and used well after 1850 by boats sailing down from the upper Tiber; the port was rebuilt by Alessandro Specchi around 1704 with a handsome ramp structure, a popular subject of 18th-c. art; note the promenade, or *Passeggiata di Ripetta* (3 A4-5), designed by Giuseppe Valadier and opened around 1840, which runs alongside the Lungotevere in Augusta at a slightly lower level.

S. Girolamo degli Illirici (13 E6). Dedicated to St. Jerome by refugees from the Illyrian region, across the Adriatic, who reached Rome in the 15th c., this church was built by Sixtus IV on the site of the church of S. Marina and rebuilt in 1588 by Martino Longhi the Elder, who also designed and built the facade in travertine, crowned with a pediment (restored, 1987-91). The Baroque interior has three chapels on each side, a false dome, and a transept: the frescoes in the tribune are by Antonio Viviani and Andrea Lilio (1588), the *Glory of the Saint* in the vault is by Paris Nogari (1588).

The Ara Pacis Augustae (detail)

The nearby church of *S. Rocco* (3 B5; 4 B1; 6 A3; 13 E6), built in 1499 by the Confraternita di S. Rocco, on the site of an 11th-c. building, was designed in its current Baroque form by Giovanni Antonio de Rossi, while the facade bears the marks of the Neoclassical reconstruction done by Giuseppe Valadier (1834).

Ara Pacis Augustae* (3 B5). This Augustan altar of peace is one of the best known and most significant pieces of Roman art from the reign of Augustus (it was dedicated in 9 B.C. to commemorate the peace that ensued after the great campaigns in Gaul and

Spain), and it was unearthed on the site of Palazzo Fiano (the monument was originally located along the segment of the Via Flaminia that lay within Mura Aureliane, or Aurelian walls) and was then enclosed within the current glass pavillion, in the 1930s; the base upon which it stands is engraved, on the side facing the Via di Ripetta, with the text of the "Res Gestae Divi Augusti," an account of the emperor's political career.

The altar comprises a rectangular enclosure wall (11.65 x 10.62 m.), inside which stands the actual altar, or "ara"; the most noteworthy scene depicted in the relief decoration – heavily restored – can be seen on the short side of the enclosure wall; you can recognize Augustus, Agrippa, Julia, and Tiberius.

Mausoleo di Augusto* (3 B5). This mausoleum of Augustus was not unearthed until 1936-38 (to tour it, you should contact the X Ripartizione del Comune), and originally stood 44 m. tall, with a mound, planted with cypress trees and surmounted by a bronze statue; on the interior was a cella containing the remains of Augustus; surrounding the central pillar – which supported the structure – lay the tombs of the most eminent members of the Julian-Claudian clan; alongside the entrance, looking south, two obelisks once stood (one now stands in the Piazza dell'Esquilino, the other in the Piazza del Quirinale) while two pillars held tablets on which was engraved the autobiography of the emperor.

Built in 27 B.C. but in ruins by late antiquity, the mausoleum was used as a quarry for building materials (the incessant quarrying has reduced it to its present size); in time it was used as a vineyard, hanging garden, amphitheater, theater, and auditorium (the hall, with excellent acoustics, is now closed to the public).

Palazzo di Giustizia (building of the ministry of justice; 3 B-C3). Better known as the Palazzaccio (an uncomplimentary nickname, evoking the heavy-handed design and decoration of the building) and now the site of the Corte Suprema di Cassazione, Italy's supreme court, this building was erected between 1888 and 1910 in massive blocks of travertine, ultimately causing the collapse of the soil beneath (restoration and shoring up has been underway since 1970). Overlooking the Tiber is the rear facade, adorned by a bronze *quadriga* by Ettore Ximenes (1907), while the main facade overlooks the nearby *Piazza Cavour* (3 B3); here, in the center, stands a *monument to*

Cavour (Stefano Galletti, 1895).

On a line with the portal of the rear elevation of the Palazzo di Giustizia runs the *Ponte Umberto I* (3 C-D3; 6 B1; 13 F5), a bridge built by Angelo Vescovali between 1885 and 1895.

Casa Madre dei Mutilati (3 C2-3). Designed by Marcello Piacentini in 1928-36, this structure is typical of the orotund style of the Fascist regime. The massive structure, made of tufa and travertine, overlooks the Piazza Adriana (over the portal, note the bronze sculptural group by Giovanni Prini), while another major elevation overlooks the Tiber; in a hall on the second floor, note the frescoes by Mario Sironi. This building is the headquarters of the national association of war invalids – Associazione Nazionale Mutilati e Invalidi di Guerra – and of a high Roman court, the Corte d'Appello di Roma.

Ponte S. Angelo* (3 D2). This is the ancient bridge, or "**Pons Aelius**" that the emperor Hadrian ordered built in A.D. 133-134 (the three central arches still stand) to connect his own mausoleum with the opposite bank of the river (Castel S. Angelo, which since incorporated that mausoleum, is described on page 173); it was restored at the behest of Nicholas V in 1447-53 following the collapse of the bridge's parapets, caused by the enormous crowd that filled Rome for the Jubilee of 1450. Popes Clement VII and Clement IX arranged to have the bridge laid out in the present spectacular manner, and the job was completed with the direct intervention of Gian Lorenzo Bernini and his school: the artist designed the statues (tradition long held that the *Angel with the Cross*, now attributed to Ercole Ferrata, was by Bernini himself; the *Angel with a Scroll* and the *Angel with a Crown of Thorns* are copies of originals) and their arrangment. From the bridge, near which the Jewish community would pay homage to the new pope during the great procession along the "Via Papalis" (see page 107) which marked the new pope's official entry into the Vaticano, there is a splendid view of the Via della Conciliazione (see page 75) and the Basilica di S. Pietro (St. Peter's cathedral; see page 76).

Ponte Vittorio Emanuele II (3 D1). Inaugurated in 1911 for the 50th anniversary of the proclamation of the united Kingdom of Italy and the International Exposition, this bridge was designed as an ideal conclusion of the Corso Vittorio Emanuele II (see page 66) toward Borgo and the Ospedale di S. Spirito in Sassia (see page 141).

Downstream, you can make out ruins of the piers of the *"Pons Neronianus"*, which collapsed or was demolished, probably in the 6th c. Roughly on the site of that bridge, Pope Julius II decided to build – parallel to the Ponte Sisto (see below) – the Ponte Giulio, but it was never built.

Ponte Principe Amedeo Savoia Aosta (3 E1). This bridge, named after a prince of the house of Savoy, was built in masonry, with travertine facing in 1939-42, and it serves the traffic that pours under the lower slopes of the Janiculum through the tunnel, or *Galleria Principe Amedeo Savoia Aosta* (2 D-E4-5), built immediately after WWII.

Ponte Mazzini (3 F2). This bridge, also built in masonry and faced in travertine, adorned with elegant lamps made of bronze, stands on a line with the prison, or Carcere di Regina Coeli.

Ponte Sisto* (7 B4). Baccio Pontelli may have designed this, the only bridge built in

out to the right onto the *Piazza Trilussa* (7 B4), once known as the Piazza di Ponte Sisto. In 1898 the *Fontana dell'Acqua Paola*, a fountain that Pope Paul V had ordered built at the end of the Via Giulia on the other side of the bridge, was erected here; this fountain was used to flood the streets during particularly hot summer days. The *Monument to Trilussa*, the pseudonym of the poet Carlo Alberto Salustri, who loved the trattorias and taverns of the surrounding areas, dates from 1954.

Ponte Garibaldi (7 C5-6). This bridge was built by Angelo Vescovali in 1884-88 on a line with the Viale di Trastevere (see page 136), and was widened in 1955-57. From the point directly over the central pier, you have a fine view of the Isola Tiberina (see below).

Isola Tiberina* (8 C1-2). This island was known as Licaonia in the Middle Ages, and later as the Isola di S. Bartolomeo, after the church that stands on the island; more recently it has been dubbed the "Isola dei

The Tiber river bending around the Isola Tiberina

Rome (1473-75) between the end of the classical era and the end of the 19th c. This bridge has four arches, is made of tufa-stone and travertine (the opening in the central pylon was used for centuries as a warning sign of flood waters), and incorporates in its structure an arch dating from Roman times (possibly the Ponte di Agrippa or the Ponte Aurelio, also known as the Ponte di Antonino), which had collapsed in A.D. 589; the bridge was widened in 1877 with a metal structure.

On a line with this bridge, the riverfront avenue, or Lungotevere della Farnesina, opens

Due Ponti," or island of two bridges (the Ponte Cestio links it to the right bank, the Ponte Fabricio to the left); it has been a holy place of worship for various deities, and was dedicated to Aesculapius, because it is said that the snake that was holy to the god of medicine, being brought to Rome from Epidaurus at the time of the plague of 293 B.C., leapt from the ship and indicated on the island the site upon which to build a temple to the god; in commemoration of that legend, there still stands today, on the east mooring area, downstream, a *statue of Aesculapius with the serpent entwined around a staff, and the head of a bull*; this figure may be a mooring bollard. This tradition of curing and medicine, enhanced by the wide-held belief that the spring on the island yielded particularly healthful water, led, at the end of the 16th c., to the construction of the first nucleus of the hospital; during the plague of 1656, the entire island was used as a quarantine area. The construction of the great embankment walls gave the island its current rhomboid shape (although at the end of the end of the 19th c. there was some talk of eliminating it entirely), which enhances its ship-like appearance, cutting through the river waters.

The bridge linking the Lungotevere degli Anguillara to the island is the *Ponte Cestio* (7 C6; 8 C1), a late-19th-c. reconstruction of the ancient bridge of that name (the central arch still survives), built in 46 a.C. by Lucius Cestius, who gave it its name; the bridge is also known as the Ponte di Graziano (after Gratian, one of the emperors who restored it) and the Ponte di S. Bartolomeo.

Overlooking the little square is the church of *S. Bartolomeo all'Isola* (8 C1), which was erected at the behest of Otto III upon the ruins of the temple of Aesculapius, rebuilt in 1583-85 (maybe by Martino Longhi the Elder) after the flood of 1557, and further renovated in 1623-24; the most recent restoration was done in 1973-76. The facade, attributed to Orazio Torriani or to Martino Longhi the Younger, features in its upper register a *fragment of mosaic* dating from work done under Pope Alexander III in 1180; the *campanile* dates from the times of the first restoration of the church (1113). Inside, the nave and two aisles are lined with columns, possibly taken from the ancient temple; the marble *well head* at the center of the stairs into the presbytery, thought to be by either Nicola d'Angelo or Pietro Vassalletto, may have been used for the health-giving spring.

A tower, or *Torre Caetani*, surviving from a medieval fortress, defends the entrance to the **Ponte Fabricio** (8 C1), a bridge that is also known as the Ponte dei Quattro Capi, or bridge of the four heads, for the two four-faced sculptures that adorn its parapets; it was also known as the "Pons Judaeorum," or bridge of the Jews, since it was near the Ghetto, or more probably because of the number of Jews who crossed it when coming here from Trastevere. The bridge, which has survived virtually intact, was built by Lucius Fabricius (62 B.C.); the 2nd-c.

restoration replaced the original travertine facing with bricks.

Ponte Rotto (8 D2). This bridge is the ancient *"Pons Aemilius"* (the first bridge made of stone), and was erected in 181-179 B.C. by Marcus Aemilius Lepidus and Marcus Fulvius Nobilioris, and completed by Publius Scipio Africanus and Lucius Mummida in 142 B.C.; it owes its modern name – literally, "broken bridge" – to the numerous collapses and subsequent restorations (in 1548-49 work was done on it by Michelangelo).

The bridge collapsed completely in 1598, and at the end of the 19th c., three arches survived; two of them were demolished for the construction of the *Ponte Palatino* (1886; 8 D1-2), which accommodates heavy traffic; from it, you can enjoy a fine view of the left bank of the river (the temple of Vesta and the temple of Fortuna Virile as well as the church of S. Maria in Cosmedin are described on page 42). The surviving arch of the ancient bridge still features the heraldic crest (dragon) of Pope Gregory XIII.

Ex Ospizio Apostolico di S. Michele a Ripa Grande (7 E-F5-6). This complex, once a hospice and now the main offices of the Ministero per i Beni Culturali e Ambientali (ministry for culture and the environment), and the Istituto Centrale per il Catalogo e la Documentazione and part of the Istituto Centrale del Restauro (two agencies concerned with documentation and restoration), stands on the right side of the Lungotevere Ripa; the construction of this riverfront boulevard resulted in the destruction of the Porto di Ripa Grande, once the largest river port in all Rome. The hospice was built, beginning in the late 17th c., by Mattia de Rossi and Carlo Fontana, as an institution for re-education and charity; in 1734-35, Ferdinando Fuga built the *Carcere Femminile*, or women's prison, toward Piazza di Porta Portese, while the church of *S. Michele*, begun in 1710-15, was completed in 1831-35.

Ponte Sublicio (7 F6). The modern bridge (Marcello Piacentini, 1914-18) commemorates the wooden bridge built in the pre-republican days by Tullius Hostilius and Ancus Marcius – or perhaps only by the latter – and the site of the legendary resistance by Publius Horatius Cocles against the Etruscan army of Lars Porsenna.

4 The City Following the Unification of Italy

When the new national government of Italy took up residence in Rome in the decade following the storming of the city, the problem arose of how to facilitate the creation of a new class of bureaucrats and administrative officials – with the structures of all the ministries and agencies that were called upon to govern a nation that had only just begun to think of itself as a nation, but that had historic needs to fulfill, needs for justice and reforms of all sorts – in an urban structure that tended to strangle expansion, in which the buildings of the new ministries still remained to be built, for the most part, or even rebuilt. Remarkable zeal and energy was expended on this task, new streets were built through the old "rioni," but above all new areas were singled out in which to build, allowing the city to expand beyond the farthest reaches of the walled perimeters, walls that were no longer needed.

A rider on horseback in the park of Villa Borghese

New quarters were built, through demolition and redefinitions of the urban space, broad green areas disappeared that for centuries, with their shady and secluded views, had been hidden jewels of the city; the immense park of Villa Ludovisi, for example, was sacrificed to make way for homes – despite the terse pages by D'Annunzio deploring the destruction, and the echoing notes of Goethe – and a new quarter (the Quartiere Boncompagni-Ludovisi, to be precise).

Outside of the city boundaries, the operation was of course less painful, but it still meant the sacrifice of a number of architectural landmarks (consider the Porta Salaria and the renovation of the entire area of what is now Piazza Fiume) in areas that were once on the edge of the city. The old roads that exited the gates of the walls, or Mura Serviane and the Mura Aureliane, took their names from the places to which they led or from the magistrates that oversaw their construction; this name in some cases was also applied to the new quarters or at least to the areas in which they stood (Nomentano, Tiburtino, etc.).

The enormous suburban villas of the ancient Roman patricians were almost entirely demolished, if we exclude a short stretch of the Via Appia Antica, while the villas of the new patricians were moved into the area slightly further out from the city in the Middle Ages and the Renaissance, to be reached only with the slow urban expansion that followed; thus a broad stretch of territory remained unoccupied, to be systematically settled by intensive development in the last decade of the 19th c. and in the first three decades of the 20th c., in nearly all directions; paradoxically, what was saved – at least in part – was the route running toward the sea that Fascist plans and other successive plans for development had always singled out for development.

The seven routes in this chapter all branch off from the main roads that set out from the Mura Aureliane, or Aurelian walls, exploring the most significant monuments and landmarks – both ancient and modern – in the extensive township area of Roma, the largest single township in all Italy.

4.1 Villa Borghese, Valle Giulia, Parioli

This route is an ideal evocation of that harmony between the city and its green areas open to the public, which according to the regulatory plans that were issued following the unification of Italy, and at least as late as the great International Exposition of 1911, should have been the product of the history, the culture, and the social life of Rome.

This linkage, although it was roundly abandoned following WWII, remains one of the most fertile ideas to emerge from the plans for Rome as a capital in the early years of the 20th c.

From Piazzale Flaminio out through the Porta del Popolo, this walking tour in its first section wanders through the park of Villa Borghese, punctuated with Neoclassical monuments and adorned with busts of famous personages, and where the Museo Borghese and the Galleria Borghese, set in the "lodge," or Casino Borghese, constitute "la regina delle raccolte private del mondo" ("the queen of the world's private art collections").

Beyond the Galleria Nazionale d'Arte Moderna, a national gallery of modern art, the route continues through the Valle Giulia, which was renovated as a quarter for the International Exposition of 1911, as far as the Mannerist structure of the Villa Giulia, which contains an Etruscan museum, the Museo Etrusco di Villa Giulia, and on to the Palazzina di Pio IV at the corner of Via Flaminia; a long detour allows us to venture into the Quartiere dei Parioli, a neighborhood that features a sizable number of residential buildings dating from the 1920s to the 1960s.

Villa Borghese* (plan 1). The splendid park was created in the 17th c. on behalf of the cardinal Scipione Borghese Caffarelli, who also had the Casino Borghese built there (see below) as a place in which to display his own art collection.

A first transformation was supervised in the 18th c. by Antonio and Mario Asprucci with Carlo Unterberger, and they clearly favored the picturesque and the Neoclassical; a further expansion was designed and supervised by Luigi Canina, who also designed, in 1827, the Roman Arch (see page 155), the Greek Propylaea (1 C1) and the Egyptian Propylaea (1 C2), and in 1830-34 the Fontana di Esculapio (fountain of Aesculapius; 1 B-C2).

Purchased by the Italian state in 1901, the villa, dedicated to King Umberto I, was donated to the city of Rome in 1903.

Casino Borghese (1 B-C6). Built between 1613 and 1617 to plans by Flaminio Ponzio and renovated at the end of the 18th c. through a distinctly Neoclassical decorative filter, this building presents two side wings united by a covered portico and a set-back central wing, with busts and statues set in niches.

Museo Borghese and Galleria Borghese*. Distributed over the ground floor and the second floor, the collections, certainly some of the most interesting in the world (the ancient marble work is accompanied by masterpieces of Renaissance and Baroque art, as well as sculpture and painting dating from the 16th to the 19th c.), were first assembled in 1608 by the cardinal Scipione, who enriched the collection of marble work and sculpture with the fine specimens given him by Pope Paul V, originating in the old St. Peter's; the collection was largely given away to France by prince Camillo Borghese under the rule of Napoleon.

The portrait gallery managed to remain intact, and here the cardinal assembled works by great artists (Raphael, Caravaggio, Botticelli); new collections flowed into it, like the collection of Olimpia Aldobrandini.

You enter the **Museo Borghese** through a portico, in which you should notice the front of a *sarcophagus with a battle between Romans and barbarians* (late-2nd c.), taken from the Basilica di S. Pietro.

In the large and richly decorated hall, there are niches with 12 *busts of emperors*; the *colossal head of Hadrian* is one of the finest idealized portraits of the emperor; the fragment of a *high relief* with a horse was integrated by Pietro Bernini as *Curtius leaping on horseback into the chasm of the Roman Forum*; on the floor, fragments of 4th-c. mosaics with *scenes of hunting in the circus* and *gladiatorial combat*.

After the Sala della Paolina (hall I), with at the center the celebrated *Venus Victorious**, a masterpiece by Antonio Canova (1805), is the Sala del Davide (hall II), which takes its name from a work carved by Gian Lorenzo Bernini in his youth, between 1623 and 1624 for the cardinal Scipione and depicting *David firing his slingshot** (the face is a self-portrait of Bernini himself).

f special note, at the center of the next oom, the Sala dell'Apollo e Dafne (hall III), the vibrant *group of Apollo and Daphne**, nother youthful masterpiece by Bernini 624), and the *statue of a boy with a duck*, aken from a Hellenistic original; on the alls, *Landscapes* by Paul Brill.

he Galleria degli Imperatori (hall IV), with, the vault, the *stories of Galataea* by omenico De Angelis, and, along the walls, 8 *busts of emperors* in porphyry and alaster (18th c.), features at the center the *ape of Proserpine* by Bernini.

the Sala dell'Ermafrodito (hall V) note e *Sleeping Hermaphrodite*, taken from a ellenistic prototype.

the Sala dell'Enea e Anchise (hall VI) we hould point out, among the various Roman culptures, *Truth Unveiled by Time* by Berni- i (ca. 1652), the *group of Aeneas and Anhises* executed by Pietro and Gian Lorenzo ernini, and a bas-relief with *Bacchanal* by rançois Duquesnoy.

eyond the Sala Egizia, the tour is comleted by the Sala del Fauno Danzante (hall II), with a *Dancing Silenus*, a Roman bronze aken from an original of the school of Lysipus, a *statue of a sleeping satyr* from Praiteles, and the *portrait of Faustina Major* rom the 2nd c.; on the walls: *Giuditta and Oloferne* by Giovanni Baglione; the *Abducon of Europa* and the *Capture of Christ* by he Cavalier d'Arpino; **Boy with a basket of ruit***, *St. Jerome* and *St. John the Baptist* by Caravaggio; the *Capture of Christ* by Dirk van Baburen.

fter the vestibule of the **Galleria Borghese**, which leads up to the Galleria degli Imperatori, hall IX contains, alongside the celerated **Deposition*** by Raphael (signature; 507; who painted the *Portrait of a young woman** and a *Portrait of man*), the *Virgin Mary with Christ Child, St. John, and Angels* by Sandro Botticelli and pupils, the *Sacred Family* by Fra Bartolomeo, the *Crucifix with Saint Jerome and Saint Christopher* attributed to Pinturicchio, and the *Virgin Mary with Christ Child* by Perugino.

hall X, decorated in the vault with the *Labors of Hercules* by Cristoforo Unterperger, note, among other things, the *Danae** by Correggio, a *Portrait of a man* by Parmigianino, the *Virgin Mary with Christ Child and Young St. John* by Andrea del Saro, *John the Baptist* by Bronzino, *Venus and Adonis bearing the honeycomb* by Lucas Cranach il Vecchio.

As you pass through halls XI-XIII (you will find paintings by Scarsellino, Garofalo, Ludovico Mazzolino and Ortolano in the first; n the second a *Portrait of a woman* by Gio-

vanni Antonio Boetraffio, a *Sacred Fami-ly* by Sodoma, a *Christ in the act of blessing* by Marco d'Oggiono; in the third a *St. Francis* and a *Madonna with Child* by Francesco Francia, a *Madonna with Child and St. Joseph and St. Giovannino* by the Landscape Kress Master and *Christ at the column* by Lorenzo Costa), you will reach the large and well-lit hall XIV (the vault was frescoed in 1624 by Giovanni Lanfranco with the *Council of the Gods*), with *Moses with the Commandments* by Guido Reni; a *Selfportrait in later life*, one in *youth* and a *Childhood portrait* by Gian Lorenzo Bernini; a *Sacred Family with Angels* by Pomarancio, the *Battle of Tullio Ostilio against the Veienti* by Cavalieri d'Arpino; the *Four Seasons* "tondi" by Francesco Albani.

In halls XV-XVII we should point out the works by Federico Barocci, Dosso Dossi

The "Madonna of the Grooms" by Caravaggio

(*Gige and Candaule; Adoration of Christ Child*), Scarsellino (*Christ with his Disciples on the way to Emmaus*), the *Adoration of the Magi* and the *Last Supper* by Jacopo Bassano, *Tobiolo and the angel* and the *Figure of a young man* by Giovanni Girolamo Savoldo, the *Resurrection of Christ* by Marco Pino, the *Nativity* by Giorgio Vasari; the *Adoration of Christ Child* by Giorgio Vasari, the *Madonnas with Child* by Sassoferrato and Pompeo Botoni.

In hall XVIII there are two masterpieces by Pieter Paul Rubens (*Weeping on the dead Christ* and *Susanna and the old men*) and the *Portrait of Marcello Sacchetti* by Pietro da

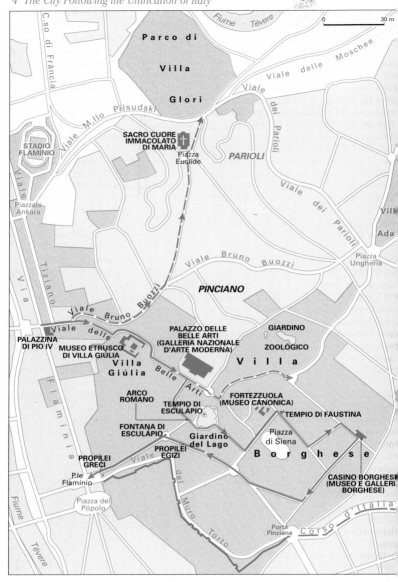

Cortona, while hall XIX features the *Escape of Enea from Troy* and *St. Jerome* by Federico Barocci, *Diana's Hunt* and the *Sibyl Cumana* by Domenichino, the *Ecstasy of St. Catherine* by Agostino Carracci and *Norandino and Lucina* by Giovanni Lanfranco. The tour ends with the hall XX, which features a number of masterpieces: *Sacred and Profane Love** painted by Titian in 1514; **Portrait of a Man*** by Antonello da Messina; *Venus Blindfolding Love*, a late work by Titian; *John the Baptist Preaching* by Bonifacio Veronese; the *Virgin Mary with Christ Child*,

signed by Giovanni Bellini, the *Flagellation of Christ* and *St. Domenick*, also by Titian.

Fortezzuola (1 B4). This is the 17th-c. Casa del Gallinaro, transformed into a medieval-style castle, probably by Luigi Canina.
The nearby *temple of Faustina*, of 1792, is a significant testimonial of the taste for specially-made ruins of that period.

Piazza di Siena (1 C4). Created by Mario and Antonio Asprucci at the end of the 18th c., on the model of Roman amphitheaters, this square, some 200 m. in length and surrounded by tall umbrella pines, is the site every year of a celebrated horse race.

Giardino del Lago (1 B-C3-4). This garden was laid out at the end of the 18th c. around a small manmade lake, with artificial structures set amidst the natural greenery (the mascarons that adorn the *fountain* on the right were created at the end of the 16th c., along with the four tritons set on the edges, done to plans drawn up by Giacomo Della Porta for the Fontana del Moro in Piazza Navona), and adorned, on the islet in the center of the body of water, by the little *temple of Aesculapius*, designed in the Ionic style by Antonio and Mario Asprucci; Luigi Canina (1826-27) designed and built the nearby *Roman Arch*.

Palazzo delle Belle Arti (1 A2-3). Cesare Bazzani built this "palace of fine arts" on occasion of the International Exposition of 1911, endowing it with a solemn classical-style facade decorated with Liberty (Italian name for Art Nouveau) motifs and celebratory friezes; the sculptures in the flower beds on either side of the stairway are by – among others – Ettore Colla, Umberto Mastroianni, and Pietro Consagra.

Galleria Nazionale d'Arte Moderna*. Established in 1883 in the Palazzo delle Esposizioni and transferred here in 1914, it was originally meant to assemble documentation and examples of Italian art of the 19th c. with clear reference to the process of formation of a national identity, in both cultural and artistic terms. The collection of Italian painting, sculpture, and graphics of the 19th and 20th c. is one of the largest such collections in existence, and is flanked by an interesting array of works by non-Italian artists.

In the **left wing of the museum**, devoted to 19th-c. painting and sculpture, the first hall documents the Neoclassical period and the subsequent Romantic phase, through works by Andrea Appiani, Francesco Podesti, Pelagio Palagi, Tomaso Minardi, Joseph Anton Koch, Antonio Canova, Pietro Tenerani, Francesco Hayez, and the Piccio; also note the *Landscapes* by A. Fontanesi, the *View Paintings* by G. Gigante, and the group of artworks donated by the Palizzi family.

Next is the collection of paintings by the Tuscan school of the Macchiaioli, with the *Battle of Custoza* by Giovanni Fattori (1880), *The Visit* by Silvestro Lega (1868), *Houses at Lerici* by Vincenzo Cabianca, and paintings

by Giovanni Boldini, Adriano Cecioni, and Telemaco Signorini.

The painters of the Neapolitan school are represented by the *Temptations of St. Anthony* by Domenico Morelli (1878), the *Battle of Dogali* by Michele Cammarano, the well-known *Luisa Sanfelice in Prison* by Gioacchino Toma (1877), and by the sculptures by Vincenzo Gemito, including the well-known *Water Carrier* from 1881.

Documenting the school of "social realism" are the works of Teofilo Patini, Vincenzo Vela, and Constantin Meunier, while among the "Divisionist" artists, note Giuseppe Pellizza, Angelo Morbelli, and Gaetano Previati. Next come the halls dedicated to Medardo Rosso, the Symbolists, and the landscape painters of the Roman Campagna, noteworthy among them, Nino Costa and Henry Coleman.

Of particular interest, among the non-Italian artists, are Auguste Rodin, Gustave Coubert, Edgar Degas, Claude Monet, and Vincent Van Gogh.

In the central interior garden, note the *Bather* by Emilio Greco (1956).

In the **right wing of the museum**, dedicated to collections of art of the 20th c., note a corridor, with reliefs by Duilio Cambellotti, that leads to hall I, in which, among other things, you should note *The Three Ages* by Gustav Klimt (1905), *Le Cabanon de Jourdan* by Paul Cézanne (1906), *Lightning* by Luigi Russolo (1909-1910), *Centaurs Fighting* by Giorgio De Chirico (1909), and

Small bronze sculpture of a ploughman

portraits by Amedeo Modigliani.

Halls II-III feature works by Umberto Boccioni, Giacomo Balla, Gino Severini, Georges Braque, Aleksandr Archipenko, Carlo Carrà, Giorgio Morandi, Piet Mondrian, Marcel Duchamp, and Hans Arp.

In the large central hall and on the veranda are examples of various aspects of figurative art between WWI and WWII: *Self-portrait* by Marino Marini (1930), *Crucifixions* by Giacomo Manzù (1939), *Solitude* by Mario Sironi (1925), *Horses* by Carlo Carrà (1927), *Sou-*

venir d'enfance à Athènes by Alberto Savinio (1930), *The Brides of the Sailors* by Massimo Campigli (1934), *Still Lifes* by Giorgio Morandi, *Mechanical Landscape* by Fillìa (1925) and artworks by Gerardo Dottori, Mario Mafai, Scipione, Antonietta Raphael Mafai, Fausto Pirandello, and Pericle Fazzini.

The succeeding halls IV-VI feature works by Filippo De Pisis, Mino Maccari, and Mario Broglio, as well as abstract art by Mauro

"Superficie 323", one of Giuseppe Capogrossi's works on display at the Galleria Nazionale d'Arte Moderna

Reggiani, Osvaldo Licini, Atanasio Soldati, and Carla Badiali and the *Angular Line*, painted in 1930 by Vasily Kandinsky.

A flight of stairs leads into the wing of the building that was added during the 1930s, where, aside from the De Chirico and Guttuso donations, there are various artistic creations, dating from the 1950s and 1960s, by Afro Basaldella, Lucio Fontana, Alberto Burri, Ettore Colla, Giuseppe Capogrossi, Emilio Vedova, Pietro Consagra, Gio Pomodoro, Daniel Spoerri, Jannis Kounellis, Piero Manzoni, Jackson Pollock, Hans Hartung, Jean Fautrier, Max Bill, Eduardo Chillida, Alexander Calder, Victor Pasmore, and Alberto Giacometti.

To the right of the Palazzo delle Belle Arti begins the Viale del Giardino Zoologico, which takes its name from the *Giardino Zoologico* (zoo; 1 A3-4-5), which covers a surface area of about 17 hectares; inside the zoo is the *Museo Civico di Zoologia*, a zoological museum, whose oldest specimens date back to the papacy of Pius VII.

Viale delle Belle Arti (1 A-B1-2-3). Designed in the context of the urban renovation done by Cesare Bazzani for the International Exposition of 1911, this avenue winds through an area known as the Valle Giulia, whose slopes are studded with academies and foreign cultural institutes.

Villa Giulia* (1 A1-2). Site of the Etruscan museum that bears its name (see below), this villa was built between 1551 and 1555, at the behest of Pope Julius III, by Bartolomeo Ammannati, Giorgio Vasari, and the Vignola, and lavishly decorated on the interior by Prospero Fontana and Taddeo Zuccari.

It presents a complex architectural structure, which develops along a longitudinal axis, punctuated by the theatrical succession of interior and exterior spaces: beyond the stern and monumental facade, with a distinct fore-wing occupying two stories, there is a succession of three courtyards, punctuated by the curving lines of the splendid **loggia** by Ammannati (signature on the pillar on the right) and the elegant *nymphaeum**, which is concluded at the bottom by the *Fontana dell'Acqua Vergine*, or fountain of the Aqua Virgo (1552-53) designed by Vasari in collaboration with Ammannati; the third courtyard was completed, with considerable modifications, only around 1750.

The garden to the right of the first courtyard is occupied by a hypothetical 19th-c. reconstruction of the little Etrusco-Italic *temple of Alatri*.

Museo Etrusco di Villa Giulia*. This museum of Etruscan archeology and art, founded in 1889 to house the pre-Roman heritage of Latium, Umbria, and southern Etruria, contains a precious and vast array of artifacts from Etruscan and Faliscan civilizations, as well as materials from Greek civilization (7th/5th c. B.C.).

The first five halls contain the materials unearthed in the necropolises and in the urban areas of Vulci (note in particular the bronze *panoply taken from the Tomba del Guerriero**, or tomb of the warrior, dating back to the 6th c. B.C.), while hall VI contains artifacts that dated from the time in which Etruscan civilization was first developing, from the necropolis Olmo Bello in Bisenzio; of particular note, at the center of the next hall (VII), are the **statues** in polyhrome terracotta **of Herakles in combat against Apollo for the doe** and *of a Goddess Latona?) with a child in her arms* (Apollo?); these were acroterial decorations from the emple of Portonaccio at Veio and are true masterpieces of Etruscan art (end of the 6th B.C.).

n halls VIII-X you can see material unearthed at Cervèteri; among the objects, here are numerous Greek vases dating om the 7th to the 6th c. B.C.; also note the plendid *Sarcofago degli Sposi**, a sarcophagus made of polychrome terracotta (ca. 30 B.C.).

fter the halls XI-XVIII – in which you can ee jewelry, votive statuettes, candelabra, omestic objects made of bronze and terracotta, mirrors, cistae, cinerary urns, and ttic and Corinthian vases (note in particular the *Oinochoe Chigi**, an oenochoe, r wine pitcher, dating back to 640-625 .C.), votive objects (depictions of hands, et, heads, etc.) and the bronze *handles* 30-520 B.C.) of the Biga di Castro, a chariot – you will climb up into the large hemicycle, hall XIX contains the interesting *astellani collection*, donated to the Italian ate in 1919; this collection contains all ategories of Greek and Italic-Etruscan ceramics, dating from the 8th to the 1st c. .C., hall XX will be dedicated to the Museo ella Villa, hall XXI contains the findings om Pyrgi (architectural and sculptural elments from temples A and B), in hall XXII ou can also find **gold leaf** works with inscriptions in Etruscan and Punico. Halls XIV and XXV are reserved for the collections of gold found in Castles (8th c. B.C. - 9th c. A.D.).

alls XXVI-XXIX feature tomb furnishings om the Faliscan territory, especially those om "Falerii Veteres" (modern-day Cìvita astellana): note the *krater with volutes* by he Pittore dell'Aurora (ca. 360-350 B.C.); alls XXX-XXXI, dedicated to the *temples of Falerii Veteres"**, document Etrusco-Italic emple decorations between the 6th and 1st B.C. and features, in the display cases, the ecorative sculpture, with interesting specimens from the 4th c. B.C.

eyond the halls XXXII-XXXIII, dedicated to the Etruscan and Etruscan-Italic material found in the ancient towns around Rome, hall XXXIV features the rich furnishings of the **Barberini tomb** and the **Bernardini tomb**, from the "Orientalizing" era, discovered near ancient "Praeneste" (now Palestrina), with refined objects made of precious metals, ivory, and bronze, from the middle of the 7th c. B.C.; from the same site comes the renowned *Ficoroni Cista**, depicting an episode from the myth of the Argonauts, created around the end of the 4th c. B.C. in Rome, as we see from the inscription on the plate on the handle ("Novios Plautios med Romai fecid, Dindia Malconia fileai dedid": literally, "Novius Plautius made me in Rome, Dindia Malconia gave me to his daughter"). Of note, in the last hall (XXXIV), are the materials taken from Hellenistic necropolises of Umbria.

Parioli (12 D-E-F5-6). This quarter, the most verdant area in Rome, long inhabited by the upper classes, began to develop between 1918 and 1924, following the International Exposition of 1911, and was laid out definitively by the regulatory plan of 1931; it acquired its present appearance following WWII.

The main thoroughfares of this quarter are the *Viale Buozzi*, which was built in 1938 and which features, after Piazza Don Minzoni, a number of interesting examples of buildings dating from 1940 to 1960, and the *Viale dei Parioli* (ca. 1888), which features small villas and mansions dating from the 1920s and 1930s; one monumental area is the exceedingly busy *Piazza Euclide*, at the center of which was inaugurated in 1952 the *church of the Sacro Cuore Immacolato di Maria*, designed by Armando Brasini.

Palazzina di Pio IV (12 F4-5). This mansion, set at the corner of Via Flaminia (see page 158), was built to plans by Pirro Ligorio (1561), around the elevation of the monumental fountain, the *Fontana dell'Acqua Vergine*, attributed to Bartolomeo Ammannati and the Vignola, and now visible at the corner of Via di Valle Giulia.

.2 The Via Flaminia and the Via Cassia

s you exit Rome heading north you will encounter a wide array of landscape and architecture, in relatively close areas; conder the areas surrounding the Via Flaminia Statale 3) and the Via Cassia (Statale 2); the ia Cassia, with its more intense and disorderly urbanization, represents a fairly chaotic development of the city, outside of any orderly design or plan, and is now lined by city structures as far as the boundary of the province of Rome. Along the Via Flaminia, on the other hand, there is still a

fairly unspoilt environment, especially outside of Rome's beltway, the Raccordo Anulare, with patches of the Roman Campagna that have disappeared elsewhere.

We recommend two routes here. The first runs along the Via Flaminia (map on the left), beginning from the Porta del Popolo; the section of this route that runs as far as the Ponte Milvio, or Milvian Bridge – a walking tour – features the sports facilities built for the Olympics of 1960 (also of interest, however is the 16th-c. church of S. Andrea; beyond the Ponte Milvio, you may wish to drive as far as the Villa "ad Gallinas Albas," also known as the Villa di Livia, and splendidly frescoed.

The second route, for which you will need to drive the whole way (map on page 159) runs from Piazzale di Ponte Milvio along the route of the old Via Cassia, reaching the medieval village of Isola Farnese and the archeological area of the Etruscan town of Veio; a short detour along the Statale 493 Via Claudia Braccianese, which follows the ancient Via Clodia, allows you to tour the church of S. Maria di Galèria, in a wonderfully intact natural setting.

Via Flaminia (12 B-C-D-E-F3-4). This road was built in 223-219 B.C. by the censor Caius Flaminius to connect Rome with "Ariminum" (Rimini); it was later extended to Ravenna (and was therefore called the Via Ravennana in the Middle Ages); in ancient times it began from the Porta Ratumena in the Mura Serviane, or Servian walls (see page 32), while following the erection of the Aurelian walls (see page 171) it began from the Porta Flaminia, now Porta del Popolo (see page 46). Of considerable importance throughout Rome's history for communications with the north, this road was studded during imperial times with monumental tombs, and beginning in the second half of the 16th c., with patrician villas – foremost among them the Casino Borghese in the Villa Borghese (see page 152) – while following WWII, the "borgate," or quarters of Làbaro and Prima Porta sprang up; over recent years, a number of factories have been built along the Grande Raccordo Anulare, Rome's beltway.

The strip of greenery running between the Via Flaminia and the Viale Tiziano is only part actually completed of the *Passeggiata Flaminia* (12 E-F4-5; 13 A-B5), a promenade designed in the years just before and after the unification of Italy. On the Via Flaminia, in 1887, the first horse-drawn trolley in Rome was inaugurated, and in 1890, the first electric trolley ran here as well.

S. Andrea* (12 F4; 13 A5). This church was founded (1552-53) shortly after the Sack of Rome of 1527 by Pope Julius III, who, while still a cardinal, had been handed over by Pope Clement VII to the Lansquenets along with other hostages as surety of a ransom; he managed to escape on St. Andrew's day (Giorno di S. Andrea); this area was chosen because, according to tradition, Cardinal Bessarion stopped here while carrying the relics of St. Andrew to Rome. The elegant design by Vignola is embellished with an oval dome and a facade made of peperino, with a triangular pediment (the campanile, however, dates from 1852); the frescoes inside, normally closed to the public, are by Sermoneta.

Stadio Flaminio (12 D-E4-5). This huge stadium, which can accommodate as many as 55,000 spectators, was built entirely in reinforced concrete in 1957-59, to a design by Pier Luigi and Antonio Nervi, on the site of the much smaller Stadio Nazionale, which was inaugurated on the 50th anniversary of the proclamation of the kingdom of Italy. Pier Luigi Nervi and Annibale Vitellozzi designed and built the successive **Palazzetto dello Sport** (a sports arena; 12 C-D4), built in 1956-58, likewise in reinforced concrete, with a capacity of 5,000 spectators.

Villaggio Olimpico (12 B-C4-5). Built to house the athletes present at the Olympic Games in 1960 by Vittorio Cafiero, Adalberto Libera, Luigi Moretti, Vincenzo Monaco, and Amedeo Luccichenti, and later converted into a residential quarter, it is made of buildings set on high cement piers.

Piazzale di Ponte Milvio (12 A-B3). Set just past the Milvian Bridge over the Tiber, after which it is named – and which is described on page 145 – this large plaza was meant to become – according to a project developed by Giuseppe Valadier in 1809 but never implemented – the triumphal entrance to the city, but also to Villa Napoleone, which the architect had intended to built at the Flaminio.
The square is now adorned by the fairly orotund *church of the Gran Madre di Dio* (12 A3), which was designed to commemorate the 1,500th anniversary of the Council of Ephesus, by Armando Brasini, and built by Clemente Busiri Vici.

The Borgata di Prima Porta. Standing on the site that was called Saxa Rubra in ancient times, this area lies outside the *Grande Raccordo Anulare*, Rome's beltway (1951-61;

from Piazzale di Ponte Milvio you get here by following the right bank of the Tiber along the Viale di Tor di Quinto and then returning onto the Via Flaminia, a high-speed road). Saxa Rubra is the site of many major historical events: this was a halting spot for Mark Antony before he entered Rome and for the army of Vespasian which marched against Vitellius; this site marked the beginning of the battle between Maxentius and Constantine, a battle which was finally resolved at the Ponte Milvio, or the Milvian Bridge; here the envoys of Pope Benedict III met with those of the antipope Anastasius and the imperial legates, in 855; here Garibaldi, retreating from Rome in 1849, called a halt.

The name Prima Porta derived from a brickwork arch, considered the earliest entrance to Rome for those arriving from the north.

Villa "ad Gallinas Albas"*. This villa belonged to the wife of Augustus, Livia, and is famous both for the statue of Augustus of Prima Porta, found here in 1863-64 and now in the Musei Vaticani, and for the splendid wall paintings, uncovered during excavations in 1951 and now reassembled in the new site of the Museo Nazionale Romano. The complex, closed to the public because of the excavation still underway, comprises large rooms with mosaic floors, a bath complex, a hypogeum decorated with the wall paintings mentioned above, and rooms with frescoes dating from the 2nd c. and polychrome marbles.

It would appear that the name of this villa, which in its entirety runs "ad Gallinas Albas et ad Lauros," derives from the belief that an eagle dropped into the lap of Livia a white hen ("gallina alba") with a branch of laurel ("lauros") in its beak; when this laurel branch wa later planted, it bloomed, and served as the source of all emperors up to Nero, whereupon it withered and died.

Via Cassia (12 A3). Probably first used by the Etruscans, but of uncertain origin (the name may come from the name of Lucius Cassius Longinus Ravilla, consul in 127 B.C., who widened it), this road split off from the Via Flaminia near the III mile, and was known as the Via Clodia in the segment running as far as La Storta, connected Rome with central Etruria, terminating at the junction with the Via Aurelia near Luni; its original military functions were replaced in the Middle Ages by religious functions, as it was used as a route by French pilgrims on their way to St. Peter's (for this reason it was called the Ruga – from "rue" – Francisca or Ruga Francigena).

The modern-day road, which for the most part follows the ancient route as far as Bolsena, runs through an area that has been pretty heavily built up as far as Isola Farnese, with an alternation of luxurious homes and illegally built multistory residential blocks.

Tomb of Nero. Set on the left side of the consular road, or Via Consolare, just past n. 735,

is one of the few Roman landmarks to be spared by the expansion of Rome in this area: the sarcophagus, dating from the second half of the 2nd c. and actually the burial site of Publius Vibius Marianus, is set upon a base and is decorated with Dioscuri, winged gryphons, and an epigraph.

Further along on the right is the Via di Grottarossa, where in 1964 the discovery was made of a sarcophagus with tomb furnishings, known as the "Mummy of Grottarossa," now in the Museo Nazionale Romano.

La Storta. This "borgata," or outlying village with a name – "the crooked one" – that refers to a detour of the Via Cassia that turned off on the left from the Via Clodia (see below), stands on the site of the last postal station before Rome, and a famous inn with a tavern. Legend has it that, in the small church here, while St. Ignatius of Loyola was saying mass, he levitated and had a mystical vision, and that as a result he was granted papal authorization to found the Company of Jesus, more commonly known as the Jesuit order.

Following the signs for Bracciano you will find yourself on the Statale Claudia Braccianese which runs along the course of the ancient *Via Clodia*, which was built at the end of the 3rd c B.C. between Rome and southern Etruria, along the route of an older Etruscan road. Near Osteria Nuova you turn to the left, and you reach *Santa Maria di Galèria*, a tiny village clustered around a square; the name of the village is a reference to the nearby Etruscan city of "Careiae," destroyed in the 9th c. by the Saracens, and revived as a settlement in the 16th c., before being definitively abandoned in the early-19th c.

In the courtyard adjoining the square, note the church of **S. Maria in Celsano**, erected above a Roman cistern; on the altar, note the panel done in the Byzantine style, while, in the apses on the side aisles, you may see two frescoes of the school of Antoniazzo Romano; along the walls are other fragments of 15th-c. frescoes.

Isola Farnese. This "borgo" or suburban village, revolves around the *Castello Farnese*, a castle that once belonged to the Orsini family, and which is documented as far back as the turn of the 11th c.

Veio*. This Etruscan city, which developed on a settlement dating back to the Iron Age was one of Rome's most dangerous enemies, and was destroyed by the general and dictator Camillus in 396 B.C.; it was however also a major trading town, as one can surmise by the size of the residential area, which covered ca. 190 hectares.

The archeological area underwent sporadic excavation in the 18th and 19th c., and was then excavated in a systematic manner from the beginning of the 20th c., yielding such remarkable finds as the famous statue of Apollo now in the Museo Etrusco di Villa Giulia. All that survives of the so-called *temple of Apollo* (though it was actually consecrated to Menerva, the Roman Minerva), which dates back to around 500 B.C. and was demolished in the 4th c. B.C., is the base.

4.3 The Via Nomentana and the Via Salaria

These two roads, which ran through here in exceedingly ancient times, and not at all far from the route of the modern road, have enjoyed a fate linked first and foremost to an industrial reawakening that at first seemed quite ordinary, but which over time took on a different aspect. The urbanized area of the Via Salaria, in particular, was built up as early as the turn of the 20th c., with major projects and improvements over time; the first section of the Via Nomentana, on the other hand, at the turn of the century, had still not been built up, and has preserved – in the various successive stretches of construction – aspects of provisional standing and experimental design.

This circular route (map on the right) follows the Via Nomentana, outside of Porta Pia, and features a number of bus lines, which can be quite useful in reaching the 19th-c. Villa Torlonia and the complex of the Byzantine basilica of S. Agnese Fuori le Mura and the late-imperial mausoleum of S. Costanza (St. Constance).

The return to the center of Rome runs first along the elegant Via Salaria, which in its first stretch skirts the broad and green park of Villa Ada, then along the Via Tagliamento, with its remarkable constructions (particularly surprising is the Quartiere Dora surrounding Piazza Mincio), and finally converging with the Mura Aureliane, or Aurelian walls, near Piazza Fiume after passing the 18th-c. Villa Albani.

Via Nomentana. Running from Rome to "Nomentum" (present-day Mentana), this road went from the Porta Collina in the Servian walls (see page 32) and from the Porta Nomentana, located just to the left of the Porta porta Pia, in the Mura Aureliane, or Aurelian walls (see page 171). In Roman times, this road was marked by its many monumental, funereal, and cemetery complexes, which served as the foundations or settings for houses of Christian worship; during the 18th and 19th c., villas were built here, and still dot the sides of the road and the surrounding areas, interspersed with residential structures and little detached villas dating from the turn of

the 20th c.; during the 1920s, urban experimentation was tried, in the form of the Città Giardino Aniene immediately across the river Aniene.

Overlooking the Piazzale di Porta Pia (5 A3), the center of which is adorned by the *Monumento al Bersagliere* (a military monument; 1932), is the *Palazzo del Ministero dei Lavori Pubblici* (a government office building; 5 A3-4; 1911-25).

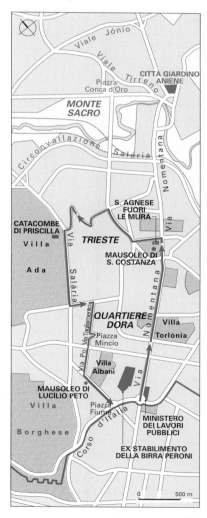

On the opposite side of the large square, the Via Ancona leads to Piazza Alessandria, and to the *Ex Stabilimento della Birra Peroni*, a former brewery, built between 1908 and 1922 and still operating as late as 1971, an elegant piece of industrial architecture.

Villa Torlonia. Converted into a public park in 1978, and now sadly abandoned to neglect and vandalism, this villa was begun by Giuseppe Valadier in 1802.

The entrance from Via Nomentana is marked by Ionic *propylaea* (1910) and is embellished with an obelisk, behind which is the *Palazzo Nobiliare*, preceded by a staircase; the building is in the Neoclassical style (1832-40); dating from the turn of the 20th c. are the *Villino Rosso* and the *Villino Medievale*, two small villas, lining the avenue that runs around the right side of the Palazzo Nobiliare (the *theater* dates back to 1841-74), and the *Casa delle Civette*, with a remarkable roof made of colored tiles, along the left-hand avenue (the *Serra Moresca*, or Moorish Greenhouse, was erected around 1840).

sort of catacomb area had sprung up. The original building, which preserves traces of Byzantine influence, underwent numerous restorations: the earliest was as early as the 6th c., under Pope Symmachus; but larger restorations were done in the 17th c., while the last one was commissioned in 1856 by Pope Pius IX.

The basilica, with the main structure of the convent, overlooks the Via Nomentana; note the apse of the nave and the 15th-c. *campanile*, while the main facade overlooks a small interior courtyard, through which you can enter the narthex.

On the interior – to which you climb up along a stairway dating from 1590, adorned with ancient fragments and artifacts – note, from the reign of Honorius I, the *matroneum*, rare in Roman churches (the women's gallery runs above the side aisles, and the arches are supported by small columns), and the apsidal **mosaic**. The main altar, set on the tomb of the martyrs Agnes and Emerenziana, is framed by a ciborium, with four porphyry columns, built at the behest of Paul V, and containing a *statue of St.*

Mosaic with wine-harvest scene in the Mausoleo di S. Costanza

With permission from the Soprintendenza Archeologica, or archeological commission, of Rome, you can tour, in subterranean chambers underneath the park, the *Catacombe Ebraiche*, or Jewish catacombs, which comprise two cemeteries dating from the 3rd and 4th c., adorned with paintings of Hebrew symbols.

S. Agnese Fuori le Mura*. Literally the church of "St. Agnes, Without the Walls," this small and exceedingly old basilica was built at the orders of Costanza, daughter of Constantine, in the 4th c., near the burial site of the martyr Agnes, where the remains of other martyrs were buried, and where a

Agnes, which Nicolas Cordier executed in 1605, working from an ancient alabaster torso; take note of the splendid *Paschal candelabrum* of the Roman school, in richly decorated marble, set to the left of the altar. The *bust of Jesus* in the 2nd chapel on the right, was for many years attributed to Michelangelo, but is now thought to be by Cordier.

From a door in the left aisle, you can descend into the *catacombs of S. Agnese*, one of the oldest and best preserved catacombs in Rome.

Mausoleo di S. Costanza*. This mausoleum was originally part of the complex of S. Agnese, and was built for Costanza and Elena, daughters of Constantine, at the turn of the 4th c. and transformed into a church in 1254. The interior is circular, and before it stand the ruins of a narthex with apse; there is a large cupola supported by twinned columns, with a diameter of 22.5 m.; the vault of the deambulatory features splendid Roman **mosaics** with a white base and various ornamental motifs (other mosaics adorn the right and left apsidioles); 15th- and 17th-c. frescoes decorate the side niches.

Via Salaria. Developing with the growth of the salt trade, toward Sabina, this road ran from the gate of Porta Salaria in the Mura Aureliane, or Aurelian walls (see page 171) and, after skirting the town of "Antemnae" (the modern Monte Antenne marks its site) – supposedly the scene of the original legendary Rape of the Sabines – it ran over the river Aniene and along the Tiber valley. Ever since ancient times, major monuments and cemetery complexes could be found there; in the area enclosed within the walled perimeter of Rome, these were canceled by the growth of the city; in the outlying area of the Roman "suburbs," some were preserved and still survive, beneath modern buildings; and this remained a predominantly agrarian area right up to the early part of the 20th c.
The modern route, which runs largely along the older route, is marked – well beyond Rome's airport – by the considerable number of small and mid-sized companies, which have led to much working-class housing. A higher general tone can be detected in the segment running toward the center of town, abounding in greenery and residential in nature.

Catacombe di Priscilla. This complex of catacombs, used as a cemetery, arrayed on two floors (plan) and with an entrance at n. 430 della Via Salaria, is one of the most notable catacombs in Rome – and certainly the most important one on the Via Salaria – and dates, at least in its art, to the 3rd c.; note in particular: the Cappella Greca, or Greek Chapel, with *scenes from the Old and New Testaments* and the *"fractio panis"* (breaking of the bread; first half of the 3rd c.?); in the area known as the Arenario, note the *Virgin Mary with Christ Child and a Prophet Pointing at a Star*, a painting in an unusual style for a cemetery area of this period; the Cubicolo della Vergine, a cubicle with *scenes from a wedding* before a bishop, and *Maternity* and one of the *Faithful in Paradise* from the second half of the 3rd c.

Villa Ada. A public park has been opened in the gardens of this villa, which was the private residence of Vittorio Emanuele II, or Victor Emmanuel II, the first king of Italy (also known as the Villa Savoia until the fall of Italy's monarchy); this, along with the Villa Doria Pamphilj, is the largest area of greenery in all Rome.

Via Tagliamento. The overall plan for this settlement, of which the most successful section lines the street, dates back to the regulatory plan of 1909 but was actually implemented in the early-1920s, and was completed in 1930.

Quartiere Dora. Known also as the Quartiere Coppedè (after Gino Coppedè, the architect who built it), this quarter comprises a group of buildings dating from the years 1919-26, which cluster around the Piazza Mincio and the curious fountain of frogs, or *Fontana delle Rane* (1920-24): this is an unusual combination of fanciful pieces of architecture, which blend a wide variety of styles.

Via Po (1 C-D6). This road is a result of the overall urban project developed under King Umberto for the area surrounding the Mura Aureliane, or Aurelian walls; dating from that period are the palazzi and little villas that line the avenue, and which the renovation undertaken in the 1960s – deriving from the changes in the functional requirements of the area – attempted to respect, preserving at least the front elevations.

Villa Albani*. A noteworthy testimonial to the antiquarian style of the 18th c., this villa was built for the cardinal Albani by Carlo Marchionni in 1747-67, and then passed into the hands of the Castelbarco family in 1817 and in 1866 to the Torlonia family, to which it still belongs. The stupendous complex (it can be toured, though only for documented reasons of scholarship, through a request to the Amministrazione Torlonia, Via della Conciliazione n. 30) comprises a series of buildings scattered throughout the spectacular garden: the "casino," or lodge, contains the Salone del Parnaso, or great hall of Parnassus, named for the fresco by Anton Raphael Mengs; the *Appartamento della Leda*, or suite of Leda, is a reconstruction of an ancient bath.
In the villa, note the surviving remains of the Albani collection and a small part of the Torlonia collection, with works of remarkable quality, including the **frescoes** detached

from the François tomb in Vulci (late-4th c. B.C.), *paintings* by Perugino, G. P. Pannini, Gherardo delle Notti, Antonie Van Dyck, Tintoretto, del Guercino, Giulio Romano, Jacques-Louis David, and Borgognone. Almost directly across from the entrance to the villa is the *mausoleum of Lucilius Petus* (to tour it, contact the X Ripartizione del Comune, Rome city government), dating back to the 1st c. B.C., and comprising a corridor and a small central chamber.

Piazza Fiume. This square was built in 1921 following the definitive demolition of the Porta Salaria, and is marked in particular by the *Palazzo della Rinascente* (department store; 1957-61), a successful modern structure inserted nicely into the historic surroundings.

The tree-lined *Corso d'Italia*, which skirts the Mura Aureliane (or Aurelian walls; see page 171), dates back to 1885; the underpasses for faster traffic were built in 1963-65.

4.4 The Via Tiburtina

The eastern area of the Roman suburb has undergone a variety of phases of development. Of all of those phases, the frantic growth of the 1980s has been the fastest, and the most surprising even to those involved: it was a development based upon the small companies of the advanced service industry, companies that found along the Via Consolare (ancient consular road) sufficient infrastructures to allow them to grow and form a compact industrial network, now known as the "Tiburtina Valley," with a clear reference to the Californian "Silicon Valley."

This walking tour begins on the east side of the Stazione Centrale di Termini, from Piazzale Tiburtino, and goes along the first stretch of the consular road, through the Città Universitaria (easily reached on the Line B of the Metropolitana, Termini-Rebibbia line), an interesting example of urban planning under Fascism, and the basilica of S. Lorenzo Fuori le Mura, the result of the fusion of two houses of worship.

Via Tiburtina (14 A-B-C3-4-5). The name comes from "Tibur" (modern-day Tivoli), toward which this road ran even in ancient times, exiting from the Porta Esquilina of the Servian walls (see page 32) and, following the erection of the Mura Aureliane (or Aurelian walls; see page 171), from the Porta Tiburtina (see below).

In imperial times, villas and aristocratic residences lined this road; at the dawn of Christianity, around the tomb of the martyr St. Lawrence, the first basilica dedicated to that saint was built; in the last years of the papacy of Pius IX it was decided to extend the railroad to the area of S. Lorenzo, which allowed for a considerable development of trade and manufacturing following the unification of Italy; the Fascist regime built rural villages (Settecamini) and housing for those evicted from the historic center (S. Basilio, Pietralata), developing into a single megalopolis in the booming growth that followed WWII.

In building the *Porta Tiburtina* (5 F6; 14 C3) the emperor Aurelian re-utilized a monumental arch erected by Augustus in 5 B.C. to support the aqueducts known as the *Aqua Marcia*, built in 144 B.C. by Quintus Marcius Rex, the *Aqua Tepula*, built in 125 B.C. by Cnaeus Servilius Caepio and Lucius Cassius Longinus, and the *Aqua Iulia*, built by Agrippa in 33 B.C.

The *Quartiere di S. Lorenzo* through which the first stretch of the Via Tiburtina runs, developed initially at the end of the 19th c., in accordance with the Humbertine checkerboard plan, as a working-class agglomeration (the roads are named after ancient Italic tribes); the neighborhood is nowadays participating and involved in the phenomenon of the growth of the service industries, resulting in a marked shift in the makeup of the population.

Città Universitaria* (14 A-B3-4). This university campus was designed by Marcello Piacentini in 1933-35, on an area of roughly 22 hectares, in accordance with a plan comprising two axes intersecting at a right angle in the Piazzale del Rettorato; the buildings, designed by the finest architects of the time, is based on a moderate classicism. The equilibrium of the original complex was modified by the stuctures added – especially behind the Rettorato – following WWII to accommodate the growing numbers of students.

The Dopolavoro Universitario, a recreational building, to the left of the main entrance on the Piazzale Aldo Moro, contains the *Teatro Ateneo* by Gaetano Minnucci; Piacentini's *Cappella della Divina Sapienza*, at the end of the first cross street on the left, was offered as a gift by Pope Pius XII in 1950-51; the *Minerva* by Arturo Martini adorns the **Piazzale del Palazzo del Rettorato**, which features the Palazzo del Rettorato, also by Piacentini, decorated in the main hall, or Aula Magna by a fresco (*Italy Between the Arts and the Sciences*) by Mario Sironi; the *Biblioteca Universitaria Alessandrina*, a library which has been installed in this building – now inadequate to contain the 1 million volumes and the roughly 16,000 periodicals of this library – was opened by Pope Alexander VII in 1670 in the Palazzo della Sapienza; the building to the right of the Palazzo del Rettorato is occupied by the Facoltà di Lettere, or department of literature.

The original structure of the *Policlinico Umberto I* (a hospital; 14 A3) was designed by Giulio Podesti in 1889-1903; the medical library has more than 150,000 volumes.

S. Lorenzo Fuori le Mura*, literally, St. Lawrence Without-the-walls. (14 B4-5). Built as a cemetery church at the orders of the

Basilica of S. Lorenzo Fuori le Mura: 12th-c. marble ciborium

emperor Constantine around A.D. 330 (the church found in the cemetery of Verano dates from that period) and rebuilt by Pelagius II in a location that ran parallel to the previous building, the basilica, which is patriarchal, was repeatedly renovated over the centuries (under Pope Clement III it formed part of the fortified citadel of "Laurentiopolis"); the area received its present-day 13th-c. appearance in the reconstruction that followed the Allied bombing of the Quartiere di S. Lorenzo (19 July 1943),

reconstruction that made it possible to eliminate the 19th-c. forms imposed upon the complex by Virginio Vespignani.

A column supporting the *statue of St. Lawrence* (Stefano Galletti, 1865) stands before the *portico* (ca. 1220), probably built by the Vassalletto; it supports a trabeation adorned by a frieze and fragments of mosaics; looming on the right is the elegant *campanile*, dating from the 12th c., but since restored.

The interior structure of the church, which was damaged by the bombing, but maintained the most noteworthy parts, clearly reveals the two different phases of construction: the Basilica Honoriana dates back to the 13th c., and has a nave and two side aisles, separated by columns of various size and origin (the capitals are medieval), while the older Basilica Pelagiana, dating from the 6th c., has been incorportated into the area of the presbytery, which occupies the nave.

On the counterfacade, take note of the *baldachin* of the tomb of the cardinal Guglielmo Fieschi, Cosmatesque, as is the *floor*, the two *ambos* * and the *Paschal candelabrum*. The Cappella di S. Tarcisio preserves 17th-c. paintings; dating from the same period is the decoration of the underground chapel, or Cappella Sotterranea di S. Ciriaca, which can be reached from the left aisle, through a door adorned on the sides by the *tomb of Gerolamo Aleandri* and the *tomb of Bernardo Guglielmi* (designed by Pietro da Cortona, busts by François Duquesnoy). In the presbytery, note the remarkable **trabeation** supported by re-used columns (dating from the 6th c.), while the *ciborium* * is the oldest signed work done by Roman marble carvers ("marmorari"; 1148); the *bishop's throne* (1254) features elegant mosaic decorations. From the adjoining *cloister* (late-12th c., but restored) – which has fragments of classical and medieval sculpture adorning its walls – you can descend to the *Catacombe di Ciriaca*.

Cimitero Monumentale del Verano (14 A-B-C5-6). This monumental cemetery was founded alongside the Basilica di S. Lorenzo, after 1804 in compliance with the Napoleonic edict that prohibited burial within inhabited centers, and was given its general layout by Giuseppe Valadier (1807-1812) and, later, by Virginio Vespignani, who did the quadriporticus and the *Cappella di S. Maria della Misericordia* (1859) at the end of the main drive (the entrance portico, adorned with colossal statues, dates back to 1880).

4.5 The Via Appia Nuova and the Via Tuscolana

Both roads run through heavily populated areas. Along the Via Tuscolana there are working-class residential quarters of various sorts; along the Via Appia Nuova, on the other hand, there has been a mushrooming growth of unregulated housing, what the Romans call "borgate spontanee" (Quarto Miglio, Statuario, etc.) that stopped developing only after WWII. The central squares, the streets, and the boulevards that join them are similar throughout this area, and date from the urban plan of 1909.

The route is a driving tour, but can also be followed by taking the S. Giovanni-Subaugusta stretch of Line A of the Rome subway, or Metropolitana (the landmarks and monuments recommended for this tour are all in the areas immediately surrounding subway stations; note the map on the right). It begins at Piazzale Appio and for the first section runs along the Via Appia Nuova, the urban segment of the Statale 7 Appia, along which you should note the modern church of S. Gaspare del Bufalo and the Parco delle Tombe della Via Latina, an archeological area that just barely escaped being steamrollered by the expansion of Rome. The second part of the tour winds along the Statale 215 Tuscolana; this road, beyond Porta Furba, runs into the extensive and heavily populated Quartiere Tuscolano (of special interest is the orotund and monumental church of S. Giovanni Bosco), ending up in Piazza di Cinecittà, near the film studios of that name.

Via Appia Nuova (9 F5-6). This road was built between the 14th and 15th c., as an alternative to the Via Appia Antica and renovated by Pope Pius VI at the end of the 18th c. The road, which begins at Porta S. Giovanni (see page 65) experienced an early and fairly controlled urban development under the regulatory plan of 1909; it was then followed by an explosive and uncontrolled development that was not brought to a halt until 1937, with a reclamation project that replaced shantytowns with high-density apartment blocks.

S. Gaspare del Bufalo. Conceived in 1975-79 and set on the enormous Piazzale dei Castelli Romani (from the Via Appia Nuova you can reach it by following the Via dei Colli Albani which runs off to the left), this church has a square plan, with a simple and integral spatial layout, accentuated by the visible structure in reinforced cement.

Parco delle Tombe della Via Latina*. This park was established in 1879, following the discovery of the early-Christian basilica of S. Stefano and of a vast necropolis dating from the second half of the 2nd c. It contains one of the few surviving patches of the Roman Campagna surounding the city walls. Along the axis of the ancient *Via Latina – a* thoroughfare that actually dates back to prehistoric times, used by the Etruscans in the colonization of the Campania region to the south, in the 8th/6th c. B.C., and which remained in use until the 14th c. A.D. as a route to Capua – you will see the *Sepolcro Barberini* (2nd c.), with part of the origina brick elevation still intact; this was where the Barberini Sarcophagus (now in the Musei Vaticani) was found; the *Tomba dei Valeri** (ca. A.D. 160), a tomb whose exterior is the product of an imaginative 19th-c. restoration, while inside there is a refined decoration based on images of the funerary world; the *Tomba dei Pancrazi* (mid-2nd c.), decorated with stuccoes and paintings with a mythological subject; in the eastern section of the park, in a somewhat secluded location, is the basilica of *S. Stefano*, with a nave and two side-aisles, with apse and baptistery, built in the mid-5th c. on the site of a Roman villa, and remaining in use as a house of worship until the 13th c.

171) and on in the direction of "Tusculum" (modern-day Tùscolo), it was rebuilt by Pope Gregory XIII at the end of the 16th c.; buildings were first built along this road under the regulatory plan of 1909. Near the walls, note the roads radiating out from the squares; after WWII the anonymous rows of buildings were built outside of the Porta Furba, which conceals on the right the *Quartiere Tuscolano*, an extensive array of residential buildings erected by INA-Casa (1950-55).

S. Giovanni Bosco. Built in 1953-58, this church dominates the chilly and pompous Piazza di S. Giovanni Bosco (from the Via

The set of a mythological film in the studios of Cinecittà

There are few traces visible of the tombs, the villas, and the catacombs that once lined the ancient route of the Via Latina, the same as the route of the modern road; note the *hypogeum* uncovered in 1955 in Via Compagni (to tour it, contact the Pontificia Commissione di Archeologia Sacra, a papal commission of religious archeology), and dating back to A.D. 315-360.

Porta Furba. The name – a corruption of the Latin term "formae," meaning aqueduct – refers to the *Acquedotto Felice*, or Aqua Felix, an aqueduct begun under Pope Gregory XIII in 1583, with the reactivation of the late-imperial Aqua Alexandrina, and completed under Pope Sixtus V with the opening of the fornix; running over the aqueduct built by Pope Sixtus runs the aqueduct built by the emperor Claudius (see page 28); you get here by driving the length of the Via dell'Arco di Travertino and then turning right into the Via Tuscolana (for that road, see below).

Via Tuscolana. A road that probably dates back to archaic times, which ran from the Porta Asinaria (see page 65) through the Mura Aureliane (or Aurelian walls; see page

Tuscolana, take a left into Viale Marco Fulvio Nobiliore) with its immense dome, surmounted by bronze statues, and a monumental facade; on the interior, with its sumptuous wealth of materials, note the bronze *Via Crucis* by Venanzo Crocetti, set against the pillars that hold up the dome, the *Sacred Heart of Jesus* by Primo Conti in the right aisle, a *Crucifix* in silver and *candelabra* in bronze, by Pericle Fazzini near the main altar, *angels* in bronze and the *Baptism of the Eunuch* by Emilio Greco in the baptistery.

Piazza di Cinecittà. The film studios after which this square is named were built at the end of the 1930s, and for the time they were the most modern studios in all of Europe. Relics of this great structure are the *Istituto Nazionale Luce* (1937-38), the *Centro Sperimentale di Cinematografia* (n. 1524; 1939), which contains the *Cineteca Nazionale* – a film archive containing roughly 50,000 Italian and non-Italian films – and a large specialty library, and the actual *Stabilimenti Cinematografici di Cinecittà* (the studios themselves; n. 1055), inaugurated in 1937.

4.6 The Via Appia Antica

Although only for a short stretch of distance, this road will allow the traveller that takes it today to have some idea of the appearance and the experience of the Roman Campagna as it must have appeared in the last few decades of the 19th c. in all directions, upon leaving Rome. All the same, it is only toward the south, along the route that can be travelled today, that the remarkable array of monuments – which could once be seen in all directions – has been sufficiently well preserved to make the length of the Via Appia Antica near the city walls one of the sights worth seeing on any visit to Rome. The route, which is really preferably a walking tour – in which case you take a bus to cover some of the longer distances, a bus which runs along the "Via Consolare," or consular road, between the Baths of Caracalla and the catacombs of S. Sebastiano – and is shown on the map on pages 168-169, starts from the Piazzale di Porta Capena, running along the first part of the Viale delle Terme di Caracalla (these structures are some of most important surviving monuments of Imperial Rome) and the Viale di Porta S. Sebastiano, and it offers some idea of the greenbelt that surrounded the city prior to the intense urbanization that followed the unification of Italy.

After exiting from Porta S. Sebastiano (a short detour toward the Porta Latina will allow you to observe one of the loveliest stretches of the Mura Aureliane, or Aurelian walls), you take the long straight road of the Via Appia Antica, a full-fledged archeological park punctuated with Roman ruins (villa of Maxentius, tomb of Cecilia Metella) and Christian monuments (catacombs of Callisto and S. Sebastiano, or Callixtus and St. Sebastian).

You may also enjoy the short detour along the Via Ardeatina toward the catacombs of Domitilla and the Fosse Ardeatine, or Ardea-tine Caves, linked to tragic events during Nazi occupation in WWII.

Parco di Porta Capena (11 B-C1-2). This park occupies the area – bounded to the NE by the cluttered Piazza di Porta Capena (see page 42) – that Guido Baccelli had planned out as a Passeggiata Archeologica or archeological stroll, with a view to connecting the monuments, from Piazza Venezia to the Via Appia Antica. The project, completed between 1887 and 1914, was heavily mangled during the 1930s by the transformation of the large avenues from walking routes to highways with heavy traffic along the Via Imperiale (the present-day Via Cristoforo Colombo: see page 175).

Terme di Caracalla*, or Baths of Caracalla (11 C-D2-3). This is one of the most impressive monumental complexes to survive from ancient Rome, and although the ruins that are visible are certainly impressive, the reconstruction – hypothetical though it may be – of the complex is of mind-boggling grandeur. Begun in A.D. 212 and inaugurated in 217, the baths were completed by Alexander Severus and restored by Aurelian (270-275), and they remained in function at least as late as the Gothic wars, when the soldiers of Vitiges, in the course of the siege of Rome, defended by Belisarius, destroyed a length of the Antonine aqueduct (see page 170) which supplied water to the baths.

The complex has a main entrance that overlooks the Via Nova, which runs parallel to the Via Appia; it originally comprised, in accordance with the standard layout of the 2nd c. (whereby the central wing was surrounded by green areas, enclosed by a perimeter wall), a frigidarium (plan on the right, 1), on either side of which were the halls of oils (2) and the halls of sands (3),

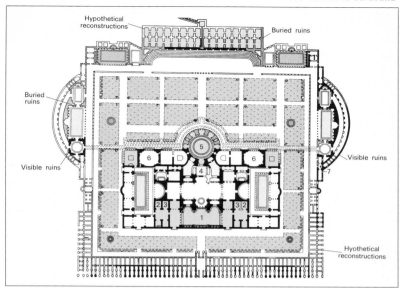

The Baths of Caracalla: plan

tepidarium (4) and a large circular calidarium (5), surrounded by open-air spaces in which to exercise (6); completing the facility were gymnasiums, exedrae, schools for gymnasts, a stadium, two libraries, and enormous underground plant structures, in one of which a mithraeum had been built (7; this is probably the largest and most lavish mithraeum in Rome).

Among the other fine objects found in these baths were, among others, the Toro Farnese and the Ercole Farnese (Farnese bull and Farnese Hercules), now in the Museo Nazionale in Naples, and the mosaic with athletes, now in the Musei Vaticani.

Ss. Nereo e Achìlleo (11 C3). Although there are records of a place of worship on this site as far back as the 4th c., the building dates from the 9th c., when Pope Leo III ordered it rebuilt on the present-day site; it

was renovated in 1475 (Pope Sixtus IV ordered the construction of the facade and the sealing up of the windows, visible beneath the plaster) and again in 1600 (the cardinal Cesare Baronio commissioned the sumptuous decoration of the interior).

The church is divided into a nave and two side-aisles (the frescoes with *stories of martyrs* are attributed to Nicolò Circignani) by unusual masonry pillars from the 15th c., and is closed off by a semicircular apse; the *enclosure* of the choir is made up of Cosmatesque fragments dating back to the 12th c., while the *main altar* is also Cosmatesque; the *episcopal throne* is by the Vassalletto family; the handsome *mosaics* in the apsidal arch are all that survive of the decorations from the time of Pope Leo III.

S. Sisto Vecchio (11 C4). This is a reconstruction of a building that probably dated

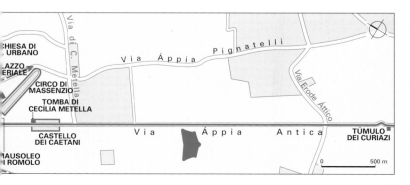

from the end of the 12th c. and the beginning of the 13th c. under Pope Innocent III (dating from that period is the handsome Romanesque *campanile*), who donated this house of worship to St. Dominick in 1219. Of the later restorations, a particularly thorough-going one was done by Filippo Raguzzini in the 18th c. Inside is a single nave (ring at n. 8) with a noteworthy **series of frescoes** (13th-14th c.), in the space between the apse of Innocent III and the 15th-c. apse on the left side of the presbytery, with scenes from the New Testament and scenes from the Apocryphal Gospels.

Via di Porta S. Sebastiano (11 C-D-E-F4-5). This road, which, along with the Viale delle Terme di Caracalla, runs the same course as the urban segment of the ancient Roman Via Appia (see page 171), begins after the *Piazzale Numa Pompilio* (11 C3-4), a major traffic interchange between EUR and the quarters to the south of the city and the area of S. Giovanni; it leads to the Porta S. Sebastiano (see below) through a setting of natural countryside that has miraculously remained intact.

Just a little beyond the mouth of this road, on the right, slightly set back, is the church of *S. Cesareo de Appia* (11 D4), rebuilt at the end of the 16th c. on the site of older buildings (ruins in underground chambers). The stern, rectangular interior, in which a nice job has been done of reassembling fragments of Cosmatesque work, features, above the bishop's throne, a fresco (*Virgin Mary with Christ Child*) dating from the 15th c., while the mosaics in the apse and on the triumphal arch were done to cartoons by the Cavalier d'Arpino.

Also affected by restoration work is the next landmark you will see, the *Casina del Cardinale Bessarione* (11 D4), or little house of the cardinal Bessarion, dating from the middle of the 15th c.

Sepolcro degli Scipioni* (11 E5). This tomb of the Scipios, unearthed as early as 1616 but re-arranged in 1926-29, is linked to one of the most influential families of the Roman republic, whose members, as the inscriptions on the tombs point out, were buried here from the beginning of the 3rd c. B.C. up to 139 B.C. (the last member of the family known to have been buried here was Scipio Hispanus). In the 3rd c., a *house* was erected atop the hypogaeum, or underground chamber; this house still shows traces of the ancient mosaic floors and of painted decorations, despite the fact that in the Middle Ages, the interior was used as a

limekiln, for the treatment of marble.

In 1831, not far from the Sepolcro degli Scipioni, the *Columbarium of Pomponio Hylas* was unearthed (to tour it, contact the X Ripartizione del Comune, Rome city government), which features a mosaic decoration in an aedicule and, in the cella, with a painted vault, numerous epitaphs from the 1st c.

Arco di Druso (11 F5). This arch of Drusus, with one monumental fornix was built be-

The arch of Drusus

tween A.D. 211 and 216, as a bridge over the Via Appia of the *Aqua Antoniniana*, an aqueduct that, splitting off from the Aqua Marcia (see page 164), supplied water to the baths of Caracalla.

Porta S. Sebastiano* (11 F5). One of the best preserved gates from the ancient Aurelian walls (see below), it takes its current name from the basilica of S. Sebastiano (see page 173), to which the Roman Via Appia led; its massive appearance was the work of Honorius, who reduced to one fornix the aperture built under Aurelian in the walled perimeter that he also ordered built, recycling the nearby arch of Drusus as a counter-gate (see above). On the exterior, the arch of the gate, restored by Belisarius and Narses with marble taken from the monuments lining the Via Appia, is flanked by two crenelated towers, and surmounted by two covered galleries and a crenelated watch rampart; on the left pier is a depiction of the Archangel Gabriel and an inscription commemorating the defeat of the Angevin troops in 1327.

In the galleries and the large turrets is the *Museo delle Mura di Roma*, which illustrates the story of the defensive fortifications of the city, from the Servian walls to the forts built after the unification of Italy.

From the museum you can set off along the charming *passeggiata*, or promenade, set amidst the greenery in a landscape that looks as much of the rest of Rome must have until the unification of Italy; it runs from Porta S. Sebastiano to the new Porta Ardeatina (see below) along the route of the **Mura Aureliane**, a ring of walls built by the emperor Aurelian, beginning in A.D. 271, in response to the growing menace of the barbarians; that menace was already quite serious. The immense ring of walls, which ran along the silhouettes of the hills, and enclosed all existing walled perimeters around the city, enlarging and expanding them (including the walled toll-gate perimeter from the age of the Flavians); the walls were completed by the death of Aurelian in A.D. 275, though some final masonry work was finished under Probus; and first under Maxentius and then, later – in response to the threat of the Goths – under the western emperor Honorius and his son Arcadius the walls were further fortified and raised, undergoing new reinforcements at the time of the Byzantines under Belisarius; they were then further restored by the popes.

The walls of Aurelian, for the construction of which the emperor did not hesitate to incorporate the structures of existing buildings (note the Anfiteatro Castrense on page 129), stood 6 m. tall, and were nearly 3.5 m. thick; about every 30 m., or 100 feet, they were equipped with a square tower, with an upper chamber suited for war machinery (in the 5th c., there were 383 towers and 116 guard houses).

After you exit through the Porta S. Sebastiano, a short detour off to the left leads you to the *Porta Latina* * (11 E6), perhaps the best preserved Roman gate; note the arch of the fornix, in radial travertine, with a cornice with moulding, and cusped crenelation.

Just inside the gate, on the left, you will see the *Oratorio di S. Giovanni in Oleo* (11 E5), built in the 5th c. on the site in which the saint supposedly emerged unharmed from a great vat of boiling oil; this oratory was partly rebuilt by Baldassarre Peruzzi or by Antonio da Sangallo the younger in the first half of the 16th c., and was restored by Francesco Borromini in the 17th c.

Continuing along the Via di Porta Latina, you can tour the church of **S. Giovanni a Porta Latina** (11 D5), which also dates back to the 5th c., but now visible in the medieval style that was the result of one of the many restorations; a portico extends before it, and it is decorated in the nave with a *series of paintings* dating from the end of the 12th c.

If you turn to the right, just outside of the gate, or Porta S. Sebastiano, you will soon reach the new *Porta Ardeatina* (11 F4), four fornices faced in brick and cut through the Aurelian walls in 1939 as the starting point of the Via Imperiale (now Via Cristoforo Colombo: see page 175), and the *Bastione Ardeatino* * (11 F3), built at the behest of Pope Paul III (1536) by Antonio da Sangallo the Younger, in the context of a very ambitious piece of urban planning – drawn up following the Sack of Rome of 1527, but soon abandoned in the face of high costs – that called for the reinforcement of the walls to Rome to withstand the new use of firearms in siege operations; to do this would have required the construction of high brick scarp walls with stone cordons.

Via Appia Antica * (11 F5). This, the old Appian Way, has been called the "regina viarum," or queen of roads, and is the most famous of all the Roman consular roads; it was built in 312 B.C. by Appius Claudius Cieco, who straightened and widened (to a width of 4.1 m.) an ancient road, creating an axis of communication southward and eastward that was of vital importance to the economic development of the city.

The modern condition of this road, which was largely abandoned after the 6th c., and was restored by Pope Pius VI in the 18th c., is linked chiefly to the plan for an archeological park, which has been the subject of much discussion since 1809, though it was not until 1988 that this park was established by the regional government of Latium (Lazio); this park should allow the public to enjoy the vast space and excellent state of the immense heritage of archeological treasures in the park, and which is now in a state of widespread neglect.

Church of Domine Quo Vadis? The structure that can now be seen is the fruit of the reconstruction, done in the 16th and 17th c., of a place of worship that dates back to the 9th c., and originally named S. Maria in Palmis; it is said that this is the site in which Jesus appeared to St. Peter, who was fleeing Rome and the persecution of Nero; it is said that when Peter asked him, "Domine, quo vadis?" (Lord, where are You going?) Christ replied: "Eo Romam iterum crucifigi" (I am going to Rome, to be crucified a second time).

Via Ardeatina. This old road connected Rome with Ardea (the modern town has the same name) capital of the rutuli; the road ran off to the right from the Via Appia Antica just beyond the ancient Roman *tomb of Priscilla*.

The *Via delle Sette Chiese*, the first cross street off to the right of the Via Ardeatina, recalls the 16th-c. devotional route – which

had stations in the four patriarchal basilicas, and in S. Lorenzo Fuori le Mura, S. Croce in Gerusalemme, and S. Sebastiano – established by St. Philip Neri.

At n. 280 you will find the **Catacombe di Domitilla**, or Catacombs of Domitilla, the largest subterranean cemetery complex in all Rome (comparable only to the cemetery complex of S. Callisto); this complex developed between the 3rd and 5th c., for a total of roughly 15 km. of tunnels, in an estate that once belonged to Flavia Domitilla (granddaughter of Vespasian); they are named after her. The catacombs also include the area known as the Hypogaeum of the Flavians, which is actually a pagan burial site, later occupied by Christians.

You can enter the catacombs through the basilica of the *Santi Nereo e Achilleo*, built toward the end of the 4th c. on the tombs of two martys, who were probably victims of the persecution ordered under Diocletian; it was not discovered until 1874 (it was devastated by the earthquake of A.D. 897); one of the columns that made up the ciborium depicts an exceedingly rare scene, that of the *Beheading of a Martyr*.

On the Via Ardeatina, after the intersection with the Via delle Sette Chiese, is the entrance to the *Fosse Ardeatine*, quarries in which, on 24 March 1944, as reprisal for the famous partisan attack in Via Rasella, 335 Italian civilians were shot by the Nazis, after being chosen at random. Behind the sacrarium, a *Museo delle Fosse Ardeatine* has been set up, with documents and memorabilia of the Nazi occupation of Rome (10 September 1943-4 June 1944).

Cappella di Reginald Pole. This chapel stands on the left side of the Via Appia Antica just past the crossroads of the Via Ardeatina; it is a round building, erected as a votive shrine to the English cardinal Reginald Pole, an opponent of the Anglican Reformation, who on this site narrowly escaped death in 1539 at the hands of the assassins of Henry VIII.

Catacombe di S. Callisto*, or Catacombs of St. Calixtus. They were built towards the end of the 2nd c., and took their name from the deacon Calixtus, who was appointed by Pope Zephyrinus to administer a burial ground linked directly to the church; when he became pope, he enlarged that burial area, making it the official funerary complex of the Roman Church (over 50 martyrs and 16 popes lie buried here). Discovered in 1849 by G.B. De Rossi, the pioneering founder of Christian archeology, the catacombs extend over a surface area of 15 hectares, with crisscrossing galleries running over a total of nearly 20 km.; the older areas are the Regione dei Papi and the Regione di S. Cecilia, while the Regione di S. Gaio and the Regione di S. Eusebio date back to the end of the 3rd c.; Regione Occidentale and Regione Liberiana date back to the 4th c.

A focal point of the tour is the *Cripta dei Papi*, or crypt of popes; here nine popes were buried (St. Pontian martyr, St. Anterote, St. Fabian martyr, St. Lucius, and St. Eutychian are mentioned in the original inscriptions in Greek). In the adjoining crypt is the tomb of St. Cecilia, with noteworthy 9th-c. *frescoes*. The Cubicoli dei Sacramenti, or cubicles of the sacraments, contain fine *frescoes* dating back to the first half of the 3rd c.; in the nearby Regione di S. Milziade (St. Miltiades) is the famous *Sarcofago del Bambino*.

Also in the complex of S. Callisto, but open only to scholars with permission from the Pontificia Commissione di Archeologia Sacra, are these *Catacombe dei Ss. Marco e Marcelliano*, catacombs that developed over the 4th c.

Via Appia Pignatelli. This 17th-c. link between the Via Appia Antica and the Via Appia Nuova (see page 166), runs through an area in which catacombs were found: the *Catacombe di Pretestato* (to tour this area, contact the Pontificia Commissione di Archeologia Sacra, a papal commission on religious archeology), that were built at the end of the 2nd c. as a pagan burial area, and then were set aside as burial ground for martyrs; and the *Jewish catacombs of Vigna Randanini**, discovered only in 1897; ruling out the catacombs of Villa Torlonia, these are the only ancient Jewish cemetery still in existence: the four funerary chambers, with paintings that might suggest an initial pagan use of the hypogaeum, are arranged in a structure resembling the one found in the Christian catacomb.

The church of **S. Urbano**, which you reach by taking the Vicolo di S. Urbano, on the left of the Via Appia Pignatelli, is a Christian construction dating from the 10th c., on the site of a temple that was probably built by Herodes Atticus (this area formed part of his landholdings); inside, of particular quality and significance are the 11th-c. *frescoes*, repainted in 1643.

Basilica di S. Sebastiano. St. Sebastian, a martyr during the reign of Diocletian, was buried on what was thought to be the site of the first burial of the apostles Peter and Paul, whose bodies had then been moved here to find haven from the destruction of Roman persecution; around the relics, a Christian necropolis gradually developed (see below), which soon had its own house of worship as well. The 4th-c. basilica was demolished, in the 17th c., to make way for a more intricate structure, assigned by the cardinal Scipione Borghese to the architect Flaminio Ponzio; it was finally completed, with the facade built by Giovanni Vasanzio, in 1613.

The interior, with a wooden *ceiling** dating from the turn of the 17th c., contains, in the Cappella delle Reliquie (or chapel of relics; plan, 1) one of the arrows that struck St. Sebastian, the column to which he was bound, and the footprints believed to have been left by Christ in the episode of the "Domine quo vadis?"; the vast *Cappella Albani* (1706-1712; 2) was built by Carlo Maratta, Alessandro Specchi, Carlo Fontana, and Filippo Barigioni (the *Saint Baptizing Philip the Arabian* to the right of the altar is by Pier Leone Ghezzi); in the *Cappella di S. Sebastiano* (3), built on a site corresponding to the tomb of the saint in the catacombs, the *statue of the Saint* was executed by Antonio Giorgetti (1671-72) to designs by Gian Lorenzo Bernini.

Catacombe di S. Sebastiano*. These catacombs of St. Sebastian, a vast cemetery complex run over four levels, the first level now having been almost entirely destroyed.

A staircase (A) leads down to the galleries, along the walls of which note the paintings of the *cycle of Jonah* (4th c.) in the Cubicolo di Giona, or cubicle of Jonah, and the crypt of St. Sebastian (Cripta di S. Sebastiano), with a *bust of the saint*, attributed to Bernini. A little further along, you will reach the Piazzuola (B), beneath which is the sandstone cavity which may be the source of the name "ad catacumbas" (from Greek "kata" and "kymbas," literally, near the cavity), upon which face the three *mausoleums* (C, D, E), established in the second half of the 2nd c., and later re-utilized by Christians. From this square you can climb up to a room (F) that was once used for funerary banquets (the graffiti, dating back to the 3rd/4th c., were the work of worshippers, who invoked the apostles). Beyond the deambulatory (G) you will find the *Platonia* (H), once the mausoleum of Quirinus, mar-

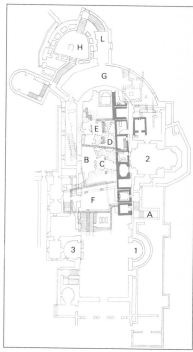

The S. Sebastiano complex

tyr, and the *Cappella di Onorio III* (L) a chapel with fine paintings from the 13th c. (note the *Slaughter of the Innocents* and the *Virgin Mary with Christ Child*).

Villa di Massenzio*, or Villa of Maxentius. This monumental complex from imperial times is one of the most interesting along the "via", and is composed of a circus and a mausoleum, set in the Roman Campagna, or countryside.

The *Circus of Maxentius* was 513 m. in length and 90 m. in width, while the "spina" in the center, which separated the two lanes of racing chariots, moving in opposite directions, and which was in ancient times adorned with the obelisk that Gian Lorenzo Bernini erected in Piazza Navona, was just short of 300 m. in length; capable of accommodating about 10,000 spectators, it was flanked by two towers (one has survived in part) and was linked to the *Imperial Palace*, which has yet to be excavated, though you can see a few ruins on the left. The **Mausoleo di Romolo**, or Mausoleum of Romulus, to the west of the circus, was built by Maxentius in memory of his son, who died before him; it was used for the burial of other members of the imperial

verted into the donjon for a castle of the Caetani clan (the Ghibelline style parapets date back to that structure, and to the work done on it in 1302).

On the right side of the road, note the little church of *S. Nicola a Capo di Bove* a fairly unusual example of Roman Gothic.

Tomb of the Curiatii (Tomba dei Curiazi). On a line with a slight shift in the route of the Via Appia Antica, which then returns to its rectilinear course, this tomb stood on a sacred site, indicated by a small hillock that contains ruins from the late republic: legend has it that this was the site of the famous battle between the Horatii and the Curiatii (the next two mount-burial sites are named for the Horatii, and also date from the late republic), but the archeological findings thus far point to ruins from a far later date.

The tomb of Cecilia Metella, along the Via Appia Antica

family; the actual tomb is circular: a corridor runs around a pillar in which there are niches for the burial urns, as there are in the walls as well. On part of the mausoleum, a villa was built in the 19th c. for the Torlonia family, once landholders in this area.

Tomb of Cecilia Metella*. One of the most noteworthy Roman monuments, and the best known landmark along the Via Appia Antica, this tomb comprises a cylindrical structure, crenelated and faced in travertine (on the interior, you can still see the burial chamber), set on a square base and adorned on the summit by a frieze in relief, with, among other features, a motif comprising bucrania (for that reason, this area is also called Capo di Bove, or "ox head"). It was built around 50 B.C. for Cecilia, daughter of Metellus, the conqueror of Crete, and wife of Crassus, a general under Caesar in Gaul, and in the Middle Ages it was con-

Villa dei Quintili*. You can tour this villa by contacting the Soprintendenza Archeologica, or archeological commission of Rome; the complex – in which you can make out the ruins of a nymphaeum, a peristyle, large halls with windows, and the arches of the aqueduct – takes its name from the wealthy brothers who became its owners under the emperor Commodus, who ordered them executed; the villa, probably the largest in the area around Rome, was then made part of the imperial estates; since the 16th c., it has become the source of countless art treasures, accumulated in it since the reign of Hadrian.

Casal Rotondo. This is the largest sepulcher of all those lining the Via Appia Antica, which is in particularly poor shape in this stretch; the tomb includes a large cylindrical structure – once faced in travertine – and surmounted by a mound.

4.7 EUR and the New Quarters to the South of the City

The Fascist regime had decided to celebrate its own 20th anniversary – and Italy's new "imperial" standing – with a universal exposition (an "Olimpiade delle Civiltà," or an "Olympiad of Civilizations," as it was described in the plan), that was meant to occupy one of the new developing areas of the city, toward the sea shore; with that in mind, the area would be equipped with structures that would then remain as permanent facilities. The first plan for the project was developed immediately following the war in Ethiopia and clearly showed the influence of international rationalist movement, though those influences were cast in the context of classical Roman architecture; the second project, developed by Marcello Piacentini in 1938 in collaboration with Gaetano Minnucci, accentuated the elements redolent of classicism.

The construction of the E42 (this was the original name of this great urban intervention; the name was later changed to EUR: Esposizione Universale di Roma, or Universal Exposition of Rome), was broken off in 1943 because of the war, and taken up again during the 1950s, with a sharp acceleration of work at the beginning of the decade, making the quarter into an elegant residential zone, and the site of a number of ministery office buildings as well.

The driving route (EUR is linked to the center of Rome by line "B" of the Metropolitana, Rome's subway system – EUR Fermi and EUR Marconi stations) runs out the new Porta Ardeatina, along the Via Cristoforo Colombo, where the pavillions of the Fiera, or fair, and the Centro Direzionale, or executive office district, offer testimony of the unattained potential of the development of the capital city.

A central feature of the tour is the quarter of EUR, a tour that includes some of the most interesting episodes of 20th-c. Italian architecture and urban planning (the buildings now cover a time span of nearly 50 years) and allows one to experience some of the most remarkable settings of Italian art note the evident reference in a number of avenues and squares to the "metaphysical painting" of Giorgio de Chirico; the classical references evident in the more monumental buildings; the heavy use of this area as a setting for many of the more memorable films of the 1960s).

Two short detours will complete the visit to the more contemporary sections of Rome: one along the Via Laurentina toward the abbey of the Tre Fontane and the Ferratella, the other, to the south of EUR, toward the satellite communities of Mostacciano and Spinaceto.

Via Cristoforo Colombo (plan 15 ,16). This road, built during the Fascist era, with the name of Via Imperiale, was conceived as a main thoroughfare running toward the quarter of E42 (the new gate, or Porta Ardeatina, which was then opened in the Mura Aureliane, or Aurelian walls, is described on page 171), and now runs on toward the seashore, cutting slightly off toward Lido di Ostia (see page 37).

Built to handle fast traffic, and basically serving as a city "highway", this road runs, on the left, near the Piazza dei Navigatori (15 C6), past one of the *mass hotels* built in 1947 – in brick and travertine – for the pilgrims of the Holy Year of Anno Santo 1950 and then converted into lower-income housing.

From the square, taking Via Genocchi you arrive in Piazza Oderico da Pordenone, crossed by the *Via delle Sette Chiese* which was the Medieval "Via Paradiso" and evokes the devout route, instituted in 1552, to visit the four Basilicas at S. Lorenzo fuori le Mura, S. Croce in Gerusalemme, S. Sebastiano, the abbey of the Tre Fontane and the Annunziatella Church.

Also on the left, beyond the buildings of the Fiera, you may note the complex of the *Centro Direzionale*, or executive office complex (15 E-F5-6), a fragment of what should one day become the Sistema Direzionale Orientale (SDO), one of the largest urban expansion projects yet laid out in Europe.

Centro Sportivo delle Tre Fontane (16 A-B3-4-5-6). Created for the Rome Olympics in 1960, this is an athletic complex with tracks and playing fields; the Via Cristoforo Colombo runs over it on an overpass before entering the EUR, running past the permanent ferris wheel of Rome's Luna Park on the left, another distinctive element of the quarter's skyline.

The name refers to the nearby **abbey of the Tre Fontane** (16 C6), linked according to tradition to the beheading of St. Paul, whose head, bouncing three times after the axe fell, supposedly generated three springs of fresh water. As a place of worship, this site dates back to the 4th or 5th c., though the monastery was founded around A.D. 625 by

Pope Honorius I, and was handed over in 1140 to the Cistercians, who began to rebuild the complex in accordance with the rules of St. Bernard; the site was abandoned after the Holy Year of 1600 because of the dangers to health, and recovery of the site began in the second half of the 19th c., when the Trappist monks reclaimed the area, planting the eucalyptus trees (the first in Rome) that still surround the abbey. Beyond the arch dedicated to Charlemagne, the *Arco di Carlo Magno*, a double entrance to the monastery, dating from the 8th or 9th c. (beneath the arch, note the *stories of*

The work involved in that development led to th undistinguished settlement of the *Ferratell* which lies off to the right of the road past th Viale dell'Umanesimo, and, a bit further on, o the opposite side of the Via Laurentina, the *m itary city of La Cecchignola.*

Piazzale delle Nazioni Unite (16 B4). Th plaza is the entryway to the EUR (Marcell Piacentini had planned to erect the Port Imperiale, or gate of empire, here), and **i** bounded by the *Palazzo dell'Istitut Nazionale della Previdenza Sociale* (right and the *Palazzo dell'Istituto Nazionale del Assicurazioni* (left), th buildings of two major s cial welfare agencies, b gun in 1940 to plans by Gi vanni Muzio, Mario Pan coni, and Giulio Pedicon the buildings bear bas-r liefs (*Maritime Glory Rome*) by Mirko Basaldell

Palazzo della Civiltà de Lavoro* (or palazzo of civ ilization based on labor; **t** B3). This building is th symbol of the quarter; fo merly named the Palazz della Civiltà Italiana, it i also known as the Co losseo Quadrato, or th square colosseum, and it i characterized by the ob sessive repetition of th arch motif (which appear 216 times), a motif that Gi vanni Guerrini, Ernest Bruno La Padula, an Mario Romano used to ce ebrate in 1938-43 this a chitectural element typic of Italian civilization.

The Palazzo della Civiltà del Lavoro, known as the "Square Colosseum"

Extending before it on th right is the *Palazzo deg Uffici dell'Ente Autonom EUR* by Gaetano Minnucci (16 B3-4), th first building to be erected in the area (1937 39); inside, there is a noteworthy fresc (*Foundation of Rome*) by Giorgio Quaron and an architectural model of the quarter

Charlemagne dating from the 12th c.), is the terracotta facade of the abbey church of the *Santi Vincenzo e Anastasio**, a Cistercian reconstruction of earlier buildings, completed by Pope Honorius III in 1221. In the stark interior, the paintings (*apostles*, of the school of Raphael, on pillars) have recently been restored.

The *Via Laurentina* (16 A-B-C-D-E-F5-6), a route of ancient origin that began from the Porta Ostiense, now the Porta S. Paolo (see page 41), runs through a sector of the city that was developed beginning 1931 and became seriously urbanized in the 1970s.

Palazzo dei Congressi* (16 C4-5). Perhap better than any other, this bulding epito mizes and represents the synthesis of mo ern styles, techniques, and materials wit the classical inspiration (Adalberto Libera 1938-54); the exterior appears as a whit cubic volume, roughly 40 m. a side, pre ceded by a large atrium decorate with par els by Gino Severini which cover the earlier frescoes by Achille Funi; the interior comprises an immense hall, surrounded by galleries and surmounted by a cross vault, and includes a large meeting hall, above which is a large open-air theater.

Piazza Guglielmo Marconi (16 C4). Marked by a *stele*, 45 m. tall and designed by Arturo Dazzi, which celebrates in 92 reliefs the invention of the radio, this square was meant to be the center of the 1942 exposition, and was intended to feature the Teatro Imperiale, a theater, on the site now occupied by the *Grattacielo Italia*, a skyscraper (1959-60).

Palazzo delle Tradizioni Popolari, or folk-ways building (16 C4). Designed by Massimo Castellazzi and Annibale Vitellozzi and built in 1939-42, this building houses the *Museo Nazionale delle Arti e Tradizioni Popolari*, a national museum of folk art and traditions, with a rich and interesting documentation and exhibit of crafts objects linked to ordinary everyday life, with special attention to the folk traditions and ways of Italy prior to the early years of the 20th c.

The large collection, assembled between 1906 and 1911 by Lamberto Loria and exhibited at a great ethnographic exhibition, the Mostra di Etnografia Italiana, held in Rome in 1911, was only established an a permanent basis here in 1956. The installation of the museum, organized typologically and thematically, works through rooms that present reconstructions of rooms and buildings, as well as documents and objects linked to the cycles of the year (Easter, Christmas, and so on) and of ordinary lives (baptism, engagement, marriage, and so forth), sections dedicated to crafts, farming, and pastoral activities, costumes (ca. 750 items), jewelry, art, and folk religion.

Palazzo delle Scienze (16 C4). Built in 1939-43, this building houses two major cultural institutions.

The **Museo Nazionale Preistorico-Etnografico "Luigi Pigorini"**, a museum of ethnography and prehistory that contains one of the largest ethnographic collections in Europe was founded in 1875, through the good offices of the paleoethnographer Luigi Pigorini, in the Palazzo del Collegio Romano, where the original core collection, comprising a noteworthy group of objects assembled by the Jesuit Athanasius Kircher in the 17th c., attracted in time an array of other finds. Moved in 1962-77 to the EUR district, it is organized in two sections dedicated respectively to Prehistory/Protohistory and to the Ethnography of non-European native cultures.

The exhibition, "A trip into the past: 8,000 years ago in the Bracciano lake", consisting of findings from a Neolithic village discovered near Anguillara Sabazia, introduces the *Prehistoric* and *Protohistoric* section, and includes a selection of Italian and European items displayed in chronological order, while thematic information panels explain the exhibits. The covered space offers speciments from the Pleistocene era (over 300,000 years ago) up to the late Iron Age (7th c. B.C.), with a collection that gradually reveals more and more regional details. There are 4 parts to the *Ethnography* section, dedicated to Africa, Oceania, Asia and Americas.

On the "black continent" there is a reconnaissance of the coasts, the discovery of its rivers and "negro art"; Oceania is represented by a symbolic trip to the Pacific Islands; Asia is reconstructed through its kaleidoscope of cultures; while Precolombian vases and Indian objects are the examples of development in the Americas.

The *Museo dell'Alto Medioevo* *, or museum of the high Middle Ages, founded in 1967, comprises a series of archeological finds, dating from the 4th to the 10th c., largely taken from the storehouses of the Museo Nazionale Romano; the collection, illustrated by explanatory panels, features materials found in two Longobard necropolises in the Marche region, marble reliefs, and ceramics, portraits from late antiquity, and a collection of Coptic fabrics. Of special note, in hall I, dedicated to materials from late antiquity, is the splendid golden *buckle*, known as a "fibula a balestra," or crossbow-style buckle (4th/6th c.), which the high officials of the army and the government used to fasten capes over their shoulders. Hall II contains *funerary furnishings* from the Longobard necropolis of Nocera Umbra (6th/7th c.), comprising domestic tools and utensils, weapons, necklaces and jewlery in gold and glass paste, ivory combs, goblets, and chalices, and fittings for horses; hall III contains materials (6th and 7th c.) from the Longobard necropolis of Castel Trosino (Ascoli Piceno).

Halls IV and V contain *reliefs from the high Middle Ages* (ciboria, ambos, presbyterial screens, well heads, capitals, and so on), dating back to the 8th to 10th c., and largely taken from churches in Rome and Latium, while in the next hall (VI) note the remains of the marble fittings of an 8th-c. church and a series of amphorae and other ceramic objects found during the excavation of a farming settlement of the high Middle Ages, in S. Cornelia near Veio.

Hall VII features an interesting mosaic floor, done in "opus sectile," and found during the excavations done at S. Rufina, near Rome; here, according to tradition, the sisters Ru-

Gold plated silver fibulas, conserved in the Museo dell'Alto Medioevo

fina and Seconda (257) were martyred. In the last hall (VIII), dedicated to *Coptic fabrics* (2nd/12th c.), there are roughly 70 pieces of cloth, used in funerary and liturgical functions.

The third floor of the building houses the *Aerofototeca*, literally archive of aerial photographs, a section of the Istituto Centrale per il Catalogo e la Documentazione, with a collection of aerial photographs of particular interest to archeologists and geographers.

Piazza Giovanni Agnelli (16 C-D5). The name of this square is a commemoration of the president of Fiat motors, who made a donation to the city of Rome of two symmetrical buildings – without windows or other apertures, but endowed with monumental entrances, and linked by a remarkable colonnade the height of the buildings – built in 1939-52 for the Turin-based car manufacturer. They are an ingenuous but magniloquent effort to translate into the rhetorical architectural style of Fascism a sense of the magnificence of the architecture of imperial Rome.

These two buildings now contain the *Museo della Civiltà Romana*, literally, the museum of Roman civilization, a collection of plaster casts depicting the most important episodes in Roman history and numerous different aspects of that civilization, as well as artifacts that illustrate the expansion of that civilization throughout the world; it also fea-

tures material presented at the Mostra Archeologica, or archeological exhibition, held at the baths of Diocletian (1911) and the Mostra Augustea della Romanità (literally, Augustan exhibition of Romanity, 1937), and was installed here by Giulio Quirino Giglioli and inaugurated in 1955.

Each of the 59 halls along which the long museum itinerary is configured is devoted to a special aspect or theme. Beyond the hall with the luminous map that illustrates the progressive Roman expansion, halls V-VII are dedicated to the legendary origins of the city and its relationship with the Mediterranean world; among other objects, these halls contain a reproduction of the *statue of the Warrior of Capestrano* (5th c. B.C.), the *Mattei sarcophagus*, reassembled with plaster casts of the original fragments, now preserved in the Vaticano and in Palazzo Mattei in Rome, and a reconstruction of the *rostral column of Caius Duilius* (260 a.C.), erected in the Foro Romano (Roman Forum) to celebrate the victory of the Romans over the Carthaginians in the naval battle of Milazzo.

We would point out, in the next halls (VIII-XXVI), the *busts of Julius Caesar* and *of the emperors of the Julian-Claudian "gens"*, the *busts of Vespasian, Domitian*, and *Antoninus Pius*, the models of *war machinery*, the cast of one side of the *arch of Marcus Aurelius* in Tripoli (A.D. 163), and models of the *mausoleum of Augustus* and the *baths of Leptis Magna*.

Beyond hall XXXVII, which contains the immense (200 sq. m.) **model of ancient Rome** depicting the appearance of the city on a scale of 1:25, hall XLV is noteworthy for the rich *treasures* of silverwork (reproductions of silver objects from Roman times), including the collection of *Hildesheim* (about 70 items from the Staatliche Museum of Berlin) and the *Esquiline collection* (from the British Museum of London).

Of special interest, in hall LI, is the complete series of *casts*, ordered in 1860 by Napoleon III, *of Trajan's column*, with reliefs that depict the emperor's campaigns against the Dacians (A.D. 101-102; A.D. 105-106).

The collection is rounded out by numerous reproductions of musical instruments and other instruments related to trade and home life, models of renowned imperial villas (Villa of Tiberius at Capri; palace of Diocletian at Split), amphitheaters, aqueducts, and nymphaeua, stelae, and inscriptions.

Archivio Centrale dello Stato (16 D4-5), or central archive of the state. Designed in 1938-42 on a line with the church of the Ss.

Pietro e Paolo, this structure comprises three buildings surrounded with colonnades and enclosing a square, in accordance with the model of the Hellenistic agora.

It contains documents of the ministries and the originals of laws and decrees of State, ever since its formation, along with the papers of the office of the prime minister.

Viale Europa (16 C-D2-3-4). This is the main thoroughfare of the quarter, and is characterized in the first section by the new office buildings of government ministries that are being moved out of the historical center (the *complex of the Ministero delle Finanze, or ministry of finance*, dates from 1957-62 a fine example of the new office buildings of EUR) and, after the intersection with the Via Cristoforo Colombo, by elegant shops.

Palazzo del Ministero delle Poste e Telecomunicazioni, building of the ministry of mail and telecommunications (16 C-D3-4). Built in the years 1969-76, since 1982 it has housed a *museum** on the history of the postal system, one of the most important on earth in that sector, which sprang from a collection begun in Florence (1878), continued in Rome after its transfer to the capital (1907) and opened to the public in 1959. It features mailboxes and mailslots (the oldest one, made of stone, dates from 1633), punches for cancelling stamps in the States of Italy, prior to unification, a fine collection of Italian and non-Italian stamps, complete with the proofs of Italian stamps from 1911 to the present day, and one of bureacratic stamps and documents; special note should be paid to the reconstruction, with the original instruments, of the transmission room used by Marconi on the yacht Elettra (in the telecommunications section), a collection of telephones, a model of the telephone built by Antonio Meucci, fine antique radios, and the *early electronic computer, ELEA 9003** built in 1956 to plans by Enrico Fermi.

Lago Artificiale (16 D-E2-3-4). This manmade lake is "foretold" by the pool, or *Piscina delle Rose* (16 D2), built in 1958-59 for the 1960 Olympics, and surrounded in part by the *Passeggiata del Giappone* (a promenade named for Japan, surrounded by 1,000 cherry trees donated by the city of Tokyo); the lake is roughly 1 km. long and 130 m. wide, at the widest point.

On the slopes of the hill that lies to the SW, is the *Giardino della Cascata* (16 D-E3), a garden that was nicely laid out, with fountains, in 1961 by Raffaele De Vico, who designed and built nearly all the public parks in the EUR.

From Largo Pella, a square near which the Via Cristoforo Colombo splits into two sections to run around the lake and up the hill atop which looms the Palazzo dello Sport (see below), you have a rapid and perspectival view of the *Palazzo dell'ENI* (16 D-E4), office building of the national power company, a 21-story skyscraper made of glass and steel, and built in 1960-62.

Palazzo dello Sport* (16 E3). This building is a successful blend of the overall style of Piacentini for the quarter as a whole, and the needs of public works in later years, and it is one of the most remarkable examples of civil engineering in the city of Rome. It was built by Pier Luigi Nervi and Marcello Piacentini in 1958-60 in place of the large arch in duralumin (aperture of 330 m.) designed by Adalberto Libera for the E42 and never built; circular in plan, it contains a sports hall capable of seating 16,000, housed under a cupola with a diameter of 100 m. and 144 ribbings.

On the right, note the *Serbatoio Idrico* (1957-59), a water tank, known locally as the Fungo, or mushroom; it contains a restaurant.

As you leave the city in the direction of Latina, you turn off from the Via Cristoforo Colombo,which, after running past the residential quarter of *Casal Palocco* which developed in the 1960s, reaches Lido di Ostia (see page 37), and you continue along the Via Pontina, made for high-speed traffic; on the right, you will pass two little townships, with distinct urban and social personalities.

Mostacciano, built from 1973 on, represents a successful blend of city construction and green countryside.

Spinaceto on the other hand, built in 1965 on city land of roughly 187 hectares, was built in the context of a plan for lower-income housing; of some interest is the plan with a "linear center" with a service "spina."

Information for Travellers:
Hotels, Restaurants, Places of interest

In the listings that follow, the information concerning hotels, restaurants, camping area resort villages, and hostels is split into 12 areas. The hotels recommended here are inc cated with official classification expressed by number of stars as required by the Italia law (from ♯♯♯ to ⋆). The restaurants listed are accompanied by the customary "fork" ra ings, TCI's traditional way of ranking restaurants (from ♦♦♦♦ to ♦). This classification is base on price, comfort, service, and appeal of the setting. Hotels and restaurants are followe by a capital letter and number (E5) followed by one (or two) bold letters (**ab**) which shoul refer you to its location on the maps, identified by a number. As of 18th December 1998 eac location's telephone code must also be dialled for local calls, indicated in the following li next to the symbol ☎. For those calling from abroad, the local code (including the 0) mus be dialled after the international code for Italy, followed by the subscriber's number. The fo lowing information has been carefully checked before going to print. We would, however, a vise readers to confirm certain data which is susceptible to change, before departure. All o servations and suggestions are gratefully accepted.

Termini, Piazza della Repubblica, Via Nazionale

Built on the site of the first train station of unified Italy, the Stazione Centrale di Termini was designed and built between 1938 and 1950 with modern criteria and structures: the two broad interior galleries feature public facilities, ticket windows, tourist offices, bars, restaurants, newsstands, bookstores, even a druggist's. This is a meeting ground for African and Slavic immigrants, either illegal or in possession of regular residence permits; the station has in recent years been converted into a little Roman casbah, often the site of violence, muggings, pursesnatchings, or acts of vandalism; strolling vendors of all races offer everything for sale, from fake Swatches to counterfeit designer purses. Around the ample square extends a neighborhood of more-or-less dignified little hotels and "pensioni," in austere palazzi from the turn of the 20th c., built to accommodate the new civil servants that were thronging Rome, the new capital of a united Italy. Trattorias and restaurants, often family-run, offer simple menus for tourists. The nearby Piazza della Repubblica, once known as the Piazza dell'Esedra, is a fundamental starting point for reaching the main points of the city;

there is an excellent network of public city tran portation, as well as a stop on the city subway, ar this is also often the jumping-off point for demo strations and processions. Le Grand Hotel, one the oldest and best-known hotels of Rome, bui at the end of the 19th c. in what was then consi ered to be one of the residential areas of the cit preserves intact its elegance.

As you enter the Via Nazionale you will fin yourself immersed in the vortex of shopping: vast array of stores offer merchandise of averag quality for tourists who are seeking Italian fas ion but at popular prices. The commercial cha acter of this street is enhanced by the publi transportation that runs along it, and furthe emphasized by the many restaurants, varie and fascinating. There is broad array of hotel from small "pensioni" all the way up to luxury h tels. The most important hotel in the area is d rectly linked to the Teatro dell'Opera through private entrance; Verdi stayed here on the oc casion of the first performance of his oper "Falstaff," in 1893.

Hotels

♯♯♯ **Le Grand Hotel.** Via Vittorio Emanuele Or lando 3, tel. 47091, fax 4747307. Number o rooms: 170. Air conditioning, elevator; spe cial parking garage for guests (5, C1, **a**).

⋆♯⋆ **Quirinale.** Via Nazionale 7, tel. 4707, fa 4820099. Number of rooms: 208. Handicap friendly. Air conditioning, elevator; specia parking garage for guests, garden (5, D1, **f**

⋆♯⋆ **Royal Santina.** Via Marsala 22, tel. 445524 fax 4941252. Number of rooms: 118. Hand icap-friendly. Air conditioning, elevator parking garage (5, D3, **e**).

⋆⋆⋆ **Alpi.** Via Castelfidardo 84/A, tel. 444124 fax 4441257. Number of rooms: 38. Lodging only; no board. Air conditioning, elevator special parking garage for guests (5, C3, **aa**).

★★ **Canada.** Via Vicenza 58, tel. 4457770, fax 4450749. Number of rooms: 70. Lodging only; no board. Air conditioning, elevator (5, C4, **n**).

★★ **Cosmopolita.** Via IV Novembre 114, tel. 69941349, fax 69941360. Number of rooms: 30. Lodging only; no board. Elevator; special parking garage for guests (4, F3, **l**).

★★ **Galileo.** Via Palestro 33, tel. 4441205, fax 4441208. Number of rooms: 38. Lodging only; no board. Air conditioning, elevator; parking area, garden (5, B-C3-4, **ac**).

★★ **Miami.** Via Nazionale 230, tel. 4817180, fax 484562. Number of rooms: 34. No dining facilities. Access for the disabled, elevator, special terms for garage (4, O6, **fp**).

★★ **Select.** Via Bachelet 6, tel. 491137, fax 4441086. Number of rooms: 19. Lodging only; no board. Air conditioning, special parking garage for guests, garden (5, C4, **j**).

★★ **Venezia.** Via Varese 18, tel. 4457101, fax 4957687. Number of rooms: 61. Lodging only; no board. Air conditioning, elevator; special parking garage for guests (5, D4, **i**).

Restaurants

🍴 **Agata e Romeo.** Via Carlo Alberto 45, tel. 4466115, fax 4465842. Closed Sunday, holiday closure varies. Air conditioning. Cuisine of Lazio and Sannio (14, C1, **rm**).

🍴 **Grappolo d'Oro.** Via Palestro 4/10, tel. 4941441. Closed Sunday, August. Air conditioning. Classical cooking – seafood (5, B3, **r**).

🍴 **Pavone.** Via Palestro 19/B, tel. 4465433, fax 4441438. Closed Saturday and Sunday lunch. Air conditioning, parking. Cuisine of Lazio and classic (5, B3, **o**).

Cafes and pastry shops

Bar del Palazzo delle Esposizioni. Via Nazionale 194, tel. 4828001. This cafe was recently renovated; you can enter, with or without a ticket to see the exhibitions in the Palazzo delle Esposizioni. It is a favorite rendezvous for cocktails and drinks.

Enoteca Trimani. Via Goito 20, tel. 4469661. This is one of the most noted retail wine shops in Italy; it still has the look and feel of a typical "bottiglieria," or wine shop-tavern of the turn of the 20th c. The family of the owners has been dealing in wine without interruption since 1820, and has its own vineyard at Anagni.

Trimani Wine Bar. Via Cernaia 37B, tel. 4469630. This wine bar opened in 1991 and is already quite popular; through the course of the year, there are numerous presentations of wines, with tasting sessions.

Museums and cultural institutions

Biblioteca del Consiglio Nazionale delle Ricerche. Piazza Aldo Moro, tel. 49933385.

Biblioteca Medica Statale. Viale del Policlinico 155, tel. 490245.

Biblioteca nazionale centrale Vittorio Emanuele II. Viale Castro Pretorio 105, tel. 4453942.

Biblioteca Universitaria Alessandrina. Piazza Aldo Moro 5, tel. 4469655.

Museo Nazionale Romano (Palazzo Massimo - Terme di Diocleziano). Piazza dei Cinquecento, largo di Villa Peretti, tel. 48903501. Closed Monday. *Weekdays and Saturday 9-1:30; holidays and Sunday 9-12:30.*

Museo numismatico della Zecca Italiana. Via XX Settembre 94, tel. 47613317. Closed August, Sunday and Monday. *Weekdays and Saturday 9-12,30.*

Palazzo delle Esposizioni. Via Nazionale 194, tel. 4745903-4828760.

Entertainment

Piccolo Eliseo. Via Nazionale 183/E, tel. 4885095.

Teatro Eliseo. Via Nazionale 183/E, tel. 4882114.

Health care facilities

Policlinico Umberto I. Viale del Policlinico 255, tel. 44701807.

Shops, crafts, and fine art

Libreria delle Esposizioni. Via Nazionale 71, tel. 4828001. In the heart of the old shopping section of Rome, this bookstore was reborn in June 1992.

Piazza del Popolo, Via del Corso, Via dei Condotti, Fontana di Trevi

The topography of this area has remained virtually intact, little marked by the slow and progressive development of the city. The streets, partially sealed off to traffic, are a reference point for shopping and center-city strolling. It is a pleasant custom among the Romans to stop for an "aperitivo" at Piazza del Popolo, and to sit at one of the many bars, taking in the three churches, the fountains, and the obelisk. There is a great bustle of pedestrians, but there is also a constant flow of cars, which stop in the large parking area beside the fountain; here, the carriages of the well-do-do and the great lords would pull up, and fairs, competitions, and horse races were held.

Via del Corso is a natural continuation of this square, and is one of the most bustling streets in Rome. Jeans stores, punk accessories shops, and neon lights have pushed aside in the last few decades the discreet and gentlemanly boutiques and shops that had previously occupied the street; there are few old shops surviving. Along this road, studded with old aristocratic palazzi, you may note a renowned movie house, one of the most luxurious hotels in Rome, and the historic cafes of the late-19th c., once a meeting spot for artists and literati, now crowded thriving bars.

Of particular interest to those fond of antiques and for discerning shoppers is the "Babbuino," as authentic Romans pronounce the name of the old Via Paolina Trifaria. Via Margutta, behind it, is the street of artists (Italy's Montmartre), chosen by painters and sculptors since the 17th c. as a place to live and to work; today, although it has lost much of its charm, it remains an interesting street to explore.

We are not far from the Piazza di Spagna, one of the most renowned squares on earth: for more than two centuries now, this has been a destination for international tourism, but also a place where wanderers and bohemians take a rest from their wanderings; it is still one of the favorite strolling sites of the Romans. The meeting place is the Barcaccia, the handsome ship-shaped fountain built by Bernini at the center of the square. The splendid 18th-c. stairway – the Spanish Steps – on the other hand, is often crowded with amateur painters, and every year this is the site of one of the most colorful events anywhere on earth (the azalea show) as well as the setting for the international "haute-couture" shows: on a remarkable runway pass the newest creations of the biggest names of high fashion; this event attracts a crowded audience from the world of entertainment and Roman aristocracy.

Piazza di Spagna has always maintained a high-society aspect: it is said that at the end of the 18th c., the quarter was largely inhabited by foreigners, out-of-towners, and "ladies of the night," and that during the muggy summer evenings, women and men who had never met would dance until the wee hours. In the designer boutiques, you will find the finest labels of Italian prêt-à-porter, while extravagance and classical style merge in the fields of fashion and design as much as in the field of fine dining: here you will see elegant period tea houses and the better sort of fast food. At the sides of the square are the favorite atelier of 1960s movie stars and princesses, and the studio of the most famous Italian designer. On the Trinità dei Monti, one of the most exclusive hotels of the capital enjoys an enviable location and a splendid panoramic view; in the surrounding areas, theaters with variety acts and cabarets are available for those who wish to spend an unusual evening.

Converging on this square is the Via dei Condotti, the best known and most popular street in Rome, which enjoyed its period of glory in the 18th c. Its cafe, Caffè Greco, which dates back to 1760, became the favorite meeting spot for artists and writers, who discussed art and literature, music and poetry here, while sipping real coffee (and not the unholy brews made of chickpeas, beans or chestnuts, and proffered in other cafes of the city of the time), and served for the first time in delicate little demitasse cups; today this cafe is crowded with tourists, who poke through the photographs, drawings, letters, and autographs that hang on the walls of the rooms, in search of nuggets of history and culture. Along the road you will find the most famous jewelry shops on earth, and the most refined boutiques, which offer a superb sampling of Italian and European high fashion. Equally fertile for fine shopping are the parallels, the Via Borgognona, the Via Frattina, and the Via della Croce (the latter, a gastronomist's paradise). In the Rione Trevi, surrounding the Piazza di Trevi, the narrow streets and little lanes are crowded each day with hundreds of tourists who arrive here from all over the world to admire Rome's most famous fountain: turning their backs on the gurgling basin, they toss the inevitable coin, which, legend has it, will assure that they return to Rome someday. All around, are strolling souvenir vendors and shops catering to the sightseeing public.

Dining throughout this area is reasonably good: there are fashionable trattorias, and restaurants with more reasonable prices, with typical regional food, wine taverns which also serve little snacks with a glass of red or white, and more-or-less affordable beer taverns; it is worth your while to make a stop at the little Viennese pastry shop in the Via Frattina to try one of their exquisite little sacher tortes; and don't forget to try their famous "bombette alla crema," as well. Hotel accommodations range from the fine luxury hotel to the less exclusive but equally refined little hotel; all enjoy a central location, fine views, and excellent service. There are night spots, for a very elite clientele.

Hotels

✦✦✦ **Hassler.** Piazza Trinità dei Monti 6, tel 699340, fax 6789991. Number of rooms 100. Handicap-friendly. Air conditioning elevator; special parking garage for guests garden (4, B3, **ag**).

✦✦✦ **D'Inghilterra.** Via Bocca di Leone 14, tel 69981, fax 69922243. Number of rooms 105. Air conditioning, elevator, special terms for garage (4, C2, **ai**).

✦✦✦ **De La Ville Intercontinental.** Via Sistina 69 tel. 67331, fax 6784213. Number of rooms 192. Air conditioning, elevator; special parking garage for guests, garden (4, B3, **an**).

✦✦✦ **Delle Nazioni.** Via Poli 7, tel. 6792441, fax 6782400. Number of rooms: 83. Lodging only; no board. Access for the disabled. Air conditioning, elevator; parking garage (4 D3, **ah**).

✦✦✦ **Plaza.** Via del Corso 126, tel. 69921111, fax 69941575. Number of rooms: 200. No dining facilities. Elevator; special parking garage for guests (4, B-C1-2, **am**).

✦✦✦ **Valadier.** Via della Fontanella 15, tel. 3611998, fax 3201558. Number of rooms: 38. Air conditioning, elevator (1, D-E1, **al**).

Cecil. ** Via F. Crispi 55/A-C, tel. 6795740, fax 6797996. Number of rooms: 41. No dining facilities. Elevator; special terms for garage (4, C4, **aq**).

Gregoriana. ** Via Gregoriana 18, tel. 6794269, fax 6784258. Number of rooms: 19. Lodging only; no board. Air conditioning, elevator; special parking garage for guests (4, C3, **aq**).

Internazionale. ** Via Sistina 79, tel. 6793047, fax 6784764. Number of rooms: 42. Lodging only; no board. Air conditioning, elevator; special parking garage for guests (4, B3, **as**).

Locarno. ** Via della Penna 22, tel. 3610841, fax 3215249. Number of rooms: 38. Lodging only; no board. Air conditioning, elevator; special parking garage for guests, garden (13, D5, **cu**).

Madrid. ** Via Mario de' Fiori 93, tel. 6991510, fax 6791653. Number of rooms: 26. Lodging only; no board. Air conditioning, elevator (4, C3, **at**).

Mozart. ** Via dei Greci 23/B, tel. 36001915, fax 36001735. Number of rooms: 31. Lodging only; no board. Air conditioning, elevator, special terms for garage (1, E1, **ao**).

Tritone. ** Via del Tritone 210, tel. 69922575, fax 6782624. Number of rooms: 43. Lodging only; no board. Air conditioning, elevator; special parking garage for guests (4, D2-3, **ap**).

Margutta. * Via Laurina 34, tel. 3223674, fax 3200395. Number of rooms: 21. Lodging only; no board. Elevator (1, E1, **au**).

Restaurants

Porto di Ripetta. Via di Ripetta 250, tel. 3612376, fax 3227089. Closed Sunday, for a certain period in August. Air conditioning. Cuisine of Tuscany/Marche (1, D-E1, **z**).

Ranieri. Via Mario dei Fiori 26, tel. 6791592, fax 69922415. Closed Sunday. Air conditioning. Classical cooking (4, B2, **v**).

Al Moro. Vicolo Bollette 13, tel. 69940736. Closed Sunday, August. Air conditioning. Roman cooking (4, E2-3, **u**).

Nino. Via Borgognona 11, tel. 6795676. Closed Sunday, August. Air conditioning. Tuscan cuisine and classical cooking (4, B-C2-3, **ri**).

Abruzzi. Via del Vaccaro 1, tel. 6793897. Closed Saturday, August. Air conditioning. Roman and Abruzzese cooking (4, E-F3, **ra**).

Buca di Ripetta. Via di Ripetta 36, tel. 3219391. Closed Sunday evening and Monday, August. Air conditioning. Tuscan and Roman cuisine (1, E1, **y**).

Mario. Via della Vite 55, tel. 6783818. Closed Sunday, August. Air conditioning. Tuscan cuisine and classical cooking (4, C2, **rt**).

Cafes and pastry shops

Alemagna. Via del Corso 181, tel. 6792887. One of the biggest and most crowded bars in Rome.

Babyngton's Tea Rooms. Piazza di Spagna 23, tel. 6786027. This is a period tearoom, with a notable atmosphere, and was opened in 1896 by Anna Maria Babyngton; you can have a genuine English tea, with the traditional biscuits and cakes.

Buccone. Via di Ripetta 19, tel. 3612154. This was the stomping ground in the 1960s for artists and intellectuals; the wine tavern and cellar – located in an 18th-c. "palazzetto," or little palazzo – has a vast assortment of wines, from Greece, Israel, and South Africa.

Caffè Ciampini. Viale della Trinità dei Monti, tel. 6785678. This cafe enjoys a remarkable location.

Caffè Greco. Via dei Condotti 86, tel. 6782554. In the old Roman civic registry, "Libro di Stato delle Anime della Parrocchia di S. Lorenzo in Lucina," there is mention of Nicola della Maddalena (1760) as the owner of this cafe. But the success of this coffee shop was the handiwork of one of the later owners, Salviani, of what we would recognize as a real cup of "caffè espresso," in little demitasse cups. Many intellectuals, who frequented the cafe in the old days, would receive mail in a distinctive wooden letterbox near the entrance; note the period furnishings.

Canova. Piazza del Popolo 16, tel. 3612231. Opened in 1952, the bar is famous for both its strategic location, and for the "aperitivi" it serves to an elite clientele (Fellini was an habitué).

Casina Valadier. Pincio, tel. 6792083. Receptions and parties are catered in this splendid villa, built by Valadier as a lodge for the Borghese family; a chilling detail – this was the officers' club for German officers under the Nazi occupation of Rome.

Pasticceria Krechel. Via Frattina 134, tel. 6780946. This pastry shop prepares all the specialties of the Viennese school of pastry-making; we should point out the sacher torte and "bombette alla crema."

Rosati. Piazza del Popolo 5, tel. 3225859. This historic Roman cafe has belonged to the Rosati family for three generations. The "Liberty" – Italian Art-Nouveau – decorations are intact; the crystal vases in the niches date from the 1920s.

Museums and cultural institutions

Accademia di Francia. Viale della Trinità dei Monti 1A, tel. 67611.

Accademia nazionale di S. Cecilia. Via Vittoria 6, tel. 3611064.

Biblioteca dell'Accademia nazionale di S. Luca. Piazza dell'Accademia di S. Luca 77, tel. 6798848.

Biblioteca Hertziana. Via Gregoriana 28, tel. 695931.

Fondazione Keats-Shelley Memorial. Piazza di Spagna 26, tel. 6784235.

Galleria Colonna. Via della Pilotta 17, tel. 6794362. Closed in August. *Saturday 9-1.*

Galleria dell'Accademia nazionale di S. Luca. Piazza dell'Accademia di S. Luca 77, tel. 6798904. Closed July and August. *Monday, Wednesday, Friday, and the last Sunday of the month 10-1.*

Galleria Pallavicini. Via XXIV Maggio 43, tel. 4827224. Not open to the public.

Museo delle Cere. Piazza dei Ss. Apostoli 67, tel. 6796482. *Open: 9-8.*

Museo nazionale delle paste alimentari. Piazza Scanderberg, tel. 69911119. *Open: 9:30-12:30 and 4-7.*

Entertainment

E.T.I. Teatro Quirino. Via Minghetti 1, tel. 6783730.

Gilda. Via Mario de' Fiori 97, tel. 6784838. Discotheque and piano bar.

Salone Margherita (Bagaglino). Via Due Macelli 75, tel. 6791439-6798269. Cabaret and variety show.

Teatro de' Servi. Via del Mortaro 22, tel. 6795130.

Teatro Due. Vicolo Due Macelli 37, tel. 6788259.

Teatro Sistina. Via Sistina 129, tel. 4826841.

Health care facilities

Ospedale di S. Giacomo. Via Canova 29, tel. 36261.

Shops, crafts, and fine art

Alinari. Via Alibert 16, tel. 6792923. Since the mid-19th c., this has been one of the most prestigious names in the field of photography and visual history.

Ansuini. Via del Babuino 150/D, tel. 36002219. For the past 130 years, it has sold fine silver, often one-of-a-kind items.

Armani. Via dei Condotti 77, tel. 6991460. High-fashion boutique.

Battistoni. Via dei Condotti 61, tel. 6786827-6794187.

Bulgari. Via dei Condotti 10, tel. 6793876. Famous jewelry, classical and modern models.

Cappelleria Radiconcini. Via del Corso 139, tel.

6791807. The most famous hat shop in Rome, has been open since 1932.

Centrocarta Vertecchi. Via della Croce 38 e 70 tel. 6783110. This is certainly the best stocke stores in Rome, for both stationery goods and fo Christmas and Easter decorations.

Fendi. Via Borgognona 36, tel. 6797641; vi Fontanella Borghese 57, tel. 6876290. High-fash ion boutique.

Fendissime, via Fontanella Borghese 56/A, te 6876391. Apparel for women.

Gucci. Via Condotti 61, tel. 6786827. Fine leathe goods, accessories, apparel for man and women

Hausmann e C. Via del Corso 406, tel. 6893194 Opened in 1893, this is one of the oldest jeweler of the center of Rome.

La Bottega del Marmoraro. Via Margutta 53/B, tel 3207660. This is a high-quality marble shop – o "marmoraro" – known and frequented among th rich and famous; aside from its marble-working a tivity, there is a collection of marble-workin tools.

Laura Biagiotti. Via Borgognona 43/44, tel 6791205. High-fashion boutique.

Perrone. Piazza di Spagna 92, tel. 6783101. Sinc 1912 this store has specialized in fine glove and hosiery for an array of famed clients.

Restauri Artistici Mario Squatriti. Via di Ripetta 29 tel. 3610232. Since 1947 this shop has done fine re storations of porcelain, ivory, terracotta, and dolls

Salvatore Ferragamo. Via Condotti 73/74, tel 6791565. Shoes and footwear; ready-to-wear.

Souleiado. Via dell'Oca 38/A, tel. 3610402. An ar ray of Provençal fabrics, directly from the regions of Avignon.

Valentino. Via Gregoriana 24, tel. 67391. High fashion. Via Condotti 12, tel. 6783656. Boutique for men. Via Bocca di Leone 15/18, tel. 6795862 Boutique for women.

Montecitorio, the Pantheon, Piazza Navona

Montecitorio is the political center of the capital of Italy. The monumental Palazzo della Curia Innocenziana, once the site of the offices of the administration of justice, has since 1870 been the site of the Camera dei Deputati, Italy's house of representatives. Nowadays, it is commonplace to see protest rallies and demonstrations held by outraged Italian citizens, in front of the building, contributing to the traffic problems in this square, already overcrowded by the large parking area around the obelisk (there are many dark-blue cars, driven by chauffeurs, carrying Italian representatives and senators). The cafes, the old "gelateria," or ice cream shop, in the Via degli Uffici del Vicario, the trattorias and the restaurants along the adjoining streets are popular with politicians, journalists, and businessmen (overlooking the square are the offices of the Rome daily newspaper, Il Tempo; not far off are the Borsa, or stock exchange, and the Camera di Commercio, or chamber of commerce). The oldest hotel in Rome, in the nearby Piazza della Rotonda, is a 15th-c. inn (or "lo-

canda"), luxuriously renovated; here both the po-et Ariosto and the composer Mascagni slept, as is announced by plaques on the facade. In the background is the Pantheon, one of the outstanding features in the area, a mute witness to the transformations of the square, which, until the end of the

8th c., had an exceedingly colorful market, which is now in the Via delle Coppelle. Crowds of tourists stop to photograph the temple and the splendid fountain, erected at the orders of Pope Gregory XI, and to go shopping in the boutiques along the adjoining streets: in the Salita de' Crescenzi, Via dela Rosetta, Via del Pantheon, Via della Maddalena, Via della Minerva, and Via del Pie' di Marmo are shops that sell curiosities, alternating with bouques that boast long histories and solid traditions (there are many stores selling religious and liturical objects); in this area you will also find the finest selection of ice cream in the city, and you will drink the finest coffee in the city. There are a great many restaurants, and they range from the most refined and costly – where you can savor first-rate sea food – down to regional-style "osterie," or taverns.

Taverns, restaurants, pizzerias selling pies by the slice, and fine delicatessens can be found in the Via dei Pàstini, where pasta of all sorts were once prepared and sold, especially the famous "trinfini," little chests full of all sorts of egg pastas, to be brought as gifts to mothers giving birth. Piazza Navona is truly one of the loveliest squares on earth, an unusual and festive outdoor parlor, that over the centuries has played the host to fesvals and athletic competitions, tours and processions (one interesting old custom is that of ooding the square on hot summer Sundays by pening the runoff pipes in the fountains). Nowadays it is colorful, with numerous artists who isplay their paintings and their gentle caricaures, sketched in a few minutes; there are wellnown, expensive bars and cafes surrounding he square (you can enjoy an excellent "gelato al rtufo," a delicious rich chocolate ice cream) nd at Christmas time, traditional stalls, selling weets, candies, plastic or clay manger scenes, like ose that in the past were sold by the "pupazari." In the surrounding area, note a delightful ice of Rome right across from S. Maria della ace, a fashionable cafe that is popular with Roan yuppies, theater people, and intellectuals. nd for those who are interested in antiques, ere is a famous antiques show every year in the a dei Coronari, once known as the "Via Recta," here the "paternostrari" or "coronari" once sold reaths ("corone") to pilgrims on their way to S. etro. The hotels in the surrounding area, are mall but exclusive, central and panoramic, rich style and atmosphere: 15th-c. inns or patrian palazzi of the 18th c. – once visited by Mazzi and Garibaldi, Sartre and Simone de Beauvoir are intact in their architectural structure, but alost all renovated on the interior, and now large-frequented by politicians and businessmen.

otels

† **Crowne Plaza Minerva.** Piazza della Minerva 69, tel. 69941888, fax 6794165. Number of rooms: 134. Access for the disabled. Air conditioning, elevator (3, F5, **g**).

★ **Colonna Palace.** Piazza di Montecitorio 12, tel. 6781341, fax 6794496. Number of rooms: 105. Lodging only; no board. Handicap-friendly. Air conditioning, elevator; special terms for garage (3, D6, **av**).

★ **Cesàri.** Via di Pietra 89/A, tel. 6792386, fax 6790882. Number of rooms: 48, 43 of which have a bath or shower. Lodging only; no board. Air conditioning, elevator (3, E6, **ax**).

★★★ **Portoghesi.** Via dei Portoghesi 1, tel. 6864231, fax 6876976. Number of rooms: 27. Lodging only; no board. Handicap-friendly. Air conditioning, elevator; special terms for garage (3, D4, **ay**).

Restaurants

🍴 **Papà Giovanni.** Via dei Sediari 4, tel. 68804807, fax 6853308. Closed Sunday, Christmas-New Year's Day, Ferragosto (15 Aug.). Air conditioning. Cuisine of Lazio (3, F4, **rh**).

🍴 **Rosetta.** Via della Rosetta 8, tel. 6861002, fax 6872852. Closed Saturday at midday and Sunday, for a certain period in August. Air conditioning. Classical cooking – seafood (3, E5, **rg**).

🍴 **Convivio.** Vicolo dell'Orso 45, tel. 6869432. Closed for lunch Saturday and Sunday, holiday closure varies. Air conditioning. Refined cuisine (3, D4, **rc**).

🍴 **El Toulà.** Via della Lupa 29/B, tel. 6873750, fax 6871115. Closed Sunday and at midday on Saturday and Monday, August. Air conditioning. Venetian cuisine (3, C5, **rl**).

🍴 **Campana.** Vicolo della Campana 18, tel. 6867820. Closed Monday, August. Air conditioning. Roman and classical cuisine – fish (3, C4, **rn**).

🍴 **Eau Vive.** Via Monterone 85, tel. 68801095. Closed Sunday, for a certain period in August. Air conditioning. French and classical cuisine (3, F4-5, **rs**).

🍴 **Buco.** Via S. Ignazio 8, tel. 6793298. Closed Monday, for a certain period in August. Air conditioning, garden. Tuscan cuisine (3, E-F6, **ro**).

🍴 **Sagrestia.** Via del Seminario 89, tel. 6797581. Closed Wednesday, Christmas, and for a certain period in August. Roman cooking – pasta dishes (3, E5, **re**).

Cafes and pastry shops

Antico Caffè della Pace. Via della Pace 3-5, tel. 6861216. In a lovely location, near the Baroque church of S. Maria della Pace, this cafe has become a meeting spot for intellectuals and artists.

Camilloni. Piazza di S. Eustachio 54, tel. 6864995. This shop is known for the excellent quality of its classical pastries and its handmade ice-creams.

Cul de Sac. Piazza di Pasquino 73, tel. 68801094. One of the most popular wine taverns in the 1970s, and the forerunner of the many "wine bars" now found in Rome; it offers over 700 different labels.

Giolitti. Via degli Uffici del Vicario 40, tel. 6794206. Opened in 1934, this is one of Rome's traditional ice-cream shops ("gelaterie"), especially popular with politicians.

La Caffettiera. Piazza di Pietra 65, tel. 6798147. Opened recently, this cafe features Neapolitan delicacies: from the classical "sfogliatella" to the rice-based "sartoù di riso," and from pastries to deep-fried "zeppole."

Sant'Eustachio. Piazza di S. Eustachio 82, tel. 6861309. Frequented by coffee connoisseurs, this bar serves everything from "espresso classico" to the "gran caffè speciale," served in a large cup, the specialty of the house.

Tre Scalini. Piazza Navona 30, tel. 68801996. Overlooking the splendid Baroque square, you can savor a wonderful "tartufo" (chocolate ice-cream) here.

Museums and cultural institutions

Accademia Ecclesiastica Pontificia. Piazza della Minerva 74, tel. 688201.

Archivio di Stato di Roma. Corso del Rinascimento 40, tel. 6864123.

Biblioteca Angelica. Piazza di S. Agostino 8, tel. 6875874.

Biblioteca Casanatense. Via di S. Ignazio 52, tel. 6798988.

Biblioteca della Fondazione Besso. Largo di Torre Argentina 11, tel. 68806290.

Biblioteca della Fondazione Primoli. Via Zanardelli 1/A, tel. 68801827.

Biblioteca Vallicelliana. Piazza della Chiesa Nuova 18, tel. 68802671.

Galleria Comunale d'Arte Moderna. Via F. Crispi 24, tel. 4742848. Closed Monday. *Weekdays and Saturday 9-7; holidays and Sunday 9-1:30.*

Galleria Doria Pamphili. Via del Collegio Romano 1/A, tel. 6797323. Closed Thursday. *10-5; guided visits by appointment 10:30-12:30.*

Museo di Roma. Piazza di S. Pantaleo 10, tel. 6875880. Closed for restoration.

Museo Napoleonico. Via Zanardelli 1, tel. 68806286. Closed Monday. *Weekdays and Saturday 9-7; holidays and Sunday 9-1.*

Entertainment

E.T.I. Teatro Valle. Via del Teatro Valle 23/A, tel. 68803794.

La Cabala Hostaria dell'Orso. Via dei Soldati 25, tel. 6864250. Discotheque and piano bar.

Tartarughino. Via della Scrofa 2, tel. 6786037. Piano Bar.

Teatro Artemide. Via dei Coronari 45, tel. 5813244.

Teatro dell'Orologio. Via dei Filippini 17, tel. 68308735.

Teatro Flaiano. Via di S. Stefano del Cacco 15, tel. 6796496.

Teatro La Scaletta. Via del Collegio Romano 1, tel. 6776360.

Teatro Rossini. Piazza S. Chiara 14, tel. 68802770.

Teatro Tor di Nona. Via degli Acquasparta 16, tel. 68805890.

Videoteatro. Vicolo degli Amatriciani 2, tel. 6867610.

Shops, crafts, and fine art

Antica Libreria Cascianelli. Largo Febo 15-16, tel. 68802806. This is the best-known store for o books in Rome; it sells Italian and non-Italian ra editions.

Bonpoint. Piazza di S. Lorenzo in Lucina 25, te 6871548. This shop opened recently, following i great success in Paris; it sells elegant and refine clothing (19th-c. style) for little ones.

Carmignani. Via della Colonna Antonina 41, t 6795449. This is a treasure chest for pipe-lover you can find the finest brands of Italian, Irish, ar English production, and the famous French Dunh

Cenci. Via di Campo Marzio 1-7, tel. 699068 This clothing shop is set in a number of rooms an old patrician "palazzetto," and it has a lo and respected tradition in the fields of men's ar women's apparel.

Ceramiche Musa. Via di Campo Marzio 39, te 6871242. Handsome and refined ceramics f floors and wall facings are manufactured with th colors and decorations of the traditional style of Vietri.

Codognotto. Via dei Pianellari 1-14, tel. 687728 This is the atelier of a remarkable individual, ce tainly one of the best-known sculptors in Rom His "ecological" creations are carved only out wood, and are lovely and even haunting.

Coloreria Poggi. Via del Gesù 74-75, Via del Pi di Marmo 40-41, tel. 6793674-6784477. Founded 1825, this art shop is rich in supplies, for studen or for professional artists.

Durante. Piazza della Rotonda 64, tel. 6795221. knife shop, founded in 1860, where you can pu chase an array of fine products, including pocl et knives with tiny files, scissors, can-openers

Fincato. Via della Colonna Antonina 34, te 6785508-6793996. Fausto Fincato has a profoun understanding and knowledge of pipes, whic has allowed him to publish a quarterly magazir and a book on the subject.

Giorgi e Febbi. Piazza della Rotonda 61-62, te 6791649. Since 1784 it has been purveying fine an hand-made fabrics (silks, cottons, and brocades to the households of famous and noble clients

Pineider. Via della Fontanella Borghese 22, te 6878369. A tradition of fine papermaking – no personalized, or embossed or printed with mono grams, names, or symbols – which dates back t 1774.

Primaria Farmacia Internazionale Caprania Piazza Capranica 96, tel. 6794680. This pharma cy dates back to 1860, and still has some of th authentic furnishings: note the antique ston drinking fountain.

Profumeria Materozzoli. Piazza di S. Lorenzo i Lucina 5, tel. 6871456. This perfumery is locate in the Palazzo Fiano Almagià, and was the firs one to open in Rome.

Tanca. Salita de' Crescenzi 10-12, tel. 6880332 Jewlery, silver, and period prints – some of th finest that can be found in Rome – in a shop tha dates back roughly 50 years.

Tebro. Via dei Prefetti 46-54, tel. 6873441. Sinc 1867, this shop has been selling refined hous hold and personal linen, both classical and mo ern, of excellent quality.

This area has preserved intact its charm, despite heavy traffic. In the unpretentious Rione Regola, once inhabited by numerous skilled artisans, you can still find numerous shops of frame-makers, gilders, goldsmiths, restorers, and upholsterers, but also clothing shops, which offer merchandise of good quality at reasonable prices. Via de' Giubbonari is one of the main shopping streets, closed to traffic and exceedingly popular with Romans, who can choose among the many restaurants and the numerous pizzerias that line the Campo de' Fiori. The square, with its age-old, thriving market place, is transformed on hot summer evenings into a large and cheerful outdoor dining hall.

The Via Giulia maintains a decidedly more elegant appearance; in the 16th c. this was the most popular road in Rome. Long and straight, the road is interrupted midway along its course by an arch covered with climbing plants; this road was built by the Farnese family to connect their palazzo to the Tiber, and is renowned in Rome for its antique shops, where you can find collector's items and hand-made furniture, but also splendid creches, which are set up in the churches at Christmas time. Nearby, elegant restaurants and little refined hotels give one the sensation of being in a place for connoisseurs.

On the opposite side of the Via Arenula, the old Jewish quarter stands out for its diversity. In 1555 a bull issued by Pope Paul IV – "Cum nimis absurdum" – established that one hour after sundown, from Easter to All Saints' Day, and two hours after sunset for the rest of the year, the five doors were to be barred shut, and no one could enter or exit. The gates were reopened under Pope Pius IX and the old section was razed to the ground at the end of the 19th c. for urbanistic and health reasons; still the Ghetto preserves the air of a secluded place, almost an island in the heart of the city; the stores too are quite similar to what they were then: wholesale clothing stores, linen shops, shops selling supplies to seamstresses (the Jews were known as skilled manufacturers of, and successful dealers in, fabrics, once the only field in which they were allowed to engage) line the dark and narrow streets of the quarter in great numbers. The restaurants offer typical Italian Jewish food: "carciofi alla giudia," a savory artichoke dish; fried mixed vegetables; "coratella coi carciofi," again artichokes; and "ali-ciotti con l'indivia," a fish dish, are among the most savory dishes; and everything is kosher. The sweets are traditional, and tend to baked goods more than pastry; note the renowned "pizza giudia" (a dough with candied fruit, almonds, raisins, and pignoli nuts) or sour black cherry pies with almond paste; nor should we overlook the "bruscolini," or peanuts, piping hot from the oven, and crunchy, at the Portico d'Ottavia.

Restaurants

🍴 **Camponeschi.** Piazza Farnese 50, tel. 6874927, fax 6865244. Closed Sunday, for a certain period in August. Air conditioning. Roman and classical cooking (VII, A5, **rw**).

🍴 **Piperno.** Monte dei Cenci 9, tel. 68806629. Closed Sunday evening and Monday, Christmas-New Year's Day, Easter, August. Air conditioning. Roman and classical cooking (7, B6, **rv**).

🍴 **Cardinale G.B..** Via delle Carceri 6, tel. 6869336. Closed Sunday, August. Air conditioning. Roman cooking (3, F2, **ru**).

🍴 **Drappo.** Vicolo del Malpasso 9, tel. 6877365. Closed Sunday, August. Air conditioning. Sardinian cooking (3, F2, **rz**).

🍴 **Pancrazio.** Piazza del Biscione 92, tel. 6861246. Closed Wednesday, for a certain period in August. Air conditioning, garden. Roman and classical cooking (7, A5, **rx**).

🍴 **Taverna Giulia.** Vicolo dell'Oro 23, on the corner of Via Giulia, tel. 6869768. Closed Sunday, August. Air conditioning. Ligurian cuisine – pasta dishes and seafood (3, E1-2, **rf**).

🍴 **Vecchia Roma.** Piazza Campitelli 18, tel. 6864604. Closed Wednesday, for a certain period in August. Air conditioning. Classical cooking – fish (8, B1-2, **rp**).

Cafes and pastry shops

Al Forno del Ghetto. Via del Portico d'Ottavia 2. Unleavened bread and oven-baked cakes, in the old Jewish tradition.

Bernasconi. Largo di Torre Argentina 1, tel. 68308141. This historic cafe and pastry shop was opened in 1851, and is one of the oldest in Rome.

Bernasconi. Piazza Cairoli 16, tel. 68806264. This small cafe and pastry shop was opened in 1926, and is always crowded; it specializes in wine and kosher products.

La Dolce Roma. Via del Portico d'Ottavia 20/B, tel. 6892196. Viennese pastries, but also American specialties (cheesecake, lemon pie).

Museums and cultural institutions

Accademia di Ungheria. Via Giulia 1, tel. 6869595.

Biblioteca dell'Istituto Nazionale di Archeologia e Storia dell'Arte. Piazza Venezia 3, tel. 6780982.

Biblioteca di Storia Moderna e Contemporanea. Via Caetani 32, tel. 6879629.

187

Biblioteca & Raccolta Teatrale del Burcardo. Via del Sudario 44, tel. 6819471.

Galleria Spada. Piazza Capo di Ferro 3, tel. 6861158. *Weekdays and Saturday 9-7; holidays and Sunday 9-1.*

Istituto dell'Enciclopedia Italiana. Piazza dell'Enciclopedia Italiana 4, tel. 68981.

Mostra della Comunità Ebraica di Roma. Lungotevere Cenci, tel. 6875051. Closed Saturday. *Monday-Thursday 9-4:30; Friday 9-2; Sunday 9-12:30.*

Musei Capitolini. Piazza del Campidoglio, tel. 67102071. Closed Monday. *9-7.*

Museo Barracco. Corso Vittorio Emanuele II 166/A, tel. 68806848. Closed Monday. *Weekdays and Saturday 9-7; holidays and Sunday 9-1.*

Museo del Palazzo di Venezia. Via del Plebiscito 118, tel. 6798865. Closed Sunday. *Open: 9-2.*

Museo del Teatro Argentina. Via dei Barbieri 21, tel. 6877390. *Open by request to the guardian.*

Museo Criminologico. Via del Gonfalone 29, tel. 68300234. *Tuesday 9-1 and 2:30-6:30; Wednesday, Friday and Saturday 9-1; Thursday 2:30-6:30.*

Entertainment

Argentina. Teatro di Roma. Largo di Torre Argentina 52, tel. 68804601-2.

Puppet Theatre. Via di Grottapinta 2, tel. 5896201.

Teatro Centrale. Via Celsa 6, tel. 6797270.

Teatro Della Cometa. Via del Teatro di Marcello 4, tel. 6784380.

Teatro Dei Satiri. Via di Grottapinta 19, tel. 68806244.

Health care facilities

Ospedale Fatebenefratelli. Piazza Fatebenefratelli 2 (Isola Tiberina), tel. 68371.

Shops, crafts, and fine art

Al Tempo Ritrovato. Piazza Farnese 103, tel. 68803749. A bookstore that sells only women's books.

Antiquariato Valligiano. Via Giulia 193, tel. 6869505. For furnishing a home, especially a vacation home, with period furniture.

Architetti Associati Farnese. Piazza Farnese 52, tel. 6896109. This is a store renowned for its terracotta, mosaico, and "piastrelle" floor coverings.

Paganini. Via d'Ara Coeli 21-33, tel. 6790305; Via d'Ara Coeli 6, tel. 6797878; Largo di Torre Agentina 7-10, tel. 6868450; Via delle Botteghe Oscure 16/A, tel. 678631. Four sales outlets for a store founded in 1948, specializing in fabrics, upholstery, and drapery.

Studio Punto Tre. Via Giulia 145, tel. 6864321. Interior decorating and design and antique furniture.

Via Veneto

Once part of the splendid Villa Ludovisi, this area developed in the late-19th c. into a varied and interesting architectural complex, which juxtaposed various architectural styles and schools; little palazzi, small villas, and luxurious buildings marked this part of the city as a place of elegance and refinement.

Via Veneto is the main thoroughfare of the area, and it runs down from Porta Pinciana to Piazza Barberini, lined with embassies, airlines offices, banks, and especially fine hotels, the best in Rome, designed and built by the most renowned architects of the end of the 19th c. The furnishings are antique, the service is impeccable, and the prices are very high. In the 1950s and 1960s, the years depicted in Fellini's "La Dolce Vita," this was the epicenter of Rome's high society: there was not a tourist, a rich Roman, a filmmaker, or a writer who did not spend at least one evening in one of the famous cafes, little windows onto the life of the zone, or in one of the exclusive nightclubs in the zone. Nowadays, several of the main nightspots are closed, while those that remain have declined considerably; the street on the whole is slipping in style, and has lost much of its charm; it remains a popular tourist destination; and sightseers stroll up and down the Via Veneto, shopping for Italian shoes in its numerous shoe stores.

At the end, Piazza Barberini, with a subway stop, funnels the chaotic traffic of Via Veneto into the Via Barberini and the Via delle Quattro Fontane.

In this area, you will find some of Rome's finest movie houses, and a renowned theater, actually inaugurated by the Duce during the Fascist era.

Hotels

‡‡‡ **Bernini-Bristol.** Piazza Barberini 23, tel 4883051, fax 4824266. Number of rooms 126. Handicap-friendly. Air conditioning elevator; special parking garage for guests (4, C5, **az**).

‡‡L **Excelsior.** Via Vittorio Veneto 125, tel. 4708, fax 4826205. Number of rooms: 327. Air conditioning, elevator; parking area, specia terms for garage (4, A5, **ba**).

★‡★ **Ambasciatori Palace.** Via Vittorio Veneto

62, tel. 47493, fax 4743601. Number of rooms: 100. Handicap-friendly. Air conditioning, elevator; special parking garage for guests (4, B5, **bg**).

⭐⭐ **Eliseo.** Via Porta Pinciana 30, tel. 4870456, fax 4819629. Number of rooms: 56. Lodging only; no board. Air conditioning, elevator; special parking garage for guests, garden (1, E4, **ct**).

⭐⭐ **G.H. Palace.** Via Vittorio Veneto 70, tel. 478719, fax 47871800. Number of rooms: 94. Access for the disabled. Air conditioning, elevator; special parking garage for guests, pool (4, B5, **bf**).

⭐⭐ **Imperiale.** Via Vittorio Veneto 24, tel. 4826351, fax 4826352. Number of rooms: 95. Handicap-friendly. Air conditioning, elevator; special parking garage for guests (4, C4, **bc**).

⭐⭐ **Londra & Cargill.** Piazza Sallustio 18, tel. 473871, fax 4746674. Number of rooms: 105. Air conditioning, elevator; parking area, garage (5, A2, **bd**).

⭐⭐ **Regina Baglioni.** Via Vittorio Veneto 72, tel. 476851, fax 485483. Number of rooms: 130. Air conditioning, elevator; parking area, special parking garage for guests (4, B5, **bb**).

⭐⭐ **Victoria.** Via Campania 41, tel. 473931, fax 4871890. Number of rooms: 110. Air conditioning, elevator; special parking garage for guests (1, E5, **be**).

⭐⭐ **Marcella.** Via Flavia 106, tel. 4746451, fax 4815832. Number of rooms: 68. Lodging only; no board. Air conditioning, elevator; parking area, special terms for garage (5, A2, **bi**).

⭐⭐ **Tea.** Via Sardegna 149, tel. 4744243, fax 4827058. Number of rooms: 35. Lodging only; no board. Air conditioning, elevator (1, D-E6, **bj**).

⭐ **Veneto.** Via Piemonte 63, tel. 42824346, fax 42814583. Number of rooms: 97. Air conditioning, elevator; special parking garage for guests (4, A6, **bh**).

estaurants

🍴 **Sans Souci.** Via Sicilia 20, tel. 4821814, fax 4821771. Closed Monday, part of August. Air conditioning. Fine cuisine of Lazio (4, A5, **sc**).

🍴 **Terrazza.** Via Ludovisi 49, tel. 478121, fax 4821584. Air conditioning. Original Mediterranean cuisine (4, B4, **w**).

🍴 **Giovanni.** Via Marche 64, tel. 4821834. Closed Friday evening and Saturday, August. Air conditioning. Classical cooking (1, E5, **se**).

🍴 **Andrea.** Via Sardegna 28, tel. 4740557. Closed Sunday and at midday on Saturday, Christmas-Epiphany (6 Jan.), for a certain period in August. Air conditioning. Roman and Abruzzese cuisine – fish and mushrooms (1, E5, **so**).

🍴🍴 **Aurora 10 da Pino il Sommelier.** Via Aurora 10, tel. 484747. Closed Monday. Air conditioning. Sicilian, Roman, classical cuisine – seafood (1, E4, **sn**).

🍴🍴 **Cesarina.** Via Piemonte 109, tel. 4880828. Closed Sunday. Air conditioning. Cooking of Romagna (1, E6, **sm**).

🍴🍴 **Girarrosto Toscano.** Via Campania 29, tel. 4821899. Closed Wednesday. Air conditioning. Tuscan cuisine (1, E5, **sd**).

🍴🍴 **Loreto.** Via A. Valenziani 19, tel. 4742454. Closed Sunday, for a certain period in August. Air conditioning. Classical cooking – seafood (5, A2, **sl**).

🍴🍴 **Peppone.** Via Emilia 60, tel. 483976. Closed Sunday (holidays and on the eve of a public holiday in August). Air conditioning. Roman cooking (4, A-B4-5, **si**).

🍴🍴 **Piccolo Mondo.** Via Aurora 39/D, tel. 485680. Closed Sunday, part of August. Air conditioning. Roman cooking (4, B4, **sh**).

🍴🍴 **Tullio.** Via S. Nicola da Tolentino 26, tel. 4874125. Closed Sunday, August. Air conditioning. Tuscan cuisine (4, C5, **sf**).

🍴 **Cantina Cantarini.** Piazza Sallustio 12, tel. 485528. Closed Sunday, Christmas-Epiphany (6 Jan.), for a certain period in August. Garden. Cooking of the Marche region – seafood (5, A-B2, **sa**).

🍴 **Colline Emiliane.** Via degli Avignonesi 22, tel. 4817538. Closed Friday, August. Air conditioning. Emilian cooking (4, C-D4, **sb**).

Cafes and pastry shops

Cafè de Paris. Via Veneto 90, tel. 4885284. First opened in 1956, this was the cafe of the Roman "Dolce Vita"; after a brief shutdown, it was opened again in December 1992.

Harry's Bar. Via Veneto 150, tel. 4742103. This bar, popular in the 1960s, is closed for renovations.

Museums and cultural institutions

Biblioteca dell'Istituto Archeologico Germanico. Via Sardegna 79, tel. 4888141.

Centro documentazione dell'USIS. Via Boncompagni 2, tel. 46742482.

Galleria nazionale d'Arte antica. Via delle Quattro Fontane 13, tel. 4814591. Closed Monday. *Tuesday and Wednesday 9-10pm; Thursday-Saturday 9-11:30pm; holidays and Sunday 9-8.*

Entertainment

Blue zone. Via Campania 37/A, tel. 4821890. Discotheque.

Jackie o'. Via Boncompagni 11, tel. 4885457. Discotheque and piano bar.

Open Gate. Via di S. Nicola da Tolentino 4, tel. 4824464. Discotheque and piano bar.

Teatro Delle Arti. Via Sicilia 59, tel. 4818598-4743564.

Shops, crafts, and fine art

Carlo Gargani. Via Lombardia 15, tel. 4743710. The finest Italian and international delicacies in a food shop that has been run for 50 years with skill and reliability, for a well-to-do clientele.

Gigli. Via Veneto, tel. 483437. This "historic" newsstand (it first opened at the turn of the 20th c.) is situated just yards from the Cafè de Paris and the Hotel Excelsior, and is open 24 hours a day.

Palombi. Via Veneto 114, tel. 4885817. The onl bakery on this renowned road, it was opened i 1913: ca. 30 types of bread, with varied pastrie and excellent croissants.

Pieroni. Via Veneto, tel. 4819697. Another "his toric" newsstand, which has stood since the tur of the 20th c. in front of the Hotel Excelsior, at th corner of Via Ludovisi, and is open at night.

Raphael Salato. Via Veneto 149, tel. 482181 This renowned shoe store is especially popula with tourists.

Via Cavour, S. Maria Maggiore, S. Giovanni in Laterano

The Esquiline, one of the largest suburbs of antiquity, is now a huge area, with quarters that are now part of the historical center, and an excellent network of public transportation.

S. Maria Maggiore and all of the surrounding quarter, with its splendid churches that are famous for their early-Christian mosaics, are largely surrounded by monumental palazzi in the style known as Umbertino, or Humbertine, after a turn-of-the-century Italian king, accommodating great numbers of the working-class, and by shops that serve the local "rione." Due to their proximity to the Stazione Termini, the hotels are aimed at people just passing through; in the Via Cavour there is an old and comfortable hotel that dates back to the late-19th c., with a nostalgic and decadent air to it, with the furnishings and decorations of the past; the service is the product of a long tradition and a professional approach. As you make your way down to the Colosseum, you will see alleys and little lanes of remarkable beauty, especially those enclosed by Roman, medieval, and Baroque buildings, and here and there, an old crafts workshop still survives. Along the Via Cavour there is a wine tavern – "enoteca" – that is particularly popular among the connoisseurs of Rome.

Another vast zone is the Quartiere di S. Giovanni, once the site of the Roman curia. Surrounding the historic Palazzi Lateranensi and the obelisk that stands in the center of the great square, modern and ancient streets are lined with old and new buildings.

The late-19th-c. Piazza Vittorio Emanuele II hosts the largest and most colorful open-air market in the city: some stands offer clothing and leather goods; more of the stands sell food at good prices. Not far away is one of the oldest ice

cream shops in Rome, almost an institution fo the inhabitants of the Esquiline. Beyond the ol walls is the market of Via Sannio, where use items of every sort are sold. Dining in this are offers mid-level and fine restaurants, with mos ly regional cuisine and affordable prices.

Hotels

★ **Atlantico.** Via Cavour 23, tel. 485951, fa 485951. Number of rooms: 74. Air cond tioning, elevator; special parking garag for guests (5, E2, **br**).

★ **Forum.** Via Tor dei Conti 25, tel. 6792440 fax 6786479. Number of rooms: 76. Air co ditioning, elevator; parking garage (8, B **bo**).

★ **Genova.** Via Cavour 33, tel. 476951, fa 4827580. Number of rooms: 91. Lodgin only; no board. Air conditioning, elevato special parking garage for guests (5, E **bm**).

★ **Massimo D'Azeglio.** Via Cavour 18, te 4870270, fax 4827386. Number of room 205. Air conditioning, elevator; parkin garage (5, E2, **bp**).

★ **Mecenate Palace Hotel.** Via Carlo Albert 3, tel. 40702024, fax 4461354. Number o rooms: 62. No dining facilities. Access fo the disabled. Special terms for garage (1 C1, **da**).

★ **Mediterraneo.** Via Cavour 15, tel. 488405 fax 4744105. Number of rooms: 268. A conditioning, elevator; special terms fo garage (5, E2, **bt**).

★ **Mondial.** Via Torino 127, tel. 472861, fa 4824822. Number of rooms: 78. Lodgin only; no board. Air conditioning, elevato parking area, parking garage (5, D1, **b**).

★ **Napoleon.** Piazza Vittorio Emanuele 10 tel. 4467264, fax 4467282. Number of room 80. Air conditioning, elevator; special par ing garage for guests (9, B4, **bn**).

★ **President.** Via Emanuele Filiberto 173, te 770121, fax 7008740. Number of rooms 180. Handicap-friendly. Air conditioning elevator; special parking garage for guest (9, D5, **bs**).

★ **Universo.** Via Principe Amedeo 5/B, te 476811, fax 4745125. Number of rooms 198. Handicap-friendly. Air conditioning elevator; special parking garage for guests (5, E2, **d**).

★★★ **Amalfi.** Via Merulana 278, tel. 4744313, fax 4820575. Number of rooms: 18. No dining facilities. Air conditioning, elevator (14, C-D1, **cb**).

★★★ **Ariston.** Via F. Turati 16, tel. 4465399, fax 4465396. Number of rooms: 97. Lodging only; no board. Air conditioning, elevator; special parking garage for guests (5, F3, **cr**).

★★★ **Borromeo.** Via Cavour 117, tel. 485856, fax 4882541. Number of rooms: 28. No dining facilities. Air conditioning, elevator; special terms for garage (8, A6, **bq**).

★★★ **Britannia.** Via Napoli 64, tel. 4883153, fax 4882343. Number of rooms: 32. Lodging only; no board. Air conditioning, elevator; parking garage, and separate special parking garage for guests (5, E1, **m**).

★★ **Centro.** Via Firenze 12, tel. 4828002, fax 4871902. Number of rooms: 38. Lodging only; no board. Air conditioning, elevator; special parking garage for guests (5, D-E1, **p**).

★★ **Nord - Nuova Roma.** Via G. Amendola 3, tel. 4885441, fax 4817163. Number of rooms: 159. Air conditioning, elevator; special terms for garage (5, D-E2, **bx**).

★★ **Richmond.** Largo C. Ricci 36, tel. 69941256, fax 69941454. Number of rooms: 13. Lodging only; no board. Air conditioning, elevator; special parking garage for guests (8, B4, **by**).

★ **Igea.** Via Principe Amedeo 97, tel. 4466911, fax 4466911. Number of rooms: 42. Lodging only; no board. Air conditioning, elevator (5, F3, **af**).

Restaurants

Bonne Nouvelle. Via del Boschetto 73, tel. 486781. Closed Sunday, for a certain period in August. Air conditioning. Cooking of Lazio – seafood (4, F5, **sq**).

Charly's Saucière. Via di S. Giovanni in Laterano 270, tel. 70495666. Closed Sunday, for a certain period in July. Air conditioning. French and Swiss cooking (9, E3, **sp**).

Mario's. Piazza del Grillo 9, tel. 6793725. Closed Sunday, Ferragosto (15 Aug.). Classical cooking – seafood (8, A4, **sv**).

Scoglio di Frisio. Via Merulana 256, tel. 4872765. Closed at midday on Saturday and Sunday. Air conditioning. Neapolitan cooking (9, A2, **su**).

Elettra. Via Principe Amedeo 74, tel. 4745397. Closed Saturday, mid-July to mid-August. Roman cooking (5, F3, **t**).

Giglio. Via Torino 137, tel. 4881606. Closed Sunday and at midday on Monday, Christmas and August. Air conditioning. Roman cooking (5, E1, **s**).

Hostaria Tempio di Mecenate. Largo Leopardi 14/18, tel. 4872653. Closed Sunday,

for a certain period between August and September. Air conditioning. Classical cooking – fish, grill (9, B3, **sw**).

Tana del Grillo. Via Alfieri 4, tel. 70453517. Closed Sunday and midday on Monday. Cooking of Ferrara (9, C3, **sr**).

Cafes and pastry shops

Cavour 313. Via Cavour 313, tel. 6785496. This is a popular meeting spot; set in an all-wood suite, in the style of the 1930s, it offers an assortment of about 500 labels of select wines.

Cipriani. Via Botta 19-23, tel. 70453930 (the number will change to 70453930). From 1906 the Cipriani cookie factory continues to make its "biscotti" in the old, time-tested fashion.

Palazzo del Freddo di Giovanni Fassi. Via Principe Eugenio 65-67, tel. 4464740. Opened in 1924, this is the most popular evening meeting place on the Esquiline.

Museums and cultural institutions

Colosseo. Piazza del Colosseo, tel. 7004261. *Summer 9-6; winter: weekdays and Saturday 9-6; Sunday 9-1.*

Foro di Augusto. Via IV Novembre 94, tel. 67102802. Closed Monday. *9-6:30.*

Foro Romano-Palatino. Largo Romolo e Remo e via di San Gregorio, tel. 6990110. *Monday to Saturday 9-6; holidays and Sunday 9-1.*

Istituto italiano per l'Africa e l'Oriente. Via Merulana 248, tel. 4874273.

Mercati Traianei - Foro di Traiano. Via IV Novembre 94, tel. 6790048. Closed Monday. *9-6:30.*

Museo degli Strumenti musicali. Piazza di S. Croce in Gerusalemme 9/A, tel. 7029862.

Museo nazionale d'Arte orientale. Via Merulana 248, tel. 4874415. Closed 1st and 3rd Monday of the month. *9-2; Tuesday and Thursday 9-7.*

Museo storico dei Granatieri di Sardegna. Piazza di S. Croce in Gerusalemme 7, tel. 7028287. Closed Sunday. *Weekdays and Saturday 9-12.*

Museo storico della Fanteria. Piazza di S. Croce in Gerusalemme 9, tel. 7027971. Closed Sunday. *Weekdays and Saturday 9-1.*

Museo storico della Lotta di Liberazione di Roma. Via Tasso 145, tel. 7003866. Closed in August. *Tuesday, Thursday, and Friday 4-7; Saturday and Sunday 9:30-12:30.*

Museo Storico Vaticano. Palazzo Lateranense, tel. 69886376. *1st Sunday of the month and every Saturday 8:45-1.*

Entertainment

Teatro dell'Opera. Via Firenze 72, tel. 4881755.

Teatro Nazionale. Via del Viminale 5, tel. 485498.

Teatro Orione. Via Tortona 7, tel. 776960.

Health care facilities

Ospedale S. Giovanni. Via Amba Aradam, tel. 77051.

Testaccio and the Aventine

Testaccio takes its name from the little man-made hill (the Monte Testaccio) that, in ancient Rome, was the dump of the nearby river port. The modern-day layout of this "rione" dates back to the early-20th c., when crowded apartment blocks were built, without terraces or balconies, at once humble and grim (the only really wide road is the Via Marmorata, named for the workshops of the marble-workers, or "marmorari" along the river). The Mattatoio, or slaughterhouse, was built between 1888 and 1891, and helped to underscore the working- or lower-class and commercial character of this neighborhood; the closeness of the Tiber contributed as well, as a channel of trade and transportation.

Most of the restaurants still maintain intact the atmosphere of the "osterie," or taverns, of bygone times: wooden tables, unassuming furnishings, often no printed menus – just a list announced aloud, and the humble cooking of "la Cucina romana" ("minestra di ceci," "rigatoni con la pajata," "gobbi alla parmigiana," "coda alla vaccinara"); the wine is often excellent, and sometimes comes from wine cellars carved out of the "Monte dei Cocci," an ancient heap of potsherds, ideal for areation.

Nowadays, however – due to the closing of the Mattatoio, or slaughterhouse (the old building is currently being used for concerts, exhibitions, and festivals), which left an area of 10 hectares open for new urban projects, and for the expansion of the city, so that the historic outskirts have moved somewhat closer to the center – this "rione" is thriving culturally: spaces have been opened for theater and poetry, music and cabaret (in Via di Monte Testaccio there are four clubs presenting Latin-American music, soul, jazz-funk, rock, and "napoletana" (a Neapolitan rock/blues); since 15 January 1993 there has been a multiplex cinema offering quality films.

The Aventine, which was also once a lower-class quarter full of shops, has undergone a different development. It is now considered to be one of the loveliest and most livable of the quarters of Rome: two distinct hills – the "grande Aventino" and the "piccolo Aventino" or the big and the little Aventine – are separated by the Viale dell'Aventino, and both characterized by the presence of marvels of histo-

ry and art, set in a natural framework of greenery; you can walk along little tree-lined streets among ancient basilicas and Art-Nouveau estates ("ville liberty"), amid schools and embassies, without encountering a single store. Just a short distance from the historical center, amid the aromas of the "giardino degli aranci," or orangerie – which becomes an open-air theater in the summer – and of the lovely Roseto Comunale, or city rose garden, there are quiet and elegant hotels and refined restaurants.

Hotels

★★★ **Domus Aventina.** Via di S. Prisca 11/B, tel. 5746135, fax 57300044. Number of rooms: 26. Lodging only; no board. Air conditioning; special terms for garage (10, A5, **bw**)

Restaurants

🍴 **Checchino dal 1887.** Via Monte Testaccio 30, tel. 5746318, fax 5743816. Closed Sunday evening and Monday, Christmas-New Year's Day, August. Roman cooking (1 D2, **sy**).

🍴 **Agustarello a Testaccio.** Via G. Branca 98, tel. 5746585. Closed Sunday and holidays, for a certain period in August. Garden. Roman cooking (10, C2, **sx**).

Cafes and pastry shops

Aldebaran. Via Galvani 54, tel. 5746013. Closed Sunday and in August. The most extraordinary list of cocktails and long drinks in the capital, made with top quality ingredients and lots of experience. Many tables in spacious rooms and outside during the summer; serves some snaks in the evening.

Barberini. Via Marmorata 41/A, tel. 5750869. Family-run excellent pastry-shop.

Museums and cultural institutions

Terme di Caracalla. Viale delle Terme di Caracalla 52, tel. 5758626. *Tuesday to Saturday 9- (summer); 9-2 hour before sunset (winter); Monday and Sunday 9-1.*

Entertainment

Teatro Anfitrione. Via di S. Saba 24, tel. 5750827.

Teatro dei Cocci. Via Galvani 69, tel. 5783502.

Teatro Vittoria. Piazza S. Maria Liberatrice 8-1, tel. 5740170.

Athletic facilities

Stadio delle Terme. Viale Baccelli, tel. 5780602.

Shops, crafts, and fine art

Volpetti. Via Marmorata 47, tel. 5742352. From an old-fashioned "salumeria" to a modern food shop specializing in cheeses, regional salami and preparations of fine foods.

he construction of the Viale di Trastevere, esigned as a great tree-lined boulevard and ow a busy noisy thoroughfare, has changed ιe metabolism and appearance of the quarter, hich was once an unbroken series of small quares and lanes. All the same, if you work our way into the lanes of the interior, it will eem, in some points, as if you have gone back ι time: old shops display merchandise along ιe sidewalks; here and there an oleander, a lau-el, or an orange tree peeps over a garden wall, r from an old kettle standing in front of a door-ay, a cat sleeps in the sun on a straw chair, a alf-hidden shop sells a handmade suit at a argain price.

ut Trastevere is famous above all for its "trat-ιrias," with their family atmospere, where ιmetimes diners or performers burst into pas-onate song; here you can sample all the spe-ιalties of "la Cucina romana": "bucatini all'am-triciana," "spaghetti alla carbonara," "abbac-hio e trippa"; lots and lots of pizzerias, all ith open-air tables, where the selection on ιe menu ranges from "bruschetta" to "crosti-ι con prosciutto" or "crostini con alici," from ιizza alla capricciosa" to "pizza alle quattro ιagioni"; there are even famous and refined ιstaurants, serving seafood, or places where ιu can sample Arab, Greek, or Indian cooking. ιd in order to enjoy the rest of the evening, ιany movie houses show movies in their orig-ιal language, sometimes quite good films, while ιnall theaters put on avant-garde productions r cabaret shows.

hen, in mid-July, the Viale di Trastevere hosts ιe traditional Festa de' Noantri, once an ex-lusively religious festival, which nowadays re-ιains a festive event for tourists and for the ιany Romans who spend the month of July in ιe city; in Piazza Mastai you will see rides for ιildren, and the shops along the boulevard sell raft products made of wicker, colorful cos-ιme jewelry, and plenty of sweets, made of al-ιonds and hazelnuts. But the most colorful spect of the quarter is the great market of ιrta Portese, which extends for ca. 1 km. from ιnte Sublicio to Ponte Testaccio; crowded ith Romans on Sunday mornings, this is a ιnuine labyrinth, where you can find anything ιu like, and where the price is set through a long and intricate haggling process. At the Cli-vo Portuense it is possible to purchase acces-sories for cars, and motorcycles and bicycles, new and used.

Although there are not enough green areas and parks in Trastevere, the Orto Botanico, or botanical gardens, are splendid, and feature more than 8,000 plants from all over the world (particularly noteworthy are the orchids). Then you need only climb up the Via Garibaldi to reach the Janicululm (Gianicolo), one of the seven wonders of Rome: here, overlooking the panoramic view of Rome, which is even more striking when viewed through the binoculars available here, you can while away a morning eating ice cream or sipping espressos in one of the open-air cafes, waiting for the traditional cannon shot to announce high noon. Not far away, you may well decide to visit one of the most handsome villas in the city: the little Vil-la Sciarra, adorned with 18th-c. statues and fountains.

Restaurants

Alberto Ciarla. Piazza S. Cosimato 40, tel. 5818668, fax 5884377. Closed Sunday, for a certain period in January and August. Air conditioning. Cuisine of Lazio – seafood (7, D4, **th**).

Paris. Piazza S. Calisto 7/A, tel. 5815378. Closed Sunday evening and Monday, Au-gust. Air conditioning, garden. Cooking of Lazio (7, D4, **tb**).

Sabatini. Piazza di S. Maria in Trastevere 13, tel. 5812026, fax 5898386. Closed Wednesday, Christmas, for a certain peri-od in August. Air conditioning. Roman and classical cooking (7, C4, **te**).

Checco er Carettiere. Via Benedetta 10, tel. 5800985. Closed Sunday evening and Monday, for a certain period in August. Air conditioning, garden. Roman cooking and seafood (7, B-C4, **ti**).

Corsetti-il Galeone. Piazza S. Cosimato 27, tel. 5809009. Air conditioning. Cuisine of Lazio and classical cooking (7, D4, **tc**).

Giggetto. Via del Portico d'Ottavia 21/A, tel. 6861105, fax 6832106. Closed Monday, Ju-ly. Roman cuisine (8, B1, **tq**).

Pastarellaro. Via di S. Crisogono 33, tel. 5810871. Closed Wednesday, for a certain period in August. Air conditioning. Roman cooking (7, D5, **tf**).

Taverna Trilussa. Via del Politeama 23, tel. 5818918. Closed Sunday evening and Monday, August. Air conditioning, garden. Roman cooking (7, C4-5, **td**).

Cafes and pastry shops

Cecere. Via Musolino 47, tel. 5811913. The "zaba-jone semifreddo" is well renowned.

Sacchetti. Piazza di S. Cosimato 61-62, tel. 5806075. This bar-pastry shop has been around for 40 years now.

Museums and cultural institutions

Accademia Americana. Via A. Masina 5, tel. 58461.

Galleria Corsini. Via della Lungara 10, tel. 68802323. Closed Monday. *Tuesday to Friday 9-7; Saturday 9-2 and Sunday 9-1.*

Museo del Folklore e dei Poeti romaneschi. Piazza di S. Egidio, tel. 5816563. Closed for restoration.

Museo Tassiano. Convento di S. Onofrio al Gianicolo. *Visits on request to the Equestrian order of S. Sepulcro of Jerusalem, tel. 068-28121.*

Entertainment

Argot Teatro. Via Del Grande 21, tel. 5898111.

Meta-teatro. Via Mameli 5, tel. 5895807.

Teatro Belli. Piazza di S. Apollonia 11/A, tel. 5894875.

Teatro la Comunità. Via Zanazzo 1, tel. 5817413.

Teatro Puff. Via Zanazzo 4, tel. 5810721.

Teatro Stanze Segrete. Via della Scala 25, tel. 5896787.

Teatro Vascello. Via Carini 72-78, tel. 5809389.

Health care facilities

Ospedale nuovo Regina Margherita. Via Morosini 30, tel. 58441.

Ospedale pediatrico del Bambin Gesù. Piazza di S. Onofrio 4, tel. 68591.

Ospedale S. Camillo. Circonvallazione Gianicolense 87, tel. 58701.

Shops, crafts, and fine art

Guaytamelli. Via del Moro 59, tel. 5880704. Here, fine craftsmen make sundials and other timepieces and directional finders, based on old models.

Innocenzi. Piazza di S. Cosimato 66, tel. 5812725. Since 1884 this shop has sold grains and vegetables of all sorts.

Valzani, Specialità Dolciarie. Via del Moro, 37/B, tel. 5803792. Sweets of all kinds, including such Roman classics as "mostaccioli," "panpepato," and "frittelle."

S. Pietro, Prati, and the Aurelio and Trionfale quarters

Via della Conciliazione, with its succession of 28 obelisks made of travertine, opens the view of the colonnade of Bernini and the giant cupola designed and built by Michelangelo. Every day, this road is packed with large motorcoaches, dropping off tourists and pilgrims about to take the classical tour. All around are palazzi dating from the Fascist era; very few buildings survived the massive demolition. There are plenty of souvenir shops, selling objects of religious iconography, images of the pope, and little models of the basilica. A luxurious hotel along the road preserves the charm and the ancient decorations of the 16th-c. palazzo in which it is set, while not far from the Città del Vaticano, or Vatican City, there are religious organizations that run pensioni and hostels, and a fair number of restaurants offering fixed-price menus.

After the tour of St. Peter's, it is pleasant to stroll through the old lanes and streets of the medieval Borgo, an old section of town that once surrounded the basilica; you can still see old "palazzetti" with little hanging terraces blooming with geranium plants, craftsmen's workshops, a few vegetable and fruit vendors, and numerous trattorias that work hard to look rustic. Borgo Pio is a favorite spot to meet friends for dinner or a drink; an old-fashioned trattoria, in Vicolo del Falco, serves original and fresh seafood specialties; note the little mineral-water fountain, carved in living stone, inside the restaurant. The gardens across from the Castel S. Angelo are the only slice of greenery in the area.

The Rione Prati was built in a hurry, after Rome was proclaimed capital of Italy; it spread out

over the vast expanses of grass, gardens, and vineyards that covered this area until 100 years ago, where the farmers and peasants would gather to drink, dance, and feast. The quarter is now fairly central, and is served by the Metropolitana, or subway, and many buslines that start at Piazza del Risorgimento. There are many elegant palazzi, and lots of office buildings, especially legal offices (at Piazzale Clodio is the Sede del Tribunale di Roma, the central court of Rome) – but there are also renowned pastry shops and noon-day restaurants, especially along the Via Cola di Rienzo, one of the great shopping streets, and the Via Ottaviano, near the terminus of the Metropolitana, with decidedly low prices. Not far off is the bike-path that runs from Viale Angelico for about 15 km. through the green countryside along the Via Flaminia.

From the neighboring Quartiere Aurelio, densely populated and commercial, the busy Statal

Aurelia runs, leading to the coast and beaches north of Rome: lining it are religious institutes and major hotels, for fairs and conferences. And for those who wish to spend a day amid nature, little lakes and fountains, hills and flower beds, there is the Villa Doria Pamphilj: you can reach it via any number of means of public transportation, it is open from dawn to dusk, and will allow you to spend a pleasant day in the enormous estate (9 sq. km.) between the Via Aurelia Antica, Porta S. Pancrazio, and the Via Vitellia.

There is more greenery high atop Monte Mario, the highest hill in Rome (138 m.); the central thoroughfare of this hill is the Via Trionfale, and that avenue is surrounded by densely populated quarters, some of them residential while others are lower-class, increasingly outlying neighborhoods. Particularly crowded is the great market, or "mercatone" of Via Andrea Doria, abounding with all sorts of fruit and vegetables, fresh meat and excellent fish and seafood. A major hotel, built at the turn of the sixties, dominates one of the finest views of the Seven Hills: the spectacular roof-garden is open even to those not staying in the hotel. A number of restaurants, on the slopes of the Monte Mario, offer fine cooking, attentive service, and a striking view.

Hotels

⁕ Cavalieri Hilton. Via Cadlolo 101, tel. 35091, fax 35092241. Number of rooms: 376. Handicap-friendly. Air conditioning, elevator; parking, parking garage, garden, pool, tennis courts (2, A1, *off map*).

⁕ Atlante Garden. Via Crescenzio 78, tel. 6872361, fax 6872315. Number of rooms: 43. Lodging only; no board. Handicap-friendly. Air conditioning, elevator; parking area, parking garage (2, B5, **ce**).

⁕ Atlante Star. Via Vitelleschi 34, tel. 6873233, fax 6872300. Number of rooms: 61. Handicap-friendly. Air conditioning, elevator; parking area, parking garage (2, B-C6, **ch**).

⁕ Cicerone. Via Cicerone 55/A, tel. 3576, fax 68801383. Number of rooms: 250. Air conditioning, elevator; parking garage (3, A-B3, **cg**).

⁕ Farnese. Via A. Farnese 30, tel. 3212553, fax 3215129. Number of rooms: 22. Lodging only; no board. Air conditioning, elevator; parking garage (13, D4, **cw**).

⁕ Giulio Cesare. Via degli Scipioni 287, tel. 3210751, fax 3211736. Number of rooms: 90. Lodging only; no board. Air conditioning, elevator; parking garage, garden (13, D5, **cy**).

⁕ Jolly Leonardo da Vinci. Via dei Gracchi 324, tel. 32499, fax 3610138. Number of rooms: 256. Handicap-friendly. Air conditioning, elevator; parking area (13, D4, **cz**).

⁕ Jolly Midas. Via Aurelia 800, tel. 66396, fax 66418457. Number of rooms: 347. Access for the disabled. Air conditioning, elevator; parking area, garden, pool, tennis courts (2, D-E1, *off map*).

⁕ Michelangelo. Via della Stazione S. Pietro 14, tel. 39366861, fax 632359. Number of rooms: 180. Air conditioning, elevator (2, E3, **co**).

⁕ Villa Pamphili. Via della Nocetta 105, tel. 5862, fax 66157747. Number of rooms: 248. Handicap-friendly. Air conditioning, elevator; parking area, garden, indoor pool and outdoor pool, tennis courts (2, F1, *off map*).

⁕ Visconti Palace. Via F. Cesi 37, tel. 3684, fax 3200551. Number of rooms: 247. Lodging only; no board. Air conditioning, elevator; parking garage (3, A3, **cf**).

★★★ Arcangelo. Via Boezio 15, tel. 6874143, fax 6893050. Number of rooms: 33. Lodging only; no board. Air conditioning, elevator; parking (3, B1, **cm**).

★★★ Columbus. Via della Conciliazione 33, tel. 6865435, fax 6864874. Number of rooms: 92. Air conditioning, elevator; parking, garden (2, D5, **ci**).

★★★ Olympic. Via Properzio 2/A, tel. 6896650, fax 68308255. Number of rooms: 53. Lodging only; no board. Air conditioning, elevator; special parking garage for guests (2, B5, **cl**).

★★★ Raganelli. Via Aurelia 734, tel. 66418012, fax 66417104. Number of rooms: 41. Elevator; parking area (2, F1, *off map*).

★★★ Sant'Anna. Via Borgo Pio 134, tel. 68801602, fax 68308717. Number of rooms: 20. Lodging only; no board. Handicap-friendly. Air conditioning, special parking garage for guests (2, C5, **cn**).

★★ Amalia. Via Germanico 66/5, tel. 39723354, fax 39723365. Number of rooms: 25. No dining facilities. Elevator; special terms for garage (2, A4, **cp**).

Camping sites and resort villages

⛺ Happy. Via Prato della Corte 1915, tel. 33626401, fax 33613800. Seasonal.

⛺ Roma. Via Aurelia 831, tel. 6623018.

⛺ Seven Hills. At Giustiniana Via Cassia 1216, tel. 30310826, fax 30310039.

Youth hostels

Ostello della Gioventù. Viale delle Olimpiadi 61, tel. 3236279; 330 beds. In summer, you must have reservations.

Restaurants

🍴 La Pergola. Via Cadlolo 101, tel. 35091, fax 39092241. Closed Sunday and Monday. Air conditioning; parking area. Fine cuisine. (2, A1, *off map*).

🍴 Les Étoiles. Via Dei Bastioni 1, tel. 6873233, fax 6872300. Air conditioning; parking, garden. Innovative and classic cuisine. (2, B-C6, **ch**).

San Luigi. Via Mocenigo 10, tel. 39720704, fax 39722421. Closed Sunday, for a certain period in August. Air conditioning. Fine cuisine (2, A3, **tm**).

Delle Vittorie. Via Montesanto 64, tel. 37352776. Closed Sunday, for a certain period in August, Christmas- New Year's Day. Garden. Roman and classical cooking (13, B3, **tt**).

Mimì. Via G. Belli 59, tel. 3210992. Closed Sunday, Christmas-New Year's Day, for a certain period in August. Air conditioning. Cooking of the Campania region (3, B2, **tp**).

Taberna dei Gracchi. Via dei Gracchi 268, tel. 3213126. Closed Sunday, and at midday on Monday, Christmas, Easter, Ferragosto (15 Aug.). Air conditioning. Classical cooking-grilled meat and fish (13, D4, **tu**).

Romolo alla Mole Adriana. Via delle Fosse di Castello 19, tel. 6861603. Closed Monday, August. Roman cooking – first courses (3, C1, **tl**).

Zì Gaetana. Via Cola di Rienzo 263, tel. 3212342. Closed Monday, for a certain period in August. Air conditioning. Roman and classical cooking – pasta dishes(2, A5, **tn**).

Cafes and pastry shops

Costantini. Piazza Cavour 16, tel. 3211502. One of the most highly reputed wine shops in Rome. More than 2000 different wines. Piero Costantini is himself a wine producer.

Ruschena. Lungotevere dei Mellini 1, tel. 3204449. This pastry shop was first opened in 1922 in the 19th-c. Palazzo Blumensthil.

Museums and cultural institutions

Museo astronomico e copernicano. Viale del Parco Mellini 84, tel. 35347056. *Wednesday and Saturday 9-1.*

Museo nazionale di Castel S. Angelo. Lungotevere Castello 50, tel. 6875036. Closed Monday. *9-9:15pm; holidays and Sunday 9-7:30.*

Museo storico nazionale dell'Arte Sanitaria. Lungotevere in Sassia 3, tel. 68352353. *Monday, Wednesday and Friday 9-12:30.*

Musei Vaticani. Città del Vaticano, tel. 69883333. *Monday to Saturday 8:45-12:45; from 16 March - 30 October, Monday - Friday: 8:45-3:45; Saturday and last Sunday of each month: 8:45-12:45pm.*

Entertainment

Auditorium di S. Cecilia. Via della Conciliazione 4, tel. 6541044.

Teatro del Borgo. Via dei Penitenzieri 11/C, tel. 6861926.

Teatro Manzoni. Via Monte Zebio 12-14, tel. 3223538.

Teatro S. Genesio. Via Podgora 1, tel. 3223432.

Health care facilities

Ospedale Oftalmico di Roma. Piazzale degli Eroi 11, tel. 317041.

Ospedale S. Carlo di Nancy. Via Aurelia 275, tel. 6381541.

Ospedale S. Filippo Neri. Via Martinotti 20, tel. 33061.

Ospedale di S. Maria della Pietà. Piazzale di S. Maria della Pietà 5, tel. 330621.

Policlinico Universitario Gemelli. Largo Gemelli 8, tel. 30151.

Shops, crafts, and fine art

Alicanti. Via Trionfale 80, tel. 39738302. Articles of all sorts for florists; this is the best known flower shop in Rome, and specializes in artificial flowers, dried flowers, and decorations.

Castroni. Via Cola di Rienzo 196, tel. 6874383. The Torrefazioni Castroni have built an "empire" roasting coffee (there are four others in Rome) that dates back to 1929.

Giuliani. Via Paolo Emilio 67/A, tel. 3243548. Quality and tradition are the hallmarks of this store of chocolate-based sweets, with almond paste and "marrons glacés" (since 1949 the best in Rome).

Parioli, Salario and Nomentano quarters

Parioli is one of the most exclusive quarters in the capital: period villas and modern buildings line elegant, silent streets, dotted with embassies and cultural institutions. Here you will find the largest parks and greenbelts in the city: Villa Ada, Villa Glori, and the splendid Villa Borghese, which – with its 9.5 hectares of land, little lakes, game parks, and bike-paths, is one of the favorite Sunday strolls of Romans; world-class equestrian events are held here; not far off is the zoo, or Giardino Zoologico, founded in 1911.
Absolutely original, in the neighboring Salario quarter, is the Quartiere Coppedè, designed

and built by the famous architect of that name following WWI: remarkable architectural creations, somewhere between Art Nouveau and Baroque, were built one alongside the other, forming a stunning setting.

There are many small Art Nouveau villas, often occupied by embassies, in the Quartiere Nomentano around the Villa Torlonia, another major green area in this district; for shopping, nearby is the Quartiere Africano (Viale Libia and Viale Eritrea).

The hotels in this area are of very high quality, with fine furnishings and excellent service, and often with great views of the parks, aimed at a first-rate clientele. Restaurants are mostly regional, with the few exceptions of a number of exclusive, fashionable places.

Hotels

⚑⚑⚑ Aldrovandi Palace. Via U. Aldrovandi 15, tel. 3223993, fax 3221435. Number of rooms: 143. Air conditioning, elevator; parking area, parking garage, garden, pool (1, A3-4, *off map*).

⚑⚑⚑ Lord Byron. Via G. de Notaris 5, tel. 3224541, fax 3220405. Number of rooms: 37. Air conditioning, elevator; special parking garage for guests, garden (12, F6, **cs**).

★⚑★ Albani. Via Adda 45, tel. 84991, fax 8499399. Number of rooms: 143. Air conditioning, elevator; parking garage (1, A-B6, *off map*).

★⚑★ Borromini. Via Lisbona 7, tel. 8841321, fax 8417550. Number of rooms: 90. Lodging only; no board. Air conditioning, elevator; parking garage (1, A6, *off map*).

★⚑★ Jolly Vittorio Veneto. Corso d'Italia 1, tel. 8495, fax 8841104. Number of rooms: 203. Handicap-friendly. Air conditioning, elevator; special parking garage for guests (1, D5, **cu**).

★⚑★ Parco dei Principi. Via Frescobaldi 5, tel. 854421, fax 8845104. Number of rooms: 200. Handicap-friendly. Air conditioning, elevator; parking garage, garden, pool (1, A6, *off map*).

★⚑★ Rivoli. Via T. Taramelli 7, tel. 3224042, fax 3227373. Number of rooms: 54. Air conditioning, elevator; parking area (1, A3, *off map*).

★★ Delle Muse. Via T. Salvini 18, tel. 8088333, fax 8085749. Number of rooms: 60. Air conditioning, elevator; special parking garage for guests, garden (1, A5, *off map*).

★★ Fenix. Viale Gorizia 5, tel. 8540741, fax 8543632. Number of rooms: 75. Air conditioning, elevator; parking garage, garden(1, A6, *off map*).

★★ Fiume. Via Brescia 5, tel. 8543000, fax 8548888. Number of rooms: 57. Lodging only; no board. Air conditioning, elevator; special parking garage for guests (5, A3, *off map*).

★★★ Helios. Via Sacco Pastore 13, tel. 8603982, fax 8604355. Number of rooms: 50. No dining facilities. Air conditioning, elevator; special terms for garage (5, A3, *off map*).

★★★ Panama. Via Salaria 336, tel. 8552558, fax 44290452. Number of rooms: 43. Lodging only; no board. Elevator; parking garage, garden (1, A6, *off map*).

★★★ Turner. Via Nomentana 29, tel. 44250077, fax 44250165. Number of rooms: 37. No dining facilities. Access for the disabled. Air conditioning, elevator; special terms for garage (5, A3, *off map*).

★★★ Villa Borghese. Via Pinciana 31, tel. 8549648, fax 8414100. Number of rooms: 28. Lodging only; no board. Special terms for garage. Garden (1, C6, **cv**).

★★★ Villa del Parco. Via Nomentana 110, tel. 44237773, fax 44237572. Number of rooms: 23. Lodging only; no board. Handicap-friendly. Air conditioning; parking, special parking garage for guests, garden (1, A6, *off map*).

★★★ Villa Florence. Via Nomentana 28, tel. 4403036, fax 4402709. Number of rooms: 33. Lodging only; no board. Access for the disabled. Air conditioning, elevator; parking area, garden (5, A5, *off map*).

Restaurants

¶¶¶ Relais le Jardin. Via G. de Notaris 5, tel. 3220404, fax 3220405. Closed Sunday, for a certain period in August. Air conditioning; parking area. Classical cooking (12, F6, **cs**).

¶¶¶ Relais la Piscine. Via Mangili 6, tel. 3216126, fax 3221435. Air conditioning; parking area. Classical cooking. (1, A3-4, *off map*).

¶¶ Bersagliere-da Raffone. Via Ancona 43, tel. 44249846. Closed Saturday, for a certain period in August. Air conditioning. Abruzzese and Roman cooking – seafood and mushrooms (5, A3, *off map*).

¶¶ Ceppo. Via Panama 2, tel. 8419696. Closed Monday, for a certain period in August. Air conditioning. Cooking of the Marche region and classical cooking (1, A6, *off map*).

¶¶ Chianti. Via Ancona 17, tel. 44291534. Closed Sunday, for a certain period in August. Air conditioning. Tuscan cuisine (5, A3, *off map*).

¶¶ Coriolano. Via Ancona 14, tel. 44249863. Closed Sunday, September. Air conditioning. Classic cuisine – fish, truffles (5, A3, *off map*).

¶¶ Hostaria da Benito. Via Flaminia Nuova 230, tel. 36307851. Closed Sunday, Ferragosto (15 Aug.). Air conditioning, garden. Classical cooking – seafood (12, A4, *off map*).

Cafes and pastry shops

Euclide. Via Civinini 119-127, tel. 8078017. One of the oldest cafes in Parioli, it offers a broad array of refreshments for parties.

197

Gatto. Via D'Ovidio 23-25, tel. 824208. From "babà" to "sfogliatella," from "struffoli" to the "pastiera," this shop offers the best of Neapolitan pastries.

Golosìa. Viale Romania 11/B, tel. 8078700. A journalist owns this store, which has 60 different moulds for chocolates, made with the finest cacao.

Natalizi. Via Po 124-126, tel. 8546213. Tradition and fine service merge with an aristocratic atmosphere. Opened in the 1920s, this shop does cocktails, catering, and buffets.

Pannocchi. Via Bergamo 56-58-60, tel. 8552109. This is a traditional pastry shop, with Triestine specialties inherited from a master pastry chef from that NE city who worked in Rome in the 1940s.

Seggiano. Via Seggiano 48-51, tel. 8123436. This is the apotheosis of Sicilian pastry: "cannoli," "cassate," marzipan fruit, and the traditional Christmas "cuccia."

Museums and cultural institutions

Catacombe di Priscilla. Via Salaria 430, tel. 86206272. Closed Monday and January. *Summer 8:30-12, 2:30-5:30; Winter 8:30-12, 2:30-5.*

Galleria Nazionale d'Arte Moderna. Viale delle Belle Arti 131, tel. 322981. Closed Monday. *Weekdays 9-10pm; Sunday 9-8.*

Museo Civico di Zoologia. Via Aldrovandi 18, tel. 3216586. Closed Monday. *9-5.*

Museo Borghese and Galleria Borghese. Piazza Scipione Borghese 5, tel. 8548577. Closed Monday. *9-10pm; Sunday and holidays 9-8.*

Museo Etrusco di Villa Giulia. Piazzale di Villa Giulia 9, tel. 3201951. Closed Monday. *9-7; Sunday 9-2.*

Entertainment

Accademia Filarmonica Romana. Via Flaminia 118, tel. 3201752.

Accademia Musicale Italiana. Via Salvini 15/A, tel. 8078141.

Piper '90. Via Tagliamento 9, tel. 8414459. Discotheque.

Scultarch. Via Taro 14, tel. 8416057-8548950.

Teatro delle Muse. Via Forlì 43, tel. 44231300.

Teatro Olimpico. Piazza Gentile da Fabriano 17, tel. 3234890-3234936.

Teatro Parioli (Sala A e B). Via Borsi 20, tel. 8083523.

Teatro Politecnico. Via Tiepolo 13/A, tel. 3611501.

Health care facilities

Centro Prevenzione Tumori Mele. Viale Regina Elena 291-295, tel. 49851.

Istituto Regina Elena. Viale Regina Elena 291-295, tel. 49851.

Ospedale Eastman. Viale Regina Elena 287/B, tel. 4453228.

Shops, crafts, and fine art

Anna Maria Fanucchi. Via De' Cavalieri 12, tel. 85354374. Another historic address in the field of a fine hand-made clothing (famous for bridal gowns).

Cerasari. Via Salaria 280-285, tel. 8416998. This has been called the "most complete delicatessen in Rome."

Crescenzi. Via Schiapparelli 21, tel. 3216411. The customers in the quarter of Parioli are quite demanding in their selection of fruit and vegetables: from leechee nuts to mangoes; but also vegetables from the Roman and other regions.

Gentilini. Via Tagliamento 62-68, tel. 8417029. The owners of this store have an important name in the context of Roman baking: they are in fact bakers of the well known makers of "biscotti" and "fette biscottate."

La Vecchia Marina. Viale Buozzi 13, tel. 8070422. Naval instruments, objects, and accessories, both old and modern; at times, you can find "historic" items.

Ricercatezze. Via Chelini 17-19-21, tel. 8078569. This is the right store where you can find all kind of fine and selective food for your exclusive gifts.

EUR and Via Appia Antica

EUR (Esposizione Universale di Roma) is an absolutely original piece of experimental urban planning: designed in the Fascist era, it constitutes one of the finest examples of the new fitting in with the structure of Rome.

Office buildings, ministry buildings, and museums cluster around the little manmade lake (where you can rent little boats by the hour) and around the Palazzo dello Sport designed by Nervi for the Olympics of 1960; at the entrance to the quarter, in Via delle Tre Fontane, is the Luna Park, which boasts the tallest ferris wheel in Europe.

The hotels and restaurants, considering the number of offices found around here and the proximity of the Aeroporto Leonardo da Vinci, target a clientele of businessmen.

The Via Appia Antica – literally, the old Appian Way – offers a charming stroll through classical antiquity and the Roman Campagna, or countryside; 12 km. in length, in many stretches it still has the ancient paving stones and runs past the most famous catacombs of Rome, as well as the cinerary remains of the era.

Beyond the gate, or Porta S. Sebastiano, there are restaurants surrounded by the occasional column or capital, artifacts that are typical of the area and of the dining experience; further along modern villas and ancient patrician homes have been renovated to cater for parties.

Hotels

‡ Aris Garden. Via Aristofane 101, tel. 52362443, fax 52352968. Number of rooms: 72. Handicap-friendly. Air conditioning, elevator; parking, garden, indoor pool and outdoor pool, tennis courts (16, F2, *off map*).

‡ Shangri Là Corsetti. Viale Algeria 141, tel. 5916441, fax 5413813. Number of rooms: 52. Air conditioning; parking area, pool (16, F3, *off map*).

‡ Sheraton Golf. Viale Parco de' Medici 22, tel. 522408, fax 52240742. Number of rooms: 285. Handicap-friendly. Air conditioning, elevator; parking area, parking garage, garden, pool, tennis courts, golf. (16, A1, *off map*).

‡ Sheraton Roma. Viale del Pattinaggio 100, tel. 5453, fax 5940689. Number of rooms: 633. Handicap-friendly. Air conditioning, elevator; parking area, special terms for garage, garden, pool, tennis courts (15, F2, *off map*).

*** Caravel. Via C. Colombo 124/C, tel. 5180789, fax 5134721. Number of rooms: 106. Lodging only; no board. Elevator; special terms for garage (15, C6, **cu**).

Restaurants

¶ Cecilia Metella. Via Appia Antica 125, tel. 5110213. Closed Monday, for a certain period in August. Air conditioning, parking area, garden. Cuisine of Lazio and classical cooking (15, C6, *off map*).

¶ Vecchia America-Corsetti. Piazza Marconi 32, tel. 5911458. Air conditioning, garden. Cuisine of Lazio and classical cooking – seafood (16, C4, **tt**).

Cafes and pastry shops

Palombini. Piazzale Adenauer 12, tel. 5911700. In particular, try the Viennese sweets, called "babbi," or "babà au rhum."

Rosanna. Viale Europa 43-45, tel. 5911994. "Mignon farciti" in all styles.

Museums and cultural institutions

Archivio Centrale dello Stato. Piazzale degli Archivi 27, tel. 920371.

Catacombe di Domitilla. Via delle Sette Chiese 282, tel. 110342. Closed Tuesday, Christmas, New Year's Day. *Summer 8:30-12, 2:30-5:30; Winter 8:30-12, 2:30-5.*

Catacombe di San Callisto. Via Appia Antica 110, 126, tel. 5136725. Closed Wednesday. *Summer 8:30-12 and 2:30-5:30; Winter 8:30-12 and 2:30-5.*

Catacombe di San Sebastiano. Via Appia Antica 136, tel. 7887035. Closed Thursday. *Summer 8:30-2, 2:30-5:30. Winter 8:30-12, 2:30-5.*

Museo nazionale dell'Alto Medioevo. Viale Lincoln 3, tel. 5925806. Closed Monday. *Weekdays 9-2, Sunday 9-1.*

Museo della Civiltà Romana. Piazza Agnelli 10, tel. 5926041. Closed Monday. *9-6:45; Sunday and holidays 9-1:30.*

Museo delle Mura di Roma. Porta S. Sebastiano 15, tel. 70475284. *Tuesday to Saturday 9-1:30; Tuesday, Thursady and Saturday also 4-7; Sunday 9-1.*

Museo delle Poste e delle Telecomunicazioni. Viale Europa 190, tel. 59582092, fax 5942039. *Monday-Friday 9-1.*

Museo nazionale delle Arti e Tradizioni Popolari. Piazza Marconi 8/10, tel. 5926148, fax 5911848; http://www.museinrete.net/mnatp, e-mail: mnatp@nexus.it. Closed Christmas, New Year's Day, First May. *Weekdays 9-2; Sunday 9-1.*

Museo nazionale preistorico etnografico Luigi Pigorini. Piazza Marconi 14, tel. 549521. Closed Monday. *Weekdays and Sunday 9-1.*

Parco delle Tombe di via Latina. Arco Travertino 151, tel. 7809255. Closed Christmas, new Year's day, First May and 15 of August. *9-1 hour before sunset.*

Sacrario e museo delle Fosse Ardeatine. Via Ardeatina 174, tel. 5136742. *Weekdays and Saturday 8:15-5:45; Sunday 8:45-5:15.*

Villa e Circo di Massenzio. Via Appia Antica 153, tel. 7801324. Closed Monday. *Summer 9-6:30; Winter 9-4:30.*

Entertainment

Tendastrisce. Via Cristoforo Colombo, tel. 5415521.

Luna Park permanente di Roma. Via delle Tre Fontane, tel. 5924747.

Health care facilities

Ospedale S. Eugenio. Piazzale dell'Umanesimo, tel. 5904.

Athletic facilities

Complesso sportivo delle Tre Fontane. Via delle Tre Fontane, tel. 5926386.

Palazzo dello Sport. Piazzale dello Sport, tel. 5925107.

Piscina delle Rose. Viale America, tel. 5926717.

Velodromo olimpico. Via della Tecnica, tel. 5925997.

Shops, crafts, and fine art

Cleto e Liliana Cellini. Viale Odescalchi 35, tel. 5131443. Here you can find excellent fresh pasta, including some curiously shaped special types.

Le Delizie Alimentari di Mauro Fronzoni. Via Vittorini 75, tel. 5002617. Excellent foods, fine service, a stunning array.

Lido di Ostia, Fiumicino, Fregene, and Veio

Except for Veio, which lies in the north along the Via Cassia, these are the main towns along the coastline, and not far from Rome.

Built in recent years along the coast, Ostia has expanded rapidly and chaotically, becoming the favorite beach of much of the population of Rome. As a beach resort, it doesn't have much to offer nowadays, and the countless buildings lining the beach makes it impossible to see the water, save for an occasional glimpse (even the lovely pine grove, or Pineta di Castel Fusano has much declined); only Ostia Antica, the ancient port of Rome, practically forgotten by time, gives us some idea of what life might have been like 2,000 years ago. All the same, because of its proximity to the city of Rome, its abundance of restaurants, and festive air that it takes on in summer, Ostia remains a pleasant destination for Romans who are willing to brave long lines of cars on the Via Cristoforo Colombo or the Via del Mare; in the numerous restaurants, you can savor mussels and crustaceans, and hotels offer affordable prices for an extended stay.

Fiumicino, located at a distance of about 25 km. from Rome at the mouth of the Via Portuense, extends around the tower that Pope Clement XIV built in 1773 on the right mouth – manmade – of the Tiber, in order to allow larger ships to moor here. Today this is an ordinary little town, well known for the proximity of the Aeroporto Leonardo da Vinci, for the little port crowded with fishing boats (the so-called Canale dei Pescatori, near which is a little marina with a few dozen yachts), and for the Fiumara Grande, the right branch of the Tiber, along whose banks are a dozen or so shipyards. The restaurants offer seafood; the best known restaurant here has a fine view of the sea, with garden dining in the summer. The hotels in this area are chiefly linked to the nearby airport, and are meant for people just passing through.

at Lido di Ostia

Hotels

★☆★ **Airport.** Viale dei Romagnoli 165, tel. 5692341, fax 5695993. Number of rooms: 259. Handicap-friendly. Air conditioning, elevator; parking garage.

★☆★ **Satellite.** Via delle Antille 49, tel. 5693841, fax 5695993. Number of rooms: 252. Handicap-friendly. Air conditioning, elevator; parking garage, pool.

★★★ **Ping Pong.** Lungomare Toscanelli 84, tel. 5601733, fax 5621236. Number of rooms: 28. Handicap-friendly. Elevator.

★★★ **Sirenetta.** Lungomare Toscanelli 46, tel. 5626700, fax 5622310. Number of rooms: 56. Elevator; parking area, garden.

Camping sites

🏕 **Internazionale di Castelfusano.** Via Litoranea al km. 1.2, tel. 5623304. Seasonal.

Restaurants

🍴 **Ferrantelli.** Via Claudio 5/7, tel. 56304269 Closed Monday (in winter also Sunday evening). Air conditioning. Classical cooking-sea food.

🍴 **Negri - da Romano e Luciano.** Via Claudio 50, tel. 5622295. Closed Wednesday in winter. Classical cooking – seafood.

🍴 **Sbarco di Enea.** At Ostia Antica, Via dei Romagnoli 675, tel. 5650253. Closed Monday, February. Garden. Classical cooking seafood.

Museums and cultural institutions

Castello di Giulio II. Ostia Antica, Piazza della Rocca 16, tel. 56358013. Closed Monday. *9-1. Tuesday and Thursday 9-4:30.*

Museo della Via Ostiense. Via R. Persichetti 3, tel. 5743193. Closed Monday. *9-1:30; Tuesday and Thursday also 2:30-4:30.*

Museo Ostiense. Scavi di Ostia Antica, tel. 56358099. Closed Monday. *9-6.*

Entertainment and leisure time

Teatro di Ostia Antica. Scavi di Ostia Antica, tel. 5650022.

Health care facilities

Ospedale di Ostia. Via Mar dei Sargassi, tel. 5666795.

at Fiumicino ✉ 0005

Hotels

★★★ **Mach 2.** Via Portuense 2467, tel. 6506394, fax 6505855. Number of rooms: 34. Access for the disabled. Air conditioning, elevator parking area.

Restaurants

🍴🍴 **Bastianelli al Molo.** Via di Torre Clementina 312, tel. 6505358, fax 6507210. Closed Monday and for a certain period in January. Refined cuisine – seafood.

🍴🍴 **Perla.** Via di Torre Clementina 214, tel. 6505038, fax 6507701. Closed Tuesday, for a certain period between August and September. Parking area, garden. Classical cooking – seafood.

🍴 **Arenella da Zì Pina.** Via di Torre Clementina 180, tel. 6505080. Closed Wednesday. Garden. Classical cooking – seafood.

🍴 **Bastianelli dal 1929.** Via di Torre Clementina 88, tel. 6505095. Closed Wednesday in low season. Air conditioning, garden. Classical cooking – seafood.

Museums and cultural institutions

Museo delle Navi. Via Guidoni 37, tel. 6529129. Closed Monday. *9-1:30; Tuesday and Thursday also 2:30-4:30.*

Hotels

★★★ **Golden Beach.** Via Gioiosa Marea 63, tel. 66560250, fax 66561095. Seasonal. Number of rooms: 35. Elevator; parking area, garden.

★★★ **Villa Fiorita.** Via Castellammare 86, tel. 66564590, fax 66560301. Number of rooms: 35. Parking area, garden.

★ **Miraggio.** Lungomare di Ponente 83, tel. 66560433, fax 66562284. Seasonal. Number of rooms: 26. Parking area, garden, private beach.

Restaurants

❘❙ **Mastino.** Via Silvi Marina 18, tel. 66560700. Closed Tuesday, Christmas- Epiphany (6 Jan.). Parking area. Roman cooking – seafood.

at Veio

Museums and cultural institutions

Area archeologica di Veio. Via Isola Farnese 64, tel. 30890116. Closed Monday. *Winter 9-2, Summer 9-7, Sunday 9-2.*

Index of Places and Things

The Città del Vaticano (Vatican City)

Rome Atlas

City key map

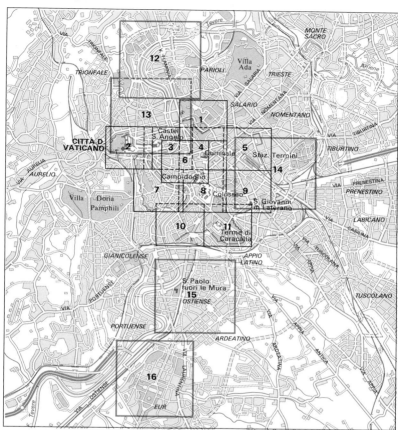

Conventional signs

⌐⌐ Ruins		Gardens
Palazzi, Museums		Cemeteries
Public buildings		Main roads
Churches		Railroads
Synagogues		Ⓜ COLOSSEO Subway lines stations
Mosques		Hotels; Restaurants
Buildings		1:7,500 (1 cm = 75 m) 1:12,500 (1 cm = 125 m)

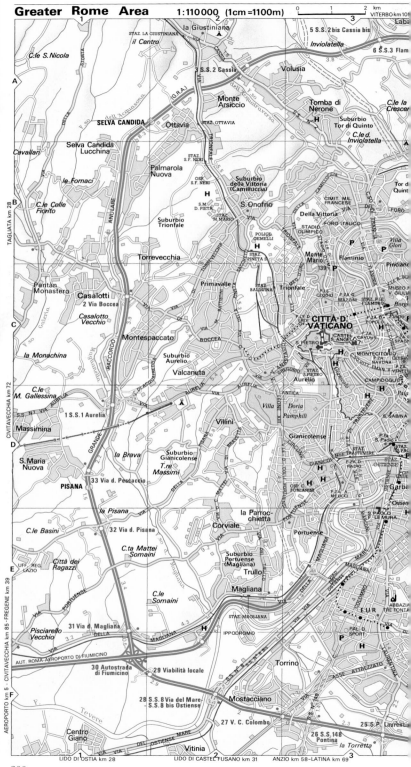

Greater Rome Area

1:110000 (1cm = 1100m)

0   1   2 km

VITERBO km 105

208

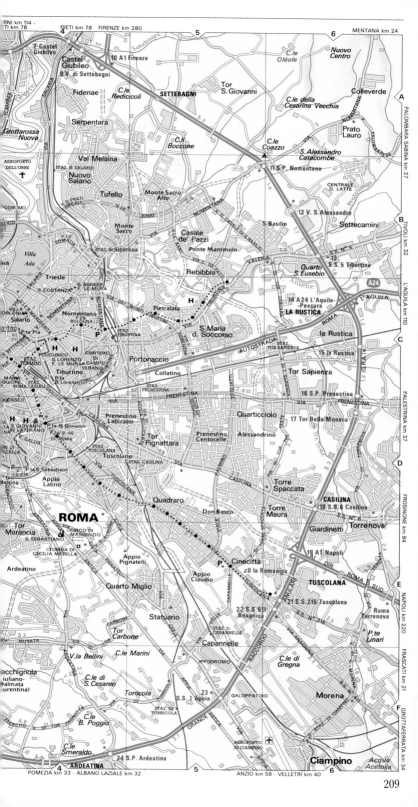

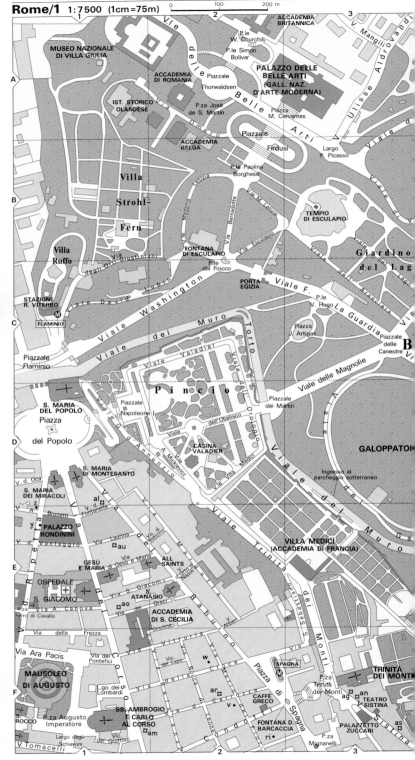

Rome/1 1:7500 (1cm=75m)

0 — 100 — 200 m

A

MUSEO NAZIONALE DI VILLA GIULIA

ACCADEMIA BRITANNICA

V. Mangili

ACCADEMIA DI ROMANIA

Piazzale Thorwaldsden

P.le W. Churchill
P.le Simón Bolivar

PALAZZO DELLE BELLE ARTI
(GALL. NAZ. D'ARTE MODERNA)

IST. STORICO OLANDESE

P.za José de S. Martin

Piazza M. Cervantes

Viale Omero

Viale delle Belle Arti

Ulisse Aldrovandi

ACCADEMIA BELGA

Piazzale Firdusi

Largo P. Picasso

V. di Villa

B

P.le Paolina Borghese

Villa Strohl-Fern

Via Madama Letizia

Viale Bernadotte

Via M. Letizia

Via Esculapio

TEMPIO DI ESCULAPIO

Giardino del Lago

Villa Ruffo

FONTANA DI ESCULAPIO

P.le del Fiocco

Viale dell'Aranciera

Via degli Orti Giustiniani

PORTA EGIZIA

Viale F.

C

STAZIONE R. VITERBO

FLAMINIO

Viale David Lubin

Viale Washington

Viale del Muro

Viale Valadier

Viale Torto

P.le V. Hugo

La Guardia

Piazza J. Artigas

Piazzale delle Canestre

B

Piazzale Flaminio

D

P i n c i o

Viale dell'

Piazzale Napoleone I

Viale delle Magnolie

Piazzale dei Martiri

GALOPPATOIO

S. MARIA DEL POPOLO

Piazza del Popolo

Viale G. d'Annunzio

Viale A. Mickiewicz

Viale dell'Obelisco

CASINA VALADIER

V.le Villa Medici

Ingresso al parcheggio sotterraneo

Viale del Muro

E

V. d. Oca

S. MARIA DI MONTESANTO

S. MARIA DEI MIRACOLI

Via Brunetti

al

Via d. Fontanelle

Vic. d. Vantaggio

PALAZZO RONDININI

Via Laurina

Via del Vantaggio

au

Via di Gesù e Maria

GESÙ E MARIA

ALL SAINTS

Via d. Greci

VILLA MEDICI
(ACCADEMIA DI FRANCIA)

OSPEDALE

S. GIACOMO

Via A. Canova

Via S. Giacomo

ao

S. ATANASIO

ACCADEMIA DI S. CECILIA

Via Vittoria

Via d. Orsoline

Via del Babuino

Via Albert

Via dei Monti Parioli

F

Via della Frezza

Via Ara Pacis

Via dei Pontefici

C

Vittoria

Vic. del Lupo

w

Piazza di

SPAGNA

Pza Trinità dei Monti

TRINITÀ DEI MONTI

MAUSOLEO DI AUGUSTO

L.go dei Lombardi

ar

CAFFÈ GRECO

an

ag

TEATRO SISTINA

S. ROCCO

P.za Augusto Imperatore

Vic. del Grottino

SS. AMBROGIO E CARLO AL CORSO

am

v

FONTANA D. BARCACCIA

ri

P.za Mignanelli

PALAZZETTO ZUCCARI

as

Via Sistina

Largo degli Schiavoni

V. Tomacelli

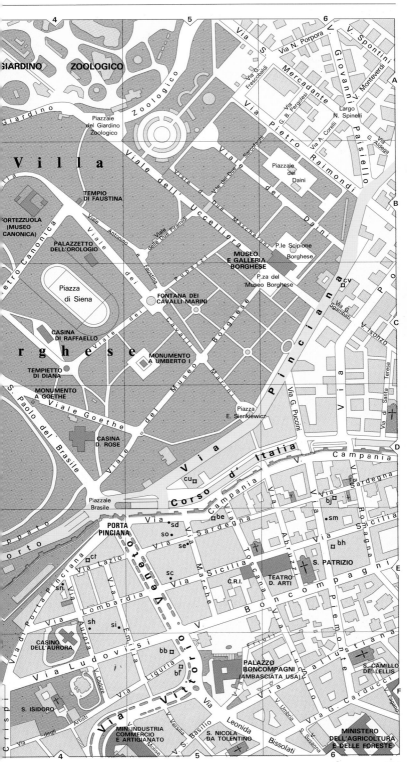

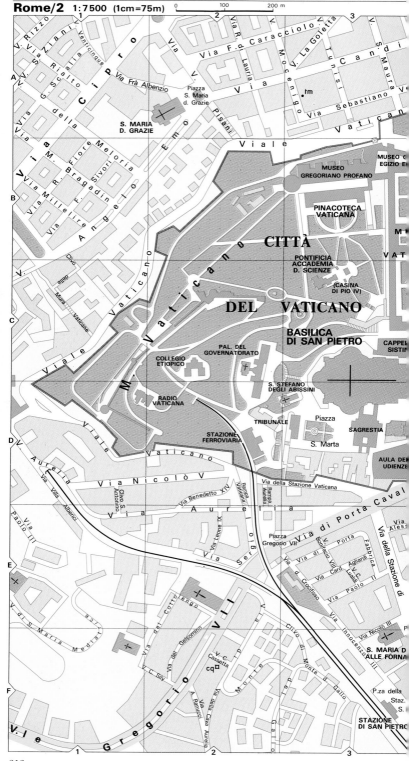

Rome/2 1:7500 (1cm=75m)

0   100   200 m

V. Rizzo
V. Ziani
V. S. Rialto
V. G. Scalia
Venticinque
Via Frà Albenzio
Via F. d. Caracciolo
V. La Goletta
V. Mocenigo
V. Tunisi
V. Maura
V. Candi
tm

Piazza
S. Maria
d. Grazie

Via   Pisani

Via   Sebastiano

S. MARIA
D. GRAZIE

Vaticano

Viale   Vaticano

Via   della
Via   M. Fiore
Meloria
Via   R. Bragadin
F. Sivori
Via   Angelo
Via   Millelire

Viale

MUSEO
EGIZIO E

MUSEO
GREGORIANO PROFANO

PINACOTECA
VATICANA

CITTÀ

M

V A T

PONTIFICIA
ACCADEMIA
D. SCIENZE

(CASINA
DI PIO IV)

Clivo
delle
Mura
Vaticane

Viale   Vaticano

DEL   VATICANO

BASILICA
DI SAN PIETRO

CAPPE
SISTI

COLLEGIO
ETIOPICO

PAL. DEL
GOVERNATORATO

RADIO
VATICANA

S. STEFANO
DEGLI ABISSINI

Viale

STAZIONE
FERROVIARIA

TRIBUNALE

Piazza

SAGRESTIA

S. Marta

Via   Vaticano

AULA DE
UDIENZE

V. Aurelia
Via Villa Albani
Via Nicolò V
Clivo S. Antonino
Via Benedetto XIV
Rampa Vaticani
Rampa Aurelia
Via della Stazione Vaticana

V. Paolo III

Via   Aurelia

Via   Leone   IX

Via della Porta Caval

Via Serio

Via   Alessia

Piazza
Gregorio VII

Via d. Crocifisso
V. Card. Agliardi
V. Boifacio VIII
Porta
Fabbrica
V. C. Iuliate
Via   Paolo   II
Via della Stazione di

V. di S. Maria Mediatr
Via del Cottolengo
Via del Gelsomino
Via Monte
Clivo di Monte d. Gallo
Via Innocenzo III
Via Nicolò III

V. C. P.
Cassetta
cq

V. C. Sily
Via della Cava Aurelia
A. Ranucci

S. MARIA D
ALLE FORNA

P.za della
Staz.
S.

STAZIONE
DI SAN PIETRO

V.le   Gregorio   VII

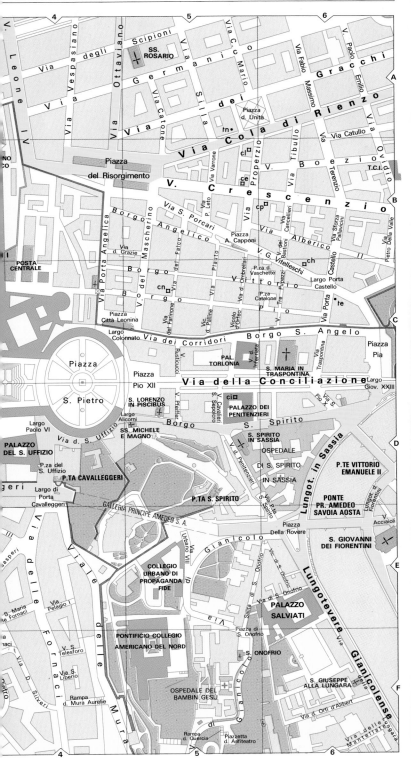

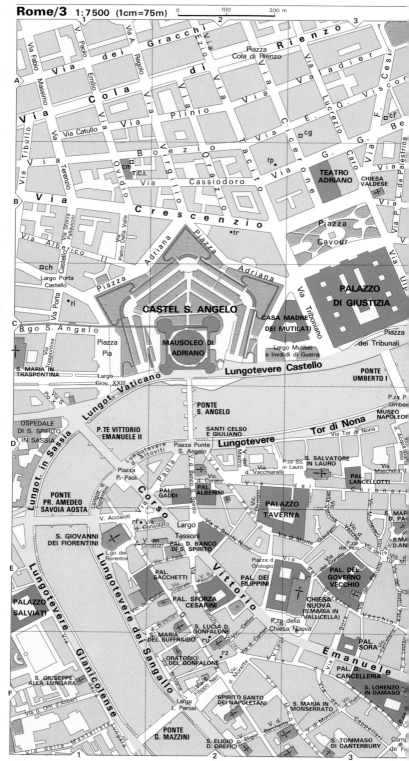

0   100   200 m

Via Fabio

Via Paolo

V. A. Regolo

Via dei Gracchi

Via A

Emilio

Via Massimo

Via Catullo

Via Cola

Via Ovidio

Via Boezio

Via Plinio

Via Virgilio

Via Orazio

Via Tacito

Piazza Cola di Rienzo

Via Cicerone

Via Rienzo

Via Valadier

V. Q. Visconti

Via F. Cesi

Via Tibullo

Via Terenzio

Via B o e z i o

Via Cassiodoro

cm

T.C.I.

V i a   C r e s c e n z i o

tp

cg

cf

G. Carlo

TEATRO ADRIANO

CHIESA VALDESE

Via Alberico

Via Castello

Via Sforza Pallavicini

Via Pietro Della Valle

Piazza Adriana

Via Adriana

Piazza Adriana

Via Adriana

•tr

Piazza Cavour

Via L. da Palestrina

ch

Largo Porta Castello

Via Porta Castello

Piazza Porta Castello

•tl

CASTEL S. ANGELO

MAUSOLEO DI ADRIANO

Via Triboniano

CASA MADRE DEI MUTILATI

PALAZZO DI GIUSTIZIA

B.go S. Angelo

Via Traspontina

Piazza Pia

Largo Mutilati e Invalidi di Guerra

Piazza dei Tribunali

S. MARIA IN TRASPONTINA

Largo Giov. XXIII

Lungotevere Castello

PONTE UMBERTO I

Lungot. Vaticano

Via Pio X

PONTE S. ANGELO

P.za P. Umber

OSPEDALE DI S. SPIRITO IN SASSIA

P.TE VITTORIO EMANUELE II

SANTI CELSO E GIULIANO

Lungotevere

Tor di Nona

MUSEO NAPOLEO

Lungot. in Sassia

Lungotevere Altoviti

Piazza Ponte S. Angelo

Via Tor di Nona

Via Acqua Sparta

Piazza P. Paoli

Via d. Banco d. S. Spirito

Via d. Vacchiarelli

Via Maschera d'

Via Corso

Via di Panico

Vic. d. Curato

P.za SS. in Lauro

S. SALVATORE IN LAURO

Via Maschera

PONTE PR. AMEDEO SAVOIA AOSTA

PAL. GADDI

PAL. ALBERINI

PAL. LANCELLOTTI

PAL. TAVERNA

PALAZZO TAVERNA

S. MAR PA

V. Acciaioli

rf•

Via d. Consolato

Largo Tassoni

PAL. D. BANCO DI S. SPIRITO

Via di Banchi Nuovi

Via di Monte Giordano

Vic. d. Vecchia

S. MA D'AN

S. GIOVANNI DEI FIORENTINI

V. dei Cimatori

Lgo dei Fiorentini

Vic. d. Palla

Piazza d. Orologio

Vic. d. Curato

PAL. SACCHETTI

PAL. DEI FILIPPINI

PAL. DEL GOVERNO VECCHIO

P.za del Fico

PALAZZO SALVIATI

Lungotevere dei Sangallo

Via Giulia

Vittorio

Via Pavone

PAL. SFORZA CESARINI

Via Sugarelli

CHIESA NUOVA (S.MARIA IN VALLICELLA)

Vecchio

Via d. Bresciani

S. MARIA DEL SUFFRAGIO

S. LUCIA D. GONFALONE

•ru

P.za della Chiesa Nuova

Emanuele

PAL. SORA

S. GIUSEPPE ALLA LUNGARA

Via d. Gonfalone

ORATORIO DEL GONFALONE

•rz

Vic. Cellini

Via Larga

PAL. D. CANCELLERIA

S. LORENZO IN DAMASO

Via degli Orti d'Alibert

Via Mantellate

Lungara

Largo L. Perosi

SPIRITO SANTO DEI NAPOLETANI

S. MARIA IN MONSERRATO

Via d. Montoro

Via Moretta

PONTE G. MAZZINI

Via Filippo Neri

S. ELIGIO D. OREFICI

V. S. Eligio

Via d. Barchetta

S. TOMMASO DI CANTERBURY

Campo de' Fi

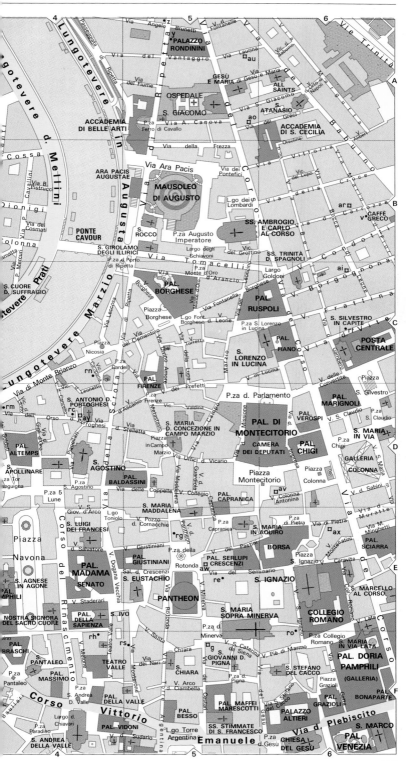

215

Rome/4   1:7500 (1cm=75m)

0   100   200 m

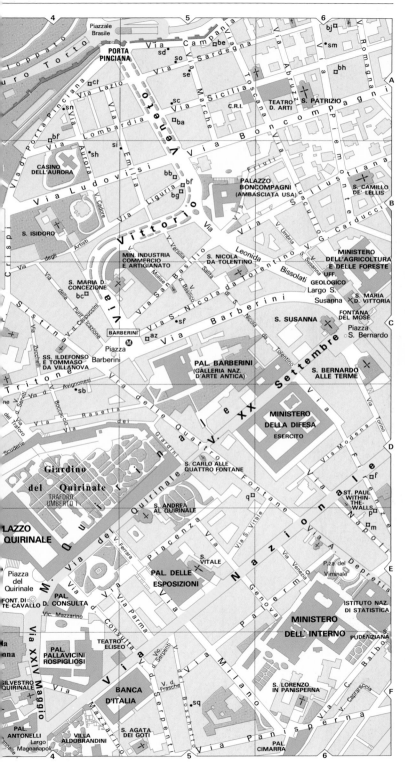

217

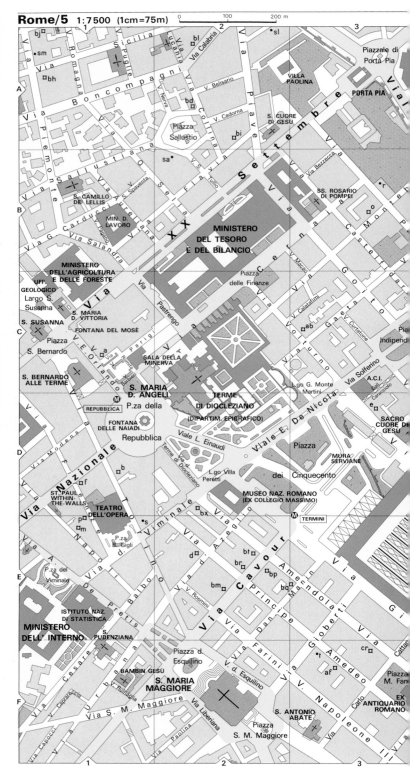

Rome/5   1:7500 (1cm=75m)

0   100   200 m

A

bj
•sm
bh

Via Sicilia
Via Puglie
V. Lucania

V. Calabria
bl
•sl

Via Boncompagni

Via Piave

Via Collina

Piazzale di
Porta Pia

Via Nerva
bd

V. Belisario

V. Cadorna

Via Piemonte

Via Romagna

Piazza
Sallustio

bi

VILLA
PAOLINA

S. CUORE
DI GESÙ

PORTA PIA

Via XX Settembre

B

Viale Sallustiana

Via Aureliana

V. Spaventa

sa•

V. Flavia

V. Tullio

Via Bezzecca

•r

Via G. Carducci

Via Salandra

S. CAMILLO
DE LELLIS

MIN. D.
LAVORO

V. Piacenza

X X

MINISTERO
DEL TESORO
E DEL BILANCIO

SS. ROSARIO
DI POMPEI

Via Castelfidardo

Via Montebello

C

MINISTERO
DELL'AGRICOLTURA
E DELLE FORESTE
UFF.
GEOLOGICO
Largo S.
Susanna
S. SUSANNA
Piazza
S. Bernardo

Via

Via

S. MARIA
D. VITTORIA
FONTANA DEL MOSÈ

V. E. Orlando

Via Parigi

Via Pastrengo

Piazza
delle Firenze

V. Maggio

V. Calatafimi

ab

Via Volturno

V. Curtatone

V. Gaeta

Piazza
Indipend

Via Goito

D

S. BERNARDO
ALLE TERME

Via Modena

M
REPUBBLICA

Via Barberini

SALA DELLA
MINERVA

S. MARIA
D. ANGELI
P.za della

FONTANA
DELLE NAIADI
Repubblica

TERME
DI DIOCLEZIANO
(DIPARTIM. EPIGRAFICO)

Viale L. Einaudi

Terme di Diocleziano

L.go Villa
Peretti

MUSEO NAZ. ROMANO
(EX COLLEGIO MASSIMO)

Viale E. De Nicola

L.go G. Monte
Martini

A.C.I.

Via Solferino

Via Caracciolo

SACRO
CUORE DI
GESÙ

Piazza

MURA
SERVIANE

dei   Cinquecento

M
TERMINI

E

Via Nazionale

b
f

ST. PAUL
WITHIN-
THE-WALLS

TEATRO
DELL'OPERA

p
m

P.za
B. Gigli

Via Napoli

•s

P.za del
Viminale

Via Viminale

bx

d

bm

V. Rosmini

Via Amendola

bt
br
bp
bq

Via Cavour

Via Principe Amendola

Via Gioberti

Gi

F

ISTITUTO NAZ.
DI STATISTICA

MINISTERO
DELL'INTERNO

S.
PUDENZIANA

Via De Pretis

Via Balbo

a

Via Cesare Balbo

V. Capuccia

V. Caporali

a

BAMBIN GESÙ

a
Via Rufiglia

Via Urbana

S. MARIA
MAGGIORE

Via S. M. Maggiore

Via Paolina

Via Liberiana

Piazza d.
Esquilino

V. d. Esquilino

V. Principe

Piazza d.
Esquilino

S. ANTONIO
ABATE

Piazza
S. M. Maggiore

Via Farini

•t
af

Via Amedeo

cr

Via Napoleone III

Via Carlo

Piazza
M. Fan

EX
ANTIQUARIO
ROMANO

Via Cattan

1   **2**   **3**

218

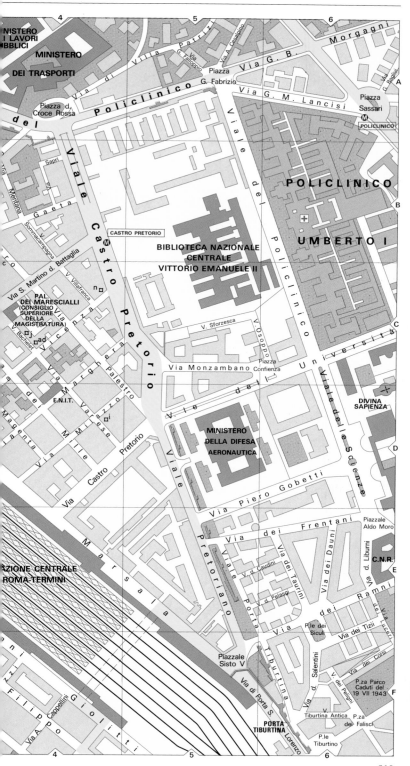

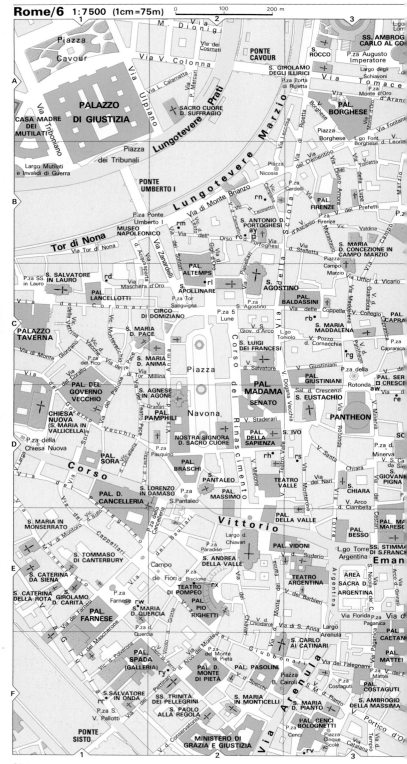

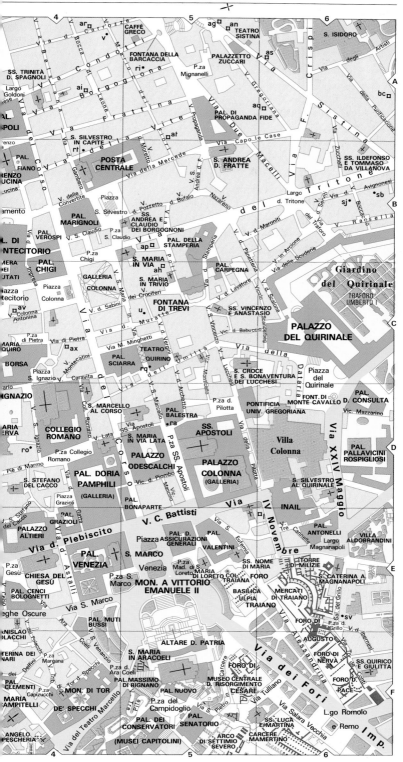

221

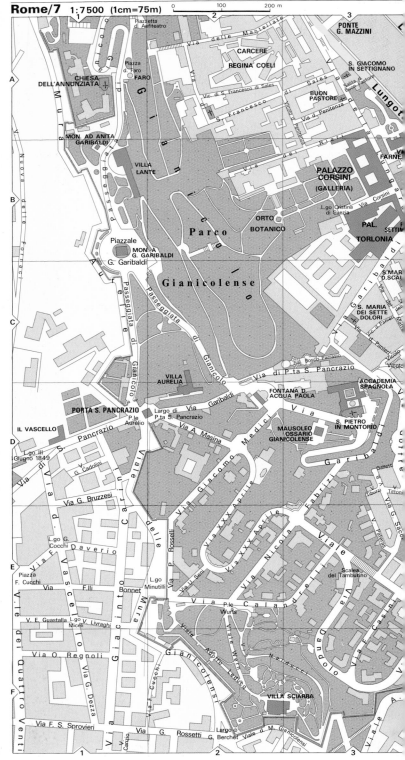

0   100   200 m

PONTE
G. MAZZINI

Piazzetta
d. Anfiteatro

Via delle Mantellate

CARCERE

REGINA COELI

S. GIACOMO
IN SETTIGNANO

Piazza
d. Faro
FARO

Vic. di S. Francesco di Sales

Salita
Buon Pastore

Lungot

CHIESA
DELL'ANNUNZIATA

Vic. d. Penitenza

BUON
PASTORE

S.
Francesco

Via d. Penitenza

MON. AD ANITA
GARIBALDI

VM
FARNE

VILLA
LANTE

Viale

PALAZZO
CORSINI

(GALLERIA)

Via Corsini

PAL.

SETTIM

Parco

ORTO
BOTANICO

L.go Cristina
di Svezia

TORLONIA

Piazzale

MON. A
G. GARIBALDI

G. Garibaldi

S.MAR
D.SCAI

Gianicolense

S. MARIA
DEI SETTE
DOLORI

Passeggiata di Gianicolo

Via di P.ta S. Pancrazio

Pal. Bosco Parrasio

ACCADEMIA
SPAGNOLA

VILLA
AURELIA

FONTANA D.
ACQUA PAOLA

Via

Garibaldi

PORTA S. PANCRAZIO

Largo di
P.ta S. Pancrazio

P.le
Aurelio

MAUSOLEO
OSSARIO
GIANICOLENSE

S. PIETRO
IN MONTORIO

IL VASCELLO

Via A. Masina

Garibaldi

Pancrazio

Via

Giacomo

Galletti

L.go III
Giugno 1849

V. Cadolini

Medici

Tiburio

Via G. Sacc

Via G. Bruzzesi

P. Rosselli

Via XXX Aprile

Fabriz

Tittoni

Viale delle

Via XXX Aprile

Nicola

Viale

L.go G.
Cocchi

Daverio

Via F.

Via XXX Aprile

Piazza
F. Cucchi

L.go
Minutilli

Via

F.lli

Bonnet

U. Seni

Scalea
del Tamburino

Via

Vascello

V. E. Guastalla

L.go V. Livraghi
Miceli

P.le Calandrelli

Wurts

Via O. Regnoli

Giacinto

Muro

Gianicolensi

Viale Adolfo Leducq

Via G. Dezza

Viale A.

Dandolo

Nanducci

Viale V.

VILLA
SCIARRA

Via F. S. Sprovieri

Via

G. Rossetti

Largo
G. Berchet

Viale d. M. Gianicolensi

Via

Viale A.

Quattro

Venti

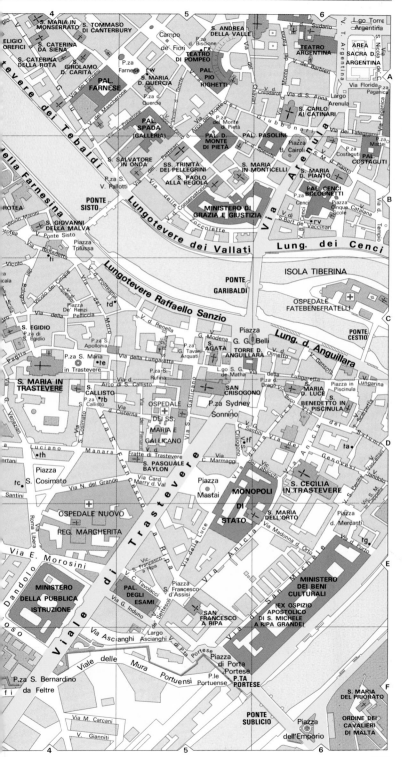

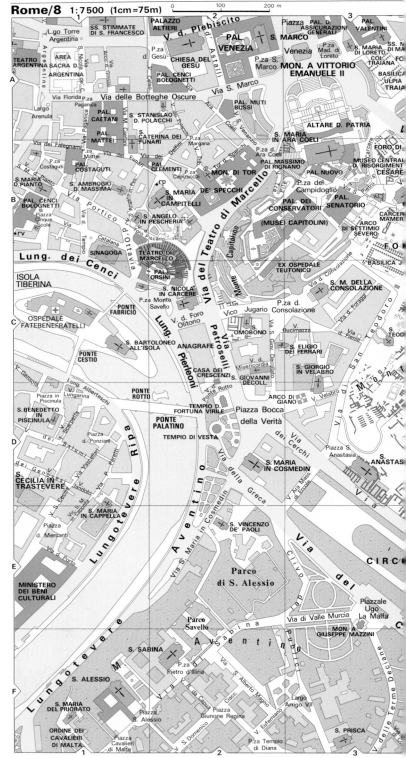

Rome/8   1:7500 (1cm=75m)

0   100   200 m

A

L.go Torre Argentina

SS. STIMMATE DI S. FRANCESCO

PALAZZO ALTIERI

Piazza PAL. D. ASSICURAZIONI GENERALI

PAL. VALENTINI

V. d. Plebiscito

PAL. VENEZIA

S. MARCO

SS. N DI MA

TEATRO ARGENTINA

AREA SACRA DI S. ARGENTINA

P.za d. Gesù

CHIESA DEL GESÙ

P.za S. Marco

Venezia

P.za Mad. di Loreto

S. MARIA DI LORETO

COL. TRAIANA

FO

Via S. Marco

MON. A VITTORIO EMANUELE II

BASILICA ULPIA TRAIA

PAL. CENCI BOLOGNETTI

Via Florida

P.za Paganica

Via delle Botteghe Oscure

PAL. MUTI BUSSI

ALTARE D. PATRIA

B

Largo Arenula

PAL. CAETANI

S. STANISLAO D. POLACCHI

S. MARIA IN ARA COELI

FORO DI

MUSEO CENTRAL D. RISORGIMENT CESARE

PAL. MATTEI

CATERINA DEI FUNARI

P.za d. Ara Coeli

PAL MASSIMO DI RIGNANO

PAL. NUOVO

Via dei Fategnami

P.za Mattei

PAL. COSTAGUTI

Via dei Funari

PAL. CLEMENTI

P.za Capizucchi

MON. DI TOR

MON. DI TOR DE' SPECCHI

P.za del Campidoglio

PAL. SENATORE

P.za Costaguti

S. AMBROGIO D. MASSIMA

S. MARIA IN CAMPITELLI

PAL. DEI CONSERVATORI

S. MARIA D. PIANTO

PAL. CENCI BOLOGNETTI

Via d. Portico d'Ottavia

S. ANGELO IN PESCHERIA

(MUSEI CAPITOLINI)

ARCO DI SETTIMIO SEVERO

CARCER MAMER

Piazza Cinque Scole

Catalana

P.za d. Piscinula

TEATRO DI MARCELLO

EX OSPEDALE TEUTONICO

BASILICA J

C

Lung. dei Cenci

SINAGOGA

PAL. ORSINI

Via d. Consolazione

S. M. DELLA CONSOLAZIONE

ISOLA TIBERINA

PONTE FABRICIO

S. NICOLA IN CARCERE

P.za Monte Savello

V. d. Foro Olitorio

Vico Jugario

Consolazione

S. TEOD

OSPEDALE FATEBENEFRATELLI

S. OMOBONO

Bucimazza

Via d. Fienili

PONTE CESTIO

S. BARTOLOMEO ALL'ISOLA

Lung. Pierleoni

S. ELIGIO DEI FERRARI

V. Gensola

Lung. Alberteschi

Lungarina

CASA DEI CRESCENZI

S. GIOVANNI DECOLL.

S. GIORGIO IN VELABRO

D

Piazza in Piscinula

PONTE ROTTO

V. d. Ponte Rotto

ARCO DI GIANO

V. Velabro

S. BENEDETTO IN PISCINULA

Piazza d. Ponziani

TEMPIO D. FORTUNA VIRILE

Piazza Bocca della Verità

PONTE PALATINO

TEMPIO DI VESTA

Via dei Cerchi

Piazza S. Anastasia

S. ANASTAS

S. CECILIA IN TRASTEVERE

S. MARIA IN CAPPELLA

S. MARIA IN COSMEDIN

Via della Greca

V. Ara Mass. di Ercole

E

Piazza d. Mercanti

Lungotevere Ripa

Via di Porto

S. VINCENZO DE' PAOLI

Parco di S. Alessio

CIRCO

MINISTERO DEI BENI CULTURALI

Piazzale Ugo La Malfa

Parco Savello

Via di Valle Murcia

MON. A GIUSEPPE MAZZINI

F

S. SABINA

Aventino

Via delle Terme Deciana

S. ALESSIO

P.za d. Pietro d'Illiria

Largo Arrigo VII

S. MARIA DEL PRIORATO

Piazza S. Alessio

Piazza Giunone Regina

S. PRISCA

ORDINE DEI CAVALIERI DI MALTA

Piazza Cavalieri di Malta

S. Domenico

P.za Tempio di Diana

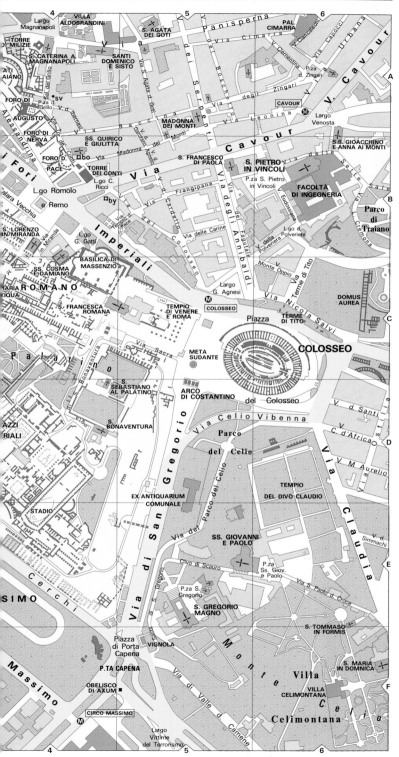

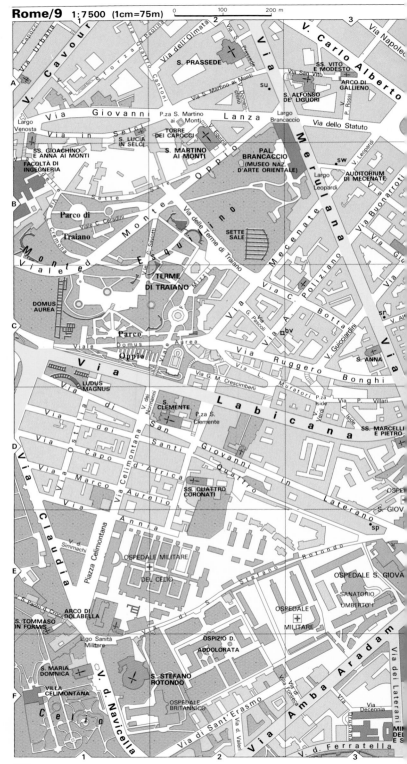

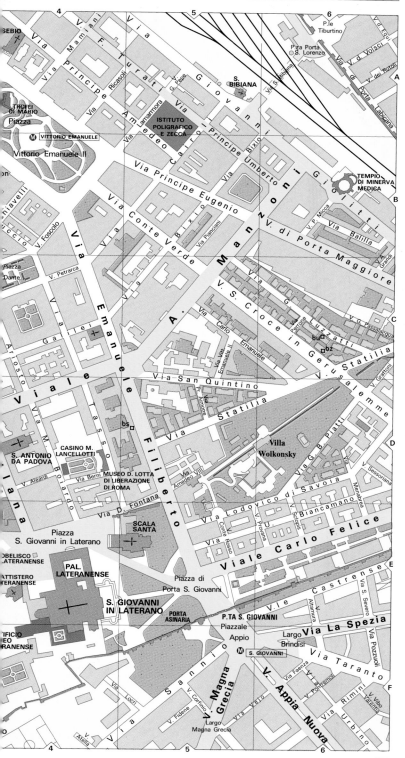

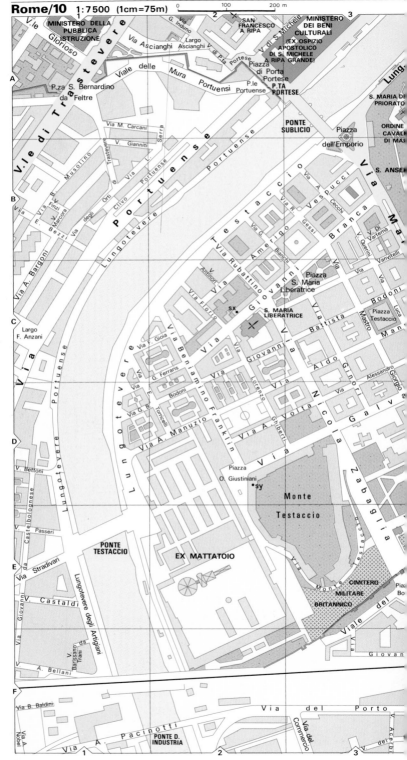

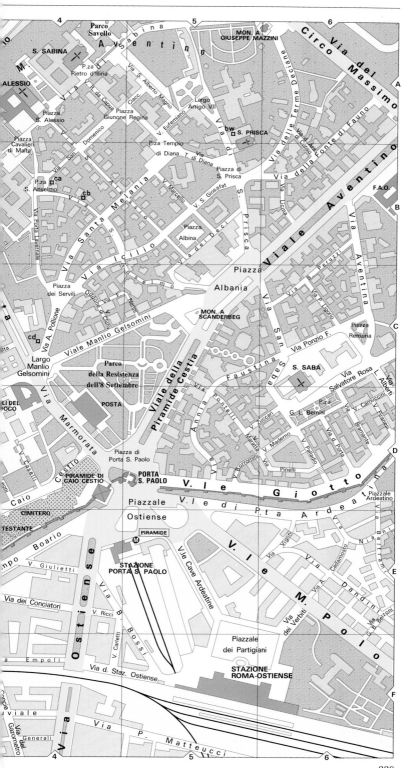

229

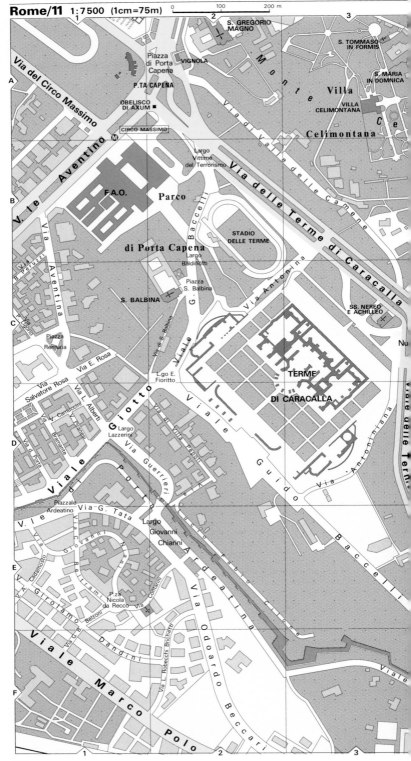

Rome/11 1:7500 (1cm=75m)

0   100   200 m

A

Via del Circo Massimo

V.le Aventino

Piazza di Porta Capena

P.TA CAPENA

VIGNOLA

S. GREGORIO MAGNO

S. TOMMASO IN FORMIS

S. MARIA IN DOMNICA

VILLA CELIMONTANA

Villa

Celimontana

Ce

OBELISCO DI AXUM

CIRCO MASSIMO

M

Largo Vittime del Terrorismo

Via di Valle delle Camene

B

V.le Aventino

B. Peruzzi

Via Aventina

F.A.O.

Parco

G. Baccelli

STADIO DELLE TERME

Via delle Terme di Caracalla

di Porta Capena

Largo Baldinotti

Piazza S. Balbina

Via Antonina

C

P. Virgilio

Piazza Remuria

S. BALBINA

Via di S. Balbina

Viale G.

L.go E. Fioritto

TERME DI CARACALLA

SS. NEREO E ACHILLEO

Nu

Via E. Rosa

Via Salvatore Rosa

Via L. Alberti

Viale Guido

D

V. Cannucini

V. Pirandi

Bramante

Via di Porta

Viale delle

Giotto

Largo Lazzerini

Via Guerrieri

Via di Villa Pepoli

Via Antoniana

Via delle Terme

E

V.le Ardeatino

Piazzale Ardeatino

Via G. Tata

Via Giovanni

Via di Porta

Largo Giovanni Chianni

Via Fabio Cilone

Via Ardeatina

Baccelli

V.le Casamasta

Via Girolamo

V. Belzoni

Via Beltrami

Dandini

P.za Nicola da Recco

Via L. Robecchi Brichetti

Via Contarini

Via Odoardo Beccari

F

Viale Marco Polo

Viale

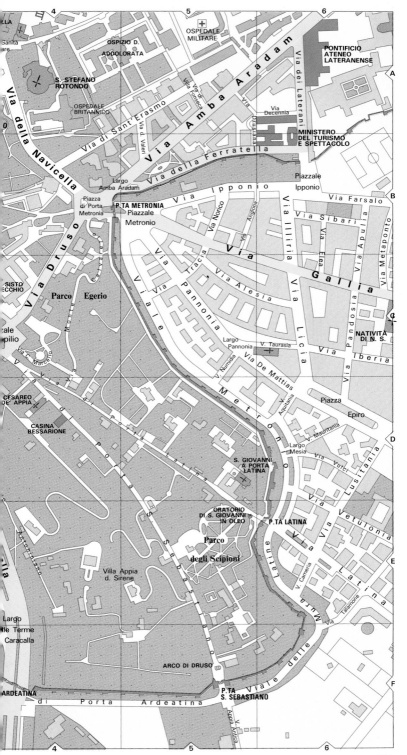

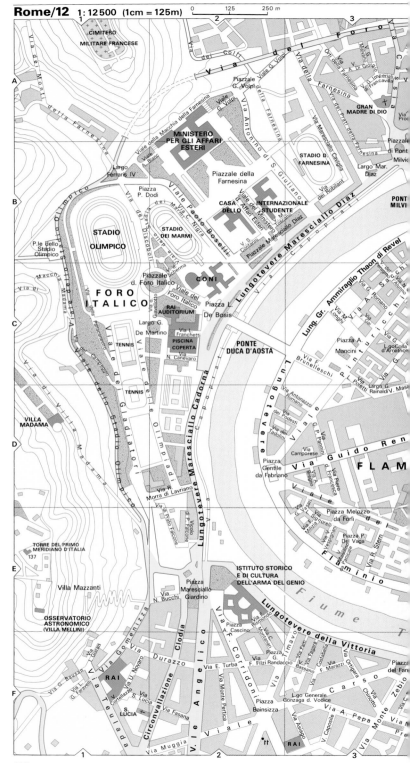

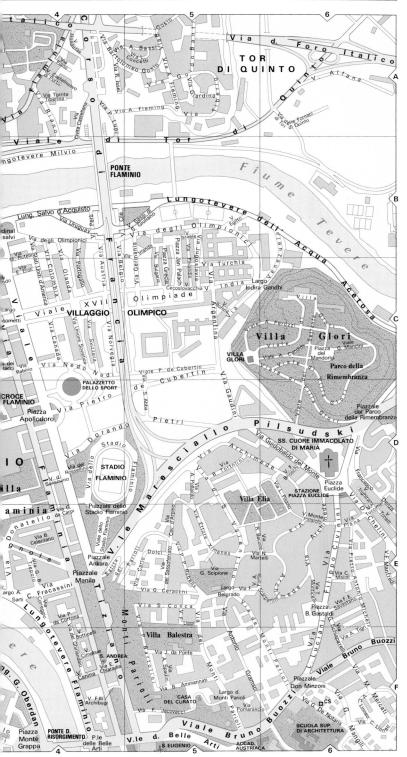

233

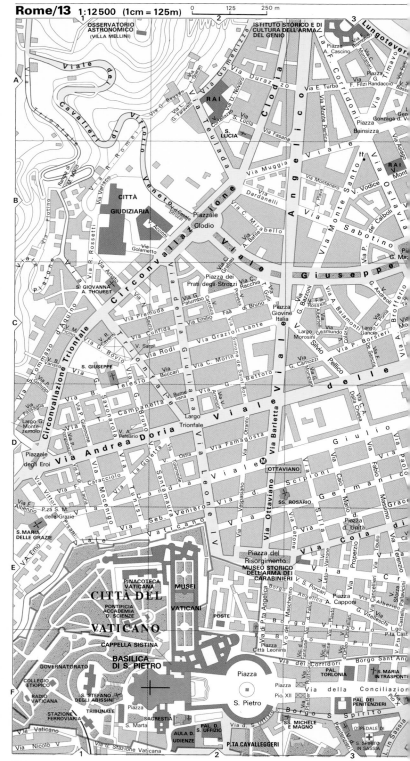

0   125   250 m

OSSERVATORIO
ASTRONOMICO
(VILLA MELLINI)

ISTITUTO STORICO E DI
CULTURA DELL'ARMA
DEL GENIO

Lungotevere

Viale dei Cavalieri

Via Trionfale

Via R. Romano

Via Vaticano

Viale Vittorio

Via G. Besuan

Via L. G. Taravelli

Via Cortolaro

Via Novaro

RAI

S. LUCIA

Via Durazzo

Via Gomenizz

Via Teulada

Via Monte Pertica

Via Fasana

Piazza
A. Cascino

Piazza
Gonzaga &

Via E. Turba

Via C.
Monteverdi

Via C. Corridoni

Via Angelo

Via Filzi Randaccio

Piazza
Bainsizza

CITTÀ
GIUDIZIARIA

Acqroni

Via Oslavia

Via Strozzi

Via Golametto

Via R. Rossetti

Piazzale
Clodio

Via C. Mirabello

Via Muggia

Via
Dardanelli

Via Monte Santo

RAI

Via Vodice

Via P. de' Calboli

Via Sabotino

Piazza
G. Mar

Giuseppe

S. GIOVANNA
A. THOURET

Circonvallazione Trionfale

Piazza dei
Prati degli Strozzi

Via C.
Racchia

Via G.
Palumbo

Via Premuda

Via C.
Grabau

Via T. Gulli

Via F.lli
Rossetti

Via A. Baiamonti

Via A. Andreoli

Viale
Giuseppe

Brofferio

Via
di Bruno

Via Emilio

Piazza
Giovine
Italia

Largo
Gancia

Via P. Borsieri

S. GIUSEPPE

Via G. Bovio

Via Cunfida

Via Rodi

Via Grazioli Lante

Via C. Morin

Via Simone de Saint Bon

Via Bettolo

Largo
Morosini

Largo

Silvio

Pellico

delle

Via Andrea Doria

Campanella

Via Buccari

Largo
Trionfale

Via Famagosta

Via Barletta

Giulio

Piazzale
degli Eroi

Via La Goletta

Via Leone

Via Otranto

Via G. Canozzi

Via
Crescenzio

Via Fabio
Massimo

Via Paolo

S. MARIA
DELLE GRAZIE

Via Tunisi

Via Sebastiano Veniero

Via Ottaviano

M

OTTAVIANO

Scipioni

Via Germanico

Grac

P.za S. M.
delle Grazie

SS. ROSARIO

Piazza
d. Unità

Via Cola

di

Piazza del
Risorgimento

MUSEO STORICO
DELL'ARMA DEI
CARABINIERI

Via Properzio

Via Tibullo

CITTÀ DEL

PINACOTECA
VATICANA

MUSEI

VATICANI

PONTIFICIA
ACCADEMIA
D. SCIENZE

POSTE

VATICANO

CAPPELLA SISTINA

BASILICA
DI S. PIETRO

GOVERNATORATO

COLLEGIO
ETIOPICO

RADIO
VATICANA

S. STEFANO
DEGLI ABISSINI

STAZIONE
FERROVIARIA

TRIBUNALE

Piazza
S. Marta

SAGRESTIA

AULA D.
UDIENZE

PAL. D.
UFFIZIO

P.TA CAVALLEGGERI

Borgo S. Porcari

Borgo Angelico

Borgo Vittorio

Borgo Pio

Piazza
Città Leonina

Piazza
A. Capponi

Via di Porta Angelica

Via Mascherino

Via del Mascherino

Piazza

S. Pietro

Piazza
Pio XII

PAL.
TORLONIA

S. MARIA
IN TRASPONTI

Via della Conciliazion

Borgo Sant'Ang

Borgo S. Spirito

PAL. DEI
PENITENZIERI

SS. MICHELE
E MAGNO

S. SPIRITO
IN SASSIA

OSPEDALE DI
S. Spirito

Via dei Corridori

Via della Stazione Vaticana

Via Nicolò V

Via Vaticano

234

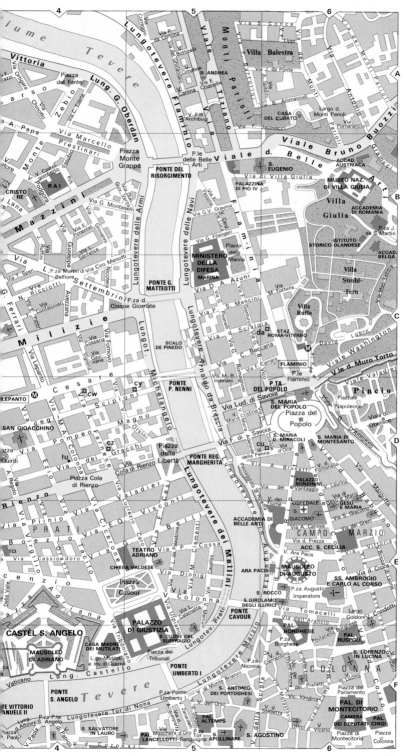

235

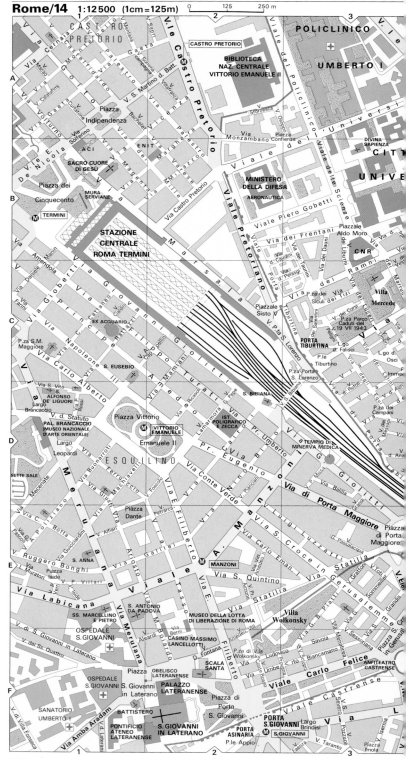

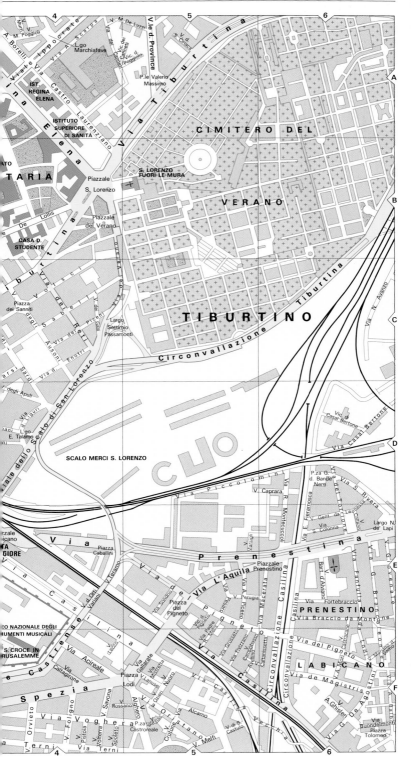

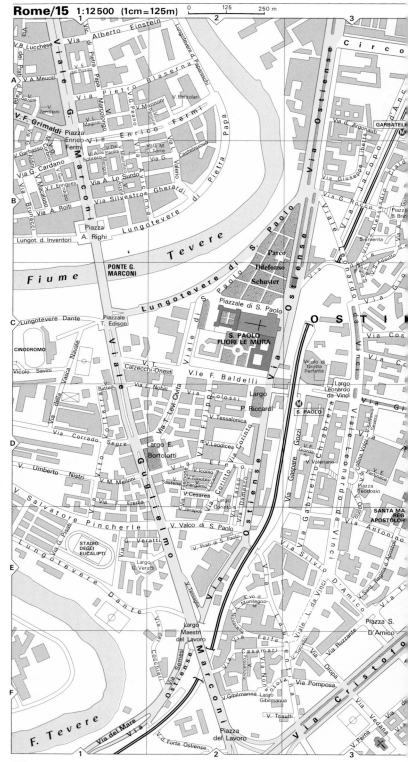

0   125   250 m

A

V. dei Prati
V. B. Lucchese
Via Alberto Einstein
V. di Pietro Papa
V. del Pozzo
Via A. Meucci
Lungotevere di Pietraschi
V. A. Meucci
P. Sereni
V. Zemboni
Via Pietro Blaserna
V. V. E. Marconi
V. G. Marinori
V. G. Peano
V. Berzolari
Circo

V. F. Grimaldi
Piazza Enrico Fermi
Via Enrico Fermi
V. Marcolongo
V. I. Magrini
V. G. Peano
Via Pietra Papa
GARBATELLI

B

V. Garbasso
V. Carbino
V. Aldini
V. Macaluso
V. G. Cardano
V. Cei
V. F. Enriques
Via A. Lo Surdo
V. A. De Gasparis
V. G. M. D. Torre
V. G. Vaiano
Castelnuovo
Via Giuseppe Iberina
Via Jacopo
Piazza B. Brin
S. emerita

Via A. Righi
Piazza A. Righi
Via Silvestro Gherardi
Lungotevere di S. Paolo
Viale Leonardo

Lungot. d. Inventori
Tevere
Parco Ildefonso Schuster

PONTE G. MARCONI
Lungotevere di S. Paolo
Piazzale di S. Paolo

Fiume

C

Lungotevere Dante
Piazzale T. Edison
Viale di S. Paolo
S. PAOLO FUORI LE MURA
O   S   T   I

CINODROMO
Viale G. Guglielmo Marconi
V. T. Calzecchi-Onesti
V.le F. Baldelli
Vicolo di Grotta Perfetta
Via Cos

Vicolo Savini
Via della Vasca Navale
Via Battelli
Via J. Nobili
Via Colossi
Largo P. Riccardi
V. Tessalonica
Largo Leonardo da Vinci

D

Via Corrado Segre
Largo E. Bortolotti
V. Laodicea
V. E. Levi Civita
Corinto
Via Corinto
Via Gaspare Gozzi
Via Giorda
V. Valeriano
V.E. Fermace
Piazza Teodosio

V. Umberto Nistri
V. M. Melloni
V. Iconio
V. Timoteo
V. Pergamo
V. Sostene
Largo Damasco
Via Gabriello Chiabrera
Collina Volpi
Via Antonino

V. Salvatore Pincherle
Via F. Eredia
V. Cesarea
V. Jerapoli
Largo Corinto
V. Valco di S. Paolo
SANTA MA REG APOSTOLOR

E

Lungotevere Dante
G. Veratti
STADIO DEGLI EUCALIPTI
Largo G. Veratti
V. Prati di S. Paolo
Via Silvio D'Amico
Viale L. da Vinci
Piazza S. D'Amico

F

Via del Mare
Largo Maestri del Lavoro
V.co di Montagnola
Via Novecana
Via Farfa
Via Casamari
Via Pomposa
Via Ruzzante
Via Orcpa
Via Sant Sabina Apostol

F. Tevere
Via Ostiense
Via Marconi
V. d. Forte Ostiense
V. Gibilmanna
Largo Gibilmanna
V. Trisulti
Piazza del Lavoro
V. Parnia
Via Cristofo
Via Vedana

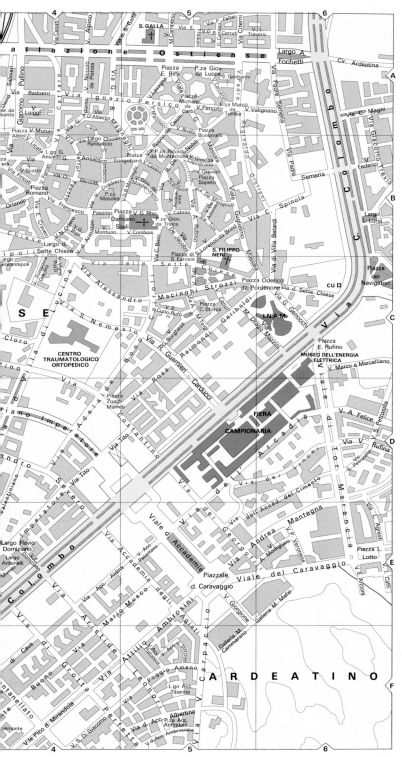

239

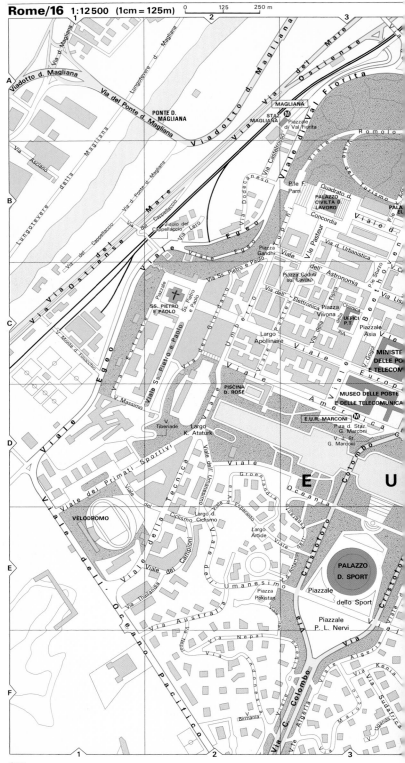

0   125   250 m

1   **2**   **3**

A   Viadotto d. Magliana
Via d. Magliana
Via d. Magliana
Lungotevere d. Magliana
Via del Ponte d. Magliana
PONTE D. MAGLIANA
Viadotto d. Magliana
Via dell Mare
Via Ostiense
Via di Val Fiorita
MAGLIANA
STAZ MAGLIANA
Piazzale di Val Fiorita
Romolo

Via Asciano
Lungotevere della Magliana

B   Lungotevere
Via del Mare
Via d. Ponte d. Magliana
Via di Cappellaccio
Vicolo del Cappellaccio
Via Dodecaneso
Via Castelrosso
Via Laro
P.le F. Parri
Quadrato d. Turismo
PALAZZO CIVILTA D. LAVORO
Concordia
V. le della
PALA EL
Via Ostiense
Via del Cappellaccio
Via d. Monte di Finocchio
Piazza Gandhi
Viale dell'
Via Eugeo
Viale Egeo
Via d. Urbanistica
V.le Pasteur
Astronomia
Piazza Caduti sul Lavoro
Via dell' Elettronica
Viale Umberto Tupini
Fisica
Piazza Chimica

C   SS. PIETRO E PAOLO
Piazzale SS. Pietro e Paolo
Via SS. Pietro e Paolo
Viale SS. Pietro e Paolo
Viale SS. Pietro e Paolo
Vivona
UFFICI P.T.
Piazzale Asia
P.le Sturzo
Via Lisa
Via della Tecnica
Largo Apollinaire
Viale Europa
MINISTE DELLE PO E TELECOM
Via Gogol
V. Monte d Finocchio
V. Massimo
V. Tiberiade
Largo K. Ataturk
PISCINA D. ROSE
MUSEO DELLE POSTE E DELLE TELECOMUNICA
V. le America
Viale dell'
Via dell'
Via della
E.U.R. MARCONI
P.za d. Staz. G. Marconi
V. d. St. G. Marconi

D   Viale dei Primati Sportivi
Viale della Tecnica
Viale dell' Umanesimo
VELODROMO
Viale
Groenlandia
V.le Esperanto
E
U
Oceania
Cristoforo Colombo

E   Viale dell' Oceano
Ciclismo
Largo d. Ciclismo
Viale dei Campioni
Viale del
Largo Artide
Viale Azia
Viale dell' Umanesimo
Piazza Pakistan
Viale
PALAZZO D. SPORT
Piazzale dello Sport
Via Thailandia
Via Australia
Piazzale P. L. Nervi
Via Cristoforo
V. Napal
Via Algeria

F   Viale dell' Oceano Pacifico
V. Birmania
Via C. Algeria
P.le Algeria
Via C. Colombo
Mare
Via Kenia
Via Sudafrica
V. Uganda

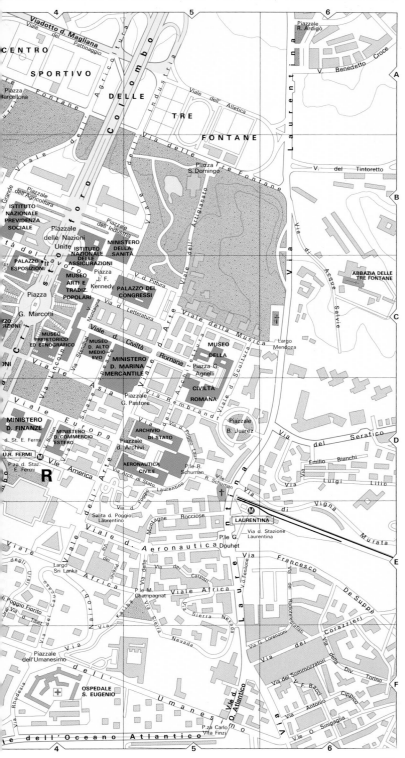

MESSICO E NUVOLE

since 1988

MEXICAN RESTAURANT
TERRACE - COCKTAIL BAR

Via dei Magazzini Generali 8
Tel. 0039 06 5741413 - 5743867
Reservations are recommended

Closed Monday

"Stop -'n'- go" CITY TOURS

9 departures daily
14 selected stops
with multilingual hostesses
Lire 20,000 for a full day

Passes for Unlimited Tours
(Roma City - Tivoli - Ostia Antica - Castelli Romani)

Special Offer

2 Days, Lire 30,000
3 Days, Lire 40,000

Tickets on board at every stop !!

CSR

McDonald's

CSR also operates tours to:

- **Tivoli** half day (a.m.) — Lire 20,000
- **Ostia Antica** half day (a.m.) — Lire 20,000
- **Castelli Romani** half day (p.m.) — Lire 20,000
- **Cerveteri** and **Tarquinia** full day — Lire 40,000

CSR Consorzio Sigthseeing Roma Ph. (06) 3217054 Fax (06) 3201978

Enoteca Cul de Sac

The modern version of this historical Roman vintage wine store opened in 1977, although its activity as an Oil and Wine shop dates back to the far-off 1900s, a period which has left its mark in the magnificent marble counter. This wine store, or 'enoteca', gave birth in Rome to the phenomenon of the Wine-Bar, offering an array of gastronomic specialties as well as an enormous selection of wines (presently around 1,400). It is located in Piazza Pasquino, (near Piazza Navona), a historical square which holds one of Rome's 'speaking' statues; the enoteca is furnished simply, in Spartan style, with a scaffolding of tubes supporting long, wooden shelves (18 meters) which display an astounding collection of wines. The room is long and narrow (hence its name 'Cul de Sac'), with rows of wooden benches, above which are hung fishing nets - the atmosphere recalls the wooden train compartments of the 1960s. The impressive list of wines is categorized according to the various regions of origin and provides, for the sake of 'beginners', a description of the characteristics of the main wines (area of production, type of grape compositions, main organoleptic characteristics). The gastronomic specialties are home-made. Worthy of special mention are the onion soup, the cream of red lentil soup, the Valtellina 'pizzoccheri' (a type of pasta dish), the 'brandade' of stockfish and the delicious home-made patè.

• *A choice of 1,400 wines, sparkling wines (spumanti) and champagne with the most important brand names in Italian Wines.*
• *Home-made gastronomic and confectionery specialties.*
• *Cheeses and salami from all around Italy.*

OPEN AFTER THE THEATER - CLOSED MONDAY (LUNCHTIME)

Roma - P.zza Pasquino, 73 • Tel. 0039 06 68.80.10.94

HB BETTOJA HOTELS

In Rome

Four four-star hotels with varied tariffs and one three-star hotel, facing or adjoining each other in the city center, near the Termini railway station, the Air Terminal and the Subway, offer their traditional and professional services for meetings, congresses, business trips and other incentives. The large number of rooms and conference halls, as well as two restaurants and the roof garden bar at Hotel Mediterraneo satisfy the most varied requirements.

MEDITERRANEO ****
Via Cavour 15 - 00184 Rome
Tel. +39 06 4884051 - Fax +39 06 4744105

MASSIMO D'AZEGLIO ****
Via Cavour 18 - 00184 Rome
Tel. +39 06 4870270 - Fax +39 06 4827386

ATLANTICO ****
Via Cavour 23 - 00184 Rome
Tel. +39 06 485951 - Fax + 39 06 485951

SAN GIORGIO ****
Via G. Amendola 61 - 00185 Rome
Tel. +39 06 4827341 - Fax + 39 06 4883191

NORD NUOVA ROMA ***
Via G. Amendola 3 - 00185 Rome
Tel. +39 06 4885441 - Fax + 39 06 4817163

RELAIS CERTOSA ****
Via Colle Ramole 2 - 50124 Florence
Tel + 39 055 2047171 - Fax +39 055 268575

In Florence

The Hotel Relais Certosa lies 500 meters from the Florence-Certosa exit of the A1 highway, in a park bordering the Certosa di Galluzzo Monastery. 5 km from the historical center, the hotel offers a free shuttle service to and from the Central Station. Equipped with conference halls, restaurants and tennis courts, this hotel is an ideal location for holding meetings and conferences in a relaxed atmosphere, surrounded by the green Tuscan countryside. Only 10 minutes from the city center.

Via del
Governo
Vecchio
51-52-53

Tel. 066861341
00186
Roma

Abbey Theatre
Irish pub
GUINNESS

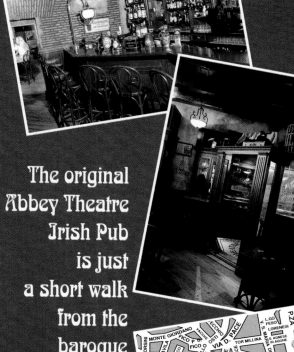

The original
Abbey Theatre
Irish Pub
is just
a short walk
from the
baroque
splendour of
Piazza Navona.

There's something new in old Rome

Is there a hotel right in the heart of Trastevere
with 170 suites that have been renovated to provide guests
with all the latest conveniences?
With a restaurant that uses produce from the proprietor's own
farm, is open for lunch, and accomodates after-theater diners?
Where you can organize an art exhibition
or a meeting for 180 people, providing hospitality, efficiency
and a large garage?
Yes, indeed. There's really something new in Trastevere.

RIPA
ALL SUITES
HOTEL

via degli orti di trastevere 1, 00153 Rome
telephone 06 58611 fax 06 5814550 e mail: ripa@uni.net

THINKING ABOUT ITALY?

*D*o you have any thoughts about this new Touring Club guidebook? Or do you want to know about any other TCI services or products? If so we want to know. Please photocopy this page (to leave the book intact), and write your comments, criticisms, and suggestions below. Then mail it (or fax it - Italy 39/2/8526331) to:

**Touring Club of Italy,
Segreteria Soci - Corso Italia, 10
20122 Milano**

....
....
....
....
....
....
....
....

Name ....

Surname ....

Address ....

City ....

Country ....

Telephone ....

DOLCI *sogni*

TOUR OPERATOR
Via Adda, 111 - 00198 Roma
Tel. +390685301758
Fax +390685301757
E-mail: *dolcisogni@uni.net*

YOUR REFERENCE IN ROME
FOR INDIVIDUALS AND GROUPS
YOUR TRAVEL AGENT IN ROME

- Booking accomodations: hotels, religious institutes, flats, b/b, residences, etc.
- Bus tour, pick up tours by car, walking tours.
- Opera and classic music. - Golf in Rome. - Flights over Rome.
- Tours at: Ostia antica, Pompei, Capri, Assisi, Florence and all over Italy.
- Bus rent. - Incentives and congress.

For further information and reservations,
please contact our site: http://www.romeguide.it